Rules of the Road for Registered Representatives

Rules of the Road for Registered Representatives

A Guide to Securities Compliance

Thomas R. Keyes
David S. Miller

New York Institute of Finance

New York London Toronto Sydney Tokyo Singapore

Library of Congress Cataloging-in-Publication Data

Keyes, Thomas R.
   Rules of the road for registered representatives: a guide to
securities compliance / Thomas R. Keyes, David S. Miller.
    p. cm.
   Includes index.
   ISBN 0-13-770314-7
   1. Brokers—Legal status, laws, etc.—United States.
2. Securities—United States. 3. Brokers—United States.
I. Miller, David Stuart. II. Title.
KF1071.K49 1991
346.73'0926—dc20
[347.306926]   90-20231
                                          CIP

This publication is designed to provide accurate and authoritative information in regard to the subject matter covered. It is sold with the understanding that the publisher is not engaged in rendering legal, accounting, or
other professional service. If legal advice or other expert assistance is
required, the services of a competent professional person should be
sought.

From a Declaration of Principles
Jointly Adopted by
a Committee of the American Bar Association
and a Committee of Publishers and Associations

In the text of this book we have presented securities laws, as well as NASD
and NYSE rules, in plain English. We reasoned that regulations presented
in the language of the workplace have a better chance of changing workplace ethics than do regulations presented in the language of lawyers. We
are aware, however, that shades of meaning may change when one trans-
lates the rhetoric of rule books into the language of laypersons. Lawyers
and regulators write as they do for good reason. Disputes about technical
points of law, therefore, should be settled by reference to the law books
and rule books, not by reference to this text. As a starting point for such
research, Appendix A includes the original text of the major rules paraphrased in the book.

To Our Wives

Nancy

and

June

Contents

Acknowledgments

Tom has long wanted to write a book presenting the rules of the securities marketplace along with the stories behind the rules. The introduction of new securities supervision requirements in early 1989 provided the opportunity to write that book. David, who had just finished writing another book with Tom, was happy with the outcome of that first project, and so was glad to sign up for another.

Among those who provided encouragement during the initial stages of this endeavor, the most important was Dennis Blitz, of Longman Financial Services Institute. Bob Johnson and Susan De Leo of AEI Investment Managers Inc. provided us with research material.

Bill Nordstrom, Peter Middleton, and Paul Litteau all read the manuscript and improved its precision with their careful and detailed comments. Their commitment to the improvement of someone else's manuscript was surprising and inspiring.

Jerome West, of Charles Schwab, and De Witt Foster, of P.A.S.S., also read drafts of the book and supported us with comments and kind words.

Merrilee Cole edited the final draft, bringing to the work her experience in the securities industry as well as her writer's eye for infelicities of grammar and style.

Each of these people improved the accuracy and clarity of the manuscript. None is responsible for remaining errors or obscurity.

We owe a special debt to Jimmy and Wanda Doyle for allowing us to spend a day in their home as they told us their painful story. They also read the original draft of the manuscript.

Finally, Tom wishes to say that thanks are due most of all to David, with whom he really enjoys working. David thanks Tom for his insight, patience, tact, infectious laughter, ideas for books to write, and facilities for writing them. Everyone should enjoy such working conditions.

Abbreviations

ADRs	*American Depositary Receipts*
Amex	*American Stock Exchange*
CBOE	*Chicago Board Options Exchange*
CBOT	*Chicago Board of Trade*
CFTC	*Commodities Futures Trading Commission*
CME	*Chicago Mercantile Exchange (Merc)*
CROP	*Compliance Registered Options Principal*
DJIA	*Dow Jones Industrial Average*
FRB	*Federal Reserve Board*
FINOP	*Financial and Operations Principal*
IAFP	*International Association of Financial Planners*
GP	*General Partner*
MPs	*Members of Parliament*
MSRB	*Municipal Securities Rulemaking Board*
NASD	*National Association of Securities Dealers*
NASDAQ	*National Association of Securities Dealers Automated Quotations*
NASDAQ/NMS	*National Association of Securities Dealers Automated Quotations/ National Market System*

NASAA	*North American Securities Administrators Association*
NMS	*National Market System*
NYSE	*New York Stock Exchange*
OCC	*Options Clearing Corporation*
OSJ	*Office of Supervisory Jurisdiction*
OTC	*Over the Counter*
ROP	*Registered Options Principal*
RR	*Registered Representative*
S & P	*Standard and Poor's Corporation*
S & P 500 Index	*Standard and Poor's Index of 500 Stocks*
SEAQ	*Stock Exchange Automated Quotations*
SEC	*Securities and Exchange Commission*
SIPC	*Securities Investor Protection Corporation*
SOES	*Small Order Execution System*
SRO	*Self-regulatory Organization*
SROP	*Senior Registered Options Principal*

Preface

Behind every rule there's a story. This fact explains the apparently perverse pleasure some take in reading securities laws and regulations. They see through the dry language to stories, sometimes tragic, of crime, crisis, and punishment. From this point of view the NASD's "Rules of Fair Practice," for example, is a set of clues to crimes against investors or other market participants. Behind today's entire regulatory structure lies the drama of the 1929 market collapse and subsequent market crises.

Most books and training programs about regulations stay close to the language of the rules and far away from the stories. The focus of such books and programs is negative. Like the Ten Commandments, their purpose is to tell you what not to do. This book takes the opposite approach. It puts the rules in plain English and turns them around—so they say what a registered representative (RR) should do, not what an RR should avoid doing. This book also includes some of the stories behind the rules.

In fact, it begins with one—the true story of Jimmy Doyle, a good man and dedicated RR whose securities violations earned him a place in the headlines and 26 months in jail. Step by step, generally with the interests of clients uppermost in his mind, Jimmy moved away from compliance regulations. Eventually, he became a classic example of why markets must have rules. The lesson of his story echoes throughout the book.

You will also read about the Great Crash of 1929 and of several subsequent market crises that affected the rules of the road. That's in Chapter 3, which is a very brief history of the stock market in the 20th century. The purpose of including a history lesson is to help make sense of the rules. They are there, in part, to head off the kinds of crises that have threatened the market with total disgrace.

When investors believe the market has lost its integrity, they take their money elsewhere. That's why the market tends to regulate itself—with a little help from the federal government. It's always been like that, with all markets throughout history. That's the story we tell in Chapter 2.

Chapters 4, 5, and 6 cover today's rules of the road, with emphasis on areas of special concern to regulators. Chapters 4 and 5 focus on rules describing the duties an RR owes to the customer and broker-dealer. Chapter 6 covers rules pertaining to the ethical responsibilities of broker-dealers.

Chapters 4, 5, and 6 include dozens of brief stories about RRs and firms that have been recently fined, suspended, barred from the industry, or taken to court for rule violations. The stories bring the abstract language of the rule manual down to earth.

Appendix I cross-references this book with securities laws and the rulebooks of the NYSE and the NASD. The appendix includes verbatim quotations from the original sources if you want to study the language behind our paraphrasing.

Appendix II is a test to see how well you can apply your knowledge of the rules of the road to situations that occur on the job. If you are an RR, answers to test questions will be available through your firm. The test contains 50 questions: The first 35 are for RRs; the final 15 are for supervisors.

As you read this book, you will notice a bias: the belief that working in the securities industry is a great adventure. Following the rules of the road is part of that adventure. Violating the rules is one way to end the adventure. If you endanger the integrity of the market, you run the risk of being excluded from it, except as a customer, for the rest of your life.

That, as you'll see, is what happened to Jimmy Doyle.

PART ONE

THE LONG VIEW

1

The Jimmy Doyle Story

In his late 50s, Jimmy Doyle has white, thinning hair and eyes so pale they might be either green or blue. He reminds you of someone, yet you aren't sure who. From a certain angle, when the light is just so, you might see a hint of Eric Sevareid's austere gravity—but only during those rare moments when Jimmy's features are quiet. In other lights you may see Jack Lemmon or Jason Robards (the resemblance is mostly in the eyes, which sparkle with amused craftiness).

Jimmy was famous for a time—back in 1977. Chances are good that you read about him, since his story was featured in *The Wall Street Journal* and syndicated columns across the country. Reporters told of his disappearance from Blue Earth, Minnesota, with $2 million of customers' bond certificates. They wrote about his mistress, a woman living in Las Vegas; about Wanda, his abandoned wife; and about his daughter (who, as his business partner, was left to face the forsaken customers). Another plausible con artist, you may have thought. Amoral. Calculating. The type that only naive clients would fail to recognize as sleazy, slick, and dangerous. Clyde Barrows in a necktie.

You certainly didn't imagine a person like yourself—law-abiding, hard-working, concerned about clients' financial well-being. But that's the way you would have seen Jimmy had you known him then.

And if you met Jimmy now, chances are good you would like him. You would probably trust him. Identify with him. Admire his knowledge of securities and his obvious love of the business—the business from which he has been banned, except as a customer, for the rest of his life.

Jimmy Doyle is small-town elite: good-humored, a natural storyteller, a dawn-to-midnight worker, a sharp trader. He's very bright but a little rough around the edges—"Them damn bonds," he says, in reference to the pilfered securities. "Your grammar is terrible," Wanda scolds. "Terrible," Jimmy smiles unabashedly. (Jimmy and Wanda eventually got back together.)

In Blue Earth, Minnesota, when times were good, Jimmy belonged to the society of lawyers, doctors, bankers, and local politicians. One suspects his companions were never bored in his company—though they may have felt off-balance, as if Jimmy were keeping a little ahead of them, controlling the conversation. A born salesman never lets up.

In 1954, Jimmy returned from the U.N. police action in Korea with a wounded left arm and a 70% disability rating. His first job was with State Bond and Mortgage in New Ulm, Minnesota. After 15 months, he moved to Minnesota Associates, where he stayed until the early 1960s. In 1962, he joined Minneapolis-based John G. Kinnard, and became a leader among the brokers who set up Kinnard's rural business.

By 1976, with 22 years in financial services, he was a vice president, a top producer, a member of the board of directors, and—as most anyone in Blue Earth could have told you—a pillar of his community. A family man. On Sundays he went to church with Wanda, well-known in the area as an accomplished singer. He was also neck-deep in questionable securities activity, and his life was about to begin unraveling. In December 1976 Jimmy would be fired from Kinnard. In December 1977 he would be in jail in Panama, Minnesota, with enough criminal charges against him to earn a potential 68 years in Leavenworth. By the end of 1978 he would be in Sandstone—Minnesota's federal prison—with murderers for neighbors.

Jimmy never saw himself as a crook. More than a decade after being fired, jailed, banned from the industry, and ostracized from his community, he acknowledged that some of his trading took place in "gray areas." But he didn't set out to amass a portfolio of customers' bonds in order to finance early retirement in Central America. After all, many of his customers *were* hunting and fishing buddies. "We took too good care of those people," he says, shaking his head. "We spoiled 'em. I don't know what the hell they're doing now."

As Jimmy sees it, he provided special services, at great cost in time and energy. Customers often left their bonds with him. "They thought they were doing us a favor," he laughs ruefully. In reality they were multiplying Jimmy's responsibilities.

In those days bonds were often issued in bearer form. Each certificate of ownership was fringed with coupons—one for each scheduled interest payment. To receive interest, the bearer of the certificate clipped the appropriate coupon and mailed it to the issuer. When Jimmy kept his customers' certificates, he did the clipping and mailing for them. To store the bonds, Jimmy maintained 12 safety deposit boxes, one for each month. Once a month, when interest came due, he would go to the bank with his scissors and clip coupons. Then he would move the certificates six boxes forward, to the month when interest would next come due. He still rubs his hands and laughs ruefully, remembering the friction of scissors on skin.

Some customers who did take delivery of certificates would bring them to Jimmy's office twice a year, usually the week before the scheduled interest payment. Of course they expected their money immediately, so Jimmy kept cash on hand to satisfy them. After paying the customer, he would send in the coupon and get the money from the issuer. Was there a charge for this service? No. Was there anything in it for Jimmy besides extra hours of work? No. Not directly, at least. When Jimmy tells the story, it sounds as innocent as small-town courtesy. But, in reality, there were serious problems with his methods. In essence, he was running his own unregistered firm in addition to acting as an RR for Kinnard. It was an extraordinary feat that he could succeed at both endeavors, but it was not something the Securities Exchange Commission or the self-regulatory organizations ever intended to happen in their marketplace.

As an RR, Jimmy was licensed to arrange (or broker) trades for Kinnard. That is, he could enter customers' buy and sell orders, and those orders would be executed through Kinnard. For that activity, he would receive a portion of Kinnard's commission. He was not authorized to buy a security in his own account (or in an account he controlled) for the purpose of selling it to a customer at a profit, but this is exactly what he did—without telling Kinnard.

There were two problems with Jimmy's methods. First, he was operating without a license. Second, he was acting in Kinnard's name but concealing the activity from his employer. Since the firm was kept in the dark about a fair portion of Jimmy's business, it might unwittingly have violated regulations—such as the requirement to keep accurate records and maintain adequate net capital. Jimmy pleased his customers, but he put Kinnard in jeopardy of punishment by regulators.

In effect, Jimmy promoted himself from Kinnard's RR position to that of a self-appointed and self-regulated broker-dealer, performing many functions of a fully registered firm: sales, record-keeping, clearing, and safe-keeping of securities. Only one thing was missing: supervision. Jimmy's business was invisible to Kinnard and to the market regulators designated by Congress to keep track of securities trading.

From Jimmy's point of view, he backed into the broker-dealer business because Kinnard wouldn't provide the service his customers wanted. Sometimes, Jimmy recalls, Kinnard would urge its brokers to round up buyers for an issue of bonds, then not acquire enough of the securities to fill all the customer orders that brokers solicited. In such situations, he simply went into the market and bought the necessary bonds himself. That seemed preferable to telling customers he wasn't able to fill the orders he had taken from them.

Not surprisingly, Kinnard management interprets Jimmy's actions differently. They believe he bought bonds on his own because he could make more money that way, at the expense of the firm and his customers.

To *The Wall Street Journal*, to Kinnard, and to the IRS, Jimmy Doyle looked like an unscrupulous fraud. To Jimmy himself—and, before he absconded with their bonds, to his customers—he was just another hard-working, personable, highly successful, main-street businessman taking care of his neighbors. As Kinnard supervisors point out, customers have a strong desire to believe in their RR. If he's right, he makes money for them. This gives an RR substantial power over customers. Like the Pied Piper, he may be able to lead others where they really ought not to go.

One should not forget, either, that Robin Hood and Jesse James are still heroes in middle America. If Jimmy Doyle, out in small-town Minnesota, occasionally bent the rules made by the big boys in Washington, D.C. and enforced by the city boys managing the firm up in Minneapolis, perhaps his customers were willing to look the other way.

The downfall of Jimmy Doyle may have begun with commodities problems. Again, there was a customer-service issue. Jimmy had to send each order on a shared wire to Kinnard. There the order was retyped and forwarded to Chicago. In a market where a few minutes can mean the difference between profit and loss, the system seemed unsatisfactory.

Jimmy wanted an unshared wire straight to Chicago so that he could get immediate quotes and faster trades. For several years he tried unsuccessfully to get Kinnard's permission to do this. Finally he arranged for a direct wire with another firm. Kinnard was upset, fearing brokers who looked up to Jimmy would follow his example.

The resulting antagonism between Jimmy and Kinnard was the first act in his dramatic decline and fall. The second act began with an innocent and routine decision by a substitute mail clerk during Thanksgiving vacation in 1976. When the clerk found an envelope from A.G. Becker addressed to a former Blue Earth resident who had moved to California, he stamped on the new address and forwarded the envelope. The regular mail sorter would have tossed the envelope into Jimmy's box. All securities-related mail went to Jimmy, whether it was addressed to him or not. The substitute clerk didn't know that.

Not receiving this particular piece of correspondence was a big problem for Jimmy. The man in California was a former customer who ordered his account closed when he moved from Blue Earth. Instead, Jimmy left the account open to use for his own trading. In fact, the envelope from A.G. Becker contained bonds Jimmy had purchased in the former customer's name, assuming the certificates would turn up as usual in his own mailbox.

Imagine the surprise of the man in California when he opened the envelope and found bonds he hadn't purchased in an account he thought was closed! Puzzled, he called Jimmy and asked what was happening. Jimmy said not to worry, just to send the bonds to him and he would straighten matters out. There had been a slip-up somewhere.

"I should've gotten right on a plane and flown out to California," Jimmy laments.

Instead of following Jimmy's instructions, the man returned the bonds to A.G. Becker. When word of the situation reached Kinnard, they fired their renegade broker who, at the time was also a vice president, top producer, and director of the firm.

Given Kinnard's concern about Jimmy's commodities business, they may have been glad for the chance to send him packing in disgrace. Moreover, the firm had already done some investigating of Jimmy's business. Having noticed apparent irregularities in customer signatures, Jimmy's supervisors called in a handwriting expert who agreed that some signatures were probably forged. Even so, there wasn't enough evidence to act on—until the bonds turned up in California.

At any rate, Jimmy was suddenly on his own with an inventory of illegally acquired bonds, a blotch on his previously impeccable record, dozens of customers with orders to execute, and an understandable concern that Kinnard would try to take those customers away from him. He began scrambling to set up a business that would allow execution of his own and his customers' trades. He also began concocting alibis to cover the cracks in his reputation. In addition, he needed convincing explanations for his Las Vegas "business trips," which were actually trysts with a mistress who lived there.

Looking back from a decade's distance, one can see that Jimmy was probably experiencing a full-scale midlife crisis. His career was in jeopardy, his marriage was breaking down, he was engaged in a long-distance affair, and his drinking was out of hand. Instead of solving problems, he was compounding them. The personal and business strategies that had worked for the first half of his life now seemed inadequate. Under intense pressure from all sides, Jimmy's universe collapsed into a black hole.

Sometimes life eerily assumes the shape of a morality tale. The name of the Las Vegas mistress was Hope.

Jimmy laughs frequently as he reminisces. He seems genuinely amused when he recounts his arrest in a Panama beauty shop. He was leaning back enjoying a hair wash when the gently massaging hands were replaced by a gun at his temple. He chuckles when he tells about the doctor with a stammer, the one who said that another round of open heart surgery (Jimmy had a near-fatal coronary several years earlier) would mean "c-c-c-c-curtains" for him. He even laughs about the murderers who were his companions at Sandstone, such as the one serving time for killing his lover. When he caught her with another man, he beheaded her with a machete—after hacking off her breasts. "He never felt any remorse," Jimmy recalls. "He thought she deserved to die. He'd have killed the man she was with, too, except the man was too fast."

One senses no remorse when Jimmy discusses his own crimes, either. At least one hears no obvious expressions of guilt. He seems comfortable recalling his adventures, except for occasional flashes of anger—often directed at lawyers. As Jimmy sees it, defense attorneys cost him a small fortune yet failed to keep him out of prison or solve his tax problems. He seems even more bitter about the lawyers who charged hefty fees for helping his former customers regain some of their money from Kinnard. As far as he's concerned, the lawyers weren't necessary. "I don't understand why they [the customers] didn't just go to Kinnard and ask for the money," he exclaims indignantly. The anger, one suspects, might be a substitute for remorse.

In Jimmy's version of the story, the lawyers are mercenary and ineffective. Kinnard's managers are devious and hostile. The customers are innocent but foolish for not going directly to Kinnard to recover their capital. Jimmy is a victim. When he took off with the bonds, he was seeking vengeance on Kinnard for thwarting his attempts to serve customers efficiently and for firing him. He wasn't trying to injure the bondholders, and didn't think they would consider him the bad guy. He was one of them, a fellow victim of managers and lawyers.

"I thought Kinnard would take the heat," he says. Even Wanda, whose perspective is in many ways markedly different from Jimmy's, takes his side in this. "They drove him to it," she says of Kinnard. Perhaps that shared perspective helps explain why she and Jimmy got back together after his 26 months in prison. After Hope left him.

"Crime doesn't pay," Wanda says summarily. Backed by her and Jimmy's experiences, the cliche sounds like revelation. Perhaps 26 months in a relatively bearable prison (it wasn't Leavenworth, which is the place the government had in mind for Jimmy) seems like mild treatment for a man who abandoned his family and stole $2 million worth of his clients' securities.

However, time in prison was only the first installment of Jimmy's payment for these crimes. Nor was he the only one who paid. "He didn't understand," his wife says bitterly, "what would happen to his family when he ran off. We were left in Blue Earth"—left to face federal agents and angry friends and financially wounded clients. Dozens of people, maybe hundreds, pay a price for crimes like Jimmy's.

When you leave the country with your customers' securities, you face more than a jail sentence. The IRS and the state department of revenue count the stolen securities as taxable income. When they catch you, your tax comes due with a vengeance. Moreover, you don't get a deduction for securities you return. You owe the tax, but you have no money to pay it. You have a jail sentence on your resume. You're out of the business you know and love. Everything you ever earn will most likely belong to the government. If you're married, your wife inherits your debts.

Jimmy still receives regular bills for back taxes. "My state bill is up to about $900,000," he laughs. "It's a joke. I don't own them that money." One suspects he's not about to hire a lawyer to help him press the point.

After completing his prison sentence, Jimmy returned briefly to Blue Earth to attend a funeral. He decided he would need a car, so he stopped by a used car lot. "Jimmy," the salesman said, "I don't believe I have anything suitable for you on this lot." "What do you mean 'suitable'?" Jimmy asked. "If you're gonna drive around this town," the salesman responded "you'll need something with bullet-proof glass."

Clearly, returning to Blue Earth was out of the question. So, Jimmy and Wanda moved to a different Minnesota town where he wasn't so well known. You might think they've started over, but they're not even in sight of their original starting point. They fell too far behind, too deep in debt.

What remains of Jimmy Doyle's two decades in the business is a love of the market, a state tax bill climbing toward $1 million, an even larger account with the IRS, a family he put through bitter experiences, and a fund of the most fascinating stories you're likely to hear in any small-town living room or cafe.

If you want to end up with spellbinding stories like Jimmy Doyle's, start by bending the rules a little, exploring the gray areas, rationalizing. All in your clients' interest, of course. You'll be amazed how easy it is to become like Jimmy—an exile from the industry with a prison record, a millionaire's tax liability, a pauper's net worth, and only a bitter memory of Hope.

2

The Market Rules

MARKET INTEGRITY

Before Jimmy Doyle packed up his customer's bonds in suitcases and fled to Costa Rica, his violations of laws and regulations were not serious enough to warrant imprisonment. That opinion is not Jimmy's alone; it is shared by investigators who looked into the case. If regulators had caught up with Jimmy before he became a thief, they would have blackballed him from the business.

Why? What had he done to deserve expulsion from the securities marketplace? Were his customers unhappy? Not until he disappeared with their bond certificates. Until then, he had worked with unusual diligence to satisfy their needs—had perhaps overindulged them. If he was satisfying his clients and not directly injuring Kinnard, what was the problem?

Jimmy didn't adhere to the standards of the securities marketplace. He was a renegade, a rogue broker who went his own way and asked no one's permission. For the most part, his business would have been legitimate had he been properly registered. As an RR, he was only allowed to take buy and sell orders from Kinnard's customers. He wasn't permitted to hold customers' cash and securities or to buy securities to sell at a higher price. Those activities are permissible only for firms registered with the SEC and subject to regulations written for broker-dealers.

Becoming properly registered may strike some as a mere formality, but it preserves the market's integrity. Was there any harm in Jimmy's operating without the knowledge and permission of managers and regulators, so long as his customers weren't hurt? Look at the impact this had on Kinnard. A broker-dealer is required to keep accurate books and to maintain a minimum amount of net capital. To be sure, Jimmy kept track of what was happening in his customers' accounts, but no one else knew that. Kinnard certainly had no idea of what he was doing in their name. Jimmy held customer securities the firm didn't know about. He kept cash it wasn't aware of. He made trades the firm couldn't supervise and charged commissions and markups that were never entered in their ledgers. Under these conditions, how could Kinnard keep complete books and records? Jimmy's undisclosed activities might have made the firm's balance sheets inaccurate. If Jimmy's accounts had been large enough and unsuccessful enough, Kinnard might have inadvertently fallen below net capital minimums without knowing that a problem was brewing.

"Who cares?" one might ask, assuming Jimmy was acting responsibly and not taking risks that jeopardized the firm's financial soundness. Certainly he was confident that his part of Kinnard's business was under control. Ultimately, everyone involved cares. Regulations may seem like annoying technicalities when customers are happy and a rogue broker's activities aren't causing his firm any obvious problems. Jimmy wasn't systematically embezzling funds, just cutting corners. But a stockbroker's decision to play broker-dealer breaks the chain of supervision that, link by link, binds the RR to the branch, the firm, the SEC, and to the society at large. That fragmentation, that loss of market integrity, is the prelude to disaster.

The Traditional Market

All markets are regulated. They have to be. However, the need for regulation may be harder to grasp in the contemporary stock market than in a traditional trading place.

For example, unlike a Medieval trade fair, the modern stock market is largely invisible to its participants. In the traditional marketplace, one can look around and see most of the participants, perhaps shake their hands and learn their names. An RR in a modern market, by contrast, deals mostly in abstractions: voices on the phone, blips on a computer screen, numbers on paper. Everything is intangible and distant— except supervisors and, perhaps, customers. The primary impact on an RR may well be pressure to produce at a given level of gross commissions, not the need to fit into a visible structure composed of other human beings. The needs of other participants in the marketplace (i.e., corporate issuers, governments, the public at large, and perhaps even the home office) seem remote.

Like Jimmy Doyle, you may have difficulty seeing beyond the pressing need to perform a particular service. Who cares how the job gets done? In reality though, practices that seem reasonable to the RR and the customer may, in fact, undermine the market. When the market collapses because scandalous behavior destroys its credibility, all participants are buried in the rubble.

For comparison's sake, consider the traditional marketplace in which the major players operate face to face. In European towns, you can see the remnants of trading places with roots in the Middle Ages. In the midst of ancient buildings, perhaps marked off by chipped and weathered columns, a space may be reserved for buyers and sellers. Early in the day farmers gather, bringing fresh vegetables or live chickens. Clothiers drape their brightly colored shirts and dresses from the ribbing underneath large umbrellas. Rug merchants roll out their wares on tables. Buyers speak directly with sellers who may also be producers.

In the intimacy of the visible marketplace, the need for integrity is obvious. Unscrupulous practice is hard to conceal. A merchant caught in violation of rules is immediately exposed for all to see. Take, for example, a scene in the novel *Sarum* (descriptively, if somewhat grandiosely, subtitled "The Novel of England"). A man named William atte Brigge is caught and punished for selling cloth that is a quarter of an inch narrower than the law requires. "By short-changing his customers this tiny fraction on the width," the novelist tells us, "he could make a modest profit even at his discounted prices."[1] William's punishment is a public spectacle. When his cart is approached by the aulnage, the man designated to enforce measurement standards, an audience of customers and fellow traders gathers. Caught red handed with his illegally trimmed cloth, William is fined and banned from the marketplace of that city and sent packing into the countryside to find a market that doesn't know his disciplinary history.[2]

A market's reputation for fairness is essential to its existence. In *Sarum*, this is obvious. What merchants would trade in a marketplace that tolerated practices like William's? The town itself, moreover, has an easily understandable stake in the market's integrity. The town's economy is synonymous with the marketplace. Without merchants and customers, the town dies. In our more diffuse society we require catastrophe on a larger scale, such as a 1929-style crash or the scheming of an Ivan Boesky, to remind us that similar rules still apply.

EVOLUTION OF THE MODERN MARKETPLACE

The securities marketplace in England and the United States was not always so different from the Medieval trade fair. To be sure, the mere existence of brokers and dealers (called brokers and jobbers in England) implies an economy far advanced beyond the marketplace of a Medieval village. Joint-stock companies with publicly traded shares were created during the growth of powerful national economies with extensive international trade. Only the conduct of business on such a large scale made possible the existence of specialized occupations such as stockbrokers.

Still, in the late seventeenth century, stockbrokers and stockjobbers gathered in something like a face-to-face market in coffee shops and along the walks and alleys in the neighborhood of London's Royal Exchange. In fact, in 1697 Parliament passed the first act to regulate this business—typically, after the market had brought itself into disrepute for insider trading and price rigging. The language of the act reveals public perceptions. It refers, for example, to "the pernicious art of stockjobbing."[3]

To restore market discipline and credibility, the act established licensing procedures, limited licenses to 100, priced them at £2 each, and required new brokers to swear they would "truly and faithfuly execute and perform the office and employment of a broker between party and party without fraud or collusion."[4] Penalties were stiff and a bit exotic by present standards. Anyone operating without a license faced three days in the pillory.

Nevertheless, the market continued to grow and evolve, and by 1720 there was a thriving trade in shares. There were perhaps 140 joint stock companies trading for a market capitalization of £4.5 million. Most market activity took place in two coffeehouses near Change Alley, a street that still exists.

Instead of waiting until the close of business to go to a bar or pub, as RRs do today, eighteenth century brokers worked at tables where they could arrange trades, eat, listen to merchants discuss their business (inside information was presumably near at hand), and follow selected stock prices in a publication called "The Course of the Exchange and Other Things." One could walk the bounds of the securities business, dodging the onrush of carriages in about a minute and a half.[5]

The market thrived in the early 1700s primarily because of the immensely popular—and historically infamous—South Sea Company. If ever a venture arose on a wing and a prayer, it was this one. Originally chartered as a government-owned operation for delivering slaves to Latin America, the company piqued no one's interest until the government conceived the clever notion of transferring ownership to public investors.

This idea was not without precedent: France had tried it earlier with the Mississippi Company, a government-owned monopoly controlling trade with the Louisiana colony. Like England, France was burdened by a huge war-related debt, and had eagerly agreed to exchange outstanding government bonds for equity in the trading company. England hoped to raise enough money from the sale of South Sea Company stock to retire its entire national debt of £31 million.

The run-up of South Sea Company stock exhibited all the familiar symptoms of speculative fever. The stock was greatly oversubscribed by investors of all sorts, from impoverished pensioners to the King himself, with royal mistresses and members of Parliament (MPs) along for the ride. Shares were sold on margin with the slenderest down payments. The company loaned money to the public with the stock as collateral; the loans were used for purchasing more shares. Friends of the company's directors received extra allocations. The directors bought and sold stock to manipulate the price upward.

During 1720, the price per share rose from £29 in January to £1,050 in June. Moreover, the speculative fever spread. Other promoters leaped onto the bandwagon with schemes ranging from perpetual-motion devices to machines for purifying salt water. One legendary operation advertised its plan for an "undertaking of great advantage, but nobody to know what it is."[6]

It was a rapidly inflating bubble that, like any other bubble, became increasingly transparent as it grew. Savvy investors began taking their profits. The prime minister, Sir Robert Walpole, bailed out at the height of the frenzy, as did other princes, dukes, and MPs. After these insiders left, the air came rushing out of the bubble. By September 1720, share prices were down to £150.

In France, the Mississippi Bubble had burst earlier in the year.

To prevent similar calamities, Parliament passed the Bubble Act. There was, of course, an inquiry. Among other damning revelations, it uncovered the Chancellor of the Exchequer's "notorious, dangerous, and infamous corruption." This corruption had helped the chancellor reap an £800,000 capital gain on his South Sea Company investment.[7] The credibility of the once booming market for shares was gone, along with the life savings of many hapless investors.

Investigations and reforms may have restored the market to good order, but they didn't restore its luster to the public. It was a long time before investors were ready to risk more adventures in buying stock. Interest in forming joint-stock companies didn't revive until well into the next century. A market without credibility is a market without business.

BEYOND THE COFFEEHOUSES

The eighteenth century in England and the United States (which, if course, wasn't the United States for most of the century) was the age in which stock exchanges were born. A New York exchange was established in 1792 by the so-called Buttonwood Agreement, signed under a prominent tree at 68-70 Wall Street. Up to this time, stockbrokers and merchants had gathered along the street and in various inns and coffee shops. The Buttonwood Agreement formalized this activity, but certainly did not establish Wall Street as the financial heart of the nation. Until the Jackson era, Philadelphia remained the home of the premier U.S. exchange, and Wall Street didn't take on its present profile as a financial complex until the outburst of economic activity during the Civil War in the early 1860s.[8]

The beginning of the exchange market in the United States was a by-product of growth. Until 1792, New York City was the temporary home of the government. Alexander Hamilton, Secretary of the Treasury and a leading figure in U.S. finance, lived on Wall Street. The market was booming, largely because of heavy trading in securities of the newly established Bank of the United States and in government debt, trading that led to the nation's first big financial scandal and to a jail term for Hamilton's close friend, William Duer.

In England, however, the first exchange opened in quieter times—between the bursting of the South Sea Bubble in 1720 and the resurgence of joint stock incorporations in the 1820s. Jonathan's, one of the coffeehouses where traders gathered, burned in 1748. When it reopened on Threadneedle Street as the New Jonathan's, its contigent of brokers began charging an entry fee to keep away less professional hangers-on, such as money lenders. Soon the sign over the door read "The Stock Exchange," and so it remained for about 30 years. In 1801 the coffeehouse exchange closed for a month to reopen as the "Stock Subscription Room," complete with a higher entrance fee, membership elections, and fines for disorderly conduct.

Also in 1801, masons began laying a foundation in Capel Court for the exchange building that lasted 150 years until outmoded communications systems made rebuilding necessary. In 1812, the membership adopted a body of rules that formed the basis of current regulation.

MARKETS AND THE COMMUNICATIONS REVOLUTION

Stock brokerage depends on communications technology. How well the market works is a measure of how quickly and accurately information and instructions pass from one point in the system to another. As communications technology changes, so does the structure of the market. As the market structure changes (increasing in scope and speed of operation), regulations change.

A U.S. investor in the 1790s, especially one who didn't live in a trade center like New York City or Philadelphia, was at the mercy of very cumbersome communications—no telephones, no telegraph, no airplanes or mail trains, no daily dissemination of market data around the country. Buying or selling securities might involve sending a letter of instructions hundreds of miles by coach to a broker. Under such circumstances, trading through a distant, centralized exchange had little appeal.

The invention of the telegraph was the first giant step toward making a truly national exchange market possible. Mr. Bell's invention was the final step. In fact, the real virtue of a centralized exchange—that it can create a high-capital, efficient, liquid marketplace—depends on rapid communications technology. Ironically, however, as the telegraph and telephone once made mammoth central markets like the New York Stock exchange workable, more recent advances in communications technology threaten to make them obsolete.

The story of the late twentieth century marketplace is, in part, a tale of fragmentation. In the United States, the United

Kingdom, and around the world, computerized quotation and clearing systems are making efficient, global trading markets possible without central exchange buildings. Roughly speaking, what we're seeing is an extension of over-the-counter trading as we know it in the United States.

Instead of sending all trades to an exchange floor for execution, the over-the-counter (OTC) market relies on a system of securities dealers that buy and sell from one another. A stock trading OTC may have several prices, depending on the dealer. Buying and selling, then, involves shopping around for the dealer offering the best price. Historically, exchanges have had the edge in efficiency over OTC markets, since trading and pricing take place in one location. One doesn't have to search for the best price of shares trading on the New York Stock Exchange (NYSE). That information is available immediately from the one firm (the *specialist*) assigned to trade that stock on the exchange floor.

In 1971 the National Association of Securities Dealers (NASD) blunted the exchange market's edge in efficiency by setting up a system of computers to track prices in the OTC market. This computer system–called NASDAQ–(National Association of Securities Dealers Automated Quotations)—put the OTC market on the map. Before the NASD's computers began recording data, it was difficult to follow OTC stock prices and no one had a solid idea of the market's daily volume. Now, prices and volume go immediately into the system and can be called up on screens in a market maker's trading room. Those with Cable television can watch the tape of OTC trades running simultaneously with the NYSE tape all day on the Financial News Network. So attractive has the OTC market become that some companies eligible for Big Board listing— Apple Computer, among others—choose to trade over the counter instead.

Moreover, the OTC market in the United States has become a global model. In 1986, when London reorganized its market under the Financial Services Act, it took its cue from NASDAQ. So thoroughly did Stock Exchange Automated Quotations (SEAQ) revolutionize trading in the United Kingdom, that the preponderance of business moved from the exchange floor to computerized trading rooms in securities firms and banks. Soon after the Big Bang, as the shake-up of the market was called, officials of the exchange began exploring new uses for their deserted floor. They have considered making it a shopping mall or a computer center.

ORIGINS OF REGULATION

All markets have generated regulations—from the small town markets of the Medieval world, through the coffeehouse trading places of eighteenth century England, to the computerized markets of the 1990s. An unregulated marketplace would be as anomalous as a sport without rules.

What is the source of market regulations? The market itself, in the first instance. The Medieval world was very clear on the absolute need for the inherently sinful descendants of Eve and Adam to be strictly governed in all their dealings. Modern capitalist economies, by contrast, have been predisposed to believe that competition makes regulation unnecessary. If left alone, Adam Smith asserted, the market will operate benignly, as if an invisible hand were directing the actions of participants. In practice, however, capitalist markets generate regulations, too. In the cool rationality of the theoretical marketplace, participants might believe that the Smithian hand is neatly arranging matters to the ultimate benefit of everyone. In the hurly-burly of the real world, however, with fortunes at stake, participants sometimes believe the market is biased against them and in favor of some other person or group. In this sense of injustice is the source of support for regulations that tip the balance away from the other fellow and toward oneself.

Medieval markets establish standards in their struggle to attract customers from one another; the marketplace we visited earlier, where William atte Brigge was punished for lying about the width of his cloth, was competing for business with the market in a nearby town. We also saw that as soon as traders grouped together in English coffeehouses they began to define the conditions of membership and expulsion. They were not about to have the reputation of their young market ruined by the riffraff that gathered at adjoining tables.

There are some risks no one is willing to take. Therefore, participants in a market develop rules to protect themselves from each other and to protect the market as a whole. Sellers must feel that competitors are not lying—about the width of their cloth, for example—to gain market share. Customers need to feel that *let the buyer beware* is not the slogan of sellers. All participants depend upon rules to protect the integrity of the market.

When a market loses its integrity, both buyers and sellers will seek safer trading places, or they will petition the government to clean up the market for them. Since all traders and customers are citizens, the government must be concerned about their needs for safety and fair treatment just as the medieval town was concerned about the integrity of its market, and as the British were concerned when the South Sea Bubble burst.

However, isn't each investor ultimately responsible for his or her losses? That's not an easy question to answer, philosophically, legally, or financially. Most of us accept responsibility for investment losses resulting from our own decisions. We don't like to lose money, but we understand that business is always a bit of a gamble. On the other hand, we are apt to feel less philosophical about our losses when we find that our unfortunate investment decisions were influenced by a broker's or promoter's lies. We don't accept with a shrug the losses caused by insiders' manipulation of prices. We're inclined to believe, in other words, that being tricked out of our money by con artists is not a legitimate part of the investment game. It makes us angry. It makes us want our money back. It makes us want to the see someone locked in the pillory or the penitentiary. Naturally, we turn to our government for help.

In the South Sea Bubble affair, misrepresentations and manipulations hurt the ordinary investor. In such cases the government often steps in to punish the offenders and change the rules of play. After all, the government has an interest in pacifying a hostile, impoverished citizenry. Such people are difficult to rule. The British government's role as regulator was complicated, however, because it was implicated in the scandal. Some shareholders who took profits and got out before the collapse were in Parliament or were part of the royal entourage. This may have given the government an even stronger motivation for attacking abuses. It needed to restore confidence in its own integrity as well as that of the marketplace. But government involvement certainly didn't increase public confidence in financial institutions.

Besides their need to maintain public confidence, governments have other reasons for intervening in markets. They depend on prosperity to lift tax revenues, for example, so they pass laws promoting profitable trade. If markets compete internationally, the government may take steps to attract foreign money into the country. Stock exchanges around the world have recently rediscovered that a stock market's reputation for fairness is very important to potential overseas investors. From the United Kingdom through Europe to Hong

Kong, governments are cleaning up and modernizing their securities markets in order to compete globally.

Markets are subject to regulation both from within and without. Participants develop rules that keep the market from becoming unfair and losing its reputation with potential customers. Governments pass laws to make markets safe for citizens and attractive to foreign investors.

RULES FROM INSIDE AND OUT

In the United States, we have a hybrid regulatory system. Securities markets make their own rules through self-regulatory organizations (SROs), such as the NYSE and the NASD. The government regulates securities markets through the SEC and sometimes the SROs and the SEC cooperate in the development of regulations. The SEC ordinarily delegates a degree of enforcement authority to the SROs, but will step in when self-regulation seems inadequate.

Perhaps nothing better symbolizes the symbiosis of market and government than Franklin Roosevelt's appointment of Joseph Kennedy, a flamboyant and highly successful trader, as the first chairman of the SEC. It may have looked like a case of assigning a fox to rule the chicken coop, since Kennedy had been involved in some of the very practices forbidden by the new regulations. But, in fact, Roosevelt's move was a shrewd recognition of the interdependence between market and community. The government needed the market's cooperation in creating stricter regulations; as a player of the game, Kennedy had a good chance of getting that cooperation. A hardcore political reformer might simply have antagonized market participants and stiffened their desire to resist government regulation.

In the joint venture of market regulation, the government is the major partner in one sense. It has the lion's share of power and authority. SROs, however, are also powerful. Securities markets are important to the government, and that gives SROs leverage with legislators. Moreover, the exchanges and the NASD employ a vast number of professionals who maintain continuous contact with the intricacies of the business. Size and knowledge give these organizations sufficient authority to cause the SEC to think carefully before it overrides an SRO decision.

During ordinary times, the SEC works by suggestion and pressure rather than the ultimate authority of the law. As we shall see in Chapter 3, however, the balance of power shifts toward the government during a market crisis. When prices drop precipitously, or when scandal erupts and tarnishes the market's image, the SEC and Congress may become an implacable rulemaking machine fueled by public anger.

THE ENDLESS CYCLE OF REGULATION

All markets are regulated, and regulations are always being reconsidered and rewritten. As competition and new technology change the market, regulators inside and outside the market struggle to keep current.

The simple rules written in London coffeehouses were utterly inadequate to protect investors whose hunger for shares was whipped to a frenzy by the South Sea Company's promoters. Regulations tailored to fit a centralized exchange market that specializes in corporate stocks are unlikely to be sufficient for a computerized nexus of markets trading stocks, bonds, stock index futures, and options. One suspects that the rules adapted to national markets are likely to need revision in the near future—under pressure of a crisis in international investment trading. There is no foreseeable end to change and regulation.

Notes

1. Rutherford, Edward, *Sarum: The Novel of England* (New York: Crown, 1987), p. 384.

2. *Ibid.*, pp. 381–384.

3. Chapman, Colin, *How the New Stock Exchange Works* (London: Century Hutchinson, 1986), p. 27.

4. *Ibid.*, pp. 27–28.

5. *Ibid.*, pp. 29–30.

6. Brinton, Crane, Christopher, John B., Wolff, Robert Lee, *A History of Civilization, 1715 to the Present*, 5th ed. (Englewood Cliffs, NJ: Prentice Hall, 1976), p. 437.

7. Chapman, *Op. Cit.* p. 31.

8. Sobel, Robert, *Panic on Wall Street: A Classic History of America's Financial Disasters—With a New Exploration of the Crash of 1987* (New York: Dutton, 1988), p. 116.

3

Industry Low Points and Regulatory Highlights

CRISIS BREEDS REGULATION

In securities markets everything is a moving target. Prices, products, technology, strategies, administrative procedures, volume, and regulations all fluctuate in the near term and evolve over the longer term. Regulations, in normal times, are subject to small changes, the steady evolution of the body of rules. This steady evolution, however, is occasionally interrupted by interludes of heavy regulatory activity. Rule-making revolutions generally sweep through the market after a crisis.

When the market is in good working order, the securities industry has considerable clout. Industry leaders can stare regulators in the eye and say convincingly, "If it ain't broke, don't fix it." But when the marketplace is in trouble, say, after a precipitous drop in stock prices or a widely publicized scandal, the industry's credibility declines. The weight of public sentiment shifts to the side of regulators and Congress. New rules go into the books.

The market gets into trouble when many investors lose money, lots of money, or when a few fortunes are made unfairly by trading on inside information or absconding with securities. The public is irate. Constituents deluge their representatives with phone calls and letters complaining about fatcat stock swindlers. Customers sue their brokers. Sometimes they shoot them. Newspapers, magazines, and television news shows are full of stories about where the money went or where the nefarious RR went. Hollywood writers whip up an anti-Wall Street melodrama, featuring a few stock heroes and villains—overanxious young broker, sleazy tycoon, public-spirited district attorney. There is widespread agreement, in short, that the market is broken. During such a crisis, the government, the self-regulatory organizations, and market participants rush to repair the damage, thereby generating a great deal of friction among themselves.

New rules arise as regulators attempt to head off a recurrence of the most recent crisis. Unfortunately—cut to the end of the story—history never repeats itself exactly. While we're looking into the rear-view mirror, afraid the past will smack us in the backside, we run head-on into the unforeseen future. Market participants are creative—they invent new strategies, new technologies, new products, and new deviations from fair practice. Rule makers always come along a little behind the rule breakers, racing to catch up.

Studying the past may not solve all our problems, but it helps us see why current rules arose and what calamities they were intended to prevent. In this chapter we'll look at four significant market breaks in the twentieth century: The Great Crash of 1929, the bear market of 1962, the bankruptcy crises of 1968, and Black Monday in 1987. In each case we'll sketch a quick picture of the crisis, then describe the rules that were

EXHIBIT 3.1.   Dow Jones Industrial Average, 1929 to 1932

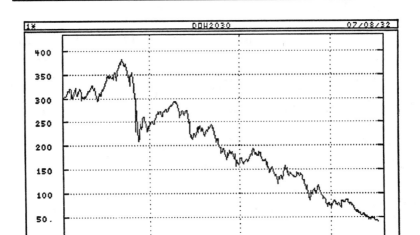

devised to protect against is recurrence. The result should be a useful outline portrait of today's regulations.

THE GREAT CRASH AND MODERN REGULATION

The best way to illustrate the most devastating of all modern bear markets is with one of those pictures worth any number of words. Exhibit 3.1, a chart of the Dow Jones Industrial Average (DJIA) during 1929 to 1932, illustrates very succinctly why the foundation for today's securities structure was laid down by Congress and the president in the 1930s.

As you can see, the magnitude of the descent from precrash highs in 1929 to the bottom of the depression in 1932 is simply staggering. Table 3.1 lists what happened to a few Blue Chip stocks.[1]

Imagine the panic investors felt when these cornerstones of the market crumbled. Imagine, too, their sense of betrayal. It

Table 3.1.
Blue Chip Stocks' Performance, 1929 to 1932

Security	High Price Sept. 3 1929*	Low Price Nov. 13, 1929	Low Price for Year 1932
American Telephone & Telegraph	304	197 1/4	70 1/4
Bethlehem Steel	140 3/8	78 1/4	7 1/4
General Electric	396 1/4	168 1/4	8 1/2
Montgomery Ward	137 7/8	49 1/4	3 1/2
National Cash Register	127 1/2	59	6 1/4
Radio Corporation of America	101	28	2 1/2

*Adjusted for stock splits and the value of rights received after
 September 3, 1929.

was not only investors—a small minority of citizens at any given time—who turned against Wall Street. In the glory days of the 1920s, the stock market symbolized the success of American capitalism. When the economy collapsed, the market quickly changed from a symbol of America's success to an emblem of its failure. People abandoned the market and stayed away for years. In 1929 over a billion shares traded on the NYSE, and a seat sold for as high as $625,000. By 1932, volume had declined to 324 million shares and the price of a seat had fallen as low as $70,000.[2] Like the Medieval market situated in the center of the walled city, Wall Street seemed to represent the heart of the community – an entire nation, in this case. So the preceding market chart, like an electrocardiogram, tracks the heartbeat of the U.S. economy; the line for 1929, not inappropriately, registers an economic version of cardiac arrest.

Though there was widespread agreement that the market was sick, there was great disagreement about its cure. Some radicals (fewer than either conservative or radical commentators would have us believe) argued for nationalization of the U.S. financial industry. Most people on Wall Street, including the aristocratic president of the NYSE, Richard Whitney, argued that the institution was a private business and should therefore be allowed to regulate itself.

However, Whitney was not without opposition in the financial industry. Members of other exchanges and OTC firms considered the NYSE a threat. In their view, govenment was a potential ally against the Big Board. Whitney even had opponents in the NYSE itself. In 1935, in fact, when business was at an extremely low ebb, Whitney was replaced by a less aristocratic and more reform-minded president, Charles Richard Gay.

By the time of Gay's election Franklin Roosevelt was president, the sweeping New Deal reforms of this legendary first 100 days were in place, and the SEC had been set up to oversee the conduct of the exchange, which nevertheless remained essentially self-regulated. On Wall Street and in Washington, D.C., the common purpose was to restore the integrity and credibility of the marketplace, not to replace it with a socialist state.

In 1933 and 1934 Congress passed a series of laws that redefined the financial industry in the United States, especially commercial and investment banking. These laws, with a few additions from the later 1930s and early 1940s, constitute the foundation of the business as we know it today—a foundation constructed in large part as a bulwark against the perceived causes of the Great Crash. Therefore, a brief look at the major pieces of legislation shows the connection between the present structure of the industry and the destructive practices of the past.

The Securities Act of 1933

The Securities Act of 1933 passed Congress because legislators wanted to make certain that public customers would have access to full and objective descriptions of businesses issuing new equity securities. Sometimes called *The Truth in Securities Act*, the 1933 legislation required new issues to be registered and to be sold only to investors who had received a prospectus including all relevant information about the business of the issuer.

The authors of the law presumed that investors would steer clear of worthless ventures so long as they were adequately described in public documents. As John Kenneth Galbraith points out, however, "No way was found of making would-be investors read what was disclosed."[3] Few customers are anxious, as you well know, to wade through the prospectuses their brokers dutifully send them. This circumstance does not, of course, relieve RRs from honoring in practice the spirit and letter of the law. Moreover, public information is there to help the sales agent as well as the customer. In a full-service broker-dealer, part of the RR's job is to recommend investments. When making such recommendations, the RR is obligated to select securities suitable to customer needs—a goal that cannot be reached in the absence of reliable information.

The Securities Exchange Act of 1934

After letting some sunshine into the new-issue market with the Securities Act of 1933, Congress tackled secondary trading and the financial industry itself in *The Securities Exchange Act of 1934*. One significant accomplishment of the 1934 legislation was to establish the five-member SEC, which is responsible for transforming the general objectives of federal securities laws into specific regulations.

As a compromise between complete self-regulation and a nationalized industry, the Securities Exchange Act was attacked by purists on both sides. William O. Douglas, for example, a staunch New Dealer who later became the third SEC chairman (and even later, of course, served as a Supreme Court Justice), thought the new legislation contained nothing "which would control the speculative craze of the American public."[4] NYSE president and spokesman Richard Whitney complained, on the other hand, that the act authorized the SEC to go beyond mere regulation of abuses and "manage exchanges and dictate brokerage practices."[5]

In the early years of SEC oversight, the commissioners struggled with the NYSE for control of market regulation. Though their spheres of control are better defined now, room still remains for disagreement between the two centers for regulatory authority. But all parties have long since conceded that the federal government has a legitimate interest in maintaining a fair, smoothly functioning exchange market. They also have conceded that the exchange can generally be relied upon to police members in the public interest.

Besides establishing federal supervision over self-regulated exchanges, the Securities Exchange Act of 1934 attacked abuses that were thought to have contributed to the great crash of 1929-1932. For one thing, the act authorizes the Federal Reserve Board (FRB) to set margin requirements and to define rules for margin accounts. It also extends the reach of full disclosure from issuers to broker-dealers and forbids market manipulation and fraudulent practices. Precisely defining market manipulation is another matter; better expressed, the distinction between permissible and impermissible manipulation is the subject of continuing debate.

Take as an example of permissible manipulation the specialist firms operating on the exchange floor. The exchange assigns each stock to a specialist firm, and that firm is charged with *making a market* in the stock. This means that specialists are sometimes required to be both buyers and sellers, if that is necessary to maintain the smooth functioning of the market in their stocks. This buying and selling is a form of benign manipulation—*benign*, the exchange presumes, since it usually affects prices only by fractions of a point and is intended to maintain order in the market. The specialists are not acting for their own benefit at customers' expense. But during the debate over exchange regulation in the 1930s, some critics of the NYSE advocated an end to the specialist system. Obviously, the system endured. So has the criticism.

Doing away with manipulation is not a simple matter of forbidding a few specific practices and punishing those who engage in them. Market participants are creative—they find new ways to manipulate prices. Or, the market itself changes so much that price manipulation becomes a byproduct of honest and open strategies. Program trading and portfolio insurance, for example, became immediately suspect when the market took its nose dive on October 19, 1987. Up until that time they seemed to be conservative practices favored by well-intentioned portfolio managers.

Bank Regulations

Congress wasn't content with writing new laws mandating full disclosure and federal regulation of exchange trading. Banks, too, were the subject of new legislation, for flaws in their practices were widely believed to have contributed to the national economic tragedy.

During the widespread expansion of securities trading in the 1920s, banks had moved into position to capture some of the flood of money flowing between investors and issuers. The most straightforward way to do that was for a commercial bank (i.e., an institution taking deposits and making loans) to create an affiliated investment bank to underwrite securities.

The initial venture of this type was The First Securities Company, founded in 1908 by The First National Bank of New York.[6] By 1931 First Securities had been joined by 284 similar institutions affiliated with national banks, and by numerous others affiliated with state banks. The combination of commercial and investment banking was not without its critics. Senator Carter Glass, for example, complained that underwriting bond offerings was too risky a business for institutions entrusted with the public's savings.

Yet, no legislation forbade the combination of commercial banking and securities underwriting until after the depression wore the polish off the financial industry's reputation. Between 1929 and 1933 8,000 banks failed in the United States, causing thousands of depositors to lose their savings.[7] Others withdrew their money from banks, fearing that the collapse was contagious. Banks, in other words, lost credibility.

With the bank market in such a state of chaos, reforms were fairly easy to institute. In 1932 Congress passed *The Federal Home Loan Banking Act* to straighten out the savings and loan industry—not, unfortunately, for the last time. After deregulation, scandal, and financial catastrophe in the 1980s, the S&L industry once again lost credibility and became vulnerable to regulatory attention.

In 1933 Congress turned its attention from the S&Ls to commercial banks, and passed *The Banking Act*. Along with additional banking laws passed in 1935, The Banking Act is better known as the *Glass-Steagall Act*, after its authors.

The most salient feature of the Glass-Steagall laws is the separation of commercial and investment banking. Under the act, commercial banks may not underwrite or deal in securities for their own accounts. They also may not affiliate with securities firms or investment trusts. Securities firms may not establish checking or savings accounts. Although Senator Glass had long argued against deposit insurance, the Banking Act created the Federal Deposit Insurance Corporation (FDIC). At least in part, this was a response to pressure from the public and from smaller banks.

Over-the-Counter Market Regulations

Federal regulation came more slowly to two other major segments of the industry, the OTC market and investment companies. Just the same, motivation for making the changes still came from the disasters of the early part of the decade, fortified by another crash in 1937.

Until 1938, when Congress passed the *Maloney Act*, OTC trading was unregulated. Even after the passage of the act, regulation rested relatively lightly on the industry. The Maloney Act's major accomplishments were to recognize the NASD's role as a self-regulatory organization and to exempt it from antitrust statutes. By 1939 the NASD had 1,500 members, and by 1941 it comprised more than 2,000 firms—30 percent of U.S. OTC dealers.

Though not as large as the NYSE, the OTC market was vigorous. In fact, the OTC and NYSE markets treated one another as enemies. This was especially true in regard to OTC trading of stocks listed on the exchange. Because the NYSE offered no volume discounts, institutional investors sometimes took their larger trades to the OTC market, where they could negotiate reduced commissions. The NYSE could not retaliate, because members were forbidden by SEC and exchange rules to trade listed stocks anywhere except on the exchange.

Further, the NYSE was not effective in convincing eligible unlisted companies to move their stock to the exchange. The usual procedure was for the American Stock Exchange (Amex) to purloin stocks from the OTC market and keep the shares until the NYSE took them. The history of the financial industry, like the history of nations, is seasoned by warfare.[8]

Investment Company Regulations

Investment companies, or investment trusts as they were commonly called at the time, started off conservatively enough in the early 1920s. As the Roaring Twenties gathered momentum, however, trusts began forming fast and furiously, often granting maximum latitude to the management and providing minimal safety for the investor.

Issuing bonds as well as stock, trusts became increasingly dependent on leverage. Sometimes one trust was formed to invest in another trust that had been formed to invest in still another—with leverage multiplied all along the chain. Furthermore, trusts were not required to disclose their investment decisions; to do so, managers argued, would prompt a run on the securities they owned.[9] As John Kenneth Galbraith notes in his classic study of the crash, the situation was reminiscent of an earlier investment debacle (mentioned in the preceding chapter of this book):

> Historians have told with wonder of one of the promotions at the time of the South Sea Bubble. It was "For an undertaking which shall in due time be revealed." The stock is said to have sold exceedingly well. As promotions the investment trusts were, on the record, even more wonderful. They were undertakings the nature of which was never to be revealed, and their stock sold exceedingly well.[10]

Disturbed by the trusts' disastrous performance in the early 1930s—losses of $3 billion on assets of $7 billion, according to a contemporary estimate—the SEC commissioned a study of the situation. Begun in 1935, the study took four years to complete and led to passage of the *Investment Company Act of 1940*. Requiring detailed disclosure and SEC regulation of investment companies, the act is the basis of current investment company regulations.

Though much has changed in the financial world since 1940, the United States has not experienced a cataclysmic bear market like the one in the early 1930s. Nor have we suffered through a depression like the one that crippled the economy during the remainder of that decade. We have also not seen revolutionary changes in securities regulations.

But the industry has scarcely stood still during the half century since the Investment Company Act of 1940. Steady fine tuning of industry regulations has occasionally given way to outbreaks of regulatory activity inspired by crisis. Like natural evolution, change in financial markets includes struggle and represents adaptation to new environments. The history of the financial markets is, in other words, a story of survival of the fittest. The next major test of fitness after the 1930s occurred during the Kennedy years. The market survived it rather handily.

THE KENNEDY CORRECTION

In 1962, in the midst of Camelot, a substantial correction interrupted the great bull market of 1941 to 1966. Stock prices increased steadily during the Eisenhower years, stumbling occasionally over bits of bad news such as presidential heart attacks and the launching of Sputnik. Starting at about 250 in 1953, the DJIA rose almost to 700 during the election campaign in 1960. That peak represented widespread optimism about the assumed victory of Richard Nixon, the candidate generally preferred by business.

As election day neared and the outcome of the contest seemed increasingly hard to predict, the DJIA dropped to 560. After Kennedy squeaked by his opponent, the market resumed its upward climb. The president's first year in office, despite problems as significant as the Bay of Pigs, was accompanied by continued bullish sentiment on Wall Street. By

EXHIBIT 3.2.   Market Performance, 1960 to 1962

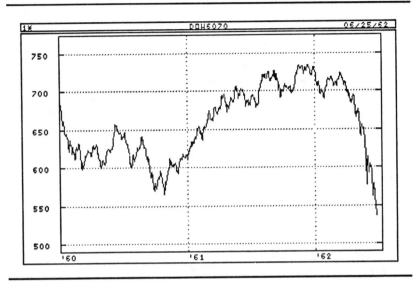

December of 1961, the DJIA had advanced above 730. Then the investment climate grew stormy.

During the first quarter of 1962, the market was buffeted by a series of moderate declines and advances. (See Exhibit 3.2.) By late March the DJIA was 723, at which point prices began to slide. Why? That's always a matter of conjecture, but the usual factors were present. The market had been ascending for a long time, and many observers thought the time for a correction had arrived. (Every bull market is accompanied by a chorus of doomsayers, who are, of course, eventually correct.) Bond yields were up, and institutional money was moving from stocks into debt securities. People were concerned about our unfavorable trade balance. The new president had campaigned, in part, on a platform of increased growth without increased inflation; but business needed more than the reassurances of a klatch of Harvard advisers to believe this was possible. There were scandals and investigations. One legislative inquiry revealed gross tampering in the new issue market, which had been a key factor in causing the run up in prices.

Most noticeable and most memorable was the confrontation between Kennedy and the steel industry in early April of 1962. Despite the administration's anti-inflation policies, the industry raised prices. In a remarkable display of presidential authority, Kennedy confronted industry leaders and "jawboned" them into rolling back prices. Although the confrontation was a great moment for President Kennedy, and should have reassured the public that he was serious about fighting inflation, it did nothing to ease suspicion that Kennedy was antibusiness. As *The Wall Street Journal* put it, "We never saw anything like it. One of the country's companies announced it was going to try to get more money for its products and promptly all hell busted loose."[11]

For whatever combination of reasons, the decline that began in March continued into April and May. Between 1962's New Year and April 30, for example, IBM lost 125 points, Litton Industries 48, and Texas Instruments 41.[12]

But the real excitement didn't come until late May. By Friday, May 24, the market was down to 611.88. On that day 6.3 million shares were traded, enough to put the tape 32 minutes behind at closing.[13] The collapse came on Monday when over nine million shares changed hands. The ticker didn't stop until an hour and 28 minutes after closing (3:30 Eastern in those days), and the DJIA fell 34.95 points to close at 576.93. Amidst comparisons between May 28 and the crash of 1929, the president declined to comment. Economic adviser Walter Heller quipped that "The market had nothing to fear but fear itself." J. Paul Getty allowed that he was buying what others were selling.[14] The *New York Times* was less sanguine, declaring that "something like an earthquake hit the stock market."[15]

The market continued falling on Tuesday. At noon, with the ticker rendered useless by the volume of trading, the DJIA was down over 48 points for the week. Then the market turned around. By the end of the day, the DJIA had won back 40 of those 48 points. On Thursday (the market was closed on Wednesday for Memorial Day), the DJIA rose over nine points to repair all the damage. Yet the slide was not over until June 25, when the market hit 524.55, a loss of 27 percent of the DJIA's value at its peak the previous December. Not until autumn did the market rally decisively and return to its bullish course.[16]

Despite the fireworks of late May and the slump that lasted through most of 1962, the regulatory aftereffects of "The Kennedy Slide" were relatively slight. The SEC conducted a study of the matter, but researchers could neither isolate the causes of the collapse nor recommend regulatory remedies. The report called attention to the disruption of normal trading on May 28 and 29—lateness of the tape, for example—and recommended that the exchanges make a joint study of ways to maintain normal functioning during heavy trading.

The Kennedy Administration responded to the crisis by pressing for tax cuts to vitalize the economy. The Federal Reserve Board lowered margin equity requirements to stimulate investment.[17] The most impressive aspect of the response was its moderation, perhaps an expression of faith in the market, the economy, and the general structure of regulation erected under the New Deal. Walter Heller's echo of FDR may have been right on the mark: Fear could have driven the market through the floor, but investors stayed relatively calm. Nevertheless, the market had some surprises in store for broker-dealers, investors, and regulators later in the decade.

MECHANICAL BREAKDOWN: 1968

The next market crisis was not precipitated by rapidly declining prices but, ironically, by steadily growing volume. We've just seen a harbinger of the problem. High turnover in late May of 1962 delayed the tape and threw the exchange into chaos. RRs stuffed orders into their pockets, hoping to execute them later. The tape lagged so far behind trading that sellers unloaded stocks at unknown prices. When the market resumed its upward course, the difficulties of May 28 and 29 were glossed over as anomalies. In retrospect they look more like portents.

The decade of the 1960s was a growth period for financial markets. It was also a time of strident controversy in the financial world, as it was in society at large.

But isn't growth good? More trading, after all, should yield more commissions for more brokers. Further, in 1964 the NYSE had taken steps to accommodate growing volume by installing a ticker capable of handling 10 million shares a day. It seemed an optimistic enough gesture, since the average trading volume at the time was only half that amount.

Yet, the exchange was not optimistic enough. Trading exceeded 10 million shares on the average day in 1967, and was near 13 million per day the next year. Stock prices were rising, new issues were abundant and popular, and the public was once again in love with the adventure of investing. To handle the crush of new customers, broker-dealers hired armies of inexperienced clerical personnel and RRs. The number of working RRs doubled between 1965 and 1968.

But all was not well. Growth was so rapid it became malignant. According to market historian Robert Sobel, the exchange floors were "hectic," specialists were "harried," and "brokerages were in a state of chaos."[18] The percentage of "fails" (trades that didn't settle in timely fashion) increased in proportion to growing volume and the mushrooming numbers of inexperienced brokerage employees. Executions were delayed, new electronic systems misbehaved, certificates arrived late or not at all. (Through the 1960s, certificates were delivered *to the money*. For every stock trade, in other words, a certificate had to be exchanged for payment. The cumbersome and time-consuming process has since been computerized.) Frustrated customers called RRs to sell stocks they had paid for, only to be told that the certificates had never arrived and the shares were not theirs to sell. Rumors abounded about Mafia infiltration, broker drug abuse, and widespread theft. Along with the increase in fails came a corresponding increase in customer complaints—up from about 3,000 in 1967 to over 14,000 in 1969.[19]

The market's credibility was in jeopardy. So, even though shareholder participation and stock prices were rising, the NYSE made changes designed to reduce the volume of fails and complaints. In the spring of 1968, under pressure from the SEC, the exchange decided to close on Wednesdays and forbid brokerage firms to advertise for new business, open new branches, or hire new RRs. This, along with a slowdown in trading, gave back office personnel a chance to catch up. In early 1969 the exchange went back to five-day weeks, but closed an hour and a half early each day. Such measures helped reduce fails and, consequently, customer frustration, but only temporarily.

As you can see in Exhibit 3.3, the bears returned to the market in 1969 and things fell apart. The Dow dropped from 969 in mid May of that year to 801 in late July—the worst decline since early in the decade. By December the DJIA was down to 770 and on May 26, 1970, it hit bottom at 631.16, a total decline of more than 330 points. Falling prices caught broker-dealers with depreciating inventories and high overhead, the latter caused by the mid-decade hiring binge. Actually losing money on commissions, over 100 securities firms liquidated in 1969.[20]

The NYSE kept a Special Trust Fund to bail out customers whose broker-dealers went belly up; it was quite proud of that

EXHIBIT 3.3.   Market Performance, 1968 to 1970

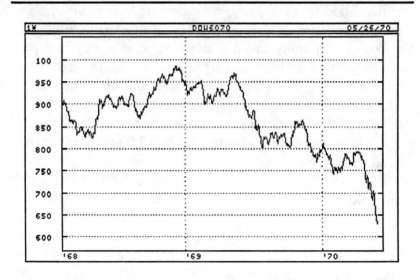

EXHIBIT 3.4.   DJIA Performance, 1970 to 1974

fact. However, the fund proved utterly inadequate to the crisis. In late 1970, therefore, Congress passed the *Securities Investor Protection Act*. Among other provisions, the act established the Securities Investor Protection Corporation (SIPC), which partially insures investors' accounts against broker-dealer bankruptcy.

Congress also called in SEC officials and charged them with a mission: increase investor protection. In response, the SEC increased broker-dealer net capital requirements and drafted the *Customer Protection Rule* (15c3-3). Under the Customer Protection Rule, firms are required to segregate customer cash and securities from their own positions. The rule also tightened limits on firms' ability to pledge customer securities as collateral.

As you can see from Exhibit 3.4, the market recovered temporarily, with the DJIA returning to 1,000 by early 1972. Then the bottom fell out. By late 1974 the DJIA had reached a new low.

The early 1970s was a turbulent time in the U.S. The Watergate scandal and the ugly end to U.S. participation in Vietnam eroded the nation's sense of purpose. Then the Arab oil embargo boosted oil prices and caused shortages that had motorists lined up at gas pumps waiting to fill their tanks with high-priced fuel. Talk of gasoline prices at $3.00 or $4.00 a gallon added fuel to the existing fear of inflation.

Besides coping with political and economic crises, broker-dealers had to worry about adapting to the rules passed in response to the problems of 1968 and 1969. Regulatory changes aimed at increasing the safety of customers' accounts significantly altered business conditions. For example, the new rules raised net-capital requirements in order to decrease the likelihood that firms would slip into bankruptcy. However, keeping more money available to meet the higher requirements substantially reduced broker-dealers' liquidity. Some broker-dealers had great difficulty adapting to the new regulatory environment. Ironically, rules written to correct current problems in the market may create the problems of the future.

QUIET EVOLUTION

An outright crisis—market crashes, scandals, failures in back office procedures, bankruptcies, and the like—may cause revolutionary changes in securities laws and rules. This was the case in the 1930s and, to a lesser degree, in the early 1970s. In addition, the ordinary evolution of the marketplace can also transform the way business is done on Wall Street. Such changes aren't so dramatic and immediate, but they can be just as sweeping. A good example of that is the growth of NASDAQ and the so-called third market since the 1960s.

The increased volume of trading in the 1960s didn't result entirely from the popularity of common stocks among individual investors. Instead of entering one by one, investors were coming into the market in groups through pools of money such as mutual funds, insurance company accounts, pensions, and trusts.

By 1969 more than 40 percent of volume on the NYSE was institutional—up from 26 percent in 1961. (The rest of the trading was carried out by individuals and exchange officials.)[21] This change in constituency put severe strains on the NYSE. It also exacerbated tensions between the NYSE and regional exchanges, between the exchange and OTC markets, between the self-regulatory organizations and the SEC, and among factions within the NYSE itself.

The major impact of institutional investors was to cause a substantial increase in the trading of large blocks of shares. Naturally, institutions wanted price breaks on such giant trades. Since NYSE rules forbade discounting, institutional investors sought lower commissions at regional exchanges and in the so-called *third market*—OTC trading of exchange-listed stocks.

In a controversial 1970 speech, President Robert W. Haack of the NYSE claimed market fragmentation was reducing the exchange's liquidity and efficiency. As a solution, Haack proposed the SEC's favored remedy: negotiated commissions. Since such price competition was anathema to most NYSE members, Haack's speech was political suicide.

Perhaps the most highly charged words in the speech, however, had nothing directly to do with commissions. Haack accused the exchange of resembling a "private club." If widely shared, such a perception would be the kiss of death. No public customer willingly invests in a market rigged to favor insiders.

Though Haack lost the presidency of the exchange, his views eventually prevailed. In April 1971 the SEC established negotiable commissions on trades greater than $500,000, and set a four-year deadline for phasing in negotiable rates on all trades. In 1975 commissions became fully negotiable. As we'll soon see, the pressures for further reform in the interests of institutional investors have not let up.

BLACK MONDAY AND ITS AFTERMATH

The period of evolutionary rule change seems to be continuing, even though something approaching a crisis atmosphere developed after Black Monday in October 1987. Moreover, the sense of crisis has been kept alive by assorted other blots on the credibility of the financial industry, including the less breathtaking nose dive taken by the stock market in October 1989, widely publicized insider trading scandals, the junk bond debacle, the S&L disaster, and general cynicism about penny stock firms. All of this, which is perhaps further compounded by worries about worldwide interest rates, recession,

EXHIBIT 3.5. DJIA Performance, 1986 to 1987

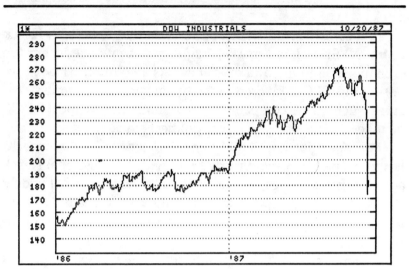

inflation, and political instability among OPEC nations, has dampened the enthusiasm of the individual investor, put a greater share of trading in the hands of institutions, and generally depressed (both economically and psychologically) RRs and other employees of U.S. broker-dealers. Changes in the marketplace since Black Monday, therefore, are well worth describing.

Descent Into Black Monday

Exhibit 3.5 of the DJIA from early 1986 through mid-October 1987 tells the story of Black Monday's unnerving impact.

The disconcerting aspect of the 1987 break in the market was not so much its magnitude as its speed. After peaking at 2722 in late August, the DJIA declined (though not without upward rallies) into October. On the Friday before October 19, the market dropped 108 points under a steady barrage of bad news about the Iran Contra affair, interest rates, the Middle East, and the dollar. It was the first one-day drop of more than 100 points. At 338 million shares traded, volume, too, set a record. The closing price of the DJIA was 2247.

Bad news continued during the weekend, and, under selling pressure in Tokyo, London, and Europe, the U.S. market opened down 200 points on Monday morning. After a brief rally, prices plunged downward throughout the day, with the market closing at 1738. The total drop for Black Monday was 508 points, or 22.61 percent. Though the market looked shaky again on Tuesday morning, the DJIA recovered during the day and closed up 103 points, at 1841. Prices rose 187 points the next day, and on Friday the DJIA closed at 1951—24 points above the closing price on the first trading day of 1987. All in all, the correction from August 25 through October 19 was about 1,000 points, or 35 percent. The phenomenal upsurge of the first half of 1987 was almost entirely erased. About 50 percent of the 1982-1987 bull market disappeared in those two unpleasant months.

Nevertheless, a sense of panic didn't set in until the spectacular plunge on October 19 and 20. On those two days, volume suddenly doubled to 600 million shares a day. Price information wasn't available. Brokers couldn't answer calls from customers desperate to sell or eager to buy. Trading mechanisms failed. On Tuesday morning, the 20th, banks withdrew credit, prompting fear that broker-dealers might be unable to settle trades with a resulting loss of capital that would force them out of business. The best-regulated, most efficient market in the world—and one of the largest—suddenly seemed inoperative. A tremor of panic shook investors around the globe.

Equity prices fell almost everywhere, except in such places as South Korea where national policy insulated the market from global events by forbidding foreign ownership of securities. The Japanese were widely expected to suffer the most debilitating long-range results, since many considered their stocks grossly overpriced. In fact, Tokyo's Nikkei Index declined less, on a percentage basis, than the DJIA. It was also much quicker to recover and exceed its precrash highs. Indeed, until the long, steep slide beginning in early 1990, Japanese stock prices seemed almost invulnerable. In Hong Kong, by contrast, the market was shut down after Black Monday and the government was forced to fund a massive bailout of a devastated securities industry. London's percentage decline was even greater than New York's.

The general collapse so unnerved U.S. investors that they got out of the market and stayed out—even after recovery, when the market regained all the ground lost in September and October 1987. Public investors, professional traders, and market makers all worried that the market had slipped into chaos.

Investors got burned, and their legislators heard them scream. The public was concerned that Wall Street, a significant piece of the economy, was broken; they wanted something done to restore its integrity. In response to pressures from individual investors, the North American Securities Administrators Association (NASAA) set up a hot line for aggrieved customers. Nevertheless, many complaints took well over a year to resolve.

The public outcry for something to be done to restore the market to smoother functioning marked a change in attitude. Back in 1971, when SIPC was established to put government muscle behind insurance protection for securities customers, there were unhappy predictions that the government would soon be dipping into the public treasury to rescue the industry. The bankruptcies of 1968 and 1969, which had prompted the formation of SIPC, were fresh in people's minds. After the 1987 debacle, however, the public seemed ready to use tax revenues to keep the securities industry afloat. (Whether the public maintains its willingness to bail out troubled financial institutions throughout the S&L fiasco remains, at this writing, to be seen.)

Meanwhile, the securities industry continues to resist tougher federal regulation. Moreover, legislators themselves worry about disruptions that might occur as the market reorganizes to conform to new rules. The favored strategy has been to alter administrative processes rather than to write new rules. Just the same, some significant changes have been made.

For a long time before Black Monday, the SEC had been nagging at the industry to institute RR retesting or continuing education. They found little support among industry or investors. Since 1986 regulators have been calling for stricter supervision of RRs by broker-dealers, changes in trading systems, and new definitions of terms related to the supervisory structure. Outrage about the market crack and continuing scandals finally created a constituency for such reforms.

For its part, the NYSE has been pushing for identification of the sources of large trades (i.e., 50,000 shares and more). To improve their ability to supervise such activity, exchanges want access to the customer's name, information that is not currently available. The NYSE has, on the other hand, been moving toward 24-hour trading as an outlet for large institutional investors who, as we'll see, have been attracted to alternative markets. To head off runaway declines, like those causing such panic on October 19 and 20 in 1987, the NYSE, Amex, and other exchanges have instituted circuit breakers and sidecars to shut off or restrict trading when the market moves too far too fast. We'll take a look at these reforms and how they have functioned in practice.

Circuit Breakers and Sidecars

The initial responses to Black Monday focused on recent innovations in trading, especially the simultaneous, computerized buying and selling of baskets of stocks on the NYSE and related index futures on Chicago's Mercantile Exchange (the Merc). Reasoning that these mammoth trades drove the market down with unnatural speed for unnecessary distances, critics called for procedural changes to restrict the offending activities.

The most Draconian of the circuit breakers has not yet been tested. This is a complete, one-hour cessation of trading if the DJIA moves 250 points below the previous day's close. After resumption, trading will stop again for two hours if the market slips another 150 points lower. The closest we have come to a test of the 250-point circuit breaker was on Friday October 13, 1989, when the market dropped 190 points on the news that a proposed takeover of United Airlines had fallen through. (Other trading restrictions, applying to other markets, did come into effect, as we'll see below.) After that experience, an NYSE panel was convened and it recommended tighter restrictions, some of which have been adopted. A proposal to halt trading after a 100-point drop has, at this writing, not been accepted.

A circuit breaker that has been tested is triggered when the Dow falls or rises 50 points during a day. When this happens, program trades can only be executed under circumstances that will not exacerbate volatility. (For instance, program sales in a down market can only occur if the last trade to change the DJIA caused upward movement.) The restrictions remain in place for the rest of the session or until the market moves back to within 25 points of its previous close. In addition, program trades are taken off the NYSE's automatic execution system for five minutes whenever S&P 500 futures contracts reach certain price limits on the Merc. This latter procedure, called a *sidecar*, is aimed at arbitrage trades triggered by differences in the price of the futures contract and the value of the stocks represented by the contract.

Both rules are designed to dampen the effects of huge trades on price volatility, a factor that keeps smaller investors out of the market. When the market is going down, for example, those enormous sell orders magnify and accelerate the downward momentum. The restrictions on program selling give traders a chance to even out the resulting imbalances in buy and sell orders, thus at least temporarily putting the brakes on the downhill movement.

Movement in the S&P futures contract price also affects trading in the contract itself as well as in the underlying stocks. During the first 10 minutes of a session, for example, trading of the contract will stop if its price moves more than five points away from the previous close. If the contract remains at the limit after the first 10 minutes of the day's trading have elapsed, suspension remains in effect for another two minutes. If the price falls 12 points, trading at a lower price is not allowed for the next half hour. After that, a one-hour cessation of trading will occur if the price drops an additional eight points. After a single-session drop of 30 points, trading of the contract is allowed only within certain limits for the remainder of the session.

Though as of this writing the market has still not tested the 250-point limit down, five- and 12-point drops in the S&P triggered trading halts on Friday, March 17, 1989, and in August of 1990, when the Iraqi invasion of Kuwait sent the market tumbling. (The 12-point limit was also tested on October 13, 1989.) No one can say for certain what might have happened had the trading restrictions not taken effect. During the Kuwait crisis, however, NYSE restrictions on program trades in conjunction with the Merc's 12-point limit on movement of the S&P 500 contract seem to have prevented free falls on more than one nervous occasion. It seems fair to say that further testing remains to be done, especially of the NYSE circuit breakers, before anyone will be in a position to draw reliable conclusions. Unfortunately, such testing cannot occur in the abstract; we have to wait for more crises to hit the market.

Trading restrictions are also in place at the Amex and on the Chicago Board of Trade (CBOT). The NASD, on the other hand, has so far declined to institute similar policies.

Institutional Pressures

The changes we've just been reviewing, circuit breakers and sidecars, are largely responses from individual investors who were frightened by the effects of volatility on their portfolios. No matter that the market rapidly recovered from Black Monday, the memory lingers of having one's already depleted net worth so severly devastated in one day. Three years later, sidecars and circuit breakers notwithstanding, individual investors are still not sufficiently confident about the market to have returned in significant numbers.

Of course, the loss of individual investors is most heavily felt by those who cater directly to them, the retail brokerage houses and their registered representatives. RRs who have prospected among individual investors both before and after Black Monday testify to the altered emotional climate among potential investors. Instead of meeting polite indifference or lack of interest, RRs now encounter a good deal of outright hostility—a measure of lingering distrust of the unpredictable, volatile market.

But what about the institutions that now account for an increasingly large fraction of the markets' capital and volume? These institutions, after all, are the users of the strategies targeted by circuit breakers and sidecars. How are they responding to the changed conditions in securities markets?

For one thing, institutions have largely dropped their support of one reform that was widely touted in the early responses to Black Monday. That reform was the extension of SEC authority over the trading of index futures, which is supervised by the Commodities Futures Trading Commission (CFTC). Since program trading and index arbitrage were blamed for excessive volatility, critics suggested that one authority should reign over all the instruments employed in such activities. As time has passed, however, institutions and the broker-dealers that represent them have backed away from their early support of extending SEC jurisdiction. They argue now that tighter supervision will restrict the market's creativity and drive away traders, thus depleting the market's liquidity.

In respect to SEC jurisdiction over index futures and in other ways, institutional investors support a different agenda from individual investors. This agenda includes some familiar items, notably the desire for special treatment that led to the establishment of negotiable commissions in the earlier 1970s. According to an article in *The Financial Times*,[22] institutions "are increasingly frustrated with what they see as anachronistic, uncompetitive exchange rules and high transaction costs." As individual investors have made their complaints known, so have their larger counterparts. According to the same article, when Bill Donaldson took over as chairman of the NYSE, one of his first courtesy calls was from "the head of equities at one of the leading and most aggressive Wall Street securities houses." The lobbying effort began immediately.

What do the institutions want from the exchange market? Predictably, they want even less costly trading fees. They also want relief from the NYSE's rule against trading listed stocks off the exchange during trading hours—a desire the exchange is trying to accommodate as part of its move toward 24-hour trading. The exchange reasons that trades now being carried out in London and on other exchanges outside the U.S. will come home if after-hours facilities are available.

Still, the more radically unhappy institutional customers have revived the long-standing argument against the NYSE's specialist system. Their complaints, to judge by the following quote from a "top executive of a Wall Street firm" interviewed for the *Financial Times* article, are not always politely phrased: "There is a firm which finds a buyer and seller. Why should we go down to the floor, use an expensive messenger who wandered over to a booth to a guy who has a God-given right to execute a trade on that security, and then get in line behind some little guy wanting to sell 10 shares?"[23]

At present, Mr. Donaldson seems unsympathetic to anti-specialist sentiment. "If the big guys are just interested in making a few bucks in the short haul, they will end up destroying the broad base of this market which is unique in the world."[24] Clearly, his job is a challenging one. To keep his marketplace whole he must hold on to the institutions and stem the exodus of individuals. No doubt the needs of the two different constituencies dovetail in some respects. The presence of numerous investors keeps the market liquid, for example, cutting trading costs and reducing risk for all concerned. Still, small and large investors are distinct groups with sometimes opposing agendas. As things stand, Mr. Donaldson's exchange teeters on the brink of the worst of all possible outcomes—losing both groups. With stakes that high, the exchange may have to reform in order to avoid withering away. We should remember, from our historical survey in Chapter 2, that the London exchange floor has been largely emptied of securities activity, which has moved to the trading rooms of the city's brokerage houses.

Markets thrive by changing to meet new conditions and overcome competition from other markets, not by standing still.

The RR's New Regulatory Role

Recent regulatory changes have tended to force supervision down the chain of command toward the RR. Beginning in 1989, for example, firms had to provide annual compliance training for RRs. (Reading this book may be a part of such training.) This is one way of putting you on notice that compliance is essential to your role in the marketplace. This pressure to know and follow the rules doesn't originate with your compliance officer, but at the top of that chain of responsibility connecting Congress to the SEC to self-regulatory bodies (e.g., the NYSE and the NASD) to RRs.

At every link in this regulatory chain, there is new emphasis on promoting ethical behavior and isolating responsibility for misdeeds. When violations occur, offenders can then be identified and excised, leaving the rest of the industry healthy. It's just another chapter in the old story of markets regulating themselves, and being regulated by governments in order to preserve their credibility with customers. There is a connection, now as always, between ethics and profit. Unfortunately, it isn't a direct connection; we have to be reminded of its reality by the occasional crisis. To weather the current crisis, legislators, regulators, exchange personnel, compliance officers, and registered representatives must all cooperate to improve the reputation of their marketplace as an efficient and ethical place for raising and investing money. With its credibility restored, Wall Street may lead the way into a future of global securities markets that trade newly devised investment instruments by means of satellites and other advanced communications technologies. Without renewed credibility, Wall Street could become just another address on a narrow passageway between empty buildings at the tip of a small island.

Notes

1. Malkiel, Burton G., *A Random Walk Down Wall Street*, 4th ed. (New York: W.W. Norton & Company, 1985), p. 44.

2. Sobel, Robert, *N.Y.S.E.* (New York: Weybright and Talley, 1975), p. 3.

3. Galbraith, John Kenneth, *The Great Crash 1929* (Boston: Houghton Mifflin, 1988), p. 166.

4. Vietor, Richard H.K., "Regulation-Defined Financial Markets: Fragmentation and Integration in Financial Services," *Wall Street and Regulation*, Samuel L. Hayes III, ed., (Boston: Harvard Business School Press, 1987), p. 21.

5. *Ibid.*, p. 22.

6. *Ibid.*, p. 14.

7. *Ibid.*, p. 16.

8. Sobel, *N.Y.S.E., Op. Cit.*, pp. 254–255.

9. Galbraith, *Op. Cit.*, p. 49.

10. *Ibid.*, p. 49.

11. Sobel, *N.Y.S.E., Op. Cit.*, p. 410.

12. *Ibid.*, p. 411.

13. *Ibid.*, p. 415.

14. *Ibid.*, p. 421.

15. Malkiel, *Op. Cit.*, p. 55.

16. Sobel, *Op. Cit.*, p. 426.

17. Sobel, *Op. Cit.*, p. 421.

18. Sobel, *N.Y.S.E., Op. Cit.*, p. 289.

19. *Ibid.*, p. 290.

20. Vietor, Richard H.K., *Op. Cit.*, p. 44.

21. Sobel, *N.Y.S.E., Op. Cit.*, p. 291.

22. "Hoping for a New Broom at the NYSE," *The Financial Times*, August 16, 1990.

23. *Ibid.*

24. *Ibid.*

PART TWO

RULES OF THE ROAD IN U.S. SECURITIES MARKETS

4

Agents and Principals

THE LAW OF AGENCY AND THE RR

The mass of rules governing the RR's actions may seem bur-densome—like stone tablets hauled down from the mountaintop and piled on one's back. The language in which they are written, scarcely more accessible than cuneiform, makes them seem an even weightier handicap. Yet, though they are numerous and sometimes obscure, the rules of the road are generally based on common sense and the duties that one human being clearly owes to another.

Becoming a registered representative means entering into a specific type of human relationship lawyers call *agency*. And all those laws and rules are about being a successful and ethical agent.

Legally speaking, an agent is a person selected to act on behalf of another person called a *principal*. The principal deter-mines what job should be done and contracts with an agent to do it. In the terminology of *Black's Law Dictionary*, an agent is "A person authorized by another to act for him, one intrusted with another's business.... One who undertakes to transact some business, or to manage some affair, for another, by the

63

authority and on account of the latter, and to render an account of it."[1] The agent, therefore, has a legal obligation to act in the principal's best interests when carrying out those assigned duties.

In the securities business, broker-dealers and RRs both have agency responsibilities. (The legal term *person* can sometimes refer to an organization as well as an individual.) When acting as brokers, firms transact business on the authority of others (customers), with a legal obligation to act in the other's best interest. The firm's agency duties also bind the RR, whether the RR acts simply as an employee or as the firm's agent. At discount securities houses RRs tend to have simple employee responsibilities. That is, they carry out their duties as the firm defines them. RRs working on contracts or housed in remote offices of full-service firms may act more as agents of the firm than as employees. When this is the case, the broker-dealer is a principal as defined above. Whether or not the RR is defined as an agent or employee does little to alter the responsibilities of the position.

The RR is a double agent, so to speak, acting on behalf of two principals—customer and broker-dealer. Serving two masters can be difficult, especially if their goals don't coincide. In large part, the rules of the road are there to help RRs serve their two masters equally, without putting one's interests ahead of the other's, and without putting self-interest ahead of either principal's legitimate needs. Whatever their short-term conflicts, customers and securities firms have the same long-range interests. As we saw in the preceding chapters, when customers aren't treated fairly they leave the market. Then everyone loses.

BROKERS, DEALERS, AND REGISTERED REPRESENTATIVES

Securities firms function in three distinct ways: as brokers, as dealers, and as investment advisers. Performing any of these functions requires registration with the SEC. Most firms act both as brokers and dealers, which accounts for the common designation, broker-dealer. In this book we are primarily concerned with the broker and dealer functions, not investment advising.

A broker, according to the *Securities and Exchange Act of 1934*, is a "person engaged in the business of effecting transactions in securities for the account of others."[2] (Though the law refers to *persons*, in the real world brokers are firms.) In other words, a broker arranges a trade between a buyer and a seller. It does not buy or sell securities in its own account and, therefore, has no inventory. The broker makes money by charging each buyer and seller a commission.

A dealer, by contrast, is a "person engaged in the business of buying and selling securities for his own account."[3] Dealers, unlike brokers, have an inventory of their own securities. Instead of receiving commissions for arranging trades, they make money by selling securities at a high enough price to cover their costs and yield a profit.

Investment advisers, of course, provide advice about the purchase and sale of securities. To receive compensation for giving advice, one must first register with the SEC according to the requirements of the *Investment Advisers Act of 1940*. Under an exemption from registration requirements, broker-dealers and their agents may also provide investment advice. Technically, they are not compensated for the advice, only for their role in actual transactions.

When a broker-dealer hires agents to carry out these trading functions, it must register those agents with the market where the securities trade; hence, the term *registered representative*.

The role of the RR is very different from that of the broker-dealer. The RR carries out the orders of the broker-dealer. The broker-dealer, on the other hand, may be a principal, trading for its own profit in its own account. Moving from the status of registered representative to the status of broker-dealer requires registration with the SEC.

Not keeping these registration requirements straight is what got Jimmy Doyle into trouble with market regulators—that, and stealing his customers' securities.

JIMMY DOYLE REVISITED

Jimmy Doyle was a registered representative, an employee of the broker-dealer John G. Kinnard. As an agent, he could arrange transactions for Kinnard's customers. Sometimes, however, he acted as a principal—buying securities, marking them up, and selling them. Since Jimmy was not registered as a broker-dealer, he was not authorized to make such transactions. No matter how fairly and efficiently he acted in his customers' behalf, Jimmy was on the wrong side of market regulations.

Jimmy's customers had authority to tell him, as their agent, to put them together with other buyers and sellers of bonds. In most cases he did so as a faithful and conscientious agent for his customers. On the other hand, he certainly did not fulfill his agency duties when he neglected to carry out customers' instructions to close their accounts. As we saw, his unauthorized trading in one former customer's account was the beginning of his end.

As double agent Jimmy was also responsible for following his employer's instructions. Kinnard had the authority to require him to report all trades so it could fulfill its obligation to keep good records. When Jimmy did not do that, he failed to carry out his duties to the broker-dealer. That, too, was a factor in his downfall.

The legal definitions given earlier imply that the agent must act on the principal's behalf, and that the principal takes responsibility for what the agent does. The agent simply carries out acts the principal would otherwise perform unassisted. Customers, for example, could sell their securities in coffee shops, if they didn't want to pay agents to assist them. Broker-dealers could save money by not hiring RRs. (As an unregistered and overworked broker-dealer, that's what Jimmy did.) Looked at this way, agency seems a pretty subservient business, a matter of following orders. In fact, law books say an agent is one sort of servant, a principal one type of master.

When you look a little closer, you see that an agent has power over the principal—power to bind that person or organization legally. The agent is literally doing the principal's work, and if it's dirty work, the principal may be held legally accountable.

Kinnard, as principal, was responsible for the actions and activities of Jimmy Doyle. Knowing that to be the case, Jimmy expected Kinnard to suffer both legally and financially when he took off with the bonds. He assumed his clients would go to Kinnard for restitution and the firm would be forced to pay. Kinnard's dilemma would be Jimmy's revenge.

That Kinnard escaped punishment for Jimmy's misdeeds is perhaps due to its immediate and vigorous cooperation in the investigation. The firm's aggressive cooperation with regulators put some distance between it and Jimmy. In effect, Kinnard convinced authorities that Jimmy had ceased acting as its agent; therefore, Jimmy no longer had the power to bind them legally through his acts. Kinnard, too, would have been punished if investigators had found the firm deficient in carrying out its supervisory duties. Principals must, in other words, be watchful of agents that act on their behalf, or they risk punishment for agents' misdeeds.

THE RR'S RESPONSIBILITY TO INDUSTRY REGULATORS

Rules of the road reflect more than the market's attempt to defend its integrity. They also reflect the will of the general public expressed through Congress. A chain of regulation links all players together, stretching from the RR through the market and Congress to the public. Regulation begins with the public's desire for an efficient and ethical securities market. To enforce this desire, the public delegates Congress authority to write laws applying to market activities. Congress, then, is the second link in the regulatory chain.

To administer securities laws, Congress creates agencies (such as the SEC authorized by the Securities Exchange Act of 1934). Their word is law, and to break certain SEC rules is to risk a term in federal prison. The SEC is the third link in the regulatory chain.

The fourth link is the market's own self-regulatory structure—exchanges and the NASD. Unlike the SEC, these organizations are not part of the government; they are private membership groups. Their regulations are not laws; they are ethical guidelines. These SROs, therefore, do not have authority to impose jail sentences. Yet, they do have authority, granted by law, to fine and expel members who violate their rules. In some cases, indeed, SRO regulations are close cousins of SEC rules, and RRs who violate such rules may find themselves sanctioned by the NASD and brought to court by the SEC.

Broker-dealers, though participants in the marketplace, are the fifth link in the chain of regulation. As members of self-regulatory organizations, firms are charged with supervising employees' compliance with SRO rules. A broker-dealer has its own rule making power. A firm can, for example, impose stricter margin requirments than market regulators demand, though of course it cannot allow lower margin payments.

The last link in the chain is the RR. Though not allowed to supervise themselves, RRs certainly are responsible for their own behavior. At present, SROs stress two methods of enforcement: adequate supervision by firms on the one hand; self-monitoring by RRs on the other. Of late, the market has not served the public interest as well as it should. Consequently, it has lost credibility. SROs have responded by tightening supervision and compliance requirements.

This book is one response to SROs' recent push for greater ethical sensitivity. More than that, it attempts to answer a long-standing SEC call for expanded education or further testing of RRs. The recent upsurge in public mistrust of the marketplace has given the SEC more leverage to institute such programs. Pushing responsibility down the chain toward the RR makes it easier to isolate and excise malefactors—to protect the industry as a whole from suffering a great loss of esteem. Focusing responsibility on the RR is a form of damage control.

The RR's Duties to the SEC

Under normal circumstances, RRs don't deal directly with the SEC. Instead, they follow instructions from their employers, who are, in turn, acting upon regulations. Firms enforce the following rules upon their RRs:

1. The duty to be accurate in filing information.

2. The duty to respond promptly and thoroughly to requests for information.

3.   The duty to pay all fines and costs incurred because of
      rule violations.

The registered representative has a duty to file accurate information as required by the SEC.

The Securities Exchange Act of 1934 requires members of
exchanges and the NASD to register with the SEC. Broker-
dealers must register by filing a form BD. RRs register with a
broker-dealer. RRs' registration requirements include filing
Form U-4, being fingerprinted, and taking the appropriate
qualification examination.

Filing false information or cheating on the test violates the
RR's duties to each link in the chain of regulation. In fact, the
information-gathering process aptly illustrates the way links of
the regulatory chain interlock.

First, the public became concerned about lack of commun-
ity control over the securities markets. The public's representatives in Congress responded by passing the 1934 act
mandating registration of securities firms with the SEC. The
SEC administers the act by delegating the paperwork to SROs.
The Series 7 exam, for example, is created by SRO committees
representing the NASD, the NYSE, the Chicago Board Options
Exchange (CBOE), and the Municipal Securities Rulemaking
Board (MSRB). The test is assembled by the New York Stock
Exchange, and administered and scored by the NASD. Each
broker-dealer distributes U-4s and sees that RRs take the
proper exams before starting work. Here are some recent
examples of what happens to RRs who fail to file accurate and
complete data.

Case 4-1 Though Dale N. Klemens filed a U-4 application claiming he had never been convicted of a felony or misdemeanor involving theft or dishonesty, he had such a conviction in 1980. For this failure to make an accurate filing, the NASD censured Klemens, fined him $5,000, and barred him from association with any NASD member in any capacity.

Case 4-2 For lying about his educational background on a U-4 application, an RR (who was not named in the announcement) was censured, fined $5,000, and barred from any association with an NASD member.

Case 4-3 The NASD determined that Beth Jill DiGiacinto and Barry Paul Sarin provided assistance to one another during the Series 7 examination. Each was fined $1,000 and suspended from association with any NASD member in any capacity for one year.

RRs register as employees of an NASD or NYSE member and, to facilitate supervision, trade only through that member. If individuals sold securities without registering with a firm, they would be unsupervised. As the following cases show, regulators do not consider trading by unregistered persons to be in the public's best interest.

Case 4-4 Watson and Taylor Investments, Inc., and registered representative A. Starke Taylor, III allegedly permitted an unregistered individual to sell limited partnership interests and receive $24,999 in commissions. The firm and Taylor were fined $15,000.

> An RR must be accurate and timely in complying with requests for information.

When regulators investigate an RR suspected of errant behavior, they request information from that individual. Failure to provide that information is itself a rule violation. Here are some cases in which failure to provide information to regulators earned RRs varying degrees of punishment:

Case 4-5   Rosanna Quinn failed three times to respond to NASD requests for information about the termination of her employment with a member firm. The NASD barred Quinn from any association with a member.

Case 4-6   Clifford Romain failed to respond to two NASD requests for information concerning compliance with the Rules of Fair Practice. Romain was fined $5,000, suspended from association with any NASD member in any capacity for two years, and required to take another qualifying exam before returning to work for a member firm.

Case 4-7   Herbert Shaw Gordon failed to respond to three NASD requests concerning various allegations made by four customers. Gordon was fined $15,000 and barred from association with any member.

Case 4-8   Judith Ann Kools failed to honor NASD requests for information regarding her employer's financial condition. Kools was suspended from association with any NASD member for six months. She and her employer were fined $3,000.

> Individual RRs and firms must pay fully and promptly any fines or costs incurred because of violations.

Part of the RR's duty to the marketplace is to comply with sanctions. Disciplinary procedures would have no meaning if they could be ignored. The following example is drawn from an NASD announcement published in January, 1989.

Case 4-9 Metropolitan Asset Securities, Ltd. and 11 of its registered employees failed to pay fines and costs in connection with violations. The NASD expelled the firm from membership and revoked the individuals' registrations.

THE RR'S DUTY AS AGENT OF THE BROKER-DEALER

Much of the NASD's leverage over registered representatives is indirect and exercised through member broker-dealers who employ RRs. This gives a broker-dealer double authority over employees: boss and enforcer. The two roles are not inherently incompatible, but occasionally an RR may feel the employer is sending mixed signals, i.e., to be more aggressive in sales but more cautious in recommendations. The apparent contradiction resolves itself if the RR is aggressive in making appropriate sales of legitimate investments, thus pleasing both sales and compliance managers, not to mention customers.

As supervisor, the broker-dealer needs complete and accurate information about RRs and their activities in the market. As agent of the broker-dealer employer, the RR is required to abide by the following four requirements:

1. Make full and prompt payment of any money owed the employer.

2. Notify the employer of any circumstance that jeopardizes the RR's ability to perform agency responsibilities. The RR must, for example, submit written notification before participating in private securities transactions or receiving compensation from another firm. All compensation must go through the employer's books.

3. Comply with market rules when executing all responsibilities assigned by the employer. As principal, the employer must exercise adequate supervision to see that its agents comply with regulations. In an underwriting, for example, the broker-dealer must not allow its employees or their associates to buy the securities at a special price. If the employee buys part of a new issue at the offering price, and the price subsequently rises rapidly in aftermarket trading, the employee must give up ownership of the security. The same is true for relatives of the employee who purchase a hot issue.

4. Abide by the firm's responsibility to charge only a *fair* markup on securities when acting as dealer.

Now we'll explain each of these requirements further, and illustrate them with case histories.

The RR's Duty to Pay Employer Promptly

Although the subhead may at first seem a mirror image of reality—isn't the employer supposed to pay the employee?—there are in fact times when the duties are reversed and the employee owes the firm money.

An RR must pay promptly and in full all money owed to the employer broker-dealer.

RRs who have accounts with their employers must pay in full and on time just like other customers. This means the broker-dealer cannot invent account procedures that favor the accounts of employees over those of public customers. The RR's compensation may include commissions or salary, but not special privileges in the marketplace.

Case 4-10 Stephen Fischer paid off an IOU to his employer with a check for $14,037.33. The check bounced. The NASD fined Fischer $20,000 and barred him from association with any NASD member in any capacity. (Fischer aggravated the infraction by failing to respond to NASD inquiries.)

Case 4-11 Francis Russo failed to pay for securities he bought in his account with his employer. Worse, he refused to pay his bill. The broker-dealer had to sell the securities at a loss. Not surprisingly, the employer fired Russo. The NASD sent him two requests for information about the firing, then fined him $10,000 and barred him from associating with any NASD member for three years.

Case 4-12 Charles Harman paid his employer for options positions in his personal account by writing a bad check for $160,000. The check bounced, as Harman knew it would. The NASD fined him $45,000 and barred him from association with any member in any capacity.

The RR's Duty to Report Outside Business Activities

You would think that selling, prospecting, reading, market watching, and account management duties assigned to an RR would be enough to keep anyone busy. Nevertheless, some ambitious RRs take on work in addition to what their employers provide. Outside work, or other market-related activities, are, in more sense than one, not just the RR's business. Moonlighting has implications for the employer and for the market as a whole.

> An RR must notify the employer of anything that jeopardizes his or her ability to perform agency responsibilities. This includes receiving compensation from another firm for securities-related business, opening an account with another firm in the RR's name or a relative's name, and participating in private securities transactions.

When a person registers to sell securities through a broker-dealer, the firm becomes responsible for supervising the employee's participation in the marketplace. Since the firm cannot supervise what it doesn't know about, RRs must obtain their employers' written permission before undertaking any outside securities business. Although this may sound simple and straightforward, in practice it can be tricky. RRs sometimes fail to report compensation or outside activities out of ignorance, not because they are trying to evade regulations.

Take compensation, for example. Any compensation an RR receives from any source within the industry must be paid directly to the employer and must go through the firm's books. Say an RR has been particularly successful selling interests in a limited partnership. As a reward, the general partner (GP) gives the RR a four-day trip to the Bahamas. Is that compensation? Yes.

Now let's say that during the trip the RR attends a conference sponsored by the International Association of Financial Planners (IAFP), and perhaps the GP arranges and pays for hotel accommodations. Or, the GP gives the RR's spouse a plane ticket to the Bahamas, which the spouse, uninterested in tropical trips, cashes in and spends on groceries. Is compensation involved in such cases? Yes. In each instance, the RR has received compensation that must be paid first to the employer and entered into the books. The value of the trip, the hotel, and the plane ticket all go into the company's records as compensation for the RR.

Are there exemptions provided under this rule? Yes, but they are few in number and involve small amounts. The wise policy is to notify your branch manager or compliance officer of anything that might be construed as compensation.

The RR's Duty to Notify the Employer of Investment Activities

Before opening or trading in a securities account with an NASD member (other than his or her employer), an RR must provide the employer with written notice and wait to receive the firm's approval. The RR must also tell the executing firm, in writing, that he or she is an RR with another member firm. This rule also applies to securities accounts the RR controls even if those accounts are not in the RR's name, and to accounts with nonmember financial institutions such as banks.

As part of its watchdog responsibilities, a broker-dealer must keep an eye on employees' transactions. This requires knowing about them even if they are made with another broker-dealer or financial institution. Therefore, an RR must receive his or her employer's approval before opening an account with another broker-dealer. Besides that, the RR must tell the other firm, in writing, about his or her status as an RR with another member. In addition, existing rules require the executing broker-dealer to notify the employer about the account and provide duplicate trade confirmations if the employer asks for them. (Note that the new rule is clearly intended to put more responsibility on the shoulders of the RR.) The corresponding NYSE rule requires stock exchange members to provide duplicate statements and confirmations to other members who employ their customers as RRs.

Like many other requirements, this one has expanded over the years—to keep up with marketplace changes and with the schemes of RRs who find novel ways to keep their transactions unsupervised. For example, some RRs have tried to hide transactions by making them in accounts bearing the names of others. (This was, you recall, one of the sins of Jimmy Doyle.) Perhaps the others whose names are most likely to be used in this way are relatives. If RRs intend to place orders in the accounts of relatives, therefore, they must obtain the employer's written permission to do so. The important consideration is not the name on the account but the identity of the person who actually controls the account and benefits (or suffers) from the activity in it.

Similarly, the NASD has recently affirmed the need for RRs to notify their employers when they open securities accounts with firms that are *not* NASD members. This practice has become a regulatory concern because of the evolution of the market. RRs are increasingly likely to open such accounts with banks, for example, and with foreign or domestic investment advisers. (In some northern states, it's easy to do business with Canadian institutions.) Since these firms don't belong to the NASD, they have no obligation to report the opening of these accounts to the RR's employer. Unless the RR does the reporting, then, the information vital to proper supervision never gets to the employer. The employer, incidentally, is responsible for making an adequate effort to insure that employees understand and comply with the reporting requirement.

> **Case 4-13** According to the NASD, Lawrence Gibson failed to notify his employer before opening a margin account that he controlled, but which was in his wife's maiden name. He also transferred a debit of $30,521.70 from that account to the accounts of two customers. For these infractions, and for refusing to respond to NASD inquiries about the activity, Gibson was fined $30,000 and suspended from association with any NASD member in any capacity, for one year. Before taking another job with a member firm, he will be required to pass another qualifying examination.

Private Securities Transactions and Dual Registration

Here are a couple of special variations on the highly ambitious practice of moonlighting: becoming involved in nonpublic offerings and the highly controversial practice of registering with more than one broker-dealer. In either case, the RR frequently is involved in too much of a good thing.

An RR must inform his or her employer in writing before entering into private securities transactions.

Regulators are uncomfortable with dual registration, but it is not universally forbidden. In some states RRs may legally register with more than one employer. In other states, however, RRs must restrict their registration to one broker-dealer or issuer. At one time the NASD proposed a ban on the practice, but withdrew the proposal in the face of widespread industry opposition. Nevertheless, RRs still must notify their employers before engaging in transactions for another firm. Each employer must state in a letter to the other that it will be responsible for activities the RR conducts on the firm's behalf.

In some circumstances, dual registration is very tempting. Say you're selling variable contracts for an insurance company that offers no other securities. To increase, or perhaps even to maintain, your business with some customers, you would like to sell limited partnerships or stocks and bonds. You don't want to move to another firm and jeopardize your standing with your insurance customers, so you register with a second broker-dealer offering other investments.

Some RRs, denied the chance to register with two broker-dealers, have taken the trouble to register as broker-dealers themselves. After spending the necessary time and money to do that, they can contract with various firms, including their former employer, to sell diverse products.

Doing business away from one's regular employer must be tempting; a lot of RRs get into trouble with regulators for doing so. The number of cases in this area may also indicate the difficulty of differentiating between allowable and forbidden business.

Sometimes, for example, RRs participate in private deals that don't seem to involve securities. It may never even occur to them to tell their employers about such arrangements. If a transaction truly doesn't involve a security, of course, it doesn't come under the jurisdiction of industry regulators and needn't be reported.

One might expect *security* to be the most thoroughly and clearly defined term in any securities law glossary. But it's not.

Take the Securities Act of 1933, for instance. Here's an obvious place to look for a definitive definition. Indeed, the act does define the term *securities*—in several ways. One definition includes "any interest or instrument commonly known as a *security*." If a number of people call something a security and treat it as a security, in other words, it is. Unfortunately, that doesn't go very far toward identifying the common characteristics of those interests or instruments people commonly treat as securities. Note especially the phrase "interest or instrument," which implies that a security may exist without an *instrument*; without, that is, a certificate, note, piece of paper, or written contract. The Securities Act of 1933 also states that a "certificate of interest or participation in a profit-sharing agreement" is a security, as is any "investment contract."[4]

The creators of the act were not interested in writing a narrow definition. Their concern was to protect as many investors as possible from as many fraudulent operators as possible. In the grip of speculative fever, too many investors hazard their life savings on the promises of unscrupulous or deluded promoters with a gift for marketing hallucinations. The ways to beguile people into parting with their money are infinite, as are schemes to evade all narrowly drafted definitions. The task of applying these definitions to novel investment schemes falls, eventually, to the courts.

Now one should remember that *the courts* does not refer to a monolithic entity. The courts are a very human system of substantial complexity and diversity. Say, for example, a disgruntled participant in a deal brings a lawsuit against the promoter. Assume the investor's lawyer claims the deal qualifies as a security according to the definitions in the 1933 Securities Act. (Actually, the plaintiff may not be an investor, but a state or even the SEC itself.) Assume, further, that you, as a registered representative, became involved in this deal to pick up spare change outside your regular employment selling variable annuities for the Amazing Benefits Insurance Company. How long will it be before the courts decide that the deal in question is actually a security and that you, therefore, should have reported your participation to Amazing Benefits? As the case winds its way through the lower court, the Appeals Court, and, perhaps, even the Supreme Court, you might hold your breath for five years or more.

The Howey Rule

Consider a case that has had important consequences for the definition of *security*: *Securities and Exchange Commission v. W.J. Howey Co.* In the early 1940s The Howey Company was a Florida citrus operation selling slices of its orange groves to investors. Most buyers fell in love with the area while vacationing at a nearby resort hotel, also owned by Howey. On average, each investor purchased a little over an acre of the grove. Each parcel was a narrow row of 48 trees. So far this looks like a straightforward real estate transaction, except, perhaps, for the rather odd division of the properties into strips.

Along with the offer of land, however, The Howey Company also promoted a service contract. Investors were told that it simply was not feasible to invest in the land without such a contract. Who, otherwise, would take care of the trees? Of course, investors were told, they were free to make arrangements with any citrus-grove service they fancied, but, conveniently, the management of Howey also operated such a service, Howey-in-the-Hills Service, Inc. Naturally, most investors bought both contracts.

When the SEC got wind of this scheme, it took Howey to court, charging it with violating the Securities Act of 1933. Specifically, the SEC accused them of using the mails and interstate commerce to offer and sell unregistered, nonexempt securities. In response, Howey claimed it was not selling a security. The District Court agreed with Howey, and the Fifth Circuit Court of Appeals agreed with the District Court.

Undeterred, the SEC took the matter to the Supreme Court, which overturned the two lower courts and ruled in 1946 that the land-plus-service arrangement constituted a security. In the process, the Court devised *The Howey Test* as a guideline for applying the definitions in the Securities Act of 1933. This test gives one a good sense of how broadly the courts will interpret the law to provide investors the protection offered by the securities market. (Justice Frankfurter's dissenting opinion is worth noting, however. He objected that the higher court had no grounds for overturning a decision upheld in two lower courts.)

According to the majority opinion, the Howey company had been offering an *investment contract*, not a combination real estate and service contract. This brought the deal under the 1933 act, which includes all investment contracts in the definition of security. Therefore, the promoter had run afoul of the SEC by not registering the offer of the contracts and filing disclosure documents. (Use of the mails and interstate commerce made the offering a federal matter; intrastate offerings may be exempt from SEC registration.)

But this begs a further question: What is an investment contract? The Securities Act of 1933 states that investment contracts are securities, but doesn't define *investment contract*. To do that, the Supreme Court relied on other cases in legal literature—notably those argued before state courts under the so-called *blue sky laws*, the state securities laws nicknamed after the notion that unsupervised hucksters will try to sell investors something as worthless as a patch of blue sky. Various state courts had determined that an investment contract is "the placing of capital or the laying out of money in a way intended to secure income or profit from its employment."[5] The crucial implication of this language is that the income or profit arises not from the investor's own efforts but from someone else's.

The purchasers of strips of Howey's groves did not, the Court ruled, simply buy land they could farm, or hire someone else to farm, or treat in any way they liked. What they really did was put up money for Howey to use, hoping to receive a share of Howey's profits. The plots, in many cases, were actually too small to be developed individually, and therefore had economic meaning only as part of the whole. "A common enterprise managed by respondents or third parties with adequate personnel and equipment is therefore essential," the court ruled, "if the investors are to achieve their paramount aim of a return on their investments. Their respective shares in this enterprise are evidenced by land sales contracts and warranty deeds, which serve as a convenient method of determining the investors' allocable shares of the profits. The resulting transfer of rights in land is purely incidental."[6]

It's especially important to note that Howey committed a violation of securities law each time it *offered* the land and service contract, even though the offer led only to a sale of land. (Some investors did contract with other service companies.) The law applies to the *offering* of securities, so violations can occur even if a sale does not.

The Howey Test was applied in 1974 in a particularly fascinating case, *SEC v. Koscot Interplanetary, Inc.* Koscot sold a line of cosmetics by using a variant of the familiar pyramid operation. It was possible, in the Koscot scheme, simply to sell cosmetics, which one purchased from the company at a discount and distributed at a higher price. The SEC never argued that such an arrangement involved a security.

But moving up from salesperson required an investment of $1,000. In return for that amount one could be promoted to supervisor, receive a greater discount on the cosmetics, and—

here's the crux of the matter—be eligible to recruit new prospects and receive a portion of their contributions to the company. The SEC argued that these transactions came within the definition of *security* and therefore had to be registered.

In deciding the case in favor of the SEC, the court applied the Howey Test, which has three elements: "First, that there is an investment of money; second, that the scheme in which an investment is made functions as a common enterprise; and third, that under the scheme, profits are derived solely from the efforts of individuals other than the investors."[7]

The first element obviously applied. The other two were applicable only through the medium of legal logic. The business was a *common enterprise* (element two) because the supervisors, in running their recruitment meetings, were dependent not on their own resources, but on scripts and guidelines provided by Koscot. A similar argument justified application of the third element—that profit be derived solely from the efforts of others.

Supervisors clearly expended their own efforts when recruiting new prospects. This had not held true of the investors in Howey, who left management of the grove entirely in the hands of a service company. According to the court, however, supervisor's efforts were "perfunctory" and had no significant impact on Koscot's ability to reap, and pass along to investors, what it described as "galactic profits." The Howey Test, the justices wrote, must be "resilient enough to encompass the egregious promotional scheme purveyed by Koscot."[8] Applying the test literally would not serve the public interest in a well-regulated market.

If this has been rather a long story, it has a succinct moral: Notify your employer of outside activities. It's quite possible to become involved in a deal that doesn't seem to you—or, for that matter, to anyone—to be definable as a security. Someday, however, that may change. What looks like a general partnership, a real estate transaction, or a pyramid selling scheme, may—especially if it loses money for investors— become a security under the scrutiny of the courts. Pyramid arrangements, in fact, have been outlawed in some states, with enforcement responsibilities assigned to the securities division.

Suddenly, perhaps long after the fact, your innocent participation in a little moonlighting venture may involve you in securities law violations. You will then be subject to fines, loss of income, loss of your profession, or loss of time because of a jail sentence. Bear this in mind if your compliance department seems to take a very conservative view of what activities are readily acceptable. Sometimes the sheriff sends a visitor to the home of the compliance officer to serve notice of a multimillion dollar law suit initiated by the state. That sort of experience puts the damper on one's desire to venture into regulatory gray areas. The following cases highlight violations the NASD has recently identified and disciplined. A variety of securities is involved. Fines tend to run high, and expulsion from the industry is frequently a part of the punishment.

Case 4-14   The NASD found that B. Lowell Denny, II sold limited partnership interests to at least six investors without notifying his employer. In addition, Denny misappropriated investor funds and failed to respond to NASD requests for information. Without admitting or denying the allegations, Denny consented to a $5,000 fine and was barred from association with any NASD member in any capacity.

Case 4-15   According to the NASD, Nick Antone engaged in securities transactions on behalf of Stern Financial Securities without notifying his employer. For his services, Antone received $23,142 from Stern. Antone and

Stern were fined $14,000 and Antone was ordered to disgorge (the SEC's unlovely way of saying "give up" or "give back") $23,740.50.

Case 4-16 Clarence E. Dawson, according to NASD allegations, acted as managing partner or general partner for a number of limited partnerships without first notifying his employer. He also used his employer's name in offering documents to imply that the firm was a sponsor, though it was not. For this and other misdeeds, Dawson was fined $30,000 and barred from associating with any NASD member in any capacity.

Case 4-17 According to the NASD, George Frederick Clark, Jr. participated in the sale of limited partnership interests without informing his employer. Proceeds totaled $525,000. Moreover, Clark allegedly violated his fiduciary responsibility to one partnership he managed by using partnership money to reimburse a client for an investment in a second partnership. Clark consented to being fined $22,000 and barred from association with any member in any capacity.

Case 4-18 Fred W. Brown, Jr. was charged by the NASD with participating in sales of limited partnership interests to at least nine individuals without first notifying his employer. Brown also failed to comply with NASD requests for information about his handling of money received from investors. Brown was fined $150,000 and barred from any association with members.

Case 4-19 Louis I. Flowers was censured by the NASD and barred from association with any member based on findings that he had offered and sold interest-bearing notes to the public without notifying his employer. Approximately 99 customers purchased notes worth more than $2.2 million. Flowers neither admitted nor denied the allegations.

Case 4-20 Gary Earl Sargent was fined $130,000 and barred from any association with any NASD member based on findings that he had, without first notifying his employer, sold approximately 330,000 shares of stock to at least 26 investors.

Case 4-21 According to the NASD, Edward G. Link violated NASD rules concerning private securities transactions by selling *money market accounts* to the public without first notifying his employer. Link neither denied nor admitted committing the violation, but consented to a $50,000 fine and was barred from any association with an NASD member.

Outside Compensation

In October 1988 the NASD adopted a new rule on receipt of compensation from outside business activities. In the NASD Manual, paragraph 2200C, Section 43, it reads like this:

> No person associated with a member in any registered capacity shall be employed by, or accept compensation from, any other person as a result of any business activity, other than a passive investment, outside the scope of his relationship with his employer firm, unless he has provided prompt written notice to the member. Such notice shall be in the form required by the member.

If you intend to moonlight at any job, in other words, you should first inform your employer. An interoffice memo suffices in most firms.

The Agent's Duty to Go by the Book

> When executing responsibilities assigned by the employer, the RR must comply with regulations affecting the broker-dealer.

As we have noted before, regulations written for the broker-dealer also bind RRs acting as the firm's agents or employees. As principal, the firm has certain marketplace responsibilities that it delegates to RRs. Consider, for example, underwriting responsibilities.

> An underwriter's duty is to make a bona fide offering of new issues to the public.

As underwriter, a firm handles the sale of a new issue to the public. As sales agents, RRs find public customers and arrange purchases. RRs should not abuse their position to profit from quick price advances in secondary trading of heavily subscribed issues. Regulations therefore forbid RRs to buy *hot issues* in their own accounts or in the accounts of relatives or associates. The practice is called *free riding and withholding*, that is, withholding shares from the public at the initial offering price and taking a free ride on the rising price in aftermarket trading. No matter how small the price increase in shares of a new issue, the RR or relative holding the securities may be required to return them. The following cases give you an idea of what happens when the NASD finds an RR guilty of free riding and withholding.

> **Case 4-22** The NASD investigated Robert Leidy and found that he "failed to make a bona fide distribution at the public asking price of securities that traded at an immediate premium in the secondary market." To get his free ride, he sold the hot issues to two customer accounts in which he had a beneficial interest. (He was further guilty of sharing in the profits and losses from these accounts without first notifying his employer—an infraction covered in the next chapter). Without confessing or denying the charges, Leidy consented to a fine of $12,626.23 and a 15-day suspension.

As soon as a rule exists, some RRs begin looking for a way around it. One scheme for getting away with free riding and withholding is to hide the transactions in someone else's account. To guard against this, regulators have continually expanded the rule to cover accounts not in the RR's name, including accounts of ever more distant relatives, trust accounts, and foreign accounts (those opened across the border in Canada, for example).

> **Case 4-23** An unnamed RR was found guilty of buying 89,000 shares of a new issue in his daughter's account, then transferring them to his account to sell after their price rose immediately in the secondary market. The RR was fined $15,000, ordered to give up more than $72,000, and suspended from any association with an NASD member for five business days.

One might wonder what's wrong with taking a position in a hot new issue. As purchaser, after all, the RR is at risk just like any other investor. No magic makes an RR able to sort out winners from losers in the firm's underwritings. A hot issue really becomes hot only in hindsight. In reality though, the RR does receive clues that are not available to the public investor. An oversubscribed offering is a good bet to become a hot issue. So as soon as the RR buys into an issue that zooms up in price, everyone screams foul and wants the lucky RR to relinquish the properous security. Of course, the RR feels cheated. If the issue had unexpectedly dropped in price, no one would have required return of the shares.

The problem, as usual, is the perceived integrity of the market. Neither issuers nor customers will enter the new issue market if underwriters offer the public only unpromising securities while saving likely winners for themselves. The ultimate penalty for not making a bona fide offering to the public is that the public eventually stops giving you business. When potential customers become totally disenchanted with one market, they can go to another—just as they switch brokers when their accounts don't prosper. Burned often enough in the stock market, customers may decide they would rather leave their money in the bank, buy fine art or real estate, or bury gold certificates under their bunkers in the prairie.

To prevent this sort of exodus from the OTC market, the NASD has been steadily tightening its underwriting rules. For example, the NASD introduced a Best Efforts Distribution Reporting Program to improve its ability to monitor new issues of non-NASDAQ securities. In addition, it instituted a special Free Riding and Withholding Program and a computerized New Issue Market Manipulation System to follow members' activities during distributions of new issues and in the aftermarket.

Why the increased surveillance? As is so often the case, scandal and disaster preceded regulatory innovation. For several years national magazines have been sniping at alleged abuses by firms that underwrite penny stocks, issues that are difficult to regulate because they are not tracked by NASDAQ computers. Under the new system the NASD receives information on members' practices in monthly reports from underwriters. According to NASD publications, tighter surveillance has improved the association's ability to regulate OTC trading.

The alleged problems in the penny stock market go a step beyond mere free riding and withholding and highlight the potential problems latent in that practice. Not content simply to hold part of a new issue and wait for its price to rise, offending underwriters manipulate the market in order to boost the value of their investments. Worse, the issues in question may be worthless. Here's a case in point:

Case 4-24 The NASD found Patten Securities Corporation of New Jersey guilty of manipulating the market for units of Horizon Capital Corporation. According to the NASD, Horizon was a blind pool company with no history, no revenues, and no income. The principals of the company were two school teachers with no relevant business experience. Corporate assets amounted to $6,000 at the time of the underwriting.

Patten initially sold 5,750,000 units of Horizon at three cents each, thus raising about $172,500. About $100,000 went to Horizon. When trading in the aftermarket was flat, Patten stepped in and bought back nearly half the issue, almost 2.5 million units. Eventually, Patten owned enough units to dominate the market and manipulate the price.

By continuously raising their bids and offers, Patten ran the aftermarket price of Horizon units up 316 percent over the public offering price. This meant customers were paying grossly inflated amounts for a most unpromising enterprise. It also meant that Patten reaped $167,000 in illegal profits. As a result of its findings, the NASD fined the firm and its president, John Patten, $50,000, ordered them to give up the illegally gotten $167,000, expelled the firm from membership, and barred Patten from any association with a member.

In an underwriting, a firm's duty to the issuer is to raise money, and its duty to the public is to offer securities at the agreed-upon price. To further this dual mission the RR, in the capacity of sales agent, finds suitable investors and arranges purchases at the offering price. For its services the firm receives appropriate compensation from which it pays the RR's commission. Bear in mind that penny stocks are not the only potential hot issues. An RR can get burned buying new blue chips too, if their aftermarket price rises just a fraction of a point over the offering price.

Fair Pricing

As we saw in the previous section, the firm and its agents are not supposed to enter into an underwriting to buy low at the initial price and sell high in the aftermarket, particularly not in an aftermarket they manipulate. This leads us to another point—the requirement that firms charge a fair markup on securities they buy and sell.

A firm will charge a fair markup, taking into consideration the actual costs of the transactions.

Since a fair markup is generally less than five percent, this rule is commonly called *the five percent rule*—commonly, but inaccurately. In some cases a fair markup may be much less than five percent; in other cases it may be much higher. What is fair changes with the difficulties and risks of trading a specific security. A very thinly traded, low-priced stock may justifiably be marked up more than five percent. An easily marketable security may perhaps be fairly marked up one percent or less.

The RR's responsibility for marking up securities varies widely from firm to firm. In wirehouses the RR may have absolutely nothing to say about the size of markups. In smaller firms, by contrast, the RR may play a significant role in determining markups. This is especially true in firms that make a market in a number of local OTC securities. In any firm, however, the amount of markup will have a significant impact on the RR. Lower than expected markups feel just like a pay cut, after all. So when markups look too slim, RRs tend to come storming into the trading room looking for explanations. We can help out by providing some explanations here.

The situation most likely to annoy the RR is called a *proceeds transaction*, which occurs when a customer sells one security and uses the proceeds of the sale to buy another security. The RR, understandably, expects the usual compensation on both the sale and the purchase, but that's not the way it works. Instead, the two transactions are treated as one trade with one commission. To be specific, the markup on the purchase is reduced by the commission or markdown on the sale.

Let's look at an example. In this case, a customer sells a security in an agency transaction. The RR's firm, in other words, is not the market maker; therefore, the RR earns a commission. The customer then buys a security in which the firm is a market maker, and the RR perhaps expects a cut of healthy markup. Since the two trades are lumped together as a proceeds transaction, however, the markup is reduced by the initial commission. Here's how it works.

Sell 200 shares @ $30	$6,000
Commission	$144
Buy 400 shares @ $14.75	$5,900
Reasonable 3% markup	$177
Markup	$177
Minus sales compensation	-144
Allowable balance	$33

Though the fair markup is three percent, the amount allowed on the buy side of this proceeds is a mere $33, i.e. the markup reduced by the sales commission. Looked at another way, the firm receives only its fair markup on the purchase. It receives, in effect, no commission on the sale—just what it would have received had the customer paid with cash instead of with money raised by selling another security.

It may seem unfair to be paid, in effect, for only half your business. But the effect of charging customers as if the two trades were only one is to encourage them to leave their money with your firm and, perhaps, to trade more often. You might think of a proceeds transaction as a sort of loss-leader.

You might also remember that the trading room is the first place to feel the heat when a firm gets caught violating the fair markup policy. RRs very seldom are sanctioned for markup violations. Here, again from the penny–stock market, is an example of what happens when a stock is marked up too steeply and the offending firm is judged to have charged an unfair markup.

Case 4-25 In an investigation of Blinder, Robinson & Co., Inc., the NASD found that the firm had unfairly and excessively marked up the stock of Telephone Express Corporation, a non-NASDAQ security. Blinder underwrote the initial offering of the stock and placed it exclusively with its own customers. Since no other dealers were involved, the NASD determined that Blinder controlled aftermarket trading in the security. In 1,328 trades they marked up the stock from 11 percent to 150 percent. For mistreating its customers in this manner, Blinder, Robinson was suspended from NASD membership for five business days. Meyer Blinder, the firm's president, and four other employees were barred from association with any NASD member for 90 days. In addition, the firm and the individuals involved were censured and fined $250,000.

SUMMARY

In this chapter we established that the apparently voluminous quantity of rules describing the ethical requirements of the registered representative flow out of the agency relationship of RR to customer and broker-dealer.

We looked in detail at the legal definition of *security*, reviewing The Howey Test and its application in the Koscot case. We saw that the SEC and the courts tend to accept the broadest definition of the term, thereby extending the protection of market rules to as many public customers as possible.

In describing the relationship of RR and employer, we defined the broker-dealer's two-fold role in the securities marketplace, the two parts of which are suggested by the hyphenated name.

As broker, the firm arranges trades for its customers who buy and sell securities. Compensation for its activities comes from commissions that the firm charges buyers and sellers. As dealer, the firm buys and sells over the counter for its own account. Compensation for the expenses of dealing in securities comes from the markup included in the selling price.

In both activities the firm is bound to act in the interests of customers and to comply with the rules designed to protect the public and maintain the credibility of the marketplace. The firm is obligated to supervise carefully the activities of its registered employees to be certain they conform with applicable laws and regulations.

When carrying out the firm's business as broker or dealer, the registered representative is bound by the law of agency and the rules of the marketplace. As the firm must supervise the RR's compliance with rules, the RR must obey the employer's legitimate directives. RRs are obligated to tell the firm about outside business activities and to follow underwriting rules.

We ended with a look at one of the most troubled areas of today's securities marketplace—the trading of so-called penny stocks. There is no better example of the way illegitimate dealing erodes the public credibility of a market. To restore that credibility and improve the protection of the public, the SEC and NASD have mounted a vigorous campaign of enforcement against fraud and manipulation among penny–stock firms.

Notes

1. Black, Henry Campbell, *Black's Law Dictionary*, Revised 4th ed. (St. Paul, MN: West Publishing Company, 1968), pp. 84–85.

2. Ratner, David L., *Securities Regulation* (St. Paul, MN: West Publishing Company, 1978), p. 149.

3. *Ibid*, p. 149.

4. Jennings, Richard W. and Marsh, Jr., Harold, *Securities Regulation: Cases and Materials*, 4th ed. (Mineola, NY: The Foundation Press, 1977), p. 224.

5. *Ibid.*, p. 224.

6. *Ibid.*, p. 226.

7. *Ibid.*, p. 231.

8. *Ibid.*, p. 235.

5

The Customer's Agent

INTRODUCTION

Some years ago stockbrokers were known as *customers' men* to signify their special responsibility to investors. How times— and terms— have changed! Now, with such diverse financial products available, a registered representative may very well not be, in the literal sense, a stockbroker. And who can still be comfortable with the gender designation in customers' man? Moreover, RRs may have any of a number of duties, trading or research, for example, that they owe to the firm rather than the customer.

Despite the changes, the term customers' man (make that *customers' agent*) is good to remember. The customer is still a principal. Along with the broker-dealer, the RR is still an agent. The rules of agency still apply.

In a sense, the RR works for the customer *and* the firm. As customer's agent, the RR is a financial version of Robinson Crusoe's man Friday—a person with special knowledge and skills necessary to help another pursue certain goals. In Crusoe's case the initial goal was survival, though as time passed Friday helped him achieve greater security and comfort as well as merely learning to survive. Though RRs may not seem to be undertaking quite so dramatic a role in the lives of their customers as Friday did, in fact they sometimes do help people make and act upon plans intended to achieve some of life's more fundamental goals, from educating children to retiring in comfort.

Consider briefly four main rules a customer's agent has to bear in mind:

1. Know your customer. When opening an account, you are required to gather essential information about your customer. You must also keep the information up to date.

2. It's the customer's money. Use it only for the customer's purposes.

3. If you recommend investments, be certain they are suitable to the customer. Describe the investments fully and truthfully, relying only on public information.

4. Enter orders only at the customer's direction, unless you have been authorized in writing to act on your own.

In these four activities—gathering information, handling money, making recommendations, and entering orders—you act as the customer's agent with the customer's objectives in mind. You are acting in your own interest only indirectly. As always, the integrity of the marketplace determines your duty. You treat customers the way they would want to be treated, which is the way you want to be treated when you're a customer. Yet, you act in your own interest, too, since your success is tied to the success of the customers and, more fundamentally, to the success of the market. No market, no customers. No customers, no commissions.

This chapter covers each of the four aspects of the RR's relationship to the customer—starting with gathering information. This discussion will apply directly to you in greater or lesser degree depending on where you work. At discount firms RRs don't make recommendations and, consequently, don't need to know their customers as fully as full-service RRs do. Further, making recommendations is not a positive requirement for any RR. Some customers take care of themselves, for the most part, even though they use a full-service broker-dealer. But when you do make recommendations, the agency duties discussed here become essential elements of your job.

KNOW YOUR CUSTOMER

Your first obligation is to gather information about your customer. How much you need to know varies, depending on the customer, the type of account, and the firm. At the very least, NASD regulations require that you record the name and address of the customer and whether or not he or she is of legal age. If account activity will be limited to money market fund transactions, that's all the information NASD rules require. If the customer intends to invest in instruments other than money funds, however, you're obligated to get more information before settlement of the first transaction in the account. To be more precise, you must make *reasonable efforts* to obtain the customer's tax or social security number, occupation, and employer's name and address. Also try to find out whether or not the customer is associated with another member of the NASD. (Chapter 4 included a discussion of regulators' interests in ensuring that firms know about their employees' financial activities.) Account records must contain the RR's signature and the signature of someone representing the firm (partner, officer, etc.).

If you work for a full-service broker-dealer and intend to make recommendations to the customer, you're required to make reasonable efforts to gather even more information before that first transaction. Specifically, find out the customer's financial status, tax situation, investment objectives, and any other information (education, experience, or other relevant factors) necessary to tailor recommendations to the individual's needs.

Making a reasonable effort to discover this information may sound like odd language. It reflects the fact that the customer isn't legally obligated to answer personal questions. By the same token, your firm isn't required to take the account of a customer if it cannot obtain information necessary to supervise the account.

The need to gather information applies to any first-time customer, even one who isn't new to the firm. An RR might inherit a customer from another RR who failed to gather or keep current all the data necessary to understand the customer's needs.

Sometimes gathering information seems pretty tedious. You naturally want to get to the transaction, then to the next phone call. Filling out new account forms runs against the grain for most salespeople. But the information you gather—about net worth, for example—can be the lifeblood of your career.

As customer's agent, at least in a full-service firm, you can do more than take orders and, perhaps, make the occasional recommendation. You are potentially in the business of helping customers define their financial objectives and take action to achieve them. This implies helping the customer deploy all available resources to meet those needs. The better you do that job, the more successful you will be in meeting your own goals. Finding out all pertinent financial facts about a customer is clearly in the RR's interest as well as that of the investor.

Gathering information can, however, be unnerving as well as tedious. Money is a touchy subject. There are people who will more readily discuss their intimate relationships than reveal the size of their paychecks and bank accounts. So, asking new customers about their income, debts, bank balances and the like can be uncomfortable. Both you and the customer may feel that this gathering of information is really prying into private affairs. In other situations the information would, in fact, be none of your business. Bear in mind, however, that doctors, as part of their information-gathering process, must ask people to take off their clothes. Psychologists probe into people's dreams, fantasies, and sexual activities. Just the same, you may find it hard to remember that your questioning is in the customer's own interests. If your job is to give customer's professional assistance in their pursuit of financial goals, you have to know the goals. You also have to know what assets they're working with. Friday had to know whether Crusoe wanted to get off the island, live like a solitary monarch, or merely survive. Is the customer hoping to multiply a cache of spare change into enough money for a cruise? Raising money to stave off underworld creditors? Saving for retirement? An RR needs to know how seriously losses or uncertainties will affect the new customer both financially and emotionally.

The fact is most experienced RRs haven't even come close to discovering all their customer's assets. According to an article in *Registered Representative*, "The typical broker controls about one-third of client assets."[1] But RRs typically think they control far more than that. Studies conducted by a firm cited in the article found that RRs thought they controlled 75 percent to 80 percent of the liquid assets of their top 25 accounts. Actually finding those assets means asking questions, not limiting yourself to taking orders or even to making recommendations. You have to develop a relationship with customers, get to know them, and be comfortable probing deeper for knowledge of their financial means and ends.

As a full service RR making recommendations, remember, you're looking for four basic pieces of information about a customer: financial status (which can include where a person's assets are invested or deposited), tax situation, objectives (including tolerance of risk), and other relevant factors. Without this information, you have no intelligent way of deciding which of your firm's recommended investments are appropriate or how much the customer can afford to put into them. In short, you're finding out who the customer is, remembering that, in a sense, the customer is your boss.

Customer files must also be kept current. Things change in portfolios and in the lives of investors. Stocks bought and held must be sold. Children finish college, and education funding drops from the priority list. Investors age and "long-term" takes on a diminished meaning; retirement planning acquires a new urgency. Keeping current with your customers improves your ability to serve as their agent.

As information gatherer, you also satisfy the needs of your other principal—the firm, represented by your supervisor. Unless the firm has the documents profiling your customer, your activities in that account can't be properly supervised. Are you using the correct trading system? That may depend on whether the customer is an individual or institutional investor. Is there too much activity in the account? Are the trades too large or too frequent? To answer those questions, your supervisor must also know the customer.

The most information you need is about investors who select more complicated, risky products—certain options strategies and direct participation programs, for example. Such investments are not suitable for every customer. Sometimes the issuer of the security requires detailed information about investors. So your supervisor is required to keep an especially sharp eye on trading in these products. Discharging that duty effectively necessitates getting information through the RR.

Options present special challenges to investor, RR, and broker-dealer. Some option strategies are risky and very complex. The volatility of the options market means investors must be especially alert to the changing status of their positions. Technically, an option is a wasting asset. If the option contract hasn't been exercised in a few weeks or months, it expires, leaving the owner with nothing. On the other side, option writers risk having the contract exercised against them, forcing them to buy or sell stock at losses that can be enormous.

Each new options customer has to acknowledge receipt of the disclosure document available from the Options Clearing Corporation (OCC). Your firm is responsible for seeing that the document gets to the customer, and may delegate that task to RRs. In other words you may be responsible for handing or mailing the disclosure document to the customer. That's how an RR can help a customer learn to use this specialized product.

You have another task: Getting your customer's signature on the options agreement. By signing, the customer acknowledges having been informed about position and exercise limits and agrees to abide by those limits.

Firms have different ways of supervising options accounts. Basically, the RR's supervisor needs to verify that the customer has received the necessary documents and has given the RR sufficient personal and financial information. Some firms ask for the customer's signature as verification that all steps have been taken; this is called *positive verification*. Other firms send the customer a document and ask for a response only if the information on the document is in some way incorrect; this is *negative verification*. The absence of a response signifies that the

RR's work has been thoroughly done. Whichever way your firm handles information gathering, you are required to keep the customer's file up to date with a periodic inquiry—about every six months.

Selling limited partnerships also involves special new-account procedures. You are required to have investors sign a subscription agreement testifying that they have the ability to assess the risks involved and that they have sufficient net worth to withstand potential losses. The greater the risk of the venture, the higher the net-worth requirement. If you lie, or encourage the customer to lie, the trade is by definition unsuitable. (A customer who must lie in order to qualify, doesn't.) You will be in trouble if the trade goes awry.

Whatever the type of account, the information the RR gathers is copied and given to all appropriate supervisors. For options, the account must be approved before the first trade is entered. In other accounts the first trade can be entered before approval. A second trade must be approved, however, unless it is entered to close the initial position. The RR who opens a bad account with, say, a large stock purchase is taking a risk. Losses come out of the RR's pocket.

Here's a cautionary tale about new accounts.

Case 5-1 An RR—we'll call him Michael—tells of opening an account for a woman who seemed to be a knowledgeable and experienced investor. Before entering her first order—a $30,000 stock purchase—she came into the office several times, always asking sophisticated questions. Yet, something about her made Michael suspicious. Worried about the size of the woman's first trade, he said it would be necessary to verify her previous account with another firm before entering the order. He gave her a receipt for her money, and she left.

As soon as she was out the door, Michael asked his operations manager to call the firm the woman named as her previous broker. Soon the manager was back looking concerned. "I have XYZ on the phone," he said. "It's about the woman with the $30,000. I think you'd better hear this yourself."

"But I asked you to call XYY," Michael said. "She told me her last account was with XYY in Middletown."

"My mistake," the manager said. "I got the right town and the wrong broker-dealer. But believe me, you'd better talk to this guy anyway."

So Michael shrugged his shoulders, picked up the phone, and compared his story with XYZ's story. A woman of the same description as Michael's new account had traded with XYZ in Middletown for a time without incident. But when one of her large new positions went down decisively, she disappeared, leaving XYZ to sell out her account and eat the loss.

His suspicions confirmed by the serendipitous call to XYZ, Michael had his operations manager call XYY. That firm gave the woman good marks as a reliable customer.

Michael wasn't about to risk having to use his commission checks to make up losses on the woman's $30,000 position. So he visited her home—taking a witness and her cash with him. In front of the witness, he returned the money, had the woman count it, and took back his receipt.

Michael's story had a happy ending for him and his firm, if not for the investor. Not all stories end so well. An RR has a very great urge to trust a prospect with $30,000 in hand, or even a prospect promising to send a check for tens of thousands of dollars. If the urge to believe is great, however, the risk of doing so is even greater. Taking a chance on a new customer may mean holding your breath for five days while you wait for the trade to settle and the check to clear. An RR should remember Michael's story when the tedium of filling out new account forms and the discomfort of asking personal questions tempts one to ease off.

IT'S THE CUSTOMER'S MONEY

Being a registered representative means having to ask people to trust you with their money. It's a breathtaking responsibility. At least it is at first. After a time on the job, one may get a bit callous about risking customers' dollars. Easy come, easy go. Be careful. As an agent, you are bound by certain rules regarding money entrusted to you by your principal, the customer:

1. Use your customer's money for your customer's purposes.
2. Treat a customer's account as the customer's. (RRs may not share in a customer's profits or losses.)
3. Trade only for your customer's objectives.

For the most part, following these injunctions is straightforward. Sometimes, however, the distinction between obeying and disobeying them is fairly subtle.

> Use your customer's money for the customer's purposes.

A customer has an account with you. One day you call the customer with a buy recommendation. She accepts. There's enough money in her account to cover the transaction and your commission. What could be simpler? Your employer keeps the customer's money, if it is registered to do so. (Not all broker-dealers are permitted to keep customer cash.) At the customer's direction, you spend the money on appropriate securities traded in appropriate amounts. No problem. But problems do sometimes arise.

Consider the following situation. You meet a customer in the evening to close a deal, and you are paid in cash. Perhaps you're on your way to the theater or a nightclub. You could lose the money, or it could be stolen. The guarding of others' cash is scary. You would like to put it someplace until the next day. Under industry regulations, however, your duty is to transfer the funds directly from the customer to your employer. You can't, for example, temporarily deposit the money in your bank account. Why not? Because money in your bank account is at risk. This is not merely an academic point. Once the money is in the bank, it's out of your control. Any funds in your account can be withdrawn by the bank to offset your debts. RRs have been known to lose customer funds that way, without having known such a loss could occur. That is one reason that commingling of an RR's funds with a customer's funds is forbidden by the Securities Exchange Act of 1934.

If your funds are commingled with a customer's funds, it's impossible to know whose money is being used for whose purposes. There is an exception to this rule: With the firm's permission, an RR may open a joint account with someone not working at the firm. Once on notice about the account, the broker-dealer can supervise activity in it.

When a customer's money winds up in an RR's account, it usually isn't the result of an innocent mistake. It's conscious misappropriation of funds. Not surprisingly, a large proportion of infractions occur in this area—far too many to include here as examples. Each month, *The Wall Street Journal* publishes several stories about misappropriated funds culled from

NYSE releases. In August 1989, for instance, seven persons were barred from the industry for misappropriation of customer funds. Without providing a guide to all ways one can steal from accounts, the following cases illustrate various ways in which RRs misuse customers' funds. Sometimes the funds simply pass through another account before reaching the intended recipient. As we've explained, however, even that is against regulations.

Case 5-2 Loney A. Martin was found to have endorsed customers' checks and deposited them to bank accounts of companies with which he was associated. He then wrote checks on those accounts payable to the intended recipients of the customers' checks. For these and other violations, Martin was fined $75,000 and barred from any association with an NASD member.

Sometimes an RR appropriates customer funds for personal use, then reimburses the customer later without, of course, letting anyone know what is going on. That seems to have happened in the following case:

Case 5-3 An RR, whom the NASD did not name, was fined $173,000 and barred from associating with any member. The NASD found that the RR had been liquidating portions of his customers' mutual funds and putting the money in his own account. He made 26 such transactions in 14 accounts, pilfering $255,643.57. Before he was caught, he restored some of the funds to some of the investors. Nevertheless, he retained $168,000.

Occasionally an RR will get customers' unwitting permission to engage in the following sort of thievery:

Case 5-4 The NASD determined that an RR, who neither admitted nor denied the charges, had talked a customer into providing documents that permitted the RR to make withdrawals from his customer's cash management account. The RR then took $175,000 from the account, and convinced the customer he was using the money to buy securities for her. In fact, he used the money for his own purposes. The NASD fined the RR $15,000, ordered him to give up $158,000, and barred him from further association with any member.

Some RRs spin a tangled web of false withdrawals, deposits, and transfers. In the following case an honest mistake in operations put two bonds into the accounts of Michael Gordon's customers. He took it from there.

Case 5-5 After two bonds were mistakenly delivered to accounts of Michael R. Gordon's customers, the RR transferred the securities to the joint account of his mother-in-law and sister-in-law. He didn't tell the relatives what he had done. Besides pilfering the bonds, he secretly bought call options in one customer's account, then canceled the transactions and recorded them in another customer's account. Finally, Gordon also failed to execute cancellations ordered by customers and changed an address without authorization. For these violations, Gordon was fined $15,000 and barred from association with an NASD member.

In Case 5-5, the RR not only misappropriated funds, but also failed to execute orders, a violation covered later in this chapter. In addition, the RR tampered with account information, an infraction discussed earlier. Why change an address? One reason is to substitute your own or a relative's address for a customer's, thus redirecting their funds or securities to your-self. Take the case of Joseph Shaddy, for example:

> **Case 5-6** The NASD found Joseph G. Shaddy guilty of a number of violations. For example, he sold shares from one account without the customer's authorization. When the customer received a confirmation of the sale, Shaddy advised that it was the result of a mistake and should be ignored. The RR also frequently changed the address of the customer's account in his employer's books without the customer's knowledge. Shaddy had his employer issue checks against the customer's credit balance and send them to his own address. He forged the customer's endorse-ment, cashed the checks, and used the funds for his own purposes.

Not all misappropriation occurs in securities accounts. Insurance premiums, too, sometimes arrive at the wrong desti-nation:

> **Case 5-7** According to the NASD, Howard E. Tate used $3,249 of his customer's insurance premiums for his own purposes instead of transferring those funds to his firm. He also failed to respond to NASD inquiries about the missing premiums. For these violations, Mr. Tate was fined $15,000 and barred from further association with NASD member firms.

> **Case 5-8** Dean I. Zorchert was charged with loaning him-self money and making withdrawals from his customers' insurance policies without telling the customers. Alto-gether he took over $9,000. Without admitting or denying the charges, Zorchert consented to being fined $10,000 and barred from associating with NASD members.

As customers' money is theirs to use, it is also theirs to risk and, sometimes, to lose. RRs may not share customer losses any more than they can share their gains. As agent, the RR is charged with carrying out investors' instructions, not with participating in the outcome of the investor's actions. The RR and the customer simply don't share accounts, unless they are joint accounts opened with prior approval from the RR's employer. This is the rule:

> Treat the customer's account as the customer's. RRs cannot share in a customer's profits or losses.

Sometimes violations of this rule are clearly meant to circumvent supervision. That was the case when Jimmy Doyle traded in the account of a former customer who had moved to California. Some violations of this rule appear to be acts of generosity, others seem like desperate sales gimmicks. Take the following case, for example:

Case 5-9 The NASD charged an unidentified registered representative with giving three customers written, notarized guarantees against losses on their purchases of a particular common stock. For issuing these guarantees, the RR was censured, fined $5,000, and suspended from association with any NASD member for 30 days.

How often can an RR provide guarantees such as those in case 5-9 without getting into financial trouble? No one is lucky forever. One day a *guaranteed* investment will go bad and the RR may be unable to cover the losses.

Case 5-10 Joseph G. Becker shared in a customer's losses by making payments to the customer's account without prior written authorization from his employer. For this, Becker was fined $1,000 and barred from associating with an NASD firm as a principal.

Sharing in a customer account also prevents your firm from keeping proper records of your own profits and losses.

Case 5-11 Jeffrey A. Kahn was fined $10,000 for opening and trading in an account in someone else's name without properly informing his firm. Because of his hidden activity, Kahn was able to withdraw profits of $42,342.50 without the knowledge of his employer. He also failed to comply with *Regulation T* requirements designating the amount of equity necessary in a margin account

MAKE SUITABLE RECOMMENDATIONS

If you are an RR with a full service broker-dealer, you may count investment recommendations among your duties to customers. Let's see how that works.

Once you've gotten all the information you need about a customer (i.e., the person's income, net worth, experience, risk tolerance, and financial objectives), the next challenge is to recommend ways that the customer can deploy available assets in order to reach his goals.

The RR's mission is to use information about each customer to craft recommendations that are suitable to that customer in every way. The *type* of investment must suit the customer's goals and risk tolerance. The *amount* of a buy recommendation must suit the customer's level of wealth. The *frequency* of buying and selling must suit the customer's objectives, not the RR's need for commissions.

We'll look at each element of a suitable recommendation: type, amount, and frequency.

Selecting suitable investments is the RR's primary concern when making recommendations.

The idea of unsuitable investment recommendations probably conjures up images of commodities straddles, uncovered options, penny stocks, and wild-cat drilling partnerships. Such investments are, however, suitable for some investors. For those investors, more conservative choices may not be suitable. Suitability is an individual matter.

One frequently hears that mutual funds are appropriate for customers whose risk tolerance and net worth are low. Obviously, however, not every one of the vast array of funds is suitable for such investors. *Mutual fund* is a very broad category of investment, and the category is not the crucial factor in determining a suitable recommendation. That factor is, instead, the specific item within the category. Income funds loaded up with junk bonds are not suited to risk-averse customers, though they may not know that. The RR is the one charged with finding, amidst all available funds, the one that will suit the investor's situation.

Let's say you have a customer seeking safety of principal and current income. This is a conservative investor, not a wealthy one—a school-teacher, perhaps. You have him in a money market fund, a good choice when the investor opened the account in a time of high interest rates, but now interest rates have begun to fall and the investor calls to ask if you can recommend an investment with a higher return at about the same risk level.

Should you move the investor's money into a long-term government bond fund? On the surface, that strategy seems to meet the investor's objectives of current income and safety of principal. After all, what could be more conservative than the debt obligations of the U.S. government? Unfortunately, the bond fund, with its fluctuating value, involves market risk and interest-rate risk; therefore, it probably wouldn't be suitable in this instance.

How about T-bills? As a principal ingredient of money-fund portfolios, they would seem to be close in nature to the investor's current holdings. They offer safety of principal, to be sure, since they are as sound as the government that backs them. We have specified that interest rates are falling, and that means existing T-bills will be increasing in value—a plus for the investor. Their yield, however, is volatile, since their value is sensitive to changes in interest rates. Again, an RR must be very careful to choose the appropriate investment for the investor within the current market conditions.

The truth is that no category of financial product meets every stated goal of any particular investor. Only specific investments match specific objectives.

Now let's say that you have just recommended an investment to one of your customers—a suitable investment.

"But," the customer asks, "What's going to happen to this fund (or bond or stock or whatever)?" If only, you think in silent response, I knew.

You can always refer to past performance—it's part of your data, to be sure—but only if you include the usual disclaimer: Past success does not necessarily predict future performance. A person may have been alive for 75 years, but that does not guarantee the person will be alive next year. So it is with stock prices, dividends, and interest rates.

A bull market may have been in progress for two years or five years or seven years—that doesn't mean it will go on for another two, five, or seven years. Interest rates may have been rising for six months, but that doesn't assure another six months of increasing rates. A company may have declared its dividend every quarter for 10 years, but fail to pay next quarter. In its previous downward move, a stock price may have bottomed at 12. This time, though, you may buy it at 13 or 14 and watch it keep sliding until the company goes bankrupt.

There are no crystal balls and no guarantees; no soothsayer sees into the future. As investors and as RRs, though, we all want to believe the opposite. The urge to predict the future, like the excessive love of money, is deadly to one's career in securities.

Your duties as an RR do not include divining the future or making only successful recommendations. Your obligation is to make *suitable* recommendations, ones that fit the customer's situation. If you learn the customer's goals, and recommend securities that fit those goals, you are doing your job as agent.

If, on the other hand, you mislead the customer about the suitability of an investment, or if you withhold any information relevant to making an informed investment decision, you are not doing your job. The customer is no longer the decision maker. You are no longer the agent. When you lie to the customer or withhold pertinent information, you take control of the decision. Instead of carrying out the customer's wishes, you are making the customer do what you want, thus standing the agent-principal relationship on its head.

Although an RR may, and indeed should, consult numerous sources of information about securities, in one sense the most significant source is the employer's research department—if there is one. This business is specialized: researchers analyze and select; RRs match the firm's products with appropriate customers. The analyst analyzes; the RR calls prospects and investors. If your firm recommends that customers buy ABC, think twice before suggesting that customers sell ABC short. This is not to say an RR should never go against the research department's recommendations. Some firms give RRs more leeway than others. Experienced RRs may have the background to justify a degree of independence from the research department, especially if the firm has only a small staff of analysts. In general, however, you should look to the research department for help and not try to be your own investment analyst.

Here's an example of what happens when an RR is found to have recommended inappropriate investments. Note that the case involves violations mentioned in the segment on information gathering.

Case 5-12   Henry Phillip Dowling was found to have carried out unsuitable limited partnership investments for three customers. In the subscription agreements signed by these customers, Dowling overstated gross income, assets, previous investment experience, and securities held by the customers. Net worth required to qualify for investment in the partnerships was $1 million. Dowling's actions, according to the NASD, caused substantial losses to the employer and potential losses for the issuer. He was fined $45,000 and barred from association with any NASD member.

Besides picking the proper security for the customer's situation, the RR has to recommend a suitable size trade for the customer's means. Similarly, you can't trade more frequently than is suitable for the account. *Churning* may seem like a pleasant alternative to prospecting, but penalties take the fun and profit right out of it.

The following case of trading too much and too often includes a reminder that your employer is required to supervise your trading for suitability.

Case 5-13 Robert W. Martin, a Paine Webber employee, was found guilty of making unsuitable trades in a customer's account that he effectively controlled. Martin executed numerous margin transactions, including options trades, although he had no reasonable grounds to believe these transactions suitable to the customer's means and goals. The NASD also found that Paine Webber failed to review and monitor Martin's frequent trades in the account, and was otherwise remiss in its duty to supervise Martin. The firm was fined $10,000; Martin was fined $30,000 and barred from association with any NASD member.

PORTFOLIO CONSIDERATIONS

When making a recommendation, the RR has to consider more than the security in question. For instance, the RR has to ask how the recommended action will affect the customer's portfolio.

Let's say your research department likes a particular speculative issue. You put your client list up on the PC screen, and find that Jeffrey Stuart is a candidate for high-risk, high-reward securities and has cash to invest.

It's a natural fit, right?

Maybe. If you call Jones every time you have a likely looking speculative recommendation you may overload his portfolio with risky issues. Finding a customer with nothing but speculative positions will probably give your supervisor apoplexy. If you create a portfolio with that much risk in it, you're asking for trouble—for your client, yourself, and your firm.

Nor is that your only portfolio consideration. As an RR, you, too, have a portfolio—the positions of all your clients. You can think of yourself as analogous to a mutual fund. If all your customers are involved in one type of security, you increase the riskiness of your own portfolio. When the security or type of security dominating your portfolio goes bad, many clients will be unhappy at the same time. At the very least, you will have to rebuild your business frequently. One firm estimates, for example, that RRs who put all their customers into options must rebuild their business every 12 to 18 months. RRs with all customers in futures must rebuild every six to nine months.

There's another problem with concentrating your business in one type of investment. On the face of it, such a portfolio calls into question the suitability of your recommendations. Can one stock really be appropriate to the needs of dozens of clients? It's not impossible; perhaps you prospect for only one type of investor. Some RRs look primarily for conservative investors they can put in mutual funds. But, an unbalanced portfolio can trigger an investigation.

The commissioner of securities in Wisconsin once discovered an RR who had 90 percent of his customers in a single, low-priced, speculative stock. All orders were marked *unsolicited*, but the commissioner was not convinced. It isn't very likely that every member of a diverse group of investors would decide, without prompting, to buy the same speculative stock.

Even if the RR had prospected only for investors suited to that security, however, the portfolio still would have suffered acutely from lack of diversification. Putting so many customers in one speculative issue is asking for trouble. A major loss in the stock's price could destroy the RR's business. Worse, if the RR were a big producer with a small broker-dealer, such a portfolio could jeopardize the entire firm.

DISCRETIONARY ACCOUNTS

For the most part, the securities business is based on oral contracts. RRs generally trade only when the customer gives the

word to do so. Some RRs may, however, decide to take on
discretionary accounts—those in which the customer gives the
RR written permission to trade without oral authorization.
Even though each trade need not be based on an oral contract,
the account is still the customer's, *not* the RR's. Any activity in
the account must further the customer's goals. No activity in
the account may be undertaken solely to achieve the RR's
goals. If activity in a discretionary account seems unsuitable in
any way, a supervisor can break the trades. The RR may have
to pay the cost of restoring earlier positions.

Discretionary accounts are plagued by two major abuses:
missing authorization papers and churning. In the case of
missing papers, regulators may act against the RR even though
the customer testifies that the RR had an oral grant of discretionary authority. Churning, of course, is inexcusable.

Here's a case involving a discretionary account:

Case 5-14 Wayne Monroe Stephens was found to be recommending, for a discretionary account, trades he had no
reasonable grounds to suppose were suitable in size and
frequency for the customer. His employer, Blackstock &
Company, was found guilty of permitting the recommendations. Stephens and his employer were each fined
$15,000.

Discretionary accounts are so tempting and so troublesome
that many firms simply do not allow them.

BOILER ROOMS

So-called *boiler-room operators* who push penny stocks over the
phone perpetrate some of the worst violations of agency duty
to customers. For almost three decades regulators proposed
regulations and sanctions to put these dangerous charlatans
out of commission. Finally, on January 1, 1990, tough new

rules were enacted. Before highlighting the significant provisions of those regulations, we'll look at the nature of the boiler room scam and its sins against customers and the market.

Typical boiler-room operations deal in highly speculative, low-priced stocks—usually penny stocks quoted only in the *Pink Sheets* (a publication for OTC dealers) and not followed by industry analysts. The operator may be the only market maker in the stock. In other words, finding reliable, current information about the security can be very difficult for almost any investor. The broker-dealer and the RR, therefore, have a high moral obligation to be certain that the stock is suitable for the customer.

The boiler-room operator shuns this obligation completely. Instead of contacting existing accounts that might be appropriate for speculative investments, the operator cold calls strangers, often long distance, and applies high-pressure tactics to force a quick buy decision. The purpose is to move a large volume of stock in a hurry and not give prospects a chance to ask a lot of embarrassing questions about the issuer or the broker-dealer.

In truth, the companies recommended by boiler-room operators are often not suitable for any investors. They are merely worthless shells created as part of the scam. The so-called management typically has no experience in the industry the company claims to be entering; the company has little or no capital; its products or services are nothing more than pipe dreams. We looked at a good example of such an operation, Horizon Capital Corporation, in Case 4-24. Horizon was a blind pool, we noted at the time, with no history, revenues, or income. Its managment consisted of a pair of schoolteachers with no relevant business experience. The company's market value was largely created by the sales force of the underwriter, Patten Securities.

The ethical broker-dealer, as opposed to the boiler-room fraud, had two primary responsibilities to the market.

1. A broker-dealer is qualified to be in the business. It implicitly proclaims its credibility simply by setting up shop. When we go to an automobile garage, we assume the mechanic knows how to fix our car. We assume pilots on commercial airlines know how to fly and are in condition to do so. Similarly, as customers of securities broker-dealers, we believe, and we have the right to believe, that our firm has the necessary expertise, and has taken the trouble to analyze the securities it recommends. This is called the *shingle theory*, after the old-time practice of putting the name of one's business on a shingle hung by the front door.[2] A securities firm, figuratively speaking, hangs out a shingle to signify its qualifications to be in the business. Customers expect those qualifications to exist. To violate those expectations is implicitly to commit fraud.

2. RRs are obligated to know their customers and to recommend only suitable transactions. Cold calling strangers to pressure them into buying large quantities of speculative securities clearly does not fulfill that obligation.

To make it more difficult for unscrupulous boiler-room operators to defraud customers, recent rule changes impose special sales practice requirements on broker-dealers who recommend and sell penny stocks, which the NASD calls *designated securities*.

Brokers and dealers must get written purchase agreements for a new customer's first three transactions in penny stocks. For purposes of the rule, penny stocks are not listed on an exchange or traded through NASDAQ. They either sell for less than $4.99 a share, or they are issued by companies with less than $2 million in tangible assets. Further, broker-dealers must obtain certain financial information from penny-stock investors and write down the basis of determining that the securities were suitable for the customer. The customer must manually sign the suitability statement prepared by the firm.

Notice how carefully the new rules define the designated securities. This should alert us to the likelihood that fraudulent broker-dealers are already looking for ways to disguise their phony offerings as something other than penny stocks. The NASD has already made it clear, as an example, that raising the value of a security above the $4.99 limit by including an inflated markup in the price will only increase the wrath of regulators.

To give customers a fighting chance against the sales onslaughts of penny-stock pirates, the new rules obligate firms handling designated securities to make a special effort to insure that prospects are suitable for the recommended trades. The customer, too, assumes some of the obligation to keep the market clean. When customers receive a broker-dealer's suitability statement, they are expected to read it before they sign it. Obviously, customers should not sign statements that contain false information about their net worth, experience, or objectives—the factors considered in determining their suitability for speculative transactions in low-priced securities. To sign such a document makes the investor a willing party to the broker-dealer's fraud. At any rate, the process should give everyone involved a little time to think before rushing into transactions that are dangerous for the RR, the customer, and the firm.

Dangerous to the firm? Yes, indeed. Joint SEC-NASD task forces are cracking down on violators. In Florida, for example, the combined efforts of the two regulatory bodies have put Florida's extensive penny-stock industry in real jeopardy, with as many as four or five firms a day going out of business in 1990. Not only in Florida, however, but across the country, unscrupulous dealers have been reminded of the danger of violating their public trust.

The following case gives some idea of just how dangerous violating rules on penny-stock transactions can be.

Case 5-15 For misconduct in the penny-stock market, the NASD dealt harshly with Marc J. Rothenberg and Joseph A. Friscia, two principals of Diversified Equities Corp., formerly a New York broker-dealer. For fraudulent markdowns and inadequate supervision, Rothenberg was barred from the industry and Friscia was suspended for a year. The two were fined $500,000 "jointly and severally."

The problems occurred in connection with an initial public offering of stock and units in Advanced Viral Research Corp. These were non-NASDAQ, OTC securities.

Diversified Equities underwrote the entire offering and placed all of it with its own customers. Having achieved complete control of the aftermarket in Viral securities, Diversified used its position to rip off its customers when it bought the securities back from them for its own account. According to the NASD, to be more specific, Diversified charged "fraudulently excessive markdowns" in 131 purchases of Viral stock or units from its customers. These markdowns ranged from 12.5 percent to 60 percent off the prevailing market price. Total loss to the customers who trusted Diversified Equities was $381,500 in lost proceeds from sales of Viral.

Friscia was also charged with inadequate supervision of the Viral transactions. It was his job to take all reasonable precautions against the perpetration of these frauds by the sales force at Diversified.

In its report on the Viral case, the NASD emphasizes that its action against Diversified is not an isolated phenomenon. "The investigation," it notes, "was carried out by the NASD's Anti-Fraud Department and is part of a concerted nationwide effort by the NASD to eliminate sales practice abuses in penny stocks. In addition to carrying out its own investigations, the NASD routinely cooperates with other self-regulatory organizations, the SEC, and criminal law enforcement agencies."[3]

RRs tempted to participate in penny-stock fraud take warning—such transactions may be hazardous to your livelihood.

THE PERILS OF INSIDER TRADING

Finally, there's insider trading to be considered; this has been a matter of great embarrassment to the securities industry during recent months. As a registered representative, you probably won't be operating in the danger zone occupied by those who naturally acquire inside information. They generally operate at higher echelons.

Nevertheless, insider trading is a serious, current concern for everyone with a stake in the market's credibility. The belief that the market is rigged by insiders will either keep the public from investing, or it will set them searching for those who claim to have the inside scoop. Neither is good for your business. Here's a relevant, simple principle to guide your actions:

> Base your recommendation only on public information.

Inside information isn't generally likely to filter down to RRs from the rarified atmosphere breathed by the likes of Ivan Boesky or Dennis Levine. Insider trades aren't set up and carried out in the offices where you work. RRs certainly aren't among the classic insiders, the corporate officers and investment bankers whose activities are regulated by the Securities Exchange Act of 1934. In short, misuse of inside information is not likely to be among your temptations as an RR.

Still, if you make recommendations, you need to guard against inadvertently using information not yet in the public domain. This raises the question of what sort of information is inappropriate for you and your customers to use.

Rumors and gossip are clearly not acceptable public information. If you call up your clients and pass along gossip, you may be abetting—however indirectly—insider trading. In fact, you stand to lose whether the gossip turns out to be true or false. If your clients act on phony tips (alleged inside information, so to speak), they may lose money in the market. Then you're in trouble with your clients.

If your sources are accurate and your clients make out like bandits, you may find yourself under investigation. Very few RRs have the emotional or financial resources to survive the rigors of an SRO investigation, trial, or grand jury hearing. It's difficult, if not impossible, to mount a successful defense while continuing to produce at a level sufficient to keep your job.

Ironically, using a rumor that proves true is liable to get you into more trouble than passing on false gossip. Even if you're resilient enough emotionally to stand up under the problems that arise when you and customers make money by trading on inside information, you may find yourself in debt for *triple damages*. The SEC has the legal right to sue you for up to three times the amount of the profits made (or losses avoided) by you and all those to whom you gave the inside information.

What, then, is *public information*? If you read it in a nationally distributed newspaper, it's public even if it's labeled gossip. "Rumors on Wall Street indicate that XYZ, Inc. is the target of takeover activity by an unnamed group of investors," and so forth. The same information taken from a national news wire is public as well. Notice, though, that publicized rumors don't necessarily reveal investors' identities. If you repeat to customers any office rumors about investors' names, you are no longer dispensing public information.

What if your client is a corporate officer with inside information? Then the client's responsibility—and yours—is to forego acting on that information until it has been released to the public. When a corporate insider asks you to put through an order based on inside information, you are placed in a double dilemma. First, you are being asked to enter a trade in anticipation of an event not known to the public. Second, you are receiving information that can't be used in recommendations to other clients. To get yourself off the horns of that dilemma, try asking the customer to clear use of the information with corporate counsel. That will often inspire a change of mind about the trade.

Insider trading wasn't considered a violation of market ethics until fairly recently, perhaps in part because it was so hard to detect before computers made supervision more powerful. Now the rigging of the market by insiders is considered a major problem, not only in the U.S. but around the globe. Japan and various European countries have been struggling with their own scandals, in part because they have no laws or regulations forbidding investors to use inside information.

This does not necessarily save misbehaving insiders—including a number of government officials in Japan—from public disgrace. Faced with widespread anger about manipulative activity, markets will certainly react by generating regulations to restore credibility with investors. If markets don't repair the damage, governments surely will. It's the familiar story told in Chapter 3 of this book.

Now for another story, a case of insider trading written up in the *Wall Street Journal*. Note especially that clients are not immune from industry regulations.

Case 5-16 William C. Banowsky was charged by the SEC for alleged insider trading violations that occurred during his employment as a director of Thrifty Corp. Without admitting or denying the truth of the charges, Banowsky agreed to pay $754,000 in fines and penalties.

According to the SEC, Banowsky recommended purchases of Thrifty stock to three persons shortly before the announcement, on May 28, 1986, that the Thrifty drugstore chain had been taken over by Pacific Lighting Corp. (now Pacific Enterprises). Banowsky made his recommendations based on public rumors combined with his knowledge that a special board meeting would possibly be held on May 22, 1986.

After Thrifty's chairman told him about the possible meeting, Banowsky telephoned his son, secretary, and father to recommend investing in Thrifty securities. During the next several days a total of 18 investors purchased Thrifty stock and call options as a result of Banowsky's initial telephone tips. According to the SEC, the investors realized profits of more than $442,000.

Under the *Insider Trading Sanctions Act*, the courts required Banowsky to pay an amount equal to the total profits plus a civil penalty of more than $311,000. The total judgment was for more than three-quarters of a million dollars.

Banowsky said, "Three years ago in the space of a single hour, I made a mistake in judgment. It has caused a lot of grief for me and others. I sincerely regret it."

Banowsky's attorney pointed out that his client had not traded for himself and had made no profit from the transactions.

When Banowsky agreed to the sanctions, he was executive vice president of National Medical Enterprises, Inc. in Los Angeles. A former chairman of the Los Angeles Chamber of Commerce, Banowsky has also served as president of Gaylord Broadcasting Co. in Dallas, president of the University of Oklahoma, and president of Pepperdine University.[4]

While Banowsky's error was his own responsibility, an alert RR can save customers from similar grief when they are tempted to trade on nonpublic information. Recommending against such action won't earn the RR a commission, but it may save the customer several hundred thousand dollars and years of grief. Moreover, such acts of integrity repay RRs indirectly by improving the long-term health of the market in which they work.

RRs can also head off potential insider-trading problems by considering what information is likely to be available about a firm rumored to be a takeover candidate. A NASDAQ company, for example, probably provides quarterly information to the public and is tracked by analysts. A thinly traded stock listed only in the *Pink Sheets* is less likely to have a strong public following. The relative anonymity of *Pink Sheet* securities makes them potentially greater risks. It also creates an opportunity for making spectacular profits in companies overlooked by mainstream investors and analysts.

Don't misread this note of caution. Not all *Pink Sheet* stocks are small and risky. Hundreds of foreign securities, some of them household names, are traded off NASDAQ's National Market System. Moreover, the NASD is, at this writing, engaged in a pilot project to improve the flow of information on these stocks. From June 1990 to June 1991 OTC market makers will have the option of listing their stocks on a computerized quote service called the *OTC Bulletin Board*. Information on the Bulletin Board includes one- or two-sided price quotes that may, at the market maker's discretion, be either firm prices or indicative prices (what you see may be only approximately what you get). The great advantage, or potential advantage, is that the quotes displayed on the Bulletin Board can be updated instantly, whereas *Pink Sheet* quotes remain static in between publication times. If the Bulletin Board succeeds, it will, in the NASD's own words, "Enable smaller companies to enjoy the benefits of a nationwide quotation medium that will help them grow to the point where they may qualify for listing on NASDAQ."[5] It may also bring greater visibility to some not-so-small American Depository Receipts (ADRs), such as Japanese banks, Volkswagen, Nestle, Deutsche Bank, Hongkong & Shanghai Bank, and others. (These stocks are excluded from NASDAQ not because they are too small, obviously, but because they don't meet SEC disclosure rules. They do, of course, satisfy disclosure regulations in their home countries.)[6]

Finally, an RR may occasionally get the chance to emulate criminal superstars by engaging in a little market manipulation. Let's say, for example, you have customers in a thinly traded issue. By submitting a batch of buy orders near the close, you can increase the likelihood that the day's trading will end with a relatively high quote. This can bring all sorts of wonderful short-term benefits. Customers will feel better. Traders will get a shot at higher month-end bonuses, which are based on stock values. The firm's net capital will get a boost, thus reducing the chance of visits from regulators with helpful suggestions on how to run the business, and there will be fewer margin calls for customers owning the stock, since the higher price will increase their equity.

On the other hand, you might find you've only put yourself out of a job.

THE RR TAKES ORDERS

Trades come about in one of two ways. Sometimes you call a customer, make a recommendation, and get a verbal go-ahead. In such cases responsibility for the trade's suitability belongs to you. Other times the customer calls with an investment idea. Perhaps you don't like the idea. If so, be sure to tell the customer how you feel and mark the order *unsolicited*.

The rules for making decisions about a customer's account arise from the agent-principal relationship of RR and customer. As principal, the customer is responsible for making decisions. The account exists for the customer's use and benefit. As customer's agent, the RR is responsible for carrying out the customer's orders. Any actions that depart from this agent-principal setup must be authorized by the customer. The rule is as follows:

> An RR enters buy and sell orders only at the customer's direction, unless the RR receives the customer's written permission, and the employer's approval, to trade at his or her own discretion in the account.

The general securities business runs, as we noted earlier, on oral contracts. Customers give verbal orders, usually on the phone, and RRs act upon them. So you, as the RR, need some sort of record that will be acceptable in court, such as a written diary or a recording.

If customers with their own ideas can get you into trouble, so can those who want your assistance in making decisions. Sometimes, for instance, a customer will ask for help in determining one or more of the five parts of an order:

1. Action
2. Amount
3. Security
4. Price
5. Time

If the customer gives you the first three elements of the trade, you can, according to the rules, assist in determining the last two. (With mutual funds, only price discretion is allowed.)

With stocks, then, the customer can ask you to buy 100 XYZ whenever you think the time is right. You can decide to enter, say, a limit order to buy 100 XYZ at $45 or an order to buy 100 XYZ at the market. A customer can tell you to sell 300 ZYX, and you can decide to sell 300 shares at the market, at the market on close, at a limit of, for example, $50 or $47 stop.

But look out. If you make a habit of choosing time and price for customers, sooner or later you'll be wrong. You'll buy after the price drops, for example, but it will keep on dropping. And dropping. And dropping. If the customer complains, you'll find that defending your decision is very tricky. You made a mistake; you made it all by yourself; what more is there to say?

To go beyond deciding time and price—to decide whether to buy or sell, to select the size of the order, or to pick the security—you need written authorization from the customer, and approval from your firm. The account will then be supervised as a discretionary account. Naturally, a grant of full discretionary authority is fraught with all sorts of perils. For this reason some firms limit discretionary activity, and some forbid it altogether.

We already saw an example of unauthorized trading in customer accounts—that was the downfall of Jimmy Doyle. Most of the violations occurring recently seem fairly straightforward. An RR makes trades in a customer's account without securing written permission to do so. This clearly violates the agent-principal relationship meant to exist between RR and customer.

Here's an example:

Case 5-17 Donald Robin Mead made an unauthorized purchase of 2,000 shares of stock for $54,502 in a customer's account. He was fined $15,000 and required to retake the qualifying examination before returning to work for another NASD member.

At least the customer knew about the account. That isn't always the case:

Case 5-18 Frances A. Devins opened an account in the name of a customer and executed a securities purchase in it without the customer's knowledge or consent. Devins also failed to respond to NASD requests for information. He was fined $15,000 and barred from any association with an NASD member firm.

Sometimes the initial deception leads to complications:

Case 5-19 Charles Edwin Paul, Jr., was found to have made an unauthorized transaction in a customer's account for a total of $6,510. Without telling his employer, Paul paid the customer $1,000 to settle the complaint and further promised to pay the remaining balance by liquidating the securities. After doing so, Paul gave the proceeds of liquidation to the customer—again without his employer's knowledge or consent. Paul also made false and misleading statements about the matter to the NASD. Without admitting or denying these charges, Paul was fined $10,000 and barred from any association with an NASD member for 60 days.

SUMMARY

Up until this point, we have focused on rules that directly affect the registered representative. We reviewed the case of Jimmy Dolye as an example of what happens to rule violators. We quickly sketched the history of markets and showed that crises in the securities industry have inspired the creation of the rules we live by. We explained the law of agency and described in some detail the agency duties RRs owe to customers and employers. In Chapter 6, we will look at the rules that directly affect the broker-dealer, and indirectly affect the individual representative.

Notes

1. Forbat, Pamela Savage, "Getting It All," *Registered Representative* (April 1990), pp. 24–28.
2. Ratner, David L., *Securities Regulations* (St. Paul, MN: West Publishing Company, 1987), pp. 155–156.
3. *Notice to Members*, National Association of Securities Dealers (April 1990), pp. 140–141.
4. Gottschalk, Jr., Earl C., "Executive Agrees to Pay Penalties on Insider Charges," *The Wall Street Journal* (March 15, 1989), p. C15.
5. *Notice to Members*, National Association of Securities Dealers (March 19, 1990), p. 95.
6. "New Electronics Bulletin Board Promises to Make Trading Foreign Stocks Easier," *The Wall Street Journal* (June 11, 1990), p. C6.

6

Rules of the Road for Broker-Dealers

INTRODUCTION

Up to this point we've concentrated on the registered representative's compliance obligations. Beginning with Jimmy Doyle, we laid out the RR's duties and surveyed the consequences of violating the rules of the road. We also reviewed the history of markets and regulations, especially the tendency of the U.S. securities market to tailor its regulations to the task of retaining or restoring credibility after crisis and scandal. Throughout, we've stressed the agency relationship—RR as agent, broker-dealer as principal—that underlies specific rules.

In this chapter our focus shifts from the RR's duties as agent to the firm's obligations as principal. As the other half of the agent-principal pair, the firm must supervise its RRs— whether they are in retail sales, underwriting, trading, or record keeping. Principals are obligated by ethics and law to supervise their agents. When agents commit rule violations, principals may be liable along with them.

> As principals in the securities marketplace, broker-dealers must obey market rules and supervise agents and employees in all areas, including sales, advertising, trading, underwriting, record keeping, and options activities.

SIMPLER TIMES, SIMPLER RULES

In Chapter 2 we briefly told the story of William atte Brigge, a merchant in the novel *Sarum*, who was expelled from the marketplace for cutting his silk too narrow. In the small, Medieval markets described in the novel, fraud is relatively transparent. When William's cloth is found wanting in width, the responsible party is easy to locate.

Similarly, in the early days of brokerage the dealer who marked up a security too steeply or manipulated prices was the man sitting in plain sight in the coffee shop handing out certificates and collecting money. Such smaller markets were dense with principals, short on agents. Assigning blame was relatively easy.

In the vaster market of modern brokerage, agents abound and may be relatively invisible even to the principals who assign their duties. Responsibility, therefore, is tougher to allocate. Imagine that William atte Brigge owned a multinational garment business with hundreds of employees selling silk in dozens of markets. Deficiencies in his product might occur because some anonymous functionary had been snipping the silk too aggressively, either purposely or by accident. Would William have been so obviously accountable?

That, of course, depends. Did William order the fraudulent scissoring? Did he let employees know the proper measurements? Did he stress the importance of adhering to regulations on width? Did he hire experienced, competent, ethical managers and give them the tools and time necessary to keep tabs on compliance in the cutting room? His culpability rises and falls with the way these questions are answered.

RULES OF THE ROAD FOR MODERN MARKETS

Jimmy Doyle's employer, John G. Kinnard, escaped punishment for ineffective supervision of its RR's irregular activities. According to Kinnard supervisors, Jimmy's violations were especially difficult to uncover. He and his customers were acting in collusion, so there were no complaints. Kinnard was the one being tricked, not investors, Nevertheless, firms too, can be fined, suspended, and expelled when their RRs go wrong. The principal does not escape culpability if it encourages or overlooks fraudulent practices, or if it establishes a supervisory system too weak to work.

The rules regarding proper supervision are tightening up. In 1986, well before the devastating market decline in autumn of 1987, the NASD went public with proposed changes in supervisory requirements. After the usual round of comments and revisions, the alterations became effective in April 1989. They clarify the qualifications and duties of supervisors, the level of supervision necessary for a given type of office, and the procedures to follow in supervising RRs.

HOW MUCH SUPERVISION IS ENOUGH?

No matter how well a firm complies with the requirement that it supervise RRs, violations occur. Supervision of each employee's every move simply isn't possible. Anyway, who would supervise the supervisor? The only fool-proof system is self-supervision by informed and ethical employees. That's why the major portion of this book is directed toward RRs; but when an RR runs afoul of regulations, what defense can keep the RR's supervisors—and his firm—out of trouble?

> A supervisor must make *reasonable* efforts to discover
> and stop RRs' violations, but the supervisor need not
> be perfect.

Examples

According to the following case, reasonable efforts to prevent
RR abuses will get a supervisor off the hook with the SEC.
Reasonable, however, is very much open to interpretation.
Our case, based on an account in *The Wall Street Journal* for
March 24, 1989, demonstrates the extent of disagreement
about how much supervision is enough:

Case 6-1   In 1985, Louis Trujillo, a supervisor for Merrill
Lynch in San Francisco, got into trouble with the SEC
because of the actions of Victor Matl, an RR in his office.
The SEC charged Matl with misleading clients, making
unauthorized trades, and churning accounts. Trujillo,
Robert Fisher (his boss), and Merrill Lynch were charged
with failure to supervise. Matl, Fisher, and Merrill settled
the case without admitting or denying guilt. Trujillo
appealed.
He won his appeal.
Trujillo's actions against Matl began in 1981, when he
wrote a letter to Fisher denouncing the RR's "unconsciona-
ble behavior." He brought up Matl's activities during every
subsequent meeting. He also told fellow workers he was
out to "nail" Matl.
When Fisher did nothing to rein in Matl, Trujillo went
over his boss's head, calling the surveillance director in
New York. By 1982, Trujillo estimated, he was spending 60
percent of his time on the Matl investigation. When Matl

was fired a year later, he told Trujillo, "You did this to me."

Though Trujillo didn't discover all of Matl's violations, the SEC concluded, he did enough. "The test," concluded Trujillo's attorney, "isn't perfection; it's reasonableness."

Some industry observers worry that the Trujillo decision implies that supervisors may be liable for not informing on superiors who seem lax in enforcing the rules. There are no cases to test that notion as yet. If the present case seems worrisome on that point, however, it provides some reassurance on another. Supervisors can make mistakes without becoming liable for fines or other penalties. A supervisor who has done a reasonably good job needn't suffer for the misdeeds of either his brokers or his bosses. Doing a reasonable job, one should note, doesn't include launching a vendetta. Setting out to "nail" an RR seems to be turning a professional matter into a personal one.

Another case ended less happily for the supervisor of an errant RR:

Case 6-2   According to the NASD, Anthony F. Valone was involved in distribution of limited partnership interests without informing his employer. Valone, an RR with Travelers Equities Sales Inc., was fined $100,000 and barred from association with any NASD member. William C. Steinberg, a registered principal, and Travelers were each fined $50,000 for failure to supervise Valone.

It could have been worse. In 1987, the NASD expelled 17 firms and suspended nine others for violating rules or failing to supervise adequately.

THE STRUCTURE OF SUPERVISION

Part of supervising effectively is putting the right people with the right tools in the right places. Recognizing this, the NASD has beefed up its guidelines for hiring supervisors and giving them adequate support. The rules stem from common sense:

> Supervisors should have the intelligence and experience to know a violation when they see one. They should have access to the rules they are enforcing. And they shouldn't have to review the behavior of too many RRs in too many different places.

The NASD has specific requirements in these areas:

- The supervisory system must cover all aspects of the firm's business, not just retail sales. This includes trading, the back office, and market services.
- Each member firm must identify to the NASD one or more compliance principals who report to senior management and are responsible for reviewing the firm's supervisory system.
- The firm must have a reasonably current compliance manual with appropriate sections available on site.
- The firm must designate at least one principal for each type of business for which it is registered.
- The firm must make reasonable efforts to insure that supervisors are qualified for their particular responsibilities. Supervisors should, for example, understand products and relevant regulations, be capable of exercising authority over those they supervise, and be expe-

rienced in the activities conducted in their office. The firm should also consider a potential supervisor's experience, employment record, and disciplinary history.

- A firm must review periodically the activities at each office, including nonbranch offices, to be certain that all customer accounts are free of abuses and irregularities. Outside contractors may perform the reviews, but this does not excuse the firm from responsibility for compliance.

- A firm must designate a supervisor for each registered representative, no matter what the RR's function.

- A firm must arrange an annual compliance session for each registered representative. Either a registered employee of the firm or a contractor may conduct the session, but it must take place in person. Phone interviews and video conferences will not suffice. The NASD does not specify topics to be covered, but an interview should include the following: (1) A review of the RR's products and procedures; (2) an opportunity for the RR to ask questions and get answers; and (3) an update on new regulations, the firm's policies, and similar topics. Interviews may be conducted individually or in groups. Each RR, not just retail salespersons, must attend such interviews. The firm must have evidence of compliance with this regulation. For that purpose, it may wish to keep records of each interview, noting date, location, attendees, and topics covered.

- Finally, a firm must designate an appropriately registered principal as supervisor in each Office of Supervisory Jurisdiction (OSJ). If, for example, RRs in the office are Series 7 licensed, the principal might have a Series 24 license. A branch office may be supervised by a registered representative. The NASD has revised its definitions of OSJ, branch office, and nonbranch office as follows.

Any location must be treated as an *Office of Supervisory Jurisdiction* if:

1. Registered persons in the office engage in retail sales or have other public contact.
2. A substantial number of registered persons work at the location or are supervised from it.
3. The location is sufficiently far away from the nearest OSJ.
4. Registered persons reporting to the office are widely dispersed geographically.
5. Securities activities conducted at the location are complex or diverse.

Any securities business location must be designated as a *branch office*, supervised by a registered representative or registered principal, if it is identified to the public by either of the following:

- A permanent exhibit booth in a shopping mall.
- Any advertising, including the phone number.

This does not include the location of a sign that advertises the firm's business and directs inquiries to a phone number or office address.

A location where registered persons offer securities for sale may be treated as a *nonbranch office* if it is identified solely by a telephone directory line listing, business cards, or letterhead. The card or letterhead must, however, contain the address and telephone number of the supervising branch or OSJ. The RRs in a nonbranch office may accept orders and communicate them to another location.

AN INVESTOR'S RIGHT TO KNOW ABOUT AN RR'S WRONGS

No matter how thoroughly a firm supervises, infractions will occur. When they do, the public has a right to know. Regulators, therefore, have recently resolved that investors will receive more information about disciplinary actions. For example, NASD member firms are required to inform the NASD when they or their employees get into trouble with a rule-making entity such as the NASD, the NYSE, the MSRB, or the CBOE.

Member firms must inform the NASD promptly and in writing if they or their employees are the subject of any disciplinary action by a clearing corporation, self-regulatory organization, commodities futures market, or government regulatory agency.

When disclosing violations to the NASD a firm must be careful to use the proper forms listed in Table 6.1.

This takes care of our discussion of the broker-dealer's responsibility to supervise and the NASD's guidelines for reasonable supervision within an adequate structure.

ADVERTISING

In an earlier discussion of the RR's duties to the firm, we described the case of Clarence Dawson, who was fined for misleading use of his employer's name in offering documents.

TABLE 6.1.

Forms Needed to Disclose Violations

Violator	Sanction	Form
Broker-dealer	Disciplinary action	Form BD
RR	Disciplinary action	Form U-4
RR	Termination	Form U-5
RR	Internal discipline	Notice of disciplinary actions
Nonregistered person	Internal discipline	Notice of disciplinary actions
Nonregistered person	Termination for cause	Notice of disciplinary actions

Note: *Internal disciplinary actions* include significant limitations the firm imposes on an employee, such as suspension, termination, withholding of commissions, or fines in excess of $2,500.

The presence of the firm's name implied that it was supervising Dawson's sale of the securities; in fact, it didn't even know the sale was taking place. Therefore, Dawson's documents were fraudulent.

Because of such problems, the NASD requires firms to supervise all advertising. An adequate supervisory system provides for the firm's prior approval of all advertising and sales literature.

All advertising and sales literature must be approved before it is used. Approval must be indicated by the signature or initials of a registered principal of the firm or someone designated to act for the principal. Options advertising must be approved by the Compliance Registered Options Principal (CROP).

The definitions of advertising and sales literature are very broad. Essentially, advertising is any material placed in any public medium. Sales literature is virtually any public communication that isn't an advertisement. Correspondence between RRs and individual customers is not considered public communication, so it isn't regulated quite as strictly as advertising and sales literature. Letters and other materials you send to customers must be approved, but not necessarily before you send them. You must also keep copies of correspondence on file for examination.

The following case of unapproved advertising involves options material:

Case 6-3 Under the CBOE rules, an RR was fined $2,500 for several violations, including unapproved advertising and sales literature. Without obtaining the firm's approval, the RR used the firm's business card and letterhead in communications with two customers, implying that he belonged to the firm's consulting group. In fact, there was no consulting group. Further, the RR sent two customers sales literature that was unauthorized by the firm. The literature included projected returns on various recommended strategies without disclosing potential risks. In assessing the fine, the disciplinary committee took into account the fact that the RR had already contributed $5,000 toward the firm's settlement with defrauded customers.

THE TRADING ROOM

The firm's supervisory obligations are not limited to keeping an eye on the sales force. The trading room, too, can be a source of problems, as recent disciplinary actions have shown. Broker-dealers have been punished for, among other infractions, allowing unregistered persons to make trading decisions for the firm, offering securities at unfair prices, illegally parking securities with other firms, misuse of the Small Order Execution System (SOES), and fraudulent reporting of trades.

Firms generally keep RRs out of the trading room and strictly prohibit RR misuse of information about order flow and order entry. For example, firm rules normally prohibit RRs from engaging in *front running*; i.e., entry of orders, for their benefit, in front of large orders for others.

Registration of Traders

> A firm must ensure that all persons involved in trading activities meet the NASD's registration requirements.

Case 6-4 All Tech Investment Group ran afoul of the NASD for a number of violations of rules regarding SOES. (We'll look at other aspects of this case later.) Andrew B. Citrynell, All Tech's executive vice president and an outspoken critic of regulations barring the use of SOES by professional traders, was fined $5,000 and suspended from supervisory duties for five days. He was charged with allowing customers, who were of course not registered with the firm, to enter orders through SOES terminals. Citrynell explained that the firm consented to this action and other sanctions only after it ran out of money and resources to fight the NASD.

Registration helps the NASD police the marketplace and protect its integrity. Failure to register, therefore, inhibits the NASD's ability to carry out its mission. Further, giving selected customers access to systems intended solely for registered professionals is discriminatory. It's a special favor to them, and gives them an edge on other investors. That, too, violates market integrity.

Maintaining the Integrity of Market Services

In a 1989 publication the NASD responded to a number of questions about the new supervision rules. The answer to a query about what must be supervised included "market services such as SOES and NASDAQ/NMS trade reporting." Misuse of these systems certainly does nothing to reassure investors about the fairness and reliability of the marketplace. Regulators are not tolerant of those who use these systems inappropriately. Here's the rule on use of SOES:

> The Small Order Execution System (SOES) is intended to facilitate execution of agency orders for public customers at the best available price with specific limits. At present, this applies to trades of 1,000 shares or less for NASDAQ/NMS securities and 500 shares or less for other NASDAQ securities.

One way firms violate the intended purpose of the system is to use it for their own trades rather than for those of public customers.

Case 6-5 The NASD found one member firm guilty of trading its proprietary accounts through SOES and failing to supervise properly its employees' use of SOES. The firm was fined $15,000 and forbidden to use SOES for 30 days.

Another violation is *order splitting*—dividing trades too large for SOES into pieces that will fit under the size limit—1,000 shares for NMS trades, 500 for others.

Case 6-6 An NASD member found guilty of improperly executing orders through SOES and failing to supervise employee use of the system was suspended from SOES participation for six months, censured, and fined $10,000. The complaint stated that the firm's president divided a 7,500-share customer order into several smaller trades to circumvent the 1,000-share limit. The firm also used SOES for proprietary trading and failed to establish, maintain, and enforce written procedures for use of the system.

Reporting Trades

> Because market integrity depends upon reliable information, firms will supervise trading room activity to see that trades are reported fully, honestly, and on time.

Though computerized systems report trades automatically, they are not tamperproof. RRs sometimes submit phony orders; traders, too, perpetrate the occasional fraud.

The NASD is understandably proud of its automated reporting system and doesn't tolerate activity that could cast doubt on its credibility. Nor will customers take kindly to the discovery that they have been buying and selling on the basis of falsified data. In commenting on a recent disciplinary action, the NASD's Market Surveillance Committee wrote that it "takes a serious view of NASDAQ/NMS trade-reporting obligations as the trade-reporting rules are critical to the continual flow of information to the NASDAQ marketplace."

Those words referred specifically to this case:

Case 6-7 William Carey, a registered representative, was fined $10,000 and suspended from association with any

NASD firm for five business days. The Market Surveillance Committee determined that he had reported 11 fictitious trades, failed to report 14 trades, and inaccurately reported four others. The NASD also censured Carey's employer, North Country Securities, Ltd., of New York, and fined the firm $20,000. In their view, the firm failed to fulfill its obligation "to establish, maintain, and enforce supervisory procedures designed to assure that associated persons complied with applicable securities laws and NASD trade-reporting rules."

In a case involving First Boston, the NASD assessed even stronger penalties for trade-reporting violations. In the securities market, it would seem, the bigger they are, the harder they fall:

Case 6-8 James B. Raphalian, a managing director of First Boston Corporation, and his employer were fined a total of $200,000 for trade-reporting violations and failure to supervise. They were charged by the NASD's Market Surveillance Committee with failing to report, or reporting inaccurately, a substantial number of NASDAQ/NMS trades during 1987 and 1988. Raphalian's fine was $50,000. In addition, he was censured and suspended for three years from supervising compliance with OTC trading regulations. The firm, also censured, was fined $150,000. As part of the settlement, the firm agreed to do the following:

- Specify procedures to supervise reporting of NASDAQ/ NMS trades.

- Designate a managing director to supervise the OTC trading department.

- File quarterly reports with the NASD on compliance with trade-reporting requirements.

One reason for fictitious trade reporting is to manipulate prices. Perhaps the most common violation of that sort is *marking the close of the market*—entering bids (real or fictitious) that raise the final quote on a security at the end of the day or at the end of the month. As we noted in a previous chapter, boosting the final bid reduces margin calls, increases profits on positions in the stock, elevates traders' bonuses, and improves the appearance of the firm's net capital. Here's what happens to firms whose employees are caught playing that game:

> **Case 6-9**   Douglas H. Levine, formerly an RR with Volpe & Covington in San Francisco, was censured and fined $15,000 for violating the NASD's antifraud rules. Levine allegedly entered fictitious trade reports at or near the close of trading, intending to manipulate the market. (Reporting purchases at the offer just before trading stops forces the price up on the last trade. This is done to raise the closing price of securities long in a firm's account.) He made 20 such reports involving five securities. Without admitting or denying allegations against it, Volpe & Covington consented to a $20,000 fine, censure, and suspension from making markets in four NASDAQ securities for periods of from one to four days. The NASD charged the firm with failure to establish and enforce a supervisory system sufficient to detect and prevent fictitious reporting. The firm also was charged with failure to require proper registration of a principal with management and supervisory responsibilities.

Fair Pricing

> Member firms must supervise trading to ensure that securities are fairly and reasonably priced.

A discussion of trading supervision naturally raises the subject of markups. Charging whatever price the market will bear is not acceptable in the securities marketplace. Prices must be fair. As we noted earlier, a fair markup on a security reflects actual difficulties involved in making transactions in that issue. Simply setting the markup below a given level, such as five percent of the sale price, does not guarantee fairness.

Consider the following case:

Case 6-10 The NASD found Charles Dean and Dean Securities, Inc. guilty of selling municipal bonds at prices that were not fair and reasonable. Conclusions were based on the pattern of markups in 16 principal transactions. In the first five sales, markups ranged from 4.2 to 7.3 percent. In the next 11 transactions, the markups rose to between 19 and 20.5 percent. Dean and the firm were fined $10,000 and ordered to give up $16,300.

Parking Violations

Regulators consider temporarily *parking* stock with another firm as a sign that someone is trying to get away with something. Parking typically is used to obscure the ownership of the securities, thus avoiding taxes or concealing the acquisition of stock in a takeover attempt.

Parking stock occurs when one firm sells shares temporarily to another firm, and agrees to repurchase the securities at a set time and price. Stock parking has been in the news lately in connection with the Ivan Boesky scandal.

Until these recent cases, parking itself was not technically illegal unless pursued as part of an otherwise illegal scheme.

On the other hand, regulators have assumed that stock parking usually is undertaken as part of a shady activity, so the practice has been, in effect, treated as if it were illegal.

There are three common reasons to park stock. One is to hide ownership of securities to escape taxes on them. A firm isn't taxed on stock parked elsewhere and temporarily registered in the other firm's name.

A second motivation for parking stock is to hide a takeover attempt. An investor who acquires five percent of a company's stock must make that fact public by filing with the SEC. Thus alerted of a possible takeover, other investors can try to profit by taking positions in the stock. This can throw a monkey wrench into otherwise smoothly operating acquisition machinery. When the information becomes public, speculation may drive up the stock's price. Further, the target company may take the opportunity to erect takeover defenses. To avoid disclosing a five percent stake in a target company, takeover artists sometimes park shares with their friends until they have the number of shares they need to achieve their goal. The parked shares aren't in the investor's name, but they are in the investor's control. This use of parking to frustrate the intent of the disclosure requirement is, of course, illegal.

A third common reason for parking stock is to give a temporary boost to a firm's capital. Before capital computations at the end of the month, a firm needing capital may try to raise money by convincing a stronger firm to buy securities temporarily.

We'll look at the specifics of two illegal parking cases. The first involves Boesky associate Boyd Jefferies; the second focuses on a Drexel employee, a junior trader whose boss reported to junk bond king Michael Milken.

Case 6-11 Boyd Jefferies first came to the SEC's attention when Ivan Boesky turned him in. In an attempt to win lenient treatment from the government, the 58-year-old Jefferies, head of Jefferies & Co. in Los Angeles, turned state's evidence. He implicated Paul Bilzerian, a real estate speculator turned takeover artist, in two illegal parking operations. According to Jefferies, Bilzerian parked shares of two takeover targets with Jefferies & Co. The target companies were Cluett Peabody & Co. and Hammermill Paper Co. Bilzerian's purpose in parking the shares, according to Jefferies, was to conceal his intention of taking the two companies over.

The two scams worked in similar ways. In the Cluett Peabody case, Bilzerian acquired control of 24 percent of the company's stock before making a tender offer for the rest. Eventually, he sold all his shares at a $7 million profit, to West Point-Pepperell, Inc., the *white knight* that came to Cluett Peabody's rescue. In the Hammermill affair, Bilzerian and others acquired a 20 percent stake in the company, made a tender offer, and eventually sold their holdings to the International Paper Co. for a profit of $58 million.

Jefferies' role was to buy shares for Bilzerian—between 400,000 and 500,000 shares in the Hammermill case—and hold them until Bilzerian was ready to buy them back. When Jefferies bought the shares, Bilzerian owned 4.9 percent of Hammermill. Further direct purchases by Bilzerian, therefore, would have triggered the SEC reporting requirement. "We didn't really make any money," Jefferies testified. "These transactions [in Cluett Peabody and in Hammermill] were really just customer accommodation, to do a favor for [Bilzerian]."

Bilzerian has been convicted for his part in the scams, and awaits sentencing. He faces a possible jail sentence of 55 years plus fines of up to $2.8 million.

Case 6-12   The first trial in the investigation of Drexel Burnham Lambert focused on a relatively minor player, an assistant trader named Lisa Jones. Jones actually was not on trial for securities violations but for allegedly lying to a federal grand jury about her role in stock parking arrangements between her employer, Drexel, and a now defunct firm, Princeton-Newport.

The government alleged that Princeton-Newport had parked the securities with Drexel to avoid taxation.

Jones came to the SEC's attention because of her place in the company's reporting structure. Her boss was a trader named Bruce Lee Newberg, whose immediate superior was Michael Milken.

In response to investigators' questions, Jones initially claimed she couldn't remember the trades in question and didn't know the meaning of *stock parking*. She stuck to that story through several rounds of testimony until the government produced a tape of her conversations with William Hale, the Princeton trader who worked opposite Jones in making the questionable arrangements. Hale, who became a witness for the prosecution, claimed he and Jones had discussed the transactions, and decided they were probably illegal. The tape bore him out.

Jones then changed her story. Claiming the tape had refreshed her memory, she admitted to participating in the trades and discussing their questionable legality with Hale. She was indicted, brought before a federal jury, and convicted of lying to investigators. Two days after indicting Jones, the government also brought charges against Newberg and other officials at Princeton-Newport.

On August 23, 1989, Jones was sentenced to 18 months in prison, and fined $50,000 for lying to the grand jury. She has fallen a long way from her $100,000 job with Drexel, where she had, according to her testimony, found the feeling of family she missed as a young runaway.

On November 6, 1989, sentences were imposed on those involved in the parking scam at higher levels than Jones: Bruce Lee Newberg, her boss at Drexel, and three partners in Princeton-Newport. Each received three months in jail plus fines ranging from $50,000 to $165,000—far lighter punishments than the courts administered to Jones. After the sentences were announced, the defendants were reported to appear "relieved" as they hugged their families.[1]

One can legitimately wonder if the disparity in punishment, a fact not lost on the press and public, isn't precisely the sort of unfairness that makes customers cynical about the market. If the legal and regulatory system works in favor of the insiders and against the smaller players, what chance, the individual investor might ask, does a mere customer have in the securities market?

A *Chinese Wall* to Keep Inside Information In

Boyd Jefferies, Ivan Boesky, Lisa Jones, Bruce Newberg, and others implicated in their machinations have become part of the market's history of crisis and regulation. Whatever the puzzling inconsistencies in their punishments, their violations have moved the SEC and the Congress to revise insider trading rules related to the 1934 Securities Exchange Act.

The SEC's particular concern is to stop leakage of information from the corporate finance area of securities firms to other departments, especially the trading desk, underwriting, and sales. In the age of the leveraged buyout, the corporate finance department is a danger zone, a gold mine of inside information. Employees involved in structuring buyouts acquire information that traders and selling RRs could use to make themselves or their customers rich.

Regulators and legislators, therefore, are trying to contain that information within the department where it belongs. In industry parlance, the SEC would like firms to surround the corporate finance department with a *Chinese Wall* impervious to insider information.

That, as you can imagine, is a tall order. But certain measures of control are now written into the law. For one thing, the SEC has a legal right to sue users of inside information for triple damages—a matter mentioned in Chapter 4. That is, anyone who trades on inside information is liable for damages of up to three times the amount made on the trades. Worse, one is liable for triple damages on the gains of anyone to whom the information is passed.

Since insider trading has created such a public scandal, you can be sure that the NASD, the SEC, and the management of broker-dealers will be searching out and punishing all offenders.

UNDERWRITING

Underwriting a new issue of securities involves special responsibilities for a broker-dealer and its registered representatives. The firm has certain obligations to the issuer whose securities it brings to the marketplace; it also has duties to customers who purchase portions of the issue. In the following discussion we'll concentrate on four underwriting responsibilities with special significance.

First, firms must exercise *due diligence* in reviewing the issuer's disclosure documents for significant omissions and misstatements. As principals, in other words, broker-dealers have a responsibility to their customers to see that issuers are in compliance with SEC disclosure requirements.

Second, a firm must offer securities to public customers at the offering price—not to its own employees at special prices. An underwriter is, however, allowed to attempt a limited degree of manipulation in order to stabilize the price of a new issue in secondary trading. This may only be done to provide a stable price, not to run the price up and create a hot issue.

Third, a firm must be certain that sales persons are properly registered even in distributions of unregistered private placements.

Finally, in contingent underwritings the firm must comply with escrow requirements that govern the handling of money received from customers before satisfaction of the minimum subscription requirement.

Due Diligence

> When acting as an underwriter, a broker-dealer must exercise *due diligence* in ascertaining that the issuer makes available to customers all relevant information about potential problems that would affect an investor.

When a broker-dealer underwrites a new issue, it assumes responsibility for disclosure of relevant information about the issuer. The firm is not doing its duty to the public if it withholds damaging information that potential investors should know. Moreover, the firm must actively attempt to discover relevant information about the issuer.

A broker-dealer, in other words, has a duty to check out a security before selling it, just as a car dealer has a moral and legal obligation not to sell automobiles that have defective brakes.

The question remains: How much due diligence is enough? Clearly, a firm can't be expected to know everything about the issuer; it can, however, be expected to have someone read through available documents to find out what might go wrong with the proposed business and ask for any important data that seems to be missing.

The due diligence requirement has a tendency to expand with time. Thirty years ago, for example, it was rare for an underwriter to scrutinize an issuer's labor contracts. Now such research is routine. After all, strikes can damage the issuer's business.

Others besides the broker-dealer have due diligence responsibilities to clients. Accountants and attorneys, for example, also must examine available information to discover potential problems. If something does go amiss, aggrieved investors may sue any and all parties with due diligence duties.

The following case focuses on an RR who was punished for several underwriting violations, including failure to disclose relevant information:

Case 6-13 Stephen M. McIntosh, a registered principal in Cedar Rapids, Iowa, was fined $9,800 along with his employer. McIntosh was also censured and suspended from employment as a general securities principal for 30 days. Among other allegations, McIntosh was charged with having sold limited partnership units to 18 customers without providing documentation disclosing that 60 percent of the general partner was owned by shareholders of his firm, and that he himself was president and director of both his firm and the general partner.

Stabilizing Bids: Allowable Price Manipulation

> The underwriter must make a bona fide offering of securities to public customers at the offering price. An underwriter may attempt to stabilize the price of the issue in secondary trading by entering bids at or below the offering price. It may not attempt to raise the market price artifically above the offering price.

Naturally, an underwriter hates to see a new issue trading below the offering price. It's tough to sell your allotment of shares and make a profit if the public can buy them cheaper elsewhere. For that reason, underwriters are allowed to bid in the secondary market to support the price. These bids are called *stabilizing bids* and can only be entered at or below the offering price. The underwriter is not allowed to bid up the price of the security in the aftermarket.

There's a built-in problem with stabilizing bids: Customers may be tempted that bought at the price sell back at the pegged price. In an underwriting syndicate, the managing firm may accompany a stabilizing bid with a provision that RRs will lose commissions on such sales and their employer lose its selling concession. This arrangement is called a *penalty bid* or *penalty syndicate bid*. It's perfectly legal, however annoying it may be to RRs and firms adversely affected by it.

There have been recent claims that trading rooms at some penny firms are refusing to carry out sell orders unless the RR brings in a buy order for the same security. Since this policy involves rejecting customers' orders to sell, it is clearly an illegal form of market manipulation. As yet there has been no disciplinary action on such claims or any other substantiation of them. We pass the information along only as an example.

There are other allegations—again, unsubstantiated—that some firms require purchasers of hot issues to fill a portion of their order in the aftermarket. This, too, would be illegal manipulation. It is certainly not consistent with the injunction to make a bona fide offering at the offering price.

Proper Registration of Salespersons

> As underwriter, the broker-dealer is responsible for seeing to proper registration of all salespersons. This holds true even if the issue is an unregistered private placement.

As part of its mission to protect investors, the SEC requires securities salespersons to register. Usually this means registering as an employee of a broker-dealer and, as you well know, passing a licensing exam. (Officers of the issuer may be able to sell the security without registering.) In this and in other ways, registration of sales representatives helps maintain the industry's credibility with customers.

For its part, a broker-dealer must rely only on registered persons and officers of the issuer to sell its securities. In a limited partnership offering, for example, the sales force will include the underwriter's registered representatives and, perhaps, the general partner of the issuer.

Salespeople must be registered even when the security itself is exempt, as are private securities offerings and intrastate offerings.

Though intrastate offerings need not be registered with the SEC in Washington, they must be registered with the state. To qualify for the intrastate exemption, a security must meet fairly stringent residence requirements applying both to the issuer and to investors. In some states salespeople may register with the issuer rather than with a broker-dealer.

If sellers violate state requirements to register the securities or the sales force, investors have the right to return the securities in exchange for the purchase price plus interest. This is called the buyer's right of *rescission*.

Case 6-14   For allegedly permitting eight unregistered persons to function as sales representatives, Copeland Securities of New York and principal Kenneth Germain were fined $10,000 each. They consented to the fine without admitting or denying the charges.

Escrow Requirements in Contingent Offerings

In a contingent offering, the underwriter must deposit customer checks immediately into an escrow account. If the contingency is not achieved, checks must be returned to customers undiminished by commissions. The underwriter may not extend credit on purchases of new issues.

There are several types of contingent offerings, including *best-efforts*, *all-or-none*, and *mini/maxi* underwritings. Such offerings are not complete until the underwriter raises a predetermined amount of money through the sale of shares. Sales are contingent upon reaching the goal. If it isn't reached, customers get their money back. To protect that money, customers' checks are kept in escrow. Once the required sum has been subscribed, customers receive their securities, and the money in escrow is divided between the issuer and the underwriters.

While in escrow, the money must not in any way be subject to the risks of the broker-dealer's business. If the minimum sum isn't reached, the money in escrow goes back to the customers with no commission subtracted.

The major temptation in contingent underwritings is to siphon off funds that should be placed in escrow. The RR might, for example, delay depositing a customer's check and use it for his or her own purposes—perhaps intending to replace the funds later. The money might be mingled with the firm's funds. As we saw earlier, this would put the money in jeopardy if, for instance, the bank placed a lien against the account. Or the checks might be transferred to the issuer before the minimum amount has accumulated.

To guard against delay of deposits, regulations specify that customer money must be placed into the escrow account by noon of the business day following receipt of the check or noon of the second day after the issuer receives the customer's subscription form. Customer's checks must be made payable to the escrow agent. On receipt of an order, a broker-dealer holding customer funds must move the subscription money from the customer's account to an escrow account.

After misappropriation of escrow money, the second most frequent violation occurs when subscriptions stall just before reaching the required minimum amount. In such cases, the broker-dealer may be tempted to loan money to insiders or favored customers in order to push subscriptions over the top. To guard against this, regulations forbid extension of credit on new issues.

Here are some examples of violations recently punished by the NASD:

Case 6-15 We'll look at the McIntosh case one last time. It provides a fair summary of the common violations of rules governing escrow arrangements. To begin with, McIntosh accepted checks that were not made payable to an escrow agent. In several offerings he failed to deposit investors' funds in an escrow account. Funds from 21 investors went into money market accounts instead. When one contingent offering failed to raise the minimum capital in the given time, McIntosh retained customers' funds instead of returning them. He was found, in one case, to have allowed funds to be used for the issuer's benefit before the contingency requirements had been satisfied. Finally, he extended credit to four customers to purchase shares of a new issue. As we mentioned in a previous case, McIntosh was fined $9,800 along with his firm, suspended for 30 days, and censured.

Case 6-16 The NASD found two registered principals guilty of violating escrow regulations in a contingent offering of limited partnership interests. Instead of depositing investors' funds in an escrow account, they commingled the funds with those in one of two accounts apparently under their control. For this the two principals were censured and each was fined $15,000. Their firm was also censured. The firm and the principals agreed to the sanctions without admitting or denying the charges.

BROKER-DEALER FINANCIAL RESPONSIBILITIES

The spectacle of broker-dealers' going bankrupt and investors' losing their capital haunts the halls of Congress. After the crises in the late 1960s, legislators put regulators on notice that the time had come for reform. With the *Securities Industry Protection Act,* Congress sent several strong messages to the SEC: (1) Establish an early-warning system to sound an alarm when firms get into hot water financially; (2) take a more active role in preventing bankruptcies; and (3) find a way to protect investors' money and securities. Congress reminded the SEC, in other words, that the public interest is not served by a securities market filled with firms teetering on the edge of bankruptcy.

For its part Congress established the *Securities Investor Protection Corporation* (SIPC) to insure the accounts of investors against the bankruptcy of the broker-dealer. As we noted earlier, SIPC guarantees accounts up to $500,000, of which $100,000 can be cash.

In response to Congressional directives, the SEC now requires firms to maintain a minimum amount of net capital. Meeting this requirement means firms must keep completely accurate and current records of their liabilities and assets so that they know their net capital. To this end, firms holding customer cash and securities must designate a registered financial and operations principal (FINOP) to supervise financial record keeping.

Broker-dealers must maintain adequate net capital, keep accurate financial records, and properly supervise financial record keeping.

Minimum Net Capital Requirements

Requirements vary with firm size and with changes in the balance sheet. Limited broker-dealers, firms that don't hold customers' cash and securities, must have at least $5,000 in net capital. Fully registered broker-dealers that do hold customer cash and securities must maintain net capital of at least

$25,000. There is a current SEC proposal to change the capital requirements to $250,000.

Moreover, firms must be certain that total unsecured debt and funds payable to customers never exceeds 15 times net capital. For example, a firm with $1.5 million in customer funds and unsecured obligations must maintain at least $100,000 net capital.

Call For Help

Net capital minimums are absolute. If a firm's capital dips below the allowable minimum, it must suspend business. Management must send RRs home, close the shop, telegraph regulators about the problem, and find a way out of their difficulties. Sometimes firms are back in business within a day or two. Firms that don't solve net capital problems, however, are out of business for good.

Broker-dealers will occasionally go broke. That's a risk that can't be regulated out of existence. So it's no sin for securities firms to have money problems. Unforeseeable occurrences can redden the ink on the balance sheets of the most respectable firms. But financially troubled firms that try to stay open for business and conceal their difficulties from regulators change themselves from guiltless victims into culprits. This sort of behavior frustrates regulators' mission, which is to keep careful watch on the industry and steer as many firms as possible away from the shoals of insolvency.

The SEC doesn't want firms routinely operating close to the allowable minimum of net capital. A 15-to-1 ratio is not a goal to achieve; it is a condition to avoid. When a broker-dealer's net capital falls under 120 percent of the minimum, it must file a Focus II or IIA report by the 10th of the next month. Focus II reports are for full broker-dealers; Focus IIA reports are for limited firms. Moreover, the firm must continue to send the Focus II or IIA report every month thereafter until it has maintained its net capital above the early warning limit for three consecutive months.

For a limited broker-dealer, in other words, net capital of less than $6,000 (120 percent of the $5,000 minimum) requires filing a Focus IIA report. For a full broker-dealer, net capital under $30,000 requires filing. For any firm with $1.5 million in unsecured obligations and payables, $120,000 of net capital is the signal to start filing the reports.

Here are some other conditions besides net capital problems that require telegraphic notification of regulators:

- When a firm can't make the deposit to the reserve account for the balance of customer payables and receivables, it's time to send a telegram and shut down the shop.

- If an independent accountant informs a firm of material inadequacies in its accounting controls, the firm must telegraph regulators immediately; moreover, within 48 hours it must draft a letter describing a plan to solve the problem.

- If a firm discovers its books are not current, it must telegraph regulators immediately and send a letter within 48 hours describing the steps being taken to bring the books up to date.

- If a firm has too much leverage in its capital structure (subordinated debt in relation to equity) for 90 consecutive days, it must telegraph regulators on the 91st day.

A Sad Story

IRA Haupt & Company was an east coast commodities broker with a track record stretching back well into the nineteenth century. The firm arranged commodities hedges for their clients. For example, an elevator operator with wheat in storage might enter into a futures contract to sell wheat at a set price during a given month. The contract would hedge the operator's risk if wheat prices were to fall. As security for the short futures position, the elevator operator would give Haupt a receipt for the grain in the elevator.

The problem for IRA Haupt involved a man named Tony D'Angelus who said he had vegetable oil stored in huge tanks. To hedge his risk on the vegetable oil, D'Angelus sold soybean oil futures and margined his position with receipts for the oil stored with American Express Warehouse Company.

In other words, as far as Haupt knew it was in a riskless position—it had in hand the receipt guaranteeing the existence of oil it could deliver against Mr. D'Angelus's contract. Since the transaction seemed so safe, the firm was not concerned that Mr. D'Angelus's account constituted a large part of its business, until the storage tanks were found to be filled with water topped of by a couple of inches of vegetable oil.

First to suffer was American Express Warehouse Company, which had issued so many receipts for the bogus oil that it went out of business. This left Haupt holding worthless receipts and Mr. D'Angelus with an unmargined short position in the futures market. Because the position was so large, neither Haupt nor D'Angelus could meet the resulting margin call for cash. Within a few days, Haupt was out of business. Eventually, D'Angelus went to jail.

A story like this one can't have a happy ending, really. But at least the principals from IRA Haupt were soon working for other broker-dealers. It is—to repeat the theme of this section—no sin to go broke in the brokerage business. Any firm can be blindsided by fraud or unpredictable catastrophe. The sin is in covering up and continuing to do business with inadequate net capital. Regulators can't abide deceit. Deceit is not in the public interest, and regulators are charged with protecting the interests of the larger community.

Examples

The following cases illustrate problems firms have had in complying with regulations that govern record keeping and minimum net capital:

> **Case 6-17** A registered principal was suspended and fined for allowing his employer to fall below the minimum net capital requirement, for failing to prepare certain books and records, and for inaccurately recording the firm's liabilities. Without admitting or denying the charges, the principal and the firm agreed to a $7,500 fine. The principal was suspended for six months from any association with an NASD member, and suspended for two years from any association with a member as a general securities principal, manager, or supervisor.

Here's another case of juggling accounts to conceal a firm's inability to maintain minimum net capital. If financial personnel don't balance the firm's bank account and keep track of receivables and loans, the firm's financial condition is unknowable. What regulators don't know about, they can't fix.

> **Case 6-18** The NASD found Rita Delaney of Salt Lake City responsible for several violations of net capital and record keeping requirements at her firm. She failed to maintain adequate net capital and neglected to reconcile the drafts receivable account and the bank statement. She also filed to adjust books and records to reflect an outstanding bank loan and to reflect the firm's perilous financial condition. For these infractions, Delaney was fined

$1,000, barred from association with any NASD member as a financial and operations principal, barred from employment in the financial and operations area, and suspended for one year from associating in any capacity with an NASD member.

As the next case shows, firms and their financial principals also get into trouble for failing to report net capital deficiencies:

Case 6-19 Julio Rodrigo Quintana and Jose Antonio Alverado, two registered principals in Miami, Florida, were fined and suspended for allowing their firm to transact business in nonexempt securities while failing to maintain minimum net capital. They failed to notify the NASD by telegraph of the net capital deficiency and of another serious problem turned up by their accountant. They also failed to file the required Focus Part IIA Report. For these and other violations, Quintana and Alverado were fined $10,000. Alverado was suspended from association with any NASD member in any capacity for 30 days. Quintana was fined $5,000, suspended from association with any NASD member as a financial and operations principal for two weeks, and required to pass the Series 27 exam before returning to work in that capacity.

SUPERVISING OPTIONS ACCOUNTS

Options exist in a world apart from stocks and bonds—not necessarily because of the risks involved, since positions differ considerably in loss potential, but because of the sophistication required to understand various strategies. Consequently, somewhat stricter rules apply to protect the public interest in the maintenance of fair and orderly options markets.

> Customers' options accounts must be properly approved before entry of the first order. Trading in customers' options accounts must be supervised by a Registered Options Principal (ROP), a Compliance Registered Options Principal (CROP), and a Senior Registered Options Principal (SROP).

Examples

What happens when firms fail to follow the stricter regulations pertaining to options accounts? The disciplinary files provide several illustrations:

Case 6-20   Registered Representative Howard H. Hampton was recently fined $50,000 for options violations committed as an employee of two firms. His branch managers and their respective firms, E.F. Hutton and Prudential Bache, were also sanctioned for failure to supervise. Hutton and branch manager John O. Roy, Jr. consented to censure and a fine of $20,000 without admitting or denying the allegations. Prudential Bache consented to a $25,000 fine and censure; Prudential Bache manager Lawrence A. Grolemund consented to censure, a $7,500 fine, and suspension from acting as a ROP from May 16 to June 6, 1988. Both managers must requalify before resuming employment as options principals.

Case 6-21   Richard Helfer and Joseph Leftoff, registered principals in New York, were suspended for a variety of infractions, including violations of options regulations. They allowed their firm to conduct options transactions without a qualified SROP, failed to identify to the NASD the firm's CROP, failed to provide customers with all required information on confirmations, and failed to have adequate supervisory procedures. For these violations and failure to comply with various regulations related to record keeping and financial responsibility, Leftoff was suspended from association with any NASD member for three months. Helfer was suspended for three months from association with any NASD member, and suspended for a year from association with any NASD member as a general securities principal, financial and operations principal, supervisor, or manager. Both consented to the sanctions without admitting or denying the charges.

SUMMARY

As principals in the securities marketplace, broker-dealers are legally responsible for the activities of their registered representatives. Firms delegate authority to carry out such activities as arranging transactions, trading, underwriting, and keeping records. But they do not thereby relinquish responsibility for seeing that these activities are carried out in compliance with market regulations.

The morality and efficiency of the securities marketplace are very much the business of each broker-dealer, primarily because maintaining a just and orderly market is a matter of public interest. In the last analysis, a firm's long-term financial health, as well the public interest, requires maintenance of market integrity. Customers will not trade in a patently corrupt or obviously undependable marketplace. When it comes to enforcing and obeying the rules of the road, therefore, public duty and private interest are one.

Notes

1. "Former Traders Get Sentences For Racketeering," *The Wall Street Journal* (November 7, 1989), p. 3D.

The Ethical Representative: Not an Oxymoron

ETHICS ON THE STREET WHERE YOU WORK

Wall Street may be the best-known street address in the United States, if not in the world. Pennsylvania Avenue, the street where the president lives, is no more familiar or evocative. Bourbon Street, the home address of New Orleans jazz, may be as great a tourist attraction and its name may stimulate similar excitement, but it lacks the connotation of power that Wall Street exudes. Fifth Avenue enjoys a similar aura of wealth and prestige, but its image isn't so clearly focused on one industry.

By the process called metonymy—in which an attribute or feature is used to name the whole, as the crown stands for monarchy—Wall Street has come to symbolize the entire securities industry. Wherever we spend our days, all of us in the securities business work, figuratively speaking, on Wall Street. Would we work anywhere else? The Street is one of the

175

world's most enthralling arenas of activity, as essential as any boardroom or state house, as diverting as any circus or casino.

As a national symbol, Wall Street compares in evocative power with the Statue of Liberty, the White House, the Golden Gate Bridge . . . Disneyworld, the Alamo, and Alcatraz. The question for us to answer, in this final chapter, is: What sort of ethical meaning does this powerful symbol have? Does Wall Street stand for just dealing and fairness for all, or greed and corruption? Are RRs generally good, ethical agents for customers, or is an *ethical stockbroker* an oxymoron, a contradiction in terms, a joke?

Obviously, we don't hold with the cynical view of the industry, but many do—that's a problem. Moreover, Wall Street does have its share of corruption. That's an even worse problem. From the new emphasis on compliance training, you can tell that regulators and broker-dealers take these problems very seriously. In that spirit we devote our final chapter to some thoughts on what it means to be an ethical RR and what obstacles are most likely to prevent an RR from being ethical.

DO THE RIGHT THING

Here's the simple message: Being ethical means doing the right thing. Beyond that simple definition, ethics gets rapidly more complex, confusing, frustrating, even downright dangerous on occasion.

Why the difficulties? Two basic reasons. First, *the right thing* is not always the obvious thing. Philosophers, saints, lawyers, and the rest of us have most likely been arguing about what the right thing is since humankind created enough words to have an argument.

Second, even if we nail down a satisfactory definition of the right thing, we find all sorts of reasons not to do it. In his classic *Confessions*, St. Augustine begs god not to save his soul immediately because he's having so much fun living sinfully. Even though he could see the right thing shimmering ahead of him like a vision of heaven, he yearned to travel the detours to hell.

Our book about the rules of the road in the securities marketplace has been about ethics for stockbrokers, of course, not for saints. In it, we have focused on the laws and regulations intended to help us recognize the right thing. We have also discussed some of the conflicts and temptations that lead us on various detours away from the right thing.

We saw, for example, that regulations determining what is right and wrong for an RR constantly evolve. Yesterday's right thing, in other words, may be today's wrong thing. Similarly, right and wrong are sometimes hard to tell apart. The definition of a security, for example, has changed over the years and is still not a model of clarity. This isn't anybody's fault. The fact is, investing is complex. As technologies and strategies change, so must our definitions. Nevertheless, if we can't clearly draw the line separating securities from nonsecurities, we aren't always going to know when we have crossed over into the territory governed by securities regulations. That is essentially the lesson of the Howey and Koscot cases we described in Chapter 4.

Conflicts of interest also make it difficult for RRs to know and do the right thing. As we also saw in Chapter 4, RRs are agents of two masters, owing allegiance both to customer and firm. The right thing for the customer and the right thing for the firm may sometimes seem to be opposites. We have a friend who recently left a job as an RR for a major firm after his commission goals were raised. In his view the only way he could generate more commissions to keep the firm happy was to churn his customers' accounts. So he quit. Perhaps the firm was right and our friend was wrong; we aren't passing judgment here. But the painful situation illustrates very aptly the potential conflict between serving customers and raising money for the firm—not to mention raising money for oneself. RRs have several masters, each with a version of the right thing. To be successful, and to be ethical, the RR has to reconcile any conflicts.

Finally, our friend's story illustrates another point: The measure of success on Wall Street is money, not good deeds. Of course, RRs are not unique in this regard. Making money is something we all have to do, unless we were born rich or have transcended the need for food and shelter. Ethics is not a study for those who live in a bell jar. It's for those of us who need to navigate through the perils of the real world. Just the same, the atmosphere on Wall Street is supercharged with thoughts of making gains and avoiding losses. This adds to the excitement, but can all too easily turn from a healthy motive for hard work to unbridled greed. At some point RRs lose their perspective and begin to believe that making money justifies any tactic that gets them to that goal. There was a little of that sort of rationalizing in the downfall of Jimmy Doyle, remember. As long as he and his clients were making money, they were willing to deal in gray areas.

These, in short, are some of the obstacles to doing right in the securities marketplace. They are very real, very insidious. They can corrupt us almost unawares. The existence of these obstacles does not change the central argument of our book—though doing the right thing isn't always easy, it is necessary. If propects don't trust us, every phone call we make will lead to rejection. In the end our marketplace either will be ethical or it will vanish like the profits of so many who bought into the Mississippi Bubble.

With this in mind, let's take a closer look at that money-charged atmosphere that makes Wall Street so attractive and dangerous.

THE OTHER SIDE OF THE STREET

As Wall Street suggests adventure, wealth, power, mastery, and the good life, it also conjures up the Crash of 1929, Black Monday, market manipulation, panic, scandal, depression, and brokers leaping from windows. To expand our metaphor, Wall Street, like any other street, has two sides. One side is sunny and inviting; one is shady and threatening. The two are not that far apart, and a person can change sides almost without noticing it has happened.

Let's face it, most of us aren't first attracted to the Wall Street environment out of any overwhelming desire to do good, as one might be attracted to the pulpit, to medicine, or even, in some cases, to journalism or politics. We come to Wall Street to do well—to make money, to share in the excitement of life in the fast lane. On either side of the street, money is the measure of our progress. "He lost his money playing the market," we hear people say, reflecting on the darker side of the street. "My daughter?" a parent says with pride, "She just took a high paying job on Wall Street." Even on the sunny side, Wall Street is about money.

These two impressions of the Street, our apparently contradictory attitudes about the securities industry, may be part of our national ambivalence about money. Money is part of the American dream of individual material success. It is the means of buying the single-family home in the suburbs, the minivan, the cabin on the lake, the BMW. But the love of money, we also say, is the root of all evil. We envy wealth and we resent it. We strive to be rich; but in popular novels, on televised soap operas, and in movies we continuously tell ourselves that riches bring unhappiness. This ambivalence can make life difficult for people who work in an industry that is, in a sense, all about money. At one extreme, making money seems to justify any means used to achieve that end. At the other extreme, making a great deal of money implies that one is corrupt, greedy, materialistic. Clearly, the happy and ethical course runs between these two extremes where the desire to make money is balanced with the desire to help customers and keep the market clean.

Our popular culture includes some very strong negative images of the financial industry, prophetic warnings about the danger that lies at the greedy extreme. The movie *Wall Street*, for example, focuses on the behavior of a broker who would do anything to land a wealthy client. Tom Wolfe's best-selling novel, *Bonfire of the Vanities*, casts a harsh light on the securities industry by chronicling the downfall of fictional bondbroker Sherman McCoy. Like Jimmy Doyle, Sherman McCoy experienced the collapse of his business and his marriage at the same time. (For melodrama's sake, he also committed a rather ambiguous murder.) In Wolfe's view of the world, more is rotten in the city of New York than one broker or one market. All systems (social, economic, religious, and political) have collapsed into a black hole of greed, cowardice, and hate.

The real world of the 1980s gave us stories almost as melodramatic and frightening as those in the movies and novels. Dennis Levine, for example, who spent 15 months in prison for insider trading, has been traveling the country warning young people to avoid his fate. He links his own ethical lapses to the widespread money-lust in the securities industry:

Wall Street was crazy in those days. These were the 1980s, remember, the decade of excess, greed, and materialism. I became a go-go guy, consumed by the high pressure, ultracompetitive world of investment banking. I was helping my clients make tens and even hundreds of millions of dollars. I served as the lead banker on Perelman's nearly $2 billion takeover of Revlon, four months of work that enabled Drexel to earn $60 million in fees. The daily exposure to such deals, the pursuit of larger and larger transactions, and the numbing effect of 60- to 100-hour work-weeks

helped erode my values and distort my judgment. In this unbe-
lievable world of billions and billions of dollars, the millions I
made by trading on nonpublic information seemed almost insig-
nificant . . . . *Perhaps it's worth noting that my legitimate success
stemmed from the same root [as the insider trading]. My ambition was so
strong it went beyond rationality.* (Emphasis added.)[1]

For Levine, the man whose confession led investigators to
Ivan Boesky, the line between legitimate money making and
greedy self-interest disappeared. He could see only the need to
do the successful thing, and lost sight entirely of the need to
do the right thing. His ambition knew no boundaries. A belief
in ethics, along with a knowledge of rules and their importance to the marketplace, sets limits on the ambition that is
necessary to achieve the highest levels of success. Perhaps the
scariest part of Levine's story is, indeed, this underlying
assumption that the worst of the bad guys are simply the best
of the good guys run amok. In doing well, they also do evil.
You could say they love Wall Street too much—not wisely, to
quote *Othello*, but too well.

That's the sort of ethical ambiguity that makes the right
thing difficult to know and to do.

Like Dennis Levine and Boesky, our friend Jimmy Doyle
fell in love with Wall Street—with the marketplace for stocks
and bonds, the constantly moving ticker tape, the ebb and
flow of interest and dividends, conversations about bull and
bear markets, the tides of emotion that sweep through the
industry as securities prices wax and wane—the whole heady
adventure of investment. Also like Levine and Boesky,
Michael Milken, Bruce Newberg, and Lisa Jones, he did not
fall in love with the regulations and the need to respect market
integrity. He traveled down an ethical detour that led to evic-
tion from Wall Street, prison, disgrace, and hopeless debt.

If Jimmy's is not a tragic story, it's one with a very
unhappy ending—certainly a story no one who loves the busi-

ness would want to live through. It shares that characteristic with the stories of Sherman McCoy, Levine, Boesky, Milken, Jones, and many of the others whose cases we have used as illustrations of the rules. Escaping the fate of these people— avoiding censure, suspension, fines, and jail—has been the subject of this book. Protecting yourself is one reason for obeying the rules of the road and staying, so to speak, on the right side of the Street.

And it can be done.

The authors of this book know a man who was called early in life to become a minister. After years of study, he was assigned to his first congregation, and quickly discovered he had no love for a life of poverty. Consequently, he left the ministry to become a stockbroker. In his new profession, he rose rapidly to become a vice president at a major Wall Street wirehouse.

Looking back on his career choice, our friend has no regrets or ethical second thoughts. He makes two points in this regard. First, a minister is, among other things, a counselor; in that role he often finds parishioners coming to him for advice about money matters. Money is frequently involved in life's spiritual matters. It can be a source of temptation, despair, and of marital unrest, to name three frequent reasons for conferences with a minister. By taking a financial counseling approach to his business as a stockbroker, our friend felt that he was continuing one aspect of his ministry. Second, his success in the securities industry has allowed him to contribute both time and money to his church, where he is a respected elder playing a significant role in the affairs of his congregation.

On Wall Street, doing well and doing good are not incompatible.

GOING TO THE MARKET ON WALL STREET

In the beginning were the coffeehouses in which businessmen and stockbrokers congregated to buy and sell shares and to discuss the important events bearing on the economy. It was a relatively small and neighborly market, not so different from traditional markets within the towns of Europe and Asia. Business was more specialized, of course—one went elsewhere for cloth or chickens or shoes. But the atmosphere and technology of trading were very similar.

When one went to Wall Street to raise money for doing business or to trade stocks and bonds, one literally went to Wall Street—on foot or by coach. Upon arrival, one might see familiar faces as well as familiar surroundings. Certainly policing such a market was a simpler matter than it is now.

Technology changed the way we trade. So did the rapid growth of population across the United States. As the geographic edge of the nation sped west, the financial, economic, and political center stayed in the east. In response to the increasing size of the nation, inspired tinkerers such as Samuel Morse and Alexander Graham Bell invented technological methods to bring us closer together.

First there was Morse's telegraph which made it possible for securities firms to branch away from Wall Street and still serve their customers' needs immediately. No longer would a request to buy or sell shares have to be written down and mailed to a stockbroker in New York. It could be encoded in any telegraph office and sent by wire to New York. Thus were the wire houses born.

Later came Bell's telephone which made direct voice communication possible.

So the market grew from the cozy groups gathered in coffee houses to become a nationwide network hooked up to

New York by cables and wires. By continued evolution, the marketplace has outgrown Wall Street—satellites and computers have created a global market, with a few cultural and political barriers yet to be removed.

Now buyers and sellers can go to the marketplace virtually from anywhere. From every state and all around the world business-people come to raise capital for their ventures. Foreign institutional investors come to diversify their portfolios with large blocks of dollar-dominated securities. Speculators and arbitragers come to the market looking for short-term, sometimes instantaneous, profits on big-ticket trades. Money managers with fiduciary responsibilities to hundreds, thousands, or hundreds of thousands of individuals bring in vast portfolios. Individuals invest their retirement funds, hoping they will grow gradually and with relative safety into a source of income for their later years.

All these diverse participants, forming a vast cross section of the nation (and the world), have something in common—the desire to enter a marketplace that is fair, honest, and efficient. They entrust their funds to registered representatives in the faith that they will not be made into fools or paupers by that person or that person's firm.

That trust has sometimes been betrayed. In 1929, 1974, and 1987 the market collapsed. The resulting whirlpool of falling prices took down the net worth of many trusting investors. In 1968, and again in 1987, the market collapsed in another way: trading mechanisms broke down. In 1968 investors paid for stock only to wait in vain for their certificates. When they were ready to sell, they found their brokers unwilling to accept their orders because the securities they purchased had never been delivered. The market had outgrown its technology.

In the mid- to late-1970s the options market outgrew its technology and capacity. Because numerous customers complained, the SEC halted the growth of the market until completion of the wide ranging special study. Expansion of trading wasn't allowed to resume until after the various options markets were reformed according to suggestions in the study.

In 1987, on October 19 and October 20, investors called their brokers in a panic wanting to sell or buy and no one answered the phone, or someone answered the phone but was unable to call up meaningful price information from an overloaded system. The market was broken.

The market also appears broken when scandals erupt over insider trading, price manipulation, or the sudden disappearance of a trusted RR who takes a couple of million dollars worth of customer bonds along to support his new life.

RULES OF THE ROAD FOR WALL STREET

As a Medieval town suffered from the loss of trade caused by suspicion of its market's reliability, so does a modern nation suffer when any of its diverse markets become creaky or corrupt. If prices collapse without warning, if market mechanisms cease to work as expected, if industry professionals mistreat their customers, potential buyers and sellers abandon the securities market. Investors suffer. Firms and RRs suffer. The larger community suffers.

To avoid such public and private pain, the nation polices the market through the SEC as well as through self-regulatory organizations such as the NASD and the various exchanges. Policing a national marketplace—let alone a global market—is something else again from riding herd on a handful of traders housed at the tip of Manhattan Island. The task is accomplished only through elaborate sets of rules with complicated systems of supervision and enforcement.

Sometimes all that apparatus may seem absurd—just an obstacle to doing business and making money for investors.

That's the way it seemed to Jimmy Doyle, who, at the time, believed he broke the rules only to service his customers.

But as we saw in Chapter 4, the RR is not only operating as the customer's agent. He is also the agent of the firm. Jimmy, as we saw, failed to fulfill his duties to the firm. The firm has its obligations to the market, and beyond the market to the general public. It can't meet those obligations without the RR's cooperation.

Acting in the public interest, then, is another reason for obeying the rules of the road. Not only is it in your immediate self-interest to avoid censure, fines, jail terms, and exile from the industry you love; it is in the interest of the surrounding society for you to help maintain the integrity of the market which so many depend upon. Of course, since loss of market integrity means loss of money (witness the way investors shunned stocks after Black Monday in 1987) it is in your long-term self-interest to obey the rules of the road.

What goes around, as they say, comes around. In the end, maintaining the health of the securities markets is in the financial best interest of all involved, whether they be principals, agents, or customers. The rules of the road are intended to help all of us get where we're going without having a disastrous accident along the way. An ethical marketplace is no oxymoron—it is an absolute necessity.

Obey, therefore, and prosper.

Notes

1. "Oh, How They Toppled on Wall Street," *Fortune* (May 21, 1990), p. 82.

APPENDIXES

APPENDIX I

THE RULES

In the text of the book, we paraphrased laws and regulations in plain English to make them as accessible as possible. This appendix cross-references our paraphrases and the original rules.

Each section of the appendix covers rule citations in one chapter. The column to the left on each page is essentially a chapter outline. The column to the right cites original rules corresponding to paraphrased versions in the chapter.

Most of the rules in the right column are from the *NASD Manual* and the *New York Stock Exchange Constitution and Rules* (The pertinent parts of these rules are reprinted here). Several references are to federal securities laws: the Securities Act of 1933 (new issues), the Securities Exchange Act of 1934 (secondary trading), and the 1988 act (insider trading).

References to the NASD and NYSE rules cite paragraph numbers, not pages. Paragraph numbers appear in the bottom outside corner of each page of the respective manuals.

References to paragraph numbers are more enduring than pages references, since the numbers remain the same even as rules change. Page numbers, of course, change with each rule revision.

Chapter Four: Agents and Principals

The RR's Duty to the SEC and SROs

File accurate information:
on applications	NASD, para. 1791
confidentiality	NASD, para. 1789
on applications	NYSE, para. 2345

on tests
Respond to requests, sanctions   NASD, para. 2205
    Fines   NYSE, para. 2351
    Suspension
    Termination

The RR's Duty to the Broker-
Dealer Employer

Pay promptly in own account   NASD, para. 4012
                                   para. 4018

Notify B-D of potential conflicts
    Private securities transactions   NASD, para. 2200
    Accounts with other firms   NASD, para. 2178
                                    NYSE, para. 2407
    Compensation to/from others   NASD, para. 2160
                                    NYSE, para. 2350
    Outside business   NASD, para. 2200C
                                    NYSE, para. 2346
Honor B-D underwriting
responsibilities
    Make bona fide offers   NASD, para. 2151.06
    Make only fair markups   NASD, para. 2154

Chapter Five: The RR's Duties
as the Customer's Agent

RR's Duties to the Customer

Know the customer   NASD, para. 2152, 2171(c)
                                     Act of 1934
                                   NYSE, para. 2405
Respect customer's money   NASD, para. 2168

	para. 2169
	NYSE, para. 2352
Profits, losses are customer's	para. 2401
Money is customer's to risk	para. 2402(a)
Trade for customer's objectives	
Recommend suitable investments	NASD, para. 2152
	NASD para. 4651
Manage discretionary accounts	NASD, para. 2165
with discretion	NYSE, para. 2408
Use only public information	NASD, para. 2159
Triple damages	Act of 1988

Chapter Six: Rules of the Road
for Broker-Dealers

Broker-Dealer Responsibilities

Supervise RRs	NASD, para. 2171(d)
	NASD, para. 2177
	NYSE, para. 2342
Supervise ads, sales Lit.	NASD, para. 2195
Supervise trading room	
Register traders	NYSE, para. 2345
	NASD, para. 2162-2166
Maintain market integrity	NASD, para. 2197
Use SOES/ITS properly	NASD, para. 2197
	para. 2501–2510
Reporting trades accurately	NASD, para. 2155
	para. 1919–1922
	para. 1867
Maintain fair pricing	NASD, para. 2156, 2158
Avoid parking violations	Court cases
Erect Chinese walls	
around corporate finance	Act of 1988

Supervise underwritings	NASD, para. 2196, 2157
Exercise due diligence	Act of 1933
Place stabilizing bids	Act of 1933
at appropriate prices	NASD, para. 2167
Register sales persons	NASD, para. 1782
	para. 1783
	para. 1785
Avoid extending credit	Act of 1934
Place money in escrow	Act of 1933
Exercise B-D financial responsibility	
Maintain minimum net capital	Act of 1934, 15c3-1
Report financial problems	Act of 1934, 17a-11
	NASD, para. 2198
	para. 4197
Keep accurate records	NASD, para. 2171(a)
	para. 4031
	para. 4041
	para. 4051
	para. 4061–4080
	Act of 1934, 17a3-17a4
Meet margin requirements	NASD, para. 2180
	para. 2180A
Supervise option trading strictly	NASD, para. 2183
	para. 2184
	para. 2191

NASD, para. 1791

Resolution of the Board of Governors

Filing of Misleading Information as to Membership or Registration

The filing with the Association of information with respect to membership or registration as a Registered Representative which is incomplete or inaccurate so as to be misleading, or which could in any way tend to mislead, or the failure to correct such filing after notice thereof, may be deemed to be conduct inconsistent with just and equitable principles of trade and when discovered may be sufficient cause for appropriate disciplinary action.

NASD, para. 1789

¶ 1789　　CONFIDENTIALITY OF EXAMINATIONS

The Corporation considers all of its Qualification Examinations to be highly confidential. The removal from an examination center, reproduction, disclosure, receipt from or passing to any person, or use for study purposes of any portion of such Qualification Examination, whether of a present or past series, or any other use which would compromise the effectiveness of the Examinations and the use in any manner and at any time of the questions or answers to the Examinations are prohibited and are deemed to be a violation of Article III, Section 1 of the Rules of Fair Practice.

NYSE, para. 2345

¶ 2345　　Employees—Registration, Approval, Records

Rule 345. (a) No member or member organization shall permit any natural person to perform regularly the duties customarily performed by (i) a registered representative, (ii) a securities lending representative, (iii) a securities trader or (iv) a direct superviser of (i), (ii) or (iii) above, unless such person shall have been registered with, qualified by and is acceptable to the Exchange.

(b) No member or member organization shall permit any natural person, other than a member or allied member, to assume the duties of an officer with the power to legally bind such member or member organization unless such member or member organization has filed an application with and received the approval of the Exchange. (*See also Rules 304 (¶ 2304) and 311 (¶ 2311).*)

Registration of Employees

.10 Employees required to be registered or approved.—See definitions of "branch office manager", "registered representative" and "registered options representative" contained in Rules 9 (¶ 2009) and 10 (¶ 2010) and Rule 700(b)(49) (¶ 2700) and Rule 342 (¶ 2342) for qualification requirements for supervisers.

A "securities lending representative" is defined as any person who has discretion to commit his member or member organization employer to any contract or agreement (written or oral) involving securities lending or borrowing activities with any other person.

A "securities trader" is defined as any person engaged in the purchase or sale of securities or other similar instruments for the account of his employer and who does not transact any business with the public.

.11 Investigation and Records.—(a) Members and member organizations shall thoroughly investigate the previous record of persons whom they contemplate employing including, (1) persons required to be registered with the Exchange, (2) persons who regularly handle or process securities or monies or maintain the books and records relating to securities or monies and (3) persons having direct supervisory responsibility over persons engaged in the activities referred to in (1) and (2) above who are not otherwise required to be registered.

Investigatory requirements for persons required to be registered with the Exchange (referred to in (a)(1) above) shall be satisfied when the member organization fulfills its obligation to verify the information contained in the Uniform Application for Securities Industry Registration or Transfer (Form U-4). Investigatory requirements pertaining to persons specified in (a)(2) and (3) above shall be satisfied if a member organization verifies the information obtained pursuant to paragraph (b) below. Notwithstanding the above, further inquiry shall be made where appropriate in light of background information developed, the position for which the person is being considered or other circumstances. Investigation and verification shall be done by a member, allied member or person designated under the provisions of Rule 342(b)(1).

(b) Members and member organizations are reminded to obtain and keep on file all information required under Rule 17a-3(a)(12) of the Securities Exchange Act of 1934 for persons included within the definition of "associated person" pursuant to Rule 17a-3(a)(12)(ii). In addition, the Exchange requires that a record be kept of whether a bonding company has ever denied or revoked, or paid out on any bond because of such person.

If an employee is registered with the Exchange, a duplicated copy of Form U-4 signed by an authorized person shall satisfy all the recordkeeping requirements of this paragraph.

.12 Applications: Applications for all natural persons required to be registered with the Exchange shall be submitted to the Exchange on Form U-4, copies of which will be supplied on request. The application for the approval of such registered person shall be completed and filed upon the candidate's employment in order that processing may be completed by the time the training period is finished. (*See .18—Filing With Agent.*)

The information contained on Form U-4 must be kept current and shall be updated by the filing with the Exchange of an amendment to that form.

.13 Agreements.—Prior to the Exchange's consideration of the application, each candidate for registration, other than a member or allied member of the Exchange shall sign an agreement(s), on a form(s) prescribed by the Exchange, which includes a pledge that the registered person will abide by the Constitution and Rules adopted pursuant thereto as these now exist and as from time to time amended.

NASD, para. 2205

¶ 2205   Reports and Inspection of Books for Purpose of Investigating Complaints

Sec. 5. For the purpose of any investigation, or determination as to filing of a complaint or any hearing of any complaint against any member of the Corporation or any person associated with a member made or held in accordance with the Code of Procedure, any Local Business Conduct Committee, any District Business Conduct

Committee, or the Board of Governors, or any duly authorized member or members of any such Committees or Board or any duly authorized agent or agents of any such Committee or Board shall have the right (1) to require any member of the Corporation or person associated with a member to report orally or in writing with regard to any matter involved in any such investigation or hearing, and (2) to investigate the books, records and accounts of any such member with relation to any matter involved in any such investigation or hearing. No member or person associated with a member shall refuse to make any report as required in this Section, or refuse to permit any inspection of books, records and accounts as may be validly called for under this Section.

[Section 5 renumbered effective September 1, 1969.]

Resolution of the Board of Governors

Suspension of Members for Failure to Furnish Information Duly Requested

1 The President is hereby directed and authorized to notify members of the Corporation who fail to provide information with respect to their business practices and/or who fail to keep membership applications and supporting documents current and/or who fail to furnish such other information or reports or other material or data duly requested by the Corporation pursuant to the powers duly vested in it by its Certificate of Incorporation, By-Laws and such other duly authorized resolutions and directives as are necessary in the conduct of the business of the Corporation, that the continued failure to furnish duly requested information, reports, data or other material, constitutes grounds for suspension from membership.

2 After (15) fifteen days notice in writing thereof, and continued failure to furnish the information, reports, data or other material as described above in paragraph 1, the President is hereby directed and authorized to suspend the membership of any such member on behalf of the Board of Governors, and to cause notification thereof in the next following membership supplement, to the effect that the membership has been suspended for failure to furnish such duly requested information.

3 Prior to such notice, in writing to the member, the Executive Committee of the Board of Governors shall be notified in writing of such contemplated action by the President.

NYSE, para. 2351

¶ 2351   Reporting Requirements

Rule 351. (a) Each member not associated with a member organization and each member organization shall promptly report to the Exchange whenever such member or member organization, or any member, allied member or registered or non-registered employee associated with such member or member organization:

(1) has violated any provision of any securities law or regulation, or any agreement with or rule or standards of conduct of any governmental agency, self-regulatory organization, or business or professional organization, or engaged in conduct which is inconsistent with just and equitable principles of trade or detrimental to the interests or welfare of the Exchange;

Administered by Member Firm Regulatory Services

(2) is the subject of any written customer complaint involving allegations of theft or misappropriation of funds or securities or of forgery;

(3) is named as a defendant or respondent in any proceeding brought by a regulatory or self-regulatory body alleging the violation of any provision of the Securities Exchange Act of 1934, or of any other Federal or state securities, insurance, or commodities statute, or of any rule or regulation thereunder, or of any agreement with, or of any provision of the constitution, rules or similar governing instruments of, any securities, insurance or commodities regulatory or self-regulatory organization;

(4) is denied registration or is expelled, enjoined, directed to cease and desist, suspended or otherwise disciplined by any securities, insurance or commodities industry regulatory or self-regulatory organization or is denied membership or continued membership in any such self-regulatory organization; or is barred from becoming associated with any member or member organization of any such self-regulatory organization;

(5) is arrested, arraigned, indicted or convicted of, or pleads guilty to, or pleads no contest to, any criminal offense (other than minor traffic violations);

(6) is a director, controlling stockholder, partner, officer or sole proprietor of, or an associated person with, a broker, dealer, investment company, investment advisor, underwriter or insurance company which was suspended, expelled or had its registration denied or revoked by any agency, jurisdiction or organization or is associated in such a capacity with a bank, trust company or other financial institution which was convicted of, or pleaded no contest to, any felony or misdemeanor;

(7) is a defendant or respondent in any securities or commodities-related civil litigation or arbitration which has been disposed of by judgment, award or settlement for an amount exceeding $5,000;

(8) is the subject of any claim for damages by a customer, broker or dealer which is settled for an amount exceeding $5,000;

(9) is, or learns that he is associated in any business or financial activity with any person who is, subject to a "statutory disqualification" as that term is defined in the Securities Exchange Act of 1934.

(10) is the subject of any disciplinary action taken by the member or member organization against any of its associated persons involving suspension, termination, the withholding of commissions or imposition of fines in excess of $2,500, or any other significant limitation on activities.

(b) Each member associated with a member organization and each allied member or registered or non-registered employee of a member or member organization shall promptly report the existence of any of the conditions set forth in paragraph (a) of this rule to the member or member organization with which such person is associated.

(c) Each approved person shall promptly report to the member organization with which such approved person is associated, whenever such approved person becomes subject to a statutory disqualification as defined in the Securities Exchange Act of 1934; and upon being so notified, or otherwise learning such fact, the member or member organization shall promptly so advise the Exchange in writing, giving the name of the person subject to the statutory disqualification and details concerning the disqualification.

(d) At such intervals and in such detail as the Exchange shall specify, each member not associated with a member organization and each member organization shall report to the Exchange statistical information regarding customer complaints relating to such matters as may be specified by the Exchange. For the purpose of this paragraph (d), "customer" includes any person other than a broker or dealer.

NASD, para. 4012

RR must pay for Securities purchases
Federal Reserve Board—Regulation T

(b) *Time periods for payment; cancellation or liquidation.*

(1) *Full cash payment.* A creditor shall obtain full cash payment for customer purchases within 7 business days of the date:

(i) any nonexempted security was purchased;

NASD, para. 4018

(c) "Customer" includes: (1) any person or persons acting jointly: (i) to or for whom a creditor extends, arranges, or maintains any credit; or (ii) who would be considered a customer of the creditor according to the ordinary usage of the trade;

(2) any partner in a firm who would be considered a customer of the firm absent with partnership relationship; and

(3) any joint venture in which a creditor participates and which would be considered a customer of the creditor if the creditor were not a participant.

NASD, para. 2200

¶ 2200   **Private Securities Transactions**

Sec. 40. (a) *Applicability*—No person associated with a member shall participate in any manner in a private securities transaction except in accordance with the requirements of this section.

(b) *Written Notice*—Prior to participating in any private securities transaction, an associated person shall provide written notice to the member with which he is associated describing in detail the proposed transaction and the person's proposed role therein and stating whether he has received or may receive selling compensation in connection with the transaction; provided however that, in the case of a series of related transactions in which no selling compensation has been or will be received, an associated person may provide a single written notice.

(c) *Transactions for Compensation*—

(1) In the case of a transaction in which an associated person has received or may receive selling compensation, a member which has received notice pursuant to Subsection (b) shall advise the associated person in writing stating whether the member:

(A) approves the person's participation in the proposed transaction; or

(B) disapproves the person's participation in the proposed transaction.

?) If the member approves a person's participation in a transaction pursuant to Sub.ection (c)(1), the transaction shall be recorded on the books and records of the member and the member shall supervise the person's participation in the transaction as if the transaction were executed on behalf of the member.

(3) If the member disapproves a person's participation pursuant to Subsection (c)(1), the person shall not participate in the transaction in any manner, directly or indirectly.

(d) *Transactions Not For Compensation*—In the case of a transaction or a series of related transactions in which an associated person has not and will not receive any selling compensation, a member which has received notice pursuant to Subsection (b) shall provide the associated person prompt written acknowledgement of said notice and may, at its discretion, require the person to adhere to specified conditions in connection with his participation in the transaction.

(e) *Definitions*—For purposes of this section, the following terms shall have the stated meanings:

(1) "Private securities transaction" shall mean any securities transaction outside the regular course or scope of an associated person's employment with a member, including, though not limited to, new offerings of securities which are not registered with the Commission, provided however that transactions subject to the notification requirements of Article III, Section 28 of the Rules of Fair Practice, transactions among immediate family members (as defined in the Interpretation of the Board of Governors on Free-Riding and Withholding) for which no associated person receives any selling compensation, and personal transactions in investment company and variable annuity securities, shall be excluded.

(2) "Selling compensation" shall mean any compensation paid directly or indirectly from whatever source in connection with or as a result of the purchase or sale of a security, including, though not limited to, commissions; finder's fees; securities or rights to acquire securities; rights of participation in profits, tax benefits, or dissolution proceeds, as a general partner or otherwise; or expense reimbursements.

[Adopted effective November 12, 1985.]

NASD, para. 2178

¶ 2178   Transactions for or by Associated Persons

Sec. 28

Determine Adverse Interest

(a) A member ("executing member") who knowingly executes a transaction for the purchase or sale of a security for the account of a person associated with another member ("employer member"), or for any account over which such associated person has discretionary authority, shall use reasonable diligence to determine that the execution of such transaction will not adversely affect the interests of the employer member.

Obligations of Executing Member

(b) Where an executing member knows that a person associated with an employer member has or will have a financial interest in, or discretionary authority over, any existing or proposed account carried by the executing member, the executing member shall:

(1) notify the employer member in writing, prior to the execution of a transaction for such account, of the executing member's intention to open or maintain such an account;

(2) upon written request by the employer member, transmit duplicate copies of confirmations, statements, or other information with respect to such account; and

(3) notify the person associated with the employer member of the executing member's intention to provide the notice and information required by paragraphs (1) and (2) of this subsection (b).

Obligations of Associated Persons Concerning an Account with a Member.

(c) A person associated with a member who opens an account or places an order for the purchase or sale of securities with another member, shall notify the executing member of his or her association with the employer member; provided, however, that if the account was established prior to the association of the person with the employer member, the associated person shall notify the executing member promptly after becoming so associated.

Obligations of Associated Persons Concerning an Account with an Investment Adviser, Bank, or Other Financial Institution

(d) A person associated with a member who opens a securities account or places an order for the purchase or sale of securities with a domestic or foreign investment adviser, bank, or other financial institution, except a member, shall:

(1) notify his or her employer member in writing, prior to the execution ot any initial transactions, of the intention to open the account or place the order; and

(2) upon written request by the employer member, request in writing and assure that the investment adviser, bank, or other financial institution provides the employer member with duplicate copies of confirmations, statements, or other information concerning the account or order;

provided, however, that if an account subject to this subsection (d) was established prior to a person's association with a member, the person shall comply with this subsection promptly after becoming so associated.

(e) Subsections (c) and (d) of this section shall apply only to an account or order in which an associated person has a financial interest or with respect to which such person has discretionary authority.

Exemption for Transactions in Investment Company Shares and Unit Investment Trusts

(f) The provisions of this section shall not be applicable to transactions in unit investment trusts and variable contracts or redeemable securities of companies registered under the Investment Company Act of 1940, as amended, or to accounts which are limited to transactions in such securities.

[Amended effective February 28, 1983; and December 15, 1986.]

NYSE, para. 2407

¶ 2407   Transactions—Employees of Exchange, Member Organizations, or Certain Non-Member Organizations

Rule 407. (a) No member or member organization shall, without the prior written consent of the employer, make:

(1) A cash or margin transaction or carry a margin account in securities or commodities in which an employee of another member or member organization is directly or indirectly interested. Except in connection with transactions of an employee in Monthly Investment Plan type accounts, duplicate reports and statements shall be sent promptly to the employer.

(2) A cash or margin transaction or carry a margin account in securities or commodities in which an employee of the Exchange, or of any corporation of which the Exchange owns the majority of the capital stock, is directly or indirectly interested.

(3) A margin transaction or carry a margin account in securities or commodities in which an employee of a bank, trust company, insurance company, or of any other corporation, association, firm or individual engaged in the business of dealing, either as broker or as principal, in stocks, bonds, or other securities in any form, bills of exchange, acceptances, or other forms of commercial paper, is directly or indirectly interested.

(b)(1) No member, allied member, registered representative or officer of a member organization shall have a securities or commodities account with respect to which he has the power, directly or indirectly, to make investment decisions, at another member organization or a non-member organization or a bank without the prior written consent of another person designated by the member or member organization under Rule 342(b)(1) to sign such consents and review such accounts.

(2) Persons having accounts referred to in (1) above shall arrange for duplicate reports and monthly statements of said accounts to be sent to another person designated by the member or member organization under Rule 342(b)(1) to review such accounts.

(3) For the purpose of this rule accounts referred to in (1) above shall include, but are not limited to, the following: (A) securities and commodities accounts carried at member or non-member organizations or at banks; (B) limited or general partnership interests in investment partnerships; (C) direct and indirect participations in joint accounts; and (D) legal interests in trust accounts, provided that with respect to trust accounts the member or member organization required to approve the account may waive the requirement to send duplicate reports and monthly statements for such accounts.

.10 Employees of Exchange.—An employee of the Exchange or any of its affiliated companies who wishes to open a securities or commodities account should apply for permission from the Secretary of the Exchange. A form of application can be obtained in the Office of the Secretary.

.20 Application of Rule 407(3).—Rule 407(3) applies to all employees of insurance companies without regard to whether they are compensated on a salary or commission basis. However, it is not considered applicable to independent insurance agents.

For the purpose of Rule 407(3), a person who is clearly designated by the Charter of By-Laws of a bank, trust company, insurance company, etc., as an officer of such institution is not considered an "employee".

NASD, para. 2160

¶ 2160   Influencing or Rewarding Employees of Others

Sec. 10. (a) No member or person associated with a member shall, directly or indirectly, give or permit to be given anything of value, including gratuities, in excess of fifty dollars per individual per year to any person, principal, proprietor, employee, agent or representative of another person where such payment or gratuity is in relation to the business of the employer of the recipient of the payment or gratuity. A gift of any kind is considered a gratuity.

(b) This section shall not apply to contracts of employment with or to compensation for services rendered by persons enumerated in subsection (a) provided that there is in existence prior to the time of employment or before the services are rendered, a written agreement between the member and the person who is to be employed to perform such services. Such agreement shall include the nature of the proposed employment, the amount of the proposed compensation, and the written consent of such person's employer or principal.

(c) A separate record of all payments or gratuities in any amount known to the member, the employment agreement referred to in subsection (b) and any employment compensation paid as a result thereof shall be retained by the member for the period specified by Rule 17a-4 of the General Rules and Regulations under the Securities Exchange Act of 1934.

NYSE, para. 2350

¶ 2350   Compensation or Gratuities to Employees of Others

Rule 350. (a) No member, allied member, member organization or employee thereof shall:

(1) employ or compensate any person for services rendered, or

(2) give any gratuity in excess of $50 per person per year to any principal, officer, or employee of the Exchange or its subsidiaries, another member or member organization, financial institution, news or financial information media, or non-member broker or dealer in securities, commodities, or money instruments,

except as specified below or with the prior written consent of the employer and in the case of floor employees the prior written consent of the employer and the Exchange.

A gift of any kind is considered a gratuity.

(b) Compensation for services rendered of up to $100 per person per year may be paid with the prior written consent of the employer, but not of the Exchange, to operations employees of the following types:

(1) A telephone clerk on the NYSE Floor who provides courtesy telephone relief to a member's clerk, or handles such a member's orders over the member's own wire.

(2) Employees who make out commission bills or prepare Exchange reports for members.

(3) A specialist's Floor clerk who maintains records for a specialist other than his employer, or provides courtesy relief to another specialist's clerk.

(4) When the service rendered by the employee exceeds that which the primary employer is obligated to furnish,

    (a) A telephone clerk who handles a member's orders transmitted over the wire of the clerk's employer.

    (b) A telephone clerk who handles orders directed by the clerk's employer to the member who receives them.

(c) *Records* shall be retained for at least three years of all such gratuities and compensation for inspection by Exchange examiners.

NASD, para. 2200C

¶ 2200C   Outside Business Activities

Sec. 43. No person associated with a member in any registered capacity shall be employed by, or accept compensation from, any other person as a result of any business activity, other than a passive investment, outside the scope of his relationship with is employer firm, unless he has provided prompt written notice to the member. Such notice shall be in the form required by the member. Activities subject to the requirements of Article III, Section 40 of the Rules of Fair Practice shall be exempted from this requirement.

NYSE, para. 2346

¶ 2346   Limitations—Employment and Association with Members and Member Organizations

Rule 346. (a) Every member not associated with a member organization must be a registered broker or dealer unless exempted by the Securities Exchange Act of 1934.

(b) Without making a written request and receiving the prior written consent of his member or member organization employer, no member, allied member or employee of a member or member organization shall at any time be engaged in any other business; or be employed or compensated by any other person; or serve as an officer, director, partner or employee of another business organization; or own any stock or have, directly or indirectly, any financial interest in any other organization engaged in any securities, financial or kindred business; provided however, that such written request and consent shall not be required with regard to stock ownership or other financial interest in any securities, financial or kindred business which is publicly owned unless a control relationship exists.

(See also requirements of Rule 311 and 350.)

(c) Prompt written notice shall be given the Exchange whenever any member or member organization knows, or in the exercise of reasonable care should know, that any person, other than a member, allied member or employee, directly or indirectly, controls, is controlled by or is under common control with such member or member organization.

(d) No member shall qualify more than one member organization for membership.

(e) Unless otherwise permitted by the Exchange every member, allied member, registered representative and officer of a member organization who is assigned or delegated any responsibility or authority pursuant to Rule 342 shall devote his entire time during business hours to the business of such member or member organization.

(f) Except as otherwise permitted by the Exchange, no member, member organization, allied member, approved person, employee or any person directly or indirectly controlling, controlled by or under common control with a member or member organization shall have associated with him or it any person who is known, or in the exercise of reasonable care should be known, to be subject to any "statutory disqualification" defined in Section 3(a)(39) of the Securities Exchange Act of 1934. Any member organization seeking permission to have such a person continue to be or become associated with it shall pay a fee in an amount to be determined by the Exchange.

● ● ● *Supplementary Material:*

.10 In connection with paragraph (e) above, the Exchange will permit a member, allied member, registered representative or officer of a member or member organization who is assigned or delegated any responsibility or authority pursuant to Rule 342 to devote less than his entire time during business hours to the business of the member or member organization in instances where such permission will not impair the protection of investors or the public interest.

NASD, para. 2151.06

¶ 2151 Art. III, Sec. 1   "Free-Riding and Withholding"
Introduction

.06 The following Interpretation of Article III, Section 1 of the Association's Rules of Fair Practice is adopted by the Board of Governors of the Association pursuant to the provisions of Article VII, Section 3(a) of the Association's By-Laws and Article I, Section 3 of the Rules of Fair Practice.

This Interpretation is based upon the premise that members have an obligation to make a bona fide public distribution at the public offering price of securities of a public offering which trade at a premium in the secondary market whenever such secondary market begins (a "hot issue") regardless of whether such securities are acquired by the member as an underwriter, as a selling group member, or from a member participating in the distribution as an underwriter or a selling group member, or otherwise. The failure to make a bona fide public distribution when there is a demand for an issue can be a factor in artificially raising the price. Thus, the failure to do so, especially when the member may have information relating to the demand for the securities or other factors not generally known to the public, is inconsistent with high standards of commercial honor and just and equitable principles of trade and leads to an impairment of public confidence in the fairness of the investment banking and securities business. Such conduct is, therefore, in violation of Article III, Section 1 of the Association's Rules of Fair Practice and this Interpretation thereof which establishes guidelines in respect to such activity.

As in the case of any other Interpretation issued by the Board of Governors of the Association, the implementation thereof is a function of the District Business Conduct Committees and the Board of Governors. Thus, the Interpretation will be applied to a given factual situation by individuals active in the investment banking and securities business who are serving on these committees or on the Board.

They will construe this Interpretation to effectuate its overall purpose to assure a public distribution of securities for which there is a public demand.

"Free-Riding and Withholding"
Interpretation of the Board of Governors

Except as provided herein, it shall be inconsistent wtih high standards of commercial honor and just and equitable principles of trade and a violation of Article III, Section 1 of the Association's Rules of Fair Practice for a member, or a person associated with a member, to fail to make a bona fide public distribution at the public offering price of securities of a public offering which trade at a premium in the secondary market whenever such secondary market begins regardless of whether such securities are acquired by the member as an underwriter, a selling group member or from a member participating in the distribution as an underwriter or selling group member, or otherwise. Therefore, it shall be a violation of Article III, Section 1 for a member, or a person associated with a member, to:

1. Continue to hold any of the securities so acquired in any of the member's accounts;

2. Sell any of the securities to any officer, director, general partner, employee or agent of the member or of any other broker/dealer, or to a person associated with the member or with any other broker/dealer, or to a member of the immediate family of any such person;

3. Sell any of the securities to a person who is a finder in respect to the public offering or to any person acting in a fiduciary capacity to the managing underwriter, including, among others, attorneys, accountants and financial consultants, or to a member of the immediate family of any such person;

4. Sell any securities to any senior officer of a bank, savings and loan institution, insurance company, registered investment company, registered investment advisory firm or any other institutional type account, domestic or foreign, or to any person in the securities department of, or to any employee or any other person who may influence or whose activities directly or indirectly involve or are related to the function of buying or selling securities for any bank, savings and loan institution, insurance company, registered investment company, registered investment advisory firm, or other institutional type account, domestic or foreign, or to a member of the immediate family of any such person;

5. Sell any securities to any account in which any person specified under paragraphs (1), (2), (3) or (4) hereof has a beneficial interest;

Provided, however, a member may sell part of its securities acquired as described above to:

(a) persons enumerated in paragraphs (3) or (4) hereof; and

(b) members of the immediate family of persons enumerated in paragraph (2) hereof provided that such person enumerated in paragraph (2) does not contribute directly or indirectly to the support of such member of the immediate family; and

(c) any account in which any person specified under paragraph (3) or (4) or subparagraph (b) of this paragraph has a beneficial interest;

if the member is prepared to demonstrate that the securities were sold to such persons in accordance with their normal investment practice with the member, that the aggregate of the securities so sold is insubstantial and not disproportionate in amount as compared to sales to members of the public and that the amount sold to any one of such persons is insubstantial in amount.

6. Sell any of the securities, at or above the public offering price, to any other broker/dealer; provided, however, a member may sell all or part of the securities acquired as described above to another member broker/dealer upon receipt from the latter in writing assurance that such purchase would be made to fill orders for bona fide public customers, other than those enumerated in paragraphs (1), (2), (3), (4) or (5) above, at the public offering price as an accommodation to them and without compensation for such.

7. Sell any of the securities to any domestic bank, domestic branch of a foreign bank, trust company or other conduit for an undisclosed principal unless:

(a) An affirmative inquiry is made of such bank, trust company or other conduit as to whether the ultimate purchasers would be persons enumerated in paragraphs (1) through (5) hereof and receives satisfactory assurance that the ultimate purchasers would not be such persons, and that the securities would not be sold in a manner inconsistent with the provisions of paragraph (6) hereof; otherwise, there shall be a rebuttable presumption that the ultimate purchasers were persons enumerated in paragraphs (1) through (5) hereof or that the securities were sold in a manner inconsistent with the provisions of paragraph (6) hereof;

(b) A recording is made on the order ticket, or its equivalent, or on some other supporting document, of the name of the person to whom the inquiry was made at the bank, trust company or other conduit as well as the substance of what was said by that person and what was done as a result thereof;

(c) The order ticket, or its equivalent, is initialed by a registered principal of the member; and

(d) Normal supervisory procedures of the member provide for a close follow-up and review of all transactions entered into with the referred to domestic bank, trust companies or other conduits for undisclosed principals to assure that the ultimate recipients of securities so sold are not persons enumerated in paragraphs (1) through (6) hereof.

8. Sell any of the securities to a foreign broker/dealer or bank unless:

(a) In the case of a foreign broker/dealer or bank which is participating in the distribution as an underwriter, the agreement among underwriters contains a provision which obligates the said foreign broker/dealer or bank not to sell any of the securities which it receives as a participant in the distribution to persons enumerated in paragraphs (1) through (5) above, or in a manner inconsistent with the provisions of paragraph (6) hereof; or

(b) In the case of sales to a foreign broker/dealer or bank which is not participating in the distribution as an underwriter, the selling member:

(i) makes an affirmative inquiry of such foreign broker/dealer or bank as to whether the ultimate purchasers would be persons enumerated in paragraphs (1) through (5) hereof and receives satisfactory assurance that the ultimate purchasers of the securities so purchased would not be such persons, and that the securities would not be sold in a manner inconsistent with the provisions of paragraph (6) hereof;

(ii) a recording is made on the order ticket, or its equivalent, or upon some other supporting document, of the name of the person to whom the inquiry was made at the foreign broker/dealer or bank as well as the substance of what was said by that person and what was done as a result thereof; and

(iii) the order ticket, or its equivalent, is initialed by a registered principal of the member.

The obligations imposed upon members in their dealings with foreign broker/dealers or banks by this paragraph 8(b) can be fulfilled by having the foreign broker/dealer or bank to which sales falling within the scope of this Interpretation are made execute Form FR-1, or a reasonable facsimile thereof. This form, which gives a blanket assurance from the foreign broker/dealer or bank that no sales will be made in contravention of the provisions of this Interpretation, can be obtained at any District Office of the Association or at the Executive Office. The acceptance of an executed Form FR-1, or other written assurance, by a member must in all instances be made in good faith. Thus, if a member knows or should have known of facts which are inconsistent with the representations received, such will not operate to satisfy the obligations imposed upon him by this paragraph.

Scope and Intent of Interpretation

In addition to the obvious scope and intent of the above provisions, the intent of the Board of Governors in the following specific situations is outlined for the guidance of members.

Issuer Directed Securities

This Interpretation shall apply to securities which are part of a public offering notwithstanding that some or all of those securities are specifically directed by the issuer to accounts which are included within the scope of paragraphs (3) through (8) above. Therefore, if a person within the scope of those paragraphs to whom securities were directed did not have an investment history with the member or registered representative from whom they were to be purchased, the member would not be permitted to sell him such securities. Also, the "disproportionate and "insubstantial" tests would apply as in all other situations. Thus, the directing of a substantial number of securities to any one person would be prohibited as would the directing of securities to such accounts in amounts which would be disproportionate as compared to sales to members of the public. This Interpretation shall also apply to securities which are part of a public offering notwithstanding that some of those securities are specifically directed by the issuer on a non-underwritten basis. In such cases, the managing underwriter of the offering shall be responsible for insuring compliance with this Interpretation in respect to those securities.

Notwithstanding the above, sales of issuer directed securities may be made to restricted persons without the required investment history after receiving permission from the Board of Governors. Permission will be given only if there is a demonstration of valid business reasons for such sales (such as sales to distributors and suppliers or key employees, who are in each case incidentally restricted persons), and the member seeking permission is prepared to demonstrate that the aggregate amount of securities so sold is insubstantial and not disproportionate as compared to sales to members of the public, and that the amount sold to any one of such persons is insubstantial in amount.

Investment Partnerships and Corporations

A member may not sell securities of a public offering which trade at a premium in the secondary market whenever such secondary market begins ("hot issue"), to the account of any investment partnership or corporation, domestic or foreign (except companies registered under the Investment Company Act of 1940) including but not limited to, hedge funds, investment clubs, and other like accounts unless the member complies with either of the following alternatives:

(A) prior to the execution of the transaction, the member has received from the account a current list of the names and business connections of all persons having any beneficial interest in the account, and if such information discloses that any person enumerated in paragraphs (1) through (4) hereof has a beneficial interest in such account, any sale of securities to such account must be consistent with the provisions of this Interpretation, or

(B) prior to the execution of the transaction, the member has obtained a copy of a current opinion from counsel admitted to practice law before the highest court of any state stating that counsel reasonably believes that no person with a beneficial interest in the account is a restricted person under this Interpretation and stating that, in providing such opinion, counsel:

(1) has reviewed and is familiar with this Interpretation;

(2) has reviewed a current list of all persons with a beneficial interest in the account supplied by the account manager;

(3) has reviewed information supplied by the account manager with respect to each person with a beneficial interest in the account, including the identity, the nature of employment, and any other business connections of such persons; and

(4) has requested and reviewed other documents and other pertinent information and made inquiries of the account manager and received responses thereto, if counsel determines that such further review and inquiry are necessary and relevant to determine the correct status of such persons under the Interpretation.

The member shall maintain a copy of the names and business connections of all persons having any beneficial interest in the account or a copy of the current opinion of counsel in its files for at least three years following the member's last sale of a new issue to the account, depending upon which of the above requirements the member elects to follow. For purposes of this section, a list or opinion shall be deemed to be current if it is based upon the status of the account as of a date not more than 18 months prior to the date of the transaction.

The term beneficial interest means not only ownership interests, but every type of direct financial interest of any persons enumerated in paragraphs (1) through (4) hereof in such account, including, without limitation, management fees based on the performance of the account.

Violations by Recipient

In those cases where a member or person associated with a member has been the recipient of securities of a public offering to the extent that such violated the Interpretation, the member or person associated with a member shall be deemed to be in violation of Article III, Section 1 of the Rules of Fair Practice and this Interpretation as well as the member who sold the securities since their responsibility in relation to the public distribution is equally as great as that of the member selling them. In those cases where a member or a person associated with a member has caused, directly or indirectly, the distribution of securities to a person falling within the restrictive provisions of this Interpretation the member or person associated with a member shall also be deemed to be in violation of Article III, Section 1 of the Rules of Fair Practice and this Interpretation. Receipt by a member or a person associated with a member of securities of a hot issue which is being distributed by an issuer itself without the assistance of an underwriter and/or selling group is also intended to be subject to the provisions of this Interpretation.

Violations by Registered Representative Executing Transaction

The obligation which members have to make a bona fide public distribution at the public offering price of securities of a hot issue is also an obligation of every person associated with a member who causes a transaction to be executed. Therefore, where sales are made by such persons in a manner inconsistent with the provisions of this Interpretation, such persons associated with a member will be considered equally culpable with the member for the violations found taking into consideration the facts and circumstances of the particular case under consideration.

Disclosure

The fact that a disclosure is made in the prospectus or offering circular that a sale of securities would be made in a manner inconsistent with this Interpretation does not take the matter out of its scope. In sum, therefore, disclosure does not affect the proscriptions of this Interpretation.

Explanation of Terms

The following explanation of terms is provided for the assistance of members. Other words which are defined in the By-Laws and Rules of Fair Practice shall, unless the context otherwise requires, have the meaning as defined therein.

Public Offering

The term public offering shall mean all distributions of securities whether underwritten or not; whether registered, unregistered or exempt from registration under the Securities Act of 1933, and whether they are primary or secondary distributions, including intrastate distributions and Regulation A issues, which sell at an immediate premium, in the secondary market. It shall not mean exempted securities as defined in Section 3(a)(12) of the Securities Exchange Act of 1934.

Immediate Family

The term immediate family shall include parents, mother-in-law or father-in-law, husband or wife, brother or sister, brother-in-law or sister-in-law, son-in-law or daughter-in-law, and children. In addition, the term shall include any other person who is supported, directly or indirectly, to a material extent by the member, person associated with the member or other person specified in paragraphs (2), (3), or (4) above.

Normal Investment Practice

Normal investment practice shall mean the history of investment of a restricted person in an account or accounts maintained with the member making the allocation. In cases where an account was previously maintained with another member, but serviced by the same registered representative as the one currently servicing the account for the member making the allocation, such earlier investment activity may be included in the restricted person's investment history. Usually the previous one-year period of securities activity is the basis for determining the adequacy of a restricted person's investment history. Where warranted, however, a longer or shorter period may be reviewed. It is the responsibility of the registered representative effecting the allocation, as well as the member, to demonstrate that the restricted person's investment history justifies the allocation of hot issues. Copies of customer account statements or other records maintained by the registered representative or the member may be utilized to demonstrate prior investment activity. In analyzing a restricted person's investment history the Association believes the following factors should be considered:

1) The frequency of transactions in the account or accounts during that period of time. Relevant in this respect are the nature and size of investments.

2) A comparison of the dollar amount of previous transactions with the dollar amount of the hot issue purchase. If a restricted person purchases $1,000 of a hot issue and his account revealed a series of purchases and sales in $100 amounts, the $1,000 purchase would not appear to be consistent with the restricted person's normal investment practice.

3) The practice of purchasing mainly hot issues would not constitute a normal investment practice. The Association does, however, consider as contributing to the establishment of a normal investment practice, the purchase of new issues which are not hot issues as well as secondary market transactions.

Disproportionate

In respect to the determination of what constitutes a disproportionate allocation, the Association uses as a guideline 10% of the member's participation in the issue, however acquired. It should be noted, however, that the 10% factor is merely a guideline and is one of a number of factors which are considered in reaching determinations of violations of the Interpretation on the basis of disproportionate allocations. These other factors include, among other things:

the size of the participation;

the offering price of the issue;

the amount of securities sold to restricted accounts; and,

the price of the securities in the aftermarket.

It should be noted that disciplinary action has been taken against members for violations of the Interpretation where the allocations made to restricted accounts were less than 10% of the member's participation. The 10% guideline is applied as to the aggregate of the allocations.

Notwithstanding the above, a normal unit of trading (100 shares or 10 bonds) will in most cases not be considered a disproportionate allocation regardless of the amount of the member's participation. This means that if the aggregate number of shares of a member's participation which is allocated to restricted accounts does not exceed a normal unit of trading, such allocation will in most cases not be considered disproportionate. For example, if a member receives 500 shares of a hot issue, he may allocate 100 shares to a restricted account even though such allocation represents 20% of that member's participation. Of course, all of the remaining shares would have to be allocated to unrestricted accounts and all other provisions of the Interpretation would have to be satisfied. Specifically, the allocation would have to be consistent with the normal investment practice of the account to which it was allocated and the member would not be permitted to sell to restricted persons who were totally prohibited from receiving hot issues.

Insubstantiality

This requirement is separate and distinct from the requirements relating to disproportionate allocations and normal investment practice. In addition, this term applies both to the aggregate of the se curities sold to restricted accounts and to each individual allocation. In other words, there could be a substantial allocation to an individual account in violation of the Interpretation and yet be no violation on that ground as to the total number of shares allocated to all accounts. The determination of whether an allocation to a restricted account or accounts is substantial is based upon, among other things, the number of shares allocated and/or the dollar amount of the purchase.

SALES BY ISSUERS IN CONVERSION OFFERINGS

Definitions

(a) For purposes of this Subsection, the following terms shall have the meanings stated:

(1) "Conversion offering" shall mean any offering of securities made as part of a plan by which a savings and loan association or other organization converts from a mutual to a stock form of ownership.

(2) "Eligible purchaser" shall mean a person who is eligible to purchase securities pursuant to the rules of the Federal Home Loan Bank Board or other governmental agency or instrumentality having authority to regulate conversion offerings.

Conditions for Exemption

(b) This Interpretation shall not apply to a sale of securities by the issuer on a non-underwritten basis to any person who would otherwise be prohibited or restricted from purchasing a hot issue security if all of the conditions of this Subsection (b) are satisfied.

Sales to Members, Associated Persons of Members and Certain Related Persons

(1) If the purchaser is a member, person associated with a member, member of the immediate family of any such person to whose support such person contributes, directly or indirectly, or an account in which a member or person associated with a member has a beneficial interest:

(A) the purchaser shall be an eligible purchaser;

(B) the securities purchased shall be restricted from sale or transfer for a period of 150 days following the conclusion of the offering; and

(C) the fact of purchase shall be reported in writing to the member where the person is associated within one day of payment.

Sales to Other Restricted Persons

(2) If the purchaser is not a person specified in Subsection (b)(1) above, the purchaser shall be an eligible purchaser.

NASD, para. 2154

¶ 2154   **Fair Prices and Commissions**

Sec. 4. In "over-the-counter" transactions, whether in "listed" or "unlisted" securities, if a member buys for his own account from his customer, or sells for his own account to his customer, he shall buy or sell at a price which is fair, taking into consideration all relevant circumstances, including market conditions with respect to such security at the time of the transaction, the expense involved, and the fact that he is entitled to a profit; and if he acts as agent for his customer in any such transaction, he shall not charge his customer more than a fair commission or service charge, taking into consideration all relevant circumstances including market conditions with respect to such security at the time of the transaction, the expense of executing the order and the value of any service he may have rendered by reason of his experience in and knowledge of such security and the market therefor.

Interpretation of the Board of Governors

NASD Mark-Up Policy

The question of fair mark-ups or spreads is one which has been raised from the earliest days of the Association. No definitive answer can be given and no interpretation can be all-inclusive for the obvious reason that what might be considered fair in one transaction could be unfair in another transaction because of different circumstances.

However, it was recognized that the amount of mark-up was at least a starting point from which an answer to the question could be sought and that progress might be made if the general practice of the business on mark-ups could be established. To find this out, the Association, in 1943, made a membership-wide questionnaire examination of mark-ups in retail or customer transactions. Questionnaires were filed by 82 per cent of the membership covering transactions which varied widely with respect to price, dollar amount, type of security, and degree of market activity. They included both listed and unlisted securities, with the latter, however, in the substantial majority. This information revealed that 47 per cent of the transactions computed were made at mark-ups of 3 per cent or less and 71 per cent of the transactions were effected at mark-ups of 5 per cent or less.

In a letter to the membership on October 25, 1943, the Board of Governors made known the results of its survey and expressed its philosophy on what constitutes a fair spread or profit. The Board stated that it would be impractical and unwise, if not impossible, to define specifically what constitutes a fair spread on each and every transaction because the fairness of a mark-up can be determined only after considering all of the relevant factors.

Under certain conditions a mark-up in excess of 5 per cent may be justified, but on the other hand, 5 per cent or even a lower rate is by no means always justified. The Board instructed District Business Conduct Committees to enforce Section 1 of Article III of the Rules of Fair Practice with respect to mark-ups, keeping in mind that 71 per cent of the transactions computed from the questionnaires were effected at a mark-up of 5 per cent or less. The philosophy which the Board expressed has since been referred to as the "5% Policy."

The Policy has been reviewed by the Board of Governors on numerous occasions and each time the Board has reaffirmed the philosophy expressed in the letter to members of October 25, 1943. The Board is aware, however, of the need for continually re-examining the mark-up policy and its application in the light of current economic conditions and with the benefit of experience gained from enforcement of the existing Policy. The Board has carefully considered the Policy adopted in 1943 and subsequent interpretations with respect thereto. It can find no justification for a change in the basic Policy. However, it recognizes that any clarification will materially aid members in complying with the Policy and the various committees in fulfilling their responsibility to exercise judgment in determining the fairness of mark-ups.

Based upon its review of the entire matter, the Board has adopted the interpretation set forth below.

The Interpretation

Article III, Section 1 of the Rules of Fair Practice states that:

"A member, in the conduct of his business, shall observe high standards of commercial honor and just and equitable principles of trade."

Article III, Section 4 of the Rules of Fair Practice states that:

"In 'over-the-counter' transactions, whether in 'listed' or 'unlisted' securities, if a member buys for his own account from his customer, or sells for his own account to his customer, he shall buy or sell at a price which is fair, taking into consideration all relevant circumstances, including market conditions with respect to such security at the time of the transaction, the expense involved, and the fact that he is entitled to a profit; and if he acts as agent for his customer in any such transaction, he shall not charge his customer more than a fair commission or service charge, taking into consideration all relevant circumstances including market conditions with respect to such security at the time of the transaction, the expense of executing the order and the value of any service he may have rendered by reason of his experience in and knowledge of such security and the market therefor."

In accordance with Article VII, Section 3(a) of the By-Laws, the following interpretation under Article III, Sections 1 and 4 of the Rules of Fair Practice has been adopted by the Board:

It shall be deemed conduct inconsistent with just and equitable principles of trade for a member to enter into any transaction with a customer in any security at any price not reasonably related to the current market price of the security or to charge a commission which is not reasonable.

A. General Considerations

Since the adoption of the "5% Policy" the Board has determined that:

1. The "5% Policy" is a guide—not a rule.

2. A member may not justify mark-ups on the basis of expenses which are excessive.

3. The mark-up over the prevailing market price is the significant spread from the point of view of fairness of dealings with customers in principal transactions. In the absence of other bona fide evidence of the prevailing market, a member's own contemporaneous cost is the best indication of the prevailing market price of a security.

4. A mark-up pattern of 5% or even less may be considered unfair or unreasonable under the "5% Policy."

5. Determination of the fairness of mark-ups must be based on a consideration of all the relevant factors, of which the percentage of mark-up is only one.

B. Relevant Factors

Some of the factors which the Board believes that members and the Association's committees should take into consideration in determining the fairness of a mark-up are as follows:

1. The type of security involved—

Some securities customarily carry a higher mark-up than others. For example, a higher percentage of mark-up customarily applies to a common stock transaction than to a bond transaction of the same size. Likewise, a higher percentage applies to sales of units of direct participation programs and condominium securities than to sales of common stock.

2. The availability of the security in the market—

In the case of an inactive security the effort and cost of buying or selling the security, or any other unusual circumstances connected with its acquisition or sale, may have a bearing on the amount of mark-up justified.

3. The price of the security—

While there is no direct correlation, the percentage of mark-up or rate of commission, generally increases as the price of the security decreases. Even where the amount of money is substantial, transactions in lower priced securities may require more handling and expense and may warrant a wider spread.

4. The amount of money involved in a transaction—

A transaction which involves a small amount of money may warrant a higher percentage of mark-up to cover the expenses of handling.

5. Disclosure—

Any disclosure to the customer, before the transaction is effected, of information which would indicate (a) the amount of commission charged in an agency transaction or (b) mark-up made in a principal transaction is a factor to be considered. Disclosure itself, however, does not justify a commission or mark-up which is unfair or excessive in the light of all other relevant circumstances.

6. The pattern of mark-ups—

While each transaction must meet the test of fairness, the Board believes that particular attention should be given to the pattern of a member's mark-ups.

7. The nature of the member's business—

The Board is aware of the differences in the services and facilities which are needed by, and provided for, customers of members. If not excessive, the cost of providing such services and facilities, particularly when they are of a continuing nature, may properly be considered in determining the fairness of a member's mark-ups.

C. Transactions to which the Policy is applicable

The Policy applies to all securities handled in the over-the-counter market, whether oil royalties or any other security, in the following types of transactions:

1. A transaction in which a member buys a security to fill an order for the same security previously received from a customer—

This transaction would include the so-called "riskless" or "simultaneous" transaction.

2. A transaction in which a member sells a security to a customer from inventory—

In such case the amount of the mark-up should be determined on the basis of the mark-up over the bona fide representative current market. The amount of profit or loss to the member from market appreciation or depreciation before, or after, the date of the transaction with the customer would not ordinarily enter into the determination of the amount or fairness of the mark-up.

3. A transaction in which a member purchases a security from a customer—

The price paid to the customer or the mark-down applied by the member must be reasonably related to the prevailing market price of the security.

4. A transaction in which the member acts as agent—

In such a case, the commission charged the customer must be fair in light of all relevant circumstances.

5. Transactions wherein a customer sells securities to, or through, a broker/dealer, the proceeds from which are utilized to pay for other securities purchased from, or through, the broker/dealer at or about the same time—

In such instances, the mark-up shall be computed in the same way as if the customer had purchased for cash and in computing the mark-up there shall be included any profit or commission realized by the dealer on the securities being liquidated, the proceeds of which are used to pay for securities being purchased.

D. Transactions to which the Policy is not applicable

To the sale of securities where a prospectus or offering circular is required to be delivered and the securities are sold at the specific public offering price.

This interpretation does no more than express what is clearly implied in Sections 1 and 4 of Article III of the Rules of Fair Practice. The interpretation is made, however, in order to emphasize the obligation which is assumed by every member of this Association in every transaction with a customer.

NASD, para. 2152

¶ 2152   **Recommendations to Customers**

Sec. 2. In recommending to a customer the purchase, sale or exchange of any security, a member shall have reasonable grounds for believing that the recommendation is suitable for such customer upon the basis of the facts, if any, disclosed by such customer as to his other security holdings and as to his financial situation and needs.

Policy of the Board of Governors

Fair Dealing With Customers

Implicit in all member and registered representative relationships with customers and others is the fundamental responsibility for fair dealing. Sales efforts must therefore be undertaken only on a basis that can be judged as being within the ethical standards of the Association's rules, with particular emphasis on the requirement to deal fairly with the public.

This does not mean that legitimate sales efforts in the securities business are to be discouraged by requirements which do not take into account the variety of circumstances which can enter into the member-customer relationship. It does mean, however, that sales efforts must be judged on the basis of whether they can be reasonably said to represent fair treatment for the persons to whom the sales efforts are directed, rather than on the argument that they result in profits to customers.

District Business Conduct Committees and the Board of Governors have interpreted the Rules of Fair Practice, taken disciplinary action and imposed penalties in many situations where members' sales efforts have exceeded the reasonable grounds of fair dealing.

Some practices that have resulted in disciplinary action and that clearly violate this responsibility for fair dealing are set forth below, as a guide to members:

Recommending Speculative Low-priced Securities

1. Recommending speculative low-priced securities to customers without knowledge of or attempt to obtain information concerning the customers' other securities holdings, their financial situation and other necessary data. The principle here is that this practice, by its very nature, involves a high probability that the recommendation will not be suitable for at least some of the persons solicited. This has particular application to high pressure telephone sales campaigns.

Excessive Trading Activity

2. Excessive activity in a customer's account, often referred to as "churning" or "overtrading." There are no specific standards to measure

excessiveness of activity in customer accounts because this must be related to the objectives and financial situation of the customer involved.

Trading in Mutual Fund Shares

3. Trading in mutual fund shares, particularly on a short-term basis. It is clear that normally these securities are not proper trading vehicles and such activity on its face may raise the question of rule violation.

Fraudulent Activity

4. Numerous instances of fraudulent conduct have been acted upon by the Association and have resulted in penalties against members. Among some of these activities are:

Fictitious Accounts

(a) Establishment of fictitious accounts in order to execute transactions which otherwise would be prohibited, such as the purchase of hot issues, or to disguise transactions which are against firm policy.

Discretionary Accounts

(b) Transactions in discretionary accounts in excess of or without actual authority from customers.

Unauthorized Transactions

(c) Causing the execution of transactions which are unauthorized by customers or the sending of confirmations in order to cause customers to accept transactions not actually agreed upon.

Misuse of Customers' Funds or Securities

(d) Unauthorized use or borrowing of customers' funds or securities.

In addition, other fraudulent activities, such as forgery, non-disclosure or misstatement of material facts, manipulations and various deceptions, have been found in violation of Association rules. These same activities are also subject to the civil and criminal laws and sanctions of Federal and State Governments.

Recommending Purchases Beyond Customer Capability

5. Recommending the purchase of securities or the continuing purchase of securities in amounts which are inconsistent with the reasonable expectation that the customer has the financial ability to meet such a commitment.

While most members are fully aware of the fairness required in dealing with customers, it is anticipated that these enumerated practices, which are not all inclusive, will be of future assistance in the training and education of new personnel.

The Securities and Exchange Commission has also recognized that brokers and dealers have an obligation of fair dealing in actions under the general anti-fraud provisions of the Federal securities laws. The Commission bases this obligation on the principle that when a securities dealer opens his business he is, in effect, representing that he will deal fairly with the public. Certain of the Commission's cases on fair dealing involve practices not covered in the foregoing illustrations. Usually, any breach of the obligation of fair dealing as determined by the Commission under the anti-fraud provisions of the securities laws could be considered a violation of the Association's Rules of Fair Practice.

NASD, 2171(c)

Information on accounts

(c) Each member shall maintain accounts of customers in such form and manner as to show the following information: name, address and whether the customer is legally of age; the signature of the registered representative introducing the account and the signature of the member or the partner, officer or manager accepting the account for the member. If the customer is associated with or employed by another member, this fact must be noted. In discretionary accounts, the member shall also record the age or approximate age and occupation of the customer as well as the signature of each person authorized to exercise discretion in such account.

NYSE, para. 2405

¶ 2405   **Diligence as to Accounts**

Rule 405. Every member organization is required through a general partner, a principal executive officer or a person or persons designated under the provisions of Rule 342(b)(1) [¶ 2342] to

(1) Use due diligence to learn the essential facts relative to every customer, every order, every cash or margin account accepted or carried by such organization and every person holding power of attorney over any account accepted or carried by such organization.

Supervision of Accounts

(2) Supervise diligently all accounts handled by registered representatives of the organization.

Approval of Accounts

(3) Specifically approve the opening of an account prior to or promptly after the completion of any transaction for the account of or with a customer, provided, however, that in the case of branch offices, the opening of an account for a customer may be approved by the manager of such branch office but the action of such branch office manager shall within a reasonable time be approved by a general partner, a principal (cont'd) executive officer or a person or persons designated under the provisions of Rule 342(b)(1) [¶ 2342]. The member, general partner, officer or designated person approving the opening of the account shall, prior to giving his approval, be personally informed as to the essential facts relative to the customer and to the nature of the proposed account and shall indicate his approval in writing on a document which is a part of the permanent records of his office or organization.

Common Sales Accounts

(4) To facilitate the isolated liquidation of securities valued at $1,000 or less registered in the name of an individual who does not have an account, and which are not part of any distribution, a member organization may sell the securities

through a common sales account set up for the specific purpose of handling such sales without sending a periodic statement to the customer as required by Rule 409, provided:

a) The customer is identified as the individual in whose name the securities are registered,

b) The securities are received by the member, at or prior to the time of the entry of the order, in the exact amount to be sold in good delivery form,

c) A confirmation is sent to each customer,

d) All proceeds of such sales are paid out on or immediately following settlement date, and

e) The record made in the common sales account includes as to each transaction: customer's name and address, name and amount of securities to be sold, date received, date sold, amount per share, total amount credited to the account, total amount of check issued to the customer and the date of disbursement.

Supplementary Material:

.10 **Application of Rule 405(1) and (3) [¶ 2405].**—In the case of a margin account carried by a member organization for a non-member corporation, definite knowledge should be had to the effect that the non-member corporation has the right under its charter and by-laws to engage in margin transactions for its own account and that the persons from whom orders and instructions are accepted have been duly authorized by the corporation to act on its behalf. It is advisable in each such case for the carrying organization to have in its possession a copy of the corporate Charter, By-laws and authorizations. Where it is not possible to obtain such documents, a member or allied member in the member organization carrying the account should prepare and sign a memorandum for its files indicating the basis upon which he believes that the corporation may properly engage in margin transactions and that the persons acting for the corporation have been duly authorized to do so.

In the case of a cash account carried for a non-member corporation, the carrying member organization should assure itself through a general partner or an officer who is a holder of voting stock that persons entering orders and issuing instructions with respect to the account do so upon the proper authority.

When an agency account is carried by a member organization its files should contain the name of the principal for whom the agent is acting and written evidence of the agent's authority.

When Estate and Trustee accounts are involved a member organization should obtain counsel's advice as to the documents which should be obtained.

Information as to the country of which a customer is a citizen is deemed to be an essential fact.

.20 See Rule 382 for information concerning the permitted allocation of responsibilities under ¶ (1) and (3) of this Rule between introducing and carrying organizations.

NASD, para. 2168

¶ 2168   Use of Fraudulent Devices

Sec. 18. No member shall effect any transaction in, or induce the purchase or sale of, any security by means of any manipulative, deceptive or other fraudulent device or contrivance.

NASD, para. 2169

¶ 2169   Customers' Securities or Funds

Sec. 19.

Improper Use

(a) No member or person associated with a member shall make improper use of a customer's securities or funds.

General Provisions

(b) Every member in the conduct of its business shall adhere to the provisions of Rule 15c3-3 promulgated under the Securities Exchange Act of 1934 with respect to obtaining possession and control of securities, and the maintenance of appropriate cash reserves. For the purposes of this Section, the definitions contained in Rule 15c3-3 shall apply.

Authorization to Lend

(c) No member shall lend, either to himself or to others, securities carried for the account of any customer, which are eligible to be pledged or loaned unless such member shall first have obtained from the customer a written authorization permitting the lending of securities thus carried by such member.

Segregation and identification of securities

(d) No member shall hold securities carried for the account of any customer which have fully paid for or which are excess margin securities unless such securities are segregated and identified by a method which clearly indicates the interest of such customer in those securities.

Prohibition against guarantees

(e) No member or person associated with a member shall guarantee a customer against loss in any securities account of such customer carried by the member or in any securities transaction effected by the member with or for such customer.

Sharing in accounts; extent permissible

(f)(1)(A) Except as provided in Subsection (f)(2) no member or person associated with a member shall share directly or indirectly in the profits or losses in any account of a customer carried by the member or any other member; provided, however, that a member or person associated with a member may share in the profits or losses in such an account if (i) such member or person associated with a member obtains prior written authorization from the member carrying the account; and (ii) the member or person associated with a member shall share in the profits or losses in any account of such customer only in direct proportion to the financial contributions made to such account by either the member or person associated with a member. (B) Exempt from the direct proportionate share limitation of subsection (f)(i)(A)(ii) are accounts of the immediate family of such member or person associated with a member. For purposes of this section, the term "immediate family" shall include parents, mother-in-law or father-in-law, husband or wife, children or any relative to whose support the member or person associated with a member otherwise contributes directly or indirectly.

(2) Notwithstanding the prohibition of subsection (f)(1), a member or person associated with a member may receive compensation based on a share in profits or gains in an account if all of the following conditions are satisfied:[1]

(A) The member or person associated with a member seeking such compensation obtains prior written authorization from the member carrying the account;

(B) The customer has at the time the account is opened either a net worth which the member or person associated with a member reasonably believes to be not less than $1,000,000, or the minimum amount invested in the account is not less than $500,000;

(C) The member or person associated with a member reasonably believes the customer is able to understand the proposed method of compensation and its risks prior to entering into the arrangement;

(D) The compensation arrangement is set forth in a written agreement executed by the customer and the member;

(E) The member or person associated with a member reasonably believes, immediately prior to entering into the arrangement, that the agreement represents an arm's-length arrangement between the parties;

(F) The compensation formula takes into account both gains and losses realized or accrued in the account over a period of at least one year; and

(G) The member has disclosed to the customer all material information relating to the arrangement including the method of compensation and potential conflicts of interest which may result from the compensation formula.

Explanation of the Board of Governors

Explanation of Paragraph (d) of Section 19 of Article III of the Rules of Fair Practice

Paragraph (d)

This paragraph requires members to segregate and identify by customers both fully paid and "excess margin" securities.

With regard to a customer's account which contains only stocks, it is general practice for firms to segregate that portion of the stocks having a market value in excess of 140% of the debit balance therein. When a customer's account contains bonds, the basis upon which the member is borrowing or can borrow on such bonds should be taken into consideration in determining the amount of securities to be segregated.

Following are three general types of segregation of customers' securities currently in use by many firms:

1. Physical segregation of securities by issue, with a separate list showing ownership of the securities by each customer. The listing, on cards or other records, should reflect all changes in ownership interests. This method is for securities in street name (not in individual customers' names), but the proportionate interests of the individual customers are indicated by the records.

2. Physical segregation of securities by issue, affixing to each certificate a tab or other identification showing the name of the beneficial owner of the certificate. This may be used for shares in street name or in the customer's name.

3. Specific segregation of all certificates of each customer in separate envelopes or folders, identified by customer, or by clipping the certificates together and identifying the customer by tab or other notation affixed to the segregated certificates.

In all the above methods, the records should note the dates when the securities are segregated. When such securities are not in the actual custody of the member, for instance, when they are in the physical possession of a correspondent firm, their location and the means by which they may be identified as belonging to each customer should be indicated on the books of the member carrying the customers' accounts.

NYSE, para. 2352

¶ 2352   **Guarantees and Sharing in Accounts**

Rule 352. (a) No member associated with a member organization as a member, allied member, registered representative or officer shall guarantee to his employer or to any other creditor carrying a customer's account, the payment of the debit balance in such account.

(b) No member organization shall guarantee or in any way represent that it will guarantee any customer against loss in any account or on any transaction; and no member, allied member, registered representative or officer shall guarantee or in any way represent that either he or his employer will guarantee any customer against loss in any account or on any transaction.

(c) No member, member organization, allied member, registered representative or officer shall, directly or indirectly, (i) take or receive or agree to take or receive a share in the profits, or (ii) share or agree to share in any losses, in any customer's account or of any transaction effected therein. The foregoing will not prohibit the participation of an allied member, a registered representative or an officer in a joint account or investment partnership provided he obtains the prior written consent of his employer.

(See Rule 93 for reporting requirements concerning participation in joint accounts by members, member organizations and allied members.)

Supplementary Material:

.10 Interest in customer accounts.—For the purposes of paragraphs (b) and (c) above, the term customer shall not be deemed to include the member or member organization or any joint, group, or syndicate account with such member or member organization.

.20 Paragraphs (a) and (c) shall not preclude a member, member organization, allied member, registered representative or officer from sharing or agreeing to share in any losses in any customer's account after the member organization has established that the loss was caused in whole or in part by the action or inaction of such member, member organization, allied member, registered representative or officer.

NYSE, para. 2401

Conduct of Accounts
(Rules and Policies Administered by Member Firm Regulatory Services)

¶ 2401   **Business Conduct**

Rule 401. Every member, allied member and member organization shall at all times adhere to the principles of good business practice in the conduct of his or its business affairs.

NYSE, para. 2402(a)

¶ 2402   Customer Protection—Reserves and Custody of
Securities
General Provisions

Rule 402. (a) Each member organization shall obtain custody and control of securities and maintain reserves as prescribed by Rule 15c3-3 promulgated under the Securities Exchange Act of 1934. For the purpose of this Rule the definitions contained in such Rule 15c3-3 shall apply.

NASD, para. 2152

¶ 2152   Recommendations to Customers

Sec. 2. In recommending to a customer the purchase, sale or exchange of any security, a member shall have reasonable grounds for believing that the recommendation is suitable for such customer upon the basis of the facts, if any, disclosed by such customer as to his other security holdings and as to his financial situation and needs.

Policy of the Board of Governors
Fair Dealing With Customers

Implicit in all member and registered representative relationships with customers and others is the fundamental responsibility for fair dealing. Sales efforts must therefore be undertaken only on a basis that can be judged as being within the ethical standards of the Association's rules, with particular emphasis on the requirement to deal fairly with the public.

This does not mean that legitimate sales efforts in the securities business are to be discouraged by requirements which do not take into account the variety of circumstances which can enter into the member-customer relationship. It does mean, however, that sales efforts must be judged on the basis of whether they can be reasonably said to represent fair treatment for the persons to whom the sales efforts are directed, rather than on the argument that they result in profits to customers.

District Business Conduct Committees and the Board of Governors have interpreted the Rules of Fair Practice, taken disciplinary action and imposed penalties in many situations where members' sales efforts have exceeded the reasonable grounds of fair dealing.

Some practices that have resulted in disciplinary action and that clearly violate this responsibility for fair dealing are set forth below, as a guide to members:

Recommending Speculative Low-priced Securities

1. Recommending speculative low-priced securities to customers without knowledge of or attempt to obtain information concerning the customers' other securities holdings, their financial situation and other necessary data. The principle here is that this practice, by its very nature, involves a high probability that the recommendation will not be suitable for at least some of the persons solicited. This has particular application to high pressure telephone sales campaigns.

Excessive Trading Activity

2. Excessive activity in a customer's account, often referred to as "churning" or "overtrading." There are no specific standards to measure excessiveness of activity in customer accounts because this must be related to the objectives and financial situation of the customer involved.

Trading in Mutual Fund Shares

3. Trading in mutual fund shares, particularly on a short-term basis. It is clear that normally these securities are not proper trading vehicles and such activity on its face may raise the question of rule violation.

Fraudulent Activity

4. Numerous instances of fraudulent conduct have been acted upon by the Association and have resulted in penalties against members. Among some of these activities are:

Fictitious Accounts

(a) Establishment of fictitious accounts in order to execute transactions which otherwise would be prohibited, such as the purchase of hot issues, or to disguise transactions which are against firm policy.

Discretionary Accounts

(b) Transactions in discretionary accounts in excess of or without actual authority from customers.

Unauthorized Transactions

(c) Causing the execution of transactions which are unauthorized by customers or the sending of confirmations in order to cause customers to accept transactions not actually agreed upon.

Misuse of Customers' Funds or Securities

(d) Unauthorized use or borrowing of customers' funds or securities.

In addition, other fraudulent activities, such as forgery, non-disclosure or misstatement of material facts, manipulations and various deceptions, have been found in violation of Association rules. These same activities are also subject to the civil and criminal laws and sanctions of Federal and State Governments.

Recommending Purchases Beyond Customer Capability

5. Recommending the purchase of securities or the continuing purchase of securities in amounts which are inconsistent with the reasonable expectation that the customer has the financial ability to meet such a commitment.

While most members are fully aware of the fairness required in dealing with customers, it is anticipated that these enumerated practices, which are not all inclusive, will be of future assistance in the training and education of new personnel.

The Securities and Exchange Commission has also recognized that brokers and dealers have an obligation of fair dealing in actions under the general anti-fraud provisions of the Federal securities laws. The Commission bases this obligation on the principle that when a securities dealer opens his business he is, in effect, representing that he will deal fairly with the public. Certain of the Commission's cases on fair dealing involve practices not covered in the foregoing illustrations. Usually, any breach of the obligation of fair dealing as determined by the Commission under the anti-fraud provisions of the securities laws could be considered a violation of the Association's Rules of Fair Practice.

NASD para. 4651

¶ 4651   Sales Practice Requirements for Certain Low-Priced Securities

Reg. § 240.15c2-6. (a) As a means reasonably designed to prevent fraudulent, deceptive, or manipulative acts or practices, it shall be unlawful for a broker or dealer to sell a designated security to, or to effect the purchase of a designated security by, any person unless:

(1) the transaction is exempt under paragraph (c) of this section; or

(2) prior to the transaction:

(i) the broker or dealer has approved the person's account for transactions in designated securities in accordance with the procedures set forth in paragraph (b) of this section; and

(ii) the broker or dealer has received from the person a written agreement to the transaction setting forth the identity and quantity of the designated security to be purchased.

(b) In order to approve a person's account for transactions in designated securities, the broker or dealer must:

(1) obtain from the person information concerning the person's financial situation, investment experience, and investment objectives;

(2) reasonably determine, based on the information required by paragraph (b)(1) of this section and any other information known by the broker-dealer, that transactions in designated securities are suitable for the person, and that the person (or the person's independent adviser in these transactions) has sufficient knowledge and experience in financial matters that the person (or the person's independent adviser in these transactions) reasonably may be expected to be capable of evaluating the risks of transactions in designated securities;

(3) deliver to the person a written statement:

(i) setting forth the basis on which the broker or dealer made the determination required by paragraph (b)(2) of this section;

(ii) stating in a highlighted format that it is unlawful for the broker or dealer to effect a transaction in a designated security subject to the provisions of paragraph (a)(2) of this section unless the broker or dealer has received, prior to the transaction, a written agreement to the transaction from the person; and

(iii) stating in a highlighted format immediately preceding the customer signature line that:

(A) the broker or dealer is required by this section to provide the person with the written statement; and

(B) the person should not sign and return the written statement to the broker or dealer if it does not accurately reflect the person's financial situation, investment experience, and investment objectives; and

(4) obtain from the person a manually signed and dated copy of the written statement required by paragraph (b)(3) of this section.

(c) For the purposes of this section, the following shall be exempt transactions—

(1) Transactions in which the price of the designated security is five dollars or more; provided, however, that if the designated security is a unit composed of one or more securities, the unit price divided by the number of components of the unit other than warrants, options, rights, or similar securities, must be five dollars or more, and any component of the unit that is a warrant, option, right, or similar securities, or a convertible security must have an exercise price or conversion price of five dollars or more.

(2) Transactions in which the purchaser is an accredited investor or an established customer of the broker or dealer.

(3) Transactions that are not recommended by the broker or dealer.

(4) Transactions by a broker or dealer:

(i) whose commissions, commission equivalents, and mark-ups from transactions in designated securities during each of the immediately preceding three months, and during eleven or more of the preceding twelve months, did not exceed five percent of its total commissions, commission-equivalents, and mark-ups from transactions in securities during those months; and

(ii) who has not been a market maker in the designated security that is the subject of the transaction in the immediately preceding twelve months.

(5) Any transaction or transactions that, upon prior written request or upon its own motion, the Commission conditionally or unconditionally exempts as not encompassed within the purposes of this section.

(d) For the purposes of this section—

(1) The term "accredited investor" shall have the same meaning as in 17 CFR 230.501(a).

(2) The term "designated security" shall mean any equity security other than a security:

(i) registered, or approved for registration upon notice of issuance, on a national securities exchange that makes transaction reports available pursuant to 17 CFR 11Aa3-1;

(ii) authorized, or approved for authorization upon notice of issuance, for quotation in the NASDAQ system;

(iii) issued by an investment company registered under the Investment Company Act of 1940;

(iv) that is a put option or call option issued by The Options Clearing Corporation; or

(v) whose issuer has net tangible assets in excess of $2,000,000, as demonstrated by financial statements dated less than fifteen months previously that the broker or dealer has reviewed and has a reasonable basis to believe are true and complete in relation to the date of the transaction with the person, and

(A) in the event the issuer is other than a foreign private issuer, are the most recent financial statements for the issuer that have been audited and reported on by an independent public accountant in accordance with the provisions of 17 CFR 210.2-02; or

(B) in the event the issuer is a foreign private issuer, are the most recent financial statements for the issuer that have been filed with the Commission; furnished to the Commission pursuant to 17 CFR 240.12g3-2(b); or prepared in accordance with generally accepted accounting principles in the country of incorporation, audited in compliance with the requirements of that jurisdiction, and reported on by an accountant duly registered and in good standing in accordance with the regulations of that jurisdiction.

(3) The term "established customer" shall mean any person for whom the broker or dealer, or a clearing broker on behalf of such broker or dealer, carries an account, and who in such account:

(i) has effected a securities transaction, or made a deposit of funds or securities, more than one year previously; or

(ii) has made three purchases of designated securities that occurred on separate days and involved different issuers.

[Adopted in Release No. 34-27160, effective January 1, 1990, 54 F.R. 35468.]

NASD, para. 2165

¶ 2165   Discretionary Accounts

Sec. 15.

Excessive transactions

(a) No member shall effect with or for any customer's account in respect to which such member or his agent or employee is vested with any discretionary power any transactions of purchase or sale which are excessive in size or frequency in view of the financial resources and character of such account.

Authorization and acceptance of account

(b) No member or registered representative shall exercise any discretionary power in a customer's account unless such customer has given prior written authorization to a stated individual or individuals and the account has been accepted by the member, as evidenced in writing by the member or the partner, officer or manager, duly designated by the member, in accordance with Section 27 of these rules.

Approval and review of transactions

(c) The member or the person duly designated shall approve promptly in writing each discretionary order entered and shall review all discretionary accounts at frequent intervals in order to detect and prevent transactions which are excessive in size or frequency in view of the financial resources and character of the account.

Exception

(d) This section shall not apply to discretion as to the price at which or the time when an order given by a customer for the purchase or sale of a definite amount of a specified security shall be executed.

NYSE, para. 2408

¶ 2408   Discretionary Power in Customers' Accounts

Rule 408. (a) No member, allied member or employee of a member organization shall exercise any discretionary power in any customer's account or accept orders for an account from a person other than the customer without first obtaining written authorization of the customer.

(b) No member, allied member or employee of a member organization shall exercise any discretionary power in any customer's account, without first notifying and obtaining the approval of another person delegated under Rule 342(b)(1) with authority to approve the handling of such accounts. Every order entered on a discretionary basis by a member, allied member or employee of a member organization must be identified as discretionary on the order at the time of entry. Such discretionary accounts shall receive frequent appropriate supervisory review by a person delegated such responsibility under Rule 342(b)(1), who is not exercising the discretionary authority. A written statement of the supervisory procedures governing such accounts must be maintained.

(c) No member or allied member or employee of a member organization exercising discretionary power in any customer's account shall (and no member organization shall permit any member, allied member, or employee thereof exercising discretionary power in any customer's account to) effect purchases or sales of securities which are excessive in size or frequency in view of the financial resources of such customer.

(d) The provisions of this rule shall not apply to discretion as to the price at which or the time when an order given by a customer for the purchase or sale of a definite amount of a specified security shall be executed.

NASD, para. 2159

¶ 2159   Use of Information Obtained in Fiduciary Capacity

Sec. 9. A member who in the capacity of paying agent, transfer agent, trustee, or in any other similar capacity, has received information as to the ownership of securities, shall under no circumstances make use of such information for the purpose of soliciting purchases, sales or exchanges except at the request and on behalf of the issuer.

NASD, para. 2171(d)

Record of written complaints

(d) Each member shall keep and preserve in each office of supervisory jurisdiction, as defined in Section 27 of these rules, either a separate file of all written complaints of customers and action taken by the member, if any, or a separate record of such complaints and a clear reference to the files containing the correspondence connected with such complaint as maintained in such office.

NASD, para. 2177

¶ 2177   Supervision

Sec. 27.

Supervisory System

(a) Each member shall establish and maintain a system to supervise the activities of each registered representative and associated person that is reasonably designed to achieve compliance with applicable securities laws and regulations, and with the rules of this Association. Final responsibility for proper supervision shall rest with the member. A member's supervisory system shall provide, at a minimum, for the following:

(1) The establishment and maintenance of written procedures as required by paragraphs (b) and (c) of this Section.

(2) The designation, where applicable, of an appropriately registered principal(s) with authority to carry out the supervisory responsibilities of the member for each type of business in which it engages for which registration as a broker-dealer is required.

(3) The designation as an office of supervisory jurisdiction (OSJ) of each location that meets the definition contained in paragraph (f) of this Section. Each member shall also designate such other OSJs as it determines to be necessary in order to supervise its registered representatives and associated persons in accordance with the standards set forth in this Section 27, taking into consideration the following factors:

(i) whether registered persons at the location engage in retail sales or other activities involving regular contact with public customers;

(ii) whether a substantial number of registered persons conduct securities activities at, or are otherwise supervised from, such location;

(iii) whether the location is geographically distant from another OSJ of the firm;

(iv) whether the member's registered persons are geographically dispersed; and

(v) whether the securities activities at such location are diverse and/or complex.

(4) The designation of one or more appropriately registered principals in each OSJ, including the main office, and one or more appropriately registered representatives or principals in each non-OSJ branch office with authority to carry out the supervisory responsibilities assigned to that office by the member.

(5) The assignment of each registered person to an appropriately registered representative(s) and/or principal(s) who shall be responsible for supervising that person's activities.

(6) Reasonable efforts to determine that all supervisory personnel are qualified by virtue of experience or training to carry out their assigned responsibilities.

(7) The participation of each registered representative, either individually or collectively, no less than annually, in an interview or meeting conducted by persons designated by the member at which compliance matters relevant to the activities of the representative(s) are discussed. Such interview or meeting may occur in conjunction with the discussion of other matters and may be conducted at a central or regional location or at the representative's(') place of business.

(8) Each member shall designate and specifically identify to the Association one or more principals who shall review the supervisory system, procedures, and inspections implemented by the member as required by this Section and take or recommend to senior management appropriate action reasonably designed to achieve the member's compliance with applicable securities laws and regulations, and with the rules of this Association.

Written Procedures

(b)(1) Each member shall establish, maintain, and enforce written procedures to supervise the types of business in which it engages and to supervise the activities of registered representatives and associated persons that are reasonably designed to achieve compliance with applicable securities laws and regulations, and with the applicable rules of this Association.

(b)(2) The member's written supervisory procedures shall set forth the supervisory system established by the member pursuant to Section 27(a) above, and shall include the titles, registration status and locations of the required supervisory personnel and the responsibilities of each supervisory person as these relate to the types of business engaged in, applicable securities laws and regulations, and the rules of this Association. The member shall maintain on an internal record the names of all persons who are designated as supervisory personnel and the dates for which such designation is or was effective. Such record shall be preserved by the member for a period of not less than three years, the first two years in an easily accessible place.

(b)(3) A copy of a member's written supervisory procedures, or the relevant portions thereof, shall be kept and maintained in each OSJ and at each location where supervisory activities are conducted on behalf of the member. Each member shall amend its written supervisory procedures as appropriate within a reasonable time after changes occur in applicable securities laws and regulations, including the rules of this Association, and as changes occur in its supervisory system, and each member shall be responsible for communicating amendments through its organization.

Internal Inspections

(c) Each member shall conduct a review, at least annually, of the businesses in which it engages, which review shall be reasonably designed to assist in detecting and preventing violations of and achieving compliance with applicable securities laws and regulations, and with the rules of this Association. Each member shall review the activities of each office, which shall include the periodic examination of customer accounts to detect and prevent irregularities or abuses and at least an annual inspection of each office of supervisory jurisdiction. Each branch office of the member shall be inspected according to a cycle which shall be set forth in the firm's written supervisory and inspection procedures. In establishing such cycle, the firm shall give consideration to the nature and complexity of the securities activities for which the location is responsible, the volume of business done, and the number of associated persons assigned to the location. Each member shall retain a written record of the dates upon which each review and inspection is conducted.

Written Approval

(d) Each member shall establish procedures for the review and endorsement by a registered principal in writing, on an internal record, of all transactions and all correspondence of its registered representatives pertaining to the solicitation or execution of any securities transaction.

Qualifications Investigated

(e) Each member shall have the responsibility and duty to ascertain by investigation the good character, business repute, qualifications, and experience of any person prior to making such a certification in the application of such person for registration with this Association. Where an applicant for registration has previously been registered with the Association, the member shall obtain from the Firm Access Query System (FAQS) or from the applicant a copy of the Uniform Termination Notice of Securities Industry Registration ("Form U-5") filed with the Association by such person's most recent previous NASD member employer, together with any amendments thereto that may have been filed pursuant to Article IV, Section 3 of the Association's By-Laws. The member shall obtain the Form U-5 as required by this section no later than sixty (60) days following the filing of the application for registration or demonstrate to the Association that it has made reasonable efforts to comply with the requirement. A member receiving a Form U-5 pursuant to this section shall review the Form U-5 and any amendments thereto and shall take such action as may be deemed appropriate.

Applicant's Responsibility

(f) Any applicant for registration who receives a request for a copy of his or her Form U-5 from a member pursuant to this section shall provide such copy to the member within two (2) business days of the request if the Form U-5 has been provided to such person by his or her former employer. If a former employer has failed to provide the Form U-5 to the applicant for registration, such person shall promptly request the Form U-5, and shall provide it to the requesting member within two (2) business days of receipt thereof. The applicant shall promptly provide any subsequent amendments to a Form U-5 he or she receives to the requesting member.

Definitions

(g)(1) "Office of Supervisory Jurisdiction" means any office of a member at which any one or more of the following functions take place:

(i) order execution and/or market making;

(ii) structuring of public offerings or private placements;

(iii) maintaining custody of customers' funds and/or securities;

(iv) final acceptance (approval) of new accounts on behalf of the member;

(v) review and endorsement of customer orders, pursuant to paragraph (d) above;

(vi) final approval of advertising or sales literature for use by persons associated with the member, pursuant to Article III, Section 35(b)(1) of the Rules of Fair Practice; or

(vii) responsibility for supervising the activities of persons associated with the member at one or more other branch offices of the member.

(2) "Branch Office" means any location identified by any means to the public or customers as a location at which the member conducts an investment banking or securities business, excluding any location identified solely in a telephone directory line listing or on a business card or letterhead, which listing, card, or letterhead also sets forth the address and telephone number of the branch office or OSJ of the firm from which the person(s) conducting business at the non-branch location are directly supervised.

NYSE, para. 2342

¶ 2342   **Offices—Approval, Supervision and Control**

Rule 342. (a) Each office, department or business activity of a member or member organization (including foreign incorporated branch offices) shall be under the supervision and control of the member or member organization establishing it and of the personnel delegated such authority and responsibility.

The person in charge of a group of employees shall reasonably discharge his duties and obligations in connection with supervision and control of the activities of those employees related to the business of their employer and compliance with securities laws and regulations.

(b) The general partners or directors of each member organization shall provide for appropriate supervisory control and shall designate a general partner or principal executive officer to assume overall authority and responsibility for internal supervision and control of the organization and compliance with securities' laws and regulations. This person shall:

(1) delegate to qualified principals or employees responsibility and authority for supervision and control of each office, department or business activity, and provide for appropriate procedures of supervision and control.

(2) establish a separate system of follow-up and review to determine that the delegated authority and responsibility is being properly exercised.

(c) The prior consent of the Exchange shall be obtained for each office established by a member or member organization, other than a main office.

(d) Qualified persons acceptable to the Exchange shall be in charge of:

(1) any office of a member or member organization,

(2) any regional or other group of offices,

(3) any sales department or activity.

(e) The amounts and types of credit extended by a member organization shall be supervised by members or allied members qualified by experience for such control in the types of business in which the member organization extends credit.

.10 Annual fee.—Each office of a member organization or corporate affiliate, other than the main office of the member organization, shall be subject during its existence to a registration fee of $50 for each calendar year or part thereof, unless specifically exempted by the Exchange. (*See Rule 321 for corporate affiliate requirements.*)

.11 Registered representative operating from residence.—With the prior approval of the Exchange, a registered representative may operate from his residence. His home address and telephone number may be advertised in any normal manner (such as business cards, local newspapers, stationery, etc.) but, in such event, the residence address shall be considered as constituting an office of his employer.

.12 Foreign branch offices.—With prior approval and under conditions set by the Exchange, a member organization may establish a foreign branch office in corporate form, provided all the stock of the corporation is owned by the member organization. Regulation & Surveillance will furnish information concerning these conditions. Continuance of the arrangement is subject to any changes in the Constitution, Rules and Regulations of the Exchange as may be thereafter adopted.

.13 Acceptability of supervisors. (a) *Generally.*—Any member, allied member or employee who is a candidate for acceptability under (d) above should have a creditable record as a registered representative or equivalent experience, and is expected to pass either the Allied Member Examination or the Branch Office Manager Examination to qualify under (d)(1) or (2), or an examination acceptable to the Exchange which demonstrates competency to supervise a specific sales department or activity to qualify under (d)(3). The examination requirement may be waived at the discretion of the Exchange. Special examinations may be arranged for persons whose principal work is in unusual fields.

(b) Compliance supervisors.—Each member not associated with a member organization and in the case of a member organization, the person (or persons) designated to direct day-to-day compliance activity (such as the Compliance Officer, Partner or Director) and each other person at the member organization directly supervising ten or more persons engaged in compliance activity should have overall knowledge of the securities laws and Exchange rules and must pass the Compliance Official Qualification Examination and, if the member or member organization does business with the public, the General Securities Sales Supervisor Qualification Examination (Series 8). Where good cause is shown, the Exchange, at its discretion, may waive all or a portion of the examination requirements. The Exchange may give consideration to the scope of the member or member organization's activity, to previous related employment, and to examination requirements of other self-regulatory organizations. In such cases, the Exchange must be satisfied that the person is qualified for the position.

.14 Experience of senior management.—Member organizations without experienced senior principals may be subject to agreements with the Exchange appropriately limiting their scope of activity.

.15 Small offices may be in the charge of a qualified principal or manager who is either resident or non-resident in that area. In the event that such a qualified supervisor is non-resident, a resident registered representative may be designated for subsidiary authority and is not required to meet a manager's examination or experience requirements.

.16 Supervision of registered representatives.—For responsibilities for supervision of customer accounts, see also Rule 405. Suggestions are included in the separately published guide to "Supervision and Management of Registered Representatives and Customer Accounts". Duties of supervisors of registered representatives should ordinarily include at least approval of new accounts and review of correspondence of registered representatives, transactions, and customer accounts. Appropriate records should be maintained evidencing the carrying out of supervisory responsibilities such as a written statement of the supervisory procedures currently in effect and initialing of correspondence, transactions, blotters, or statements reviewed in the supervisory process.

.17 Member organizations shall provide for the supervision and control of each general ledger bookkeeping account and account of like function on the basis specified in Rule 440.20.

.20 Information requests.—In connection with its investigation of anomalous trading activity and for other purposes, the Exchange from time to time requests from members and member organizations detailed information regarding trades effected by the member or member organization in specified NYSE listed securities and related financial instruments during a specified period. Each member not associated with a member organization and each member organization shall comply with each such request by the date required by the Exchange.

.21 Trade review and investigation.—In order to help assure its compliance with the provisions of the Securities Exchange Act of 1934, the rules under that act and the rules of the Exchange prohibiting insider trading and manipulative and deceptive devices, each member not associated with a member organization and each member organization, in addition to carrying out such other supervisory procedures as may be necessary to discharge its supervisory responsibilities as to compliance with Federal Securities laws and rules and Exchange rules generally shall:

(a) Subject trades in NYSE listed securities and in related financial investments which are effected for the account of the member or member organization or for the accounts of members, allied members or employees of the member or member organization and their family members (including trades reported by other members or member organizations pursuant to Rules 406 and 407) to review procedures that the member or member organization determines to be reasonably designed to identify trades that may violate the provisions of the Securities Exchange Act of 1934, the rules under that act or the rules of the Exchange prohibiting insider trading and manipulative and deceptive devices, and

(b) Conduct promptly an internal investigation into any such trade that appears that it may have violated those laws and rules in order to determine whether it did violate those laws and rules.

The Exchange, at its discretion, may exclude from these review and investigation requirements particular classes of persons, trades, securities and related financial instruments.

.22 Definition of related financial instrument.—For the purpose of Paragraphs .20 and .21, "related financial instrument" means:

(a) Any stock underlying an NYSE listed stock option or included in an index stock group underlying an NYSE listed index stock group option,

(b) Any stock option on an NYSE listed stock,

(c) Any index stock (bond) group option on a stock (bond) group that includes an NYSE listed stock (bond),

(d) Any futures contract on a stock (bond) group that includes an NYSE listed stock (bond), and

(e) Any option on any such futures contract.

.30 Annual Report.—By April 1 of each year, each member not associated with a member organization and each member organization shall prepare, and each member organization shall submit to its chief executive officer or managing partner, a report on the member or member organization's supervision and compliance effort during the preceding year. The report shall include:

(a) A tabulation of the reports pertaining to customer complaints and internal investigations made to the Exchange during the preceding year pursuant to Rules 351(d) and (e)(ii),

(b) Identification and analysis of significant compliance problems, plans for future systems or procedures to prevent and detect violations and problems, and an assessment of the preceding year's efforts of this nature, and

(c) Discussion of the preceding year's compliance efforts, new procedures, educational programs, etc. in each of the following areas:

(i) Antifraud and trading practices,

(ii) Investment banking activities,

(iii) Sales practices,

(iv) Books and records,

(v) Finance and operations, and

(vi) Supervision.

If any of these areas do not apply to the member or member organization, the report should so state.

NASD, para. 2195

¶ 2195   Communications With the Public

Sec. 35.

(a) Definitions

(1) Advertisement—For purposes of this section and any interpretation thereof, "advertisement" means material published, or designed for use in, a newspaper, magazine or other periodical, radio, television, telephone or tape recording, videotape display, signs or billboards, motion pictures, telephone directories (other than routine listings), or other public media.

(2) Sales Literature—For purposes of this section and any interpretation thereof, "sales literature" means any written communication distributed or made generally available to customers or the public, which communication does not meet the foregoing definition of "advertisement". Sales literature includes, but is not limited to, circulars, research reports, market letters, performance reports or summaries, form letters, standard forms of options worksheets, seminar texts, and reprints or excerpts of any other advertisement, sales literature or published article.

(b) Approval and Recordkeeping

(1) Each item of advertising and sales literature shall be approved by signature or initial, prior to use, by a registered principal (or his designee) of the member. In the case of advertising or sales literature pertaining to options, the approval must be by the Compliance Registered Options Principal or his designee.

(2) A separate file of all advertisements and sales literature, including the name(s) of the person(s) who prepared them and/or approved their use, shall be maintained for a period of three years from the date of each use.

(c) Filing Requirements and Review Procedures

(1) Advertisements and sales literature concerning registered investment companies (including mutual funds, variable contracts and unit investment trusts) shall be filed with the Association's Advertising Department within 10 days of first use or publication by any member. Filing in advance of use is recommended. Members are not required to file advertising and sales literature which have previously been filed and which are used without change.

(2) Advertisements pertaining to options, and other options-related communications to persons who have not received the appropriate current disclosure document(s), shall be submitted to the Association's Advertising Department for review at least ten days prior to use (or shorter period as the Department may allow in exceptional circumstances), unless such advertisement or communication is submitted to and approved by a registered securities exchange or other regulatory body having substantially the same standards with respect to options advertising as set forth in this Section. The Association shall, within the ten-day review period specified herein, in the

absence of highly unusual circumstances, either notify the member of its views with respect to the material filed or indicate that its comments are being withheld pending further analysis or the receipt of additional information.

(3) Advertising and sales literature concerning public direct participation programs as defined in Article III, Section 34 of the Rules of Fair Practice shall be filed with the Association's Advertising Department for review within 10 days of first use or publication. Filing in advance of use is recommended. Members need not file for review advertising and sales literature which has been filed by the sponsor, general partner or underwriter of the program or by another member.

(4) (A) Each member of the Association which has not previously filed advertisements with the Association (or with a registered securities exchange having standards comparable to those contained in this section) shall file its initial advertisement with the Association's Advertising Department at least ten days prior to use and shall continue to file its advertisements at least ten days prior to use for a period of one year.

(B) Each member which, on the effective date of this section, had been filing advertisements with the Association (or with a registered securities exchange having standards comparable to those contained in this section) for a period of less than one year shall continue to file its advertisements, at least ten days prior to use, until the completion of one year from the date the first advertisement was filed with the Association or such exchange.

(C) Except for advertisements related to municipal securities, direct participation programs or investment company securities, members subject to the requirements of subparagraphs (c)(3)(A) or (c)(3)(B) of this section may, in lieu of filing with the Association, file advertisements on the same basis, and for the same time periods specified in those subparagraphs, with any registered securities exchange having standards comparable to those contained in this section.

(5) Notwithstanding the foregoing provisions, any District Business Conduct Committee of the Association, upon review of a member's advertising and/or sales literature, and after determining that the member has departed and there is a reasonable likelihood that the member will again depart from the standards of this section, may require that such member file all advertising and/or sales literature, or the portion of such member's material which is related to any specific types or clases of securities or services, with the Association's Advertising Department and/or the District Committee, at least ten days prior to use.

The Committee shall notify the member in writing of the types of material to be filed and the length of time such requirement is to be in effect. The requirement shall not exceed one year, however, and shall not take effect until 30 days after the member receives the written notice, during which time the member may request a hearing before the District Business Conduct Committee, and any such hearing shall be held in reasonable conformity with the hearing and appeal procedures of the Code of Procedure.

(6) In addition to the foregoing requirements, every member's advertising and sales literature shall be subject to a routine spot-check procedure. Upon written request from the Association's Advertising Department, each member shall promptly submit the material requested. Members will not be required to submit material under this procedure which has been previously submitted pursuant to one of the foregoing requirements and, except for material related to municipal securities or investment company securities, the procedure will not be applied to members who have been, within the preceding calendar year, subjected to a spot-check by a registered securities exchange or other self-regulatory organization utilizing comparable procedures.

(7) The following types of material are excluded from the foregoing filing requirements and spot-check procedures:

(A) Advertisements or sales literature solely related to changes in a member's name, personnel, location, ownership, offices, business structure, officers or partners, telephone or teletype numbers, or concerning a merger with, or acquisition by, another member;

(B) Advertisements or sales literature which do no more than identify the NASDAQ symbol of the member and/or of a security in which the member is a NASDAQ registered market maker;

(C) Advertisements or sales literature which do no more than identify the member and/or offer a specific security at a stated price;

(D) Material sent to branch offices or other internal material that is not distributed to the public;

(E) Prospectus, preliminary prospectuses, offering circulars and similar documents used in connection with an offering of securities which has been registered or filed with the Securities and Exchange Commission or any state, or which is exempt from such registration, except that an investment company prospectus published pursuant to Rule 482 under the Securities Act of 1933 shall not be considered a prospectus for purposes of this exclusion;

(F) Advertisements prepared in accordance with Section 2(10)(b) of the Securities Act of 1933, as amended, or any rule thereunder, such as Rule 134, unless such advertisements are related to options, direct participation programs or securities issued by registered investment companies.

(8) Material which refers to investment company securities or options solely as part of a listing of products and/or services offered by the member, is excluded from the requirements of paragraphs (c)(1) and (c)(2) of this section.

(d) Standards Applicable to Communications With the Public

(1) General Standards

(A) All member communications with the public shall be based on principles of fair dealing and good faith and should provide a sound basis for evaluating the facts in regard to any particular security or securities or type of security, industry discussed, or service offered. No material fact or qualification may be omitted if the omission, in the light of the context of the material presented, would cause the advertising or sales literature to be misleading.

(B) Exaggerated, unwarranted or misleading statements or claims are prohibited in all public communications of members. In preparing such literature, members must bear in mind that inherent in investment are the risks of fluctuating prices and the uncertainty of dividends, rates of return and yield, and no member shall, directly or indirectly, publish, circulate or distribute any public communication that the member knows or has reason to know contains any untrue statement of a material fact or is otherwise false or misleading.

(C) When sponsoring or participating in a seminar, forum, radio or television interview, or when otherwise engaged in public appearances or speaking activities which may not constitute advertisements, members and persons associated with members shall nevertheless follow the standards of paragraph (d) of this section.

(2) Specific Standards

In addition to the foregoing general standards, the following specific standards apply:

(A) Necessary Data: Advertisements and sales literature shall contain the name of the member, the person or firm preparing the material, if other than the member, and the date on which it is first published, circulated or distributed (except that, in advertisements, only the name of the member need be stated; and except also that, in any so-called "blind" advertisement used for recruiting personnel, the name of the member may be omitted). If the information in the material is not current, this fact should be stated.

(B) Recommendations: In making a recommendation, whether or not labeled as such, a member must have a reasonable basis for the recommendation and must disclose the price at the time the recommendation is made, as well as any of the following situations which are applicable:

(i) that the member usually makes a market in the securities being recommended, or in the underlying security if the recommended security is an option, and/or that the member or associated persons will sell to or buy from customers on a principal basis;

(ii) that the member and/or its officers or partners own options, rights or warrants to purchase any of the securities of the issuer whose securities are recommended, unless the extent of such ownership is nominal;

(iii) that the member was manager or co-manager of a public offering of any securities of the recommended issuer within the last 3 years.

The member shall also provide, or offer to furnish upon request, available investment information supporting the recommendation.

A member may use material referring to past recommendations if it sets forth all recommendations as to the same type, kind, grade or classification of securities made by a member within the last year. Longer periods of years may be covered if they are consecutive and include the most recent year. Such material must also name each security recommended and give the date and nature of each recommendation (e.g., whether to buy or sell), the price at the time of the recommendation, the price at which or the price range within which the recommendation was to be acted upon, and indicate the general market conditions during the period covered.

Also permitted is material which does not make any specific recommendation but which offers to furnish a list of all recommendations made by a member within the past year or over longer periods of consecutive years, including the most recent year, if this list contains all the information specified in the previous paragraph. Neither the list of recommendations, nor material offering such list, shall imply comparable future performance. Reference to the results of a previous specific recommendation, including such a reference in a follow-up research report or market letter, is prohibited if the intent or the effect is to show the success of a past recommendation, unless all of the foregoing requirements with respect to past recommendations are met.

(C) Claims and Opinions: Communications with the public must not contain promises of specific results, exaggerated or unwarranted claims or unwarranted superlatives, opinions for which there is no reasonable basis, or forecasts of future events which are unwarranted, or which are not clearly labeled as forecasts.

(D) Testimonials: In testimonials concerning the quality of a firm's investment advice, the following points must be clearly stated in the communication:

(i) The testimonial may not be representative of the experience of other clients.

(ii) The testimonial is not indicative of future performance or success.

(iii) If more than a nominal sum is paid, the fact that it is a paid testimonial must be indicated.

(iv) If the testimonial concerns a technical aspect of investing, the person making the testimonial must have knowledge and experience to form a valid opinion.

(E) Offers of Free Service: Any statement to the effect that any report, analysis, or other service will be furnished free or without any charge must not be made unless such report, analysis or other service actually is or will be furnished entirely free and without condition or obligation.

(F) Claims for Research Facilities: No claim or implication may be made for research or other facilities beyond those which the member actually possesses or has reasonable capacity to provide.

(G) Hedge Clauses: No cautionary statements or caveats, often called hedge clauses, may be used if they are misleading or are inconsistent with the content of the material.

(H) Recruiting Advertising: Advertisements in connection with the recruitment of sales personnel must not contain exaggerated or unwarranted claims or statements about opportunities in the investment banking or securities business and should not refer to specific earnings figures or ranges which are not reasonable under the circumstances.

(I) Periodic Investment Plans: Communications with the public should not discuss or portray any type of continuous or periodic investment plan without disclosing that such a plan does not assure a profit and does not protect against loss in declining markets. In addition, if the material deals specifically with the principles of dollar-cost averaging, it should point out that since such a plan involves continuous investment in securities regardless of fluctuating price levels of such securities, the investor should consider his financial ability to continue his purchases through periods of low price levels.

(J) References to Regulatory Organizations: Communications with the public shall not make any reference to membership in the Association or to registration or regulation of the securities being offered, or of the underwriter, sponsor, or any member or associated person, which reference could imply endorsement or approval by the Association or any federal or state regulatory body.

References to membership in the Association or Securities Investors Protection Corporation shall comply with all applicable By-Laws and Rules pertaining thereto.

(K) Identification of Sources: Statistical tables, charts, graphs or other illustrations used by members in advertising or sales literature should disclose the source of the information if not prepared by the member.

(e) Standards Applicable to Investment Company-Related Communications

In addition to the provisions of paragraph (d) of this section, members' public communications concerning investment company securities shall conform to all applicable rules of the SEC, as in effect at the time the material is used.

(f) Standards Applicable to Options-Related Communications

In addition to the provisions of subsection (d) of this Section, members' public communications concerning options shall conform to the following provisions:

(1) As there may be special risks attendant to some options transactions and certain options transactions involve complex investment strategies, these factors should be reflected in any communication which includes any discussion of the uses or advantages of options. Therefore, any statement referring to the opportunities or advantages presented by options should be balanced by a statement of the corresponding risks. The risk statement should reflect the same degree of specificity as the statement of opportunities, and broad generalities should be avoided. Thus, a statement such as, "by purchasing options, an investor has an opportunity to earn profits while limiting his risk of loss," should be balanced by a statement such as, "Of course, an options investor may lose the entire amount committed to options in a relatively short period of time."

(2) It should not be suggested that speculative option strategies are suitable for most investors, or for small investors and statements suggesting the certain availability of a secondary market for options should not be made.

(3) (A) Except as provided in subparagraph (B) below, no written material with respect to options issued by The Options Clearing Corporation ("OCC") may be sent to any person prior to or at the same time with the written material the appropriate current options disclosure document(s) is (are) sent to such person.

(B) Advertisements and other options-related communications may only be used (and copies of the advertisements may only be sent to persons who have not received the appropriate disclosure document) if the material meets the requirements of Rules 134 or 134a under the Securities Act of 1933, as these Rules have been interpreted as applying to OCC options. Under Rules 134 and 134a advertisements are limited to general descriptions of the security being offered and of its issuer and to descriptions regarding the general nature of standardized options markets or options strategies. Advertisements under this Rule shall state the name and address of the person from whom (a) current dis closure document(s) may be obtained (this would usually be the member sponsoring the advertisement). Such advertisements might have the following characteristics: (i) The text of the advertisement may contain a brief description of OCC options, including a statement that the issuer of every OCC option is The Options Clearing Corporation. The text may also contain a brief description of the general attributes and method of operation of The Options Clearing Corporation and/or a description of any of the options traded in different markets, including a discussion of how the price of an option is determined; (ii) The advertisement may include any statement or legend required by any state law or administrative authority; (iii) Advertising designs and devices including borders, scrolls, arrows, pointers, multiple and combined logos and unusual type faces and lettering as well as attention-getting headlines and photographs and other graphics may be used, provided such material is not misleading.

(C) Advertisements and other written communications used prior to delivery of the appropriate disclosure document(s) shall not contain recommendations, or past or projected performance figures, including annualized rates of return.

(4) Communications which contain comparisons, recommendations, statistics or other technical data, or claims made on behalf of options programs or the options expertise of sales persons, shall include, or offer to provide upon request, supporting documentation and shall refer to the current disclosure document(s) available upon request.

(5) Communications concerning an options program (i.e., an investment plan employing the systematic use of one or more options strategies) shall disclose the cumulative history of the program or its unproven nature, and its underlying assumptions.

(6) Standard forms of options worksheets, if adopted by a member for any particular options strategy, must, in addition to compliance with the other applicable provisions of this Section, be uniformly used by such member for that strategy.

(7) Communications which contain projected performance figures or records of the performance of past recommendations or of actual transactions shall disclose all relevant costs, including commissions and interest charges (if applicable with regard to margin transactions) and copies of such communications shall be kept at a place easily accessible to the sales office for the accounts or customers involved.

(8) Communications containing projected performance figures must also:

(A) be plausible and intended as a source of reference or a comparative device to be used in the development of a recommendation;

(B) discuss the risks involved in the proposed transactions and not suggest certainty of future performance;

(C) identify all material assumptions made in such calculations (e.g., "assume options exercised", etc.);

(D) clearly establish parameters relating to such performance figures e.g., to indicate exercise price of option, purchase price of the underlying security and its market price, option premium, anticipated dividends, etc.);

(E) if related to annualized rates of return, be based upon not less than a sixty-day experience, clearly display any formulas used in making the calculations, and include a statement to the effect that the annualized returns cited might be achieved only if the parameters described can be duplicated and there is no certainty of doing so.

(9) Communications containing records or statistics relating to the performance of past recommendations or of actual transactions shall, in addition to complying with other applicable provisions of this section, state that the results presented should not and cannot be viewed as an indicator of future performance, and shall disclose all material assumptions used in the process of annualization if annualized rates of return are used. A Registered Options Principal shall determine that the record or statistics fairly present the status of the recommendations or transactions reported upon and shall initial the report.

[Section 35 amended effective August 2, 1983 and July 1, 1988.]

NYSE, para. 2345

Rule 345.   **Registration of Employees**

.10 **Employees required to be registered or approved.**—See definitions of "branch office manager", "registered representative" and "registered options representative" contained in Rules 9 (¶ 2009) and 10 (¶ 2010) and Rule 700(b)(49) (¶ 2700) and Rule 342 (¶ 2342) for qualification requirements for supervisers.

A "securities lending representative" is defined as any person who has discretion to commit his member or member organization employer to any contract or agreement (written or oral) involving securities lending or borrowing activities with any other person.

A "securities trader" is defined as any person engaged in the purchase or sale of securities or other similar instruments for the account of his employer and who does not transact any business with the public.

.15 Qualifications

(1) **Candidates for registration.**—(a) Candidates for registration, shall qualify by meeting the training requirement and by passing a qualification examinations, as applicable, which is acceptable to the Exchange.

(b) Training and Examination waivers.—Where good cause is shown, the training and/or examination requirement for a candidate for registration may be waived at the discretion of the Exchange. Consideration may be given to previous related employment and to training and/or examination requirements of other self-regulatory organizations. In such cases, the Exchange must be satisfied that the candidate is qualified for registration.

(2) Registered representatives.— The training requirement for registered representative candidates is four months. Such candidates shall pass a qualifying examination acceptable to the Exchange.

(3) Limited registration.—Applications as limited purpose registered representative candidates will be considered by the Exchange for those duly qualified persons whose activities are limited solely to the solicitation or handling of the sale or purchase of: investment company securities and variable contracts, insurance premium funding program, direct participation programs, and municipal securities, among other limited registration categories. Limited purpose registered representative candidates shall qualify by satisfying a two-month training requirement and passing a qualification examination acceptable to the Exchange.

(4) Registered options representative.—Each registred representative who transacts any business with the public in option contracts shall qualify as a"Registered Options Representative" by satisfying the four month training requirement and passing a qualification examination acceptable to the Exchange. (*See Rule 700(b)(49)*.)

(5) Securities traders and their direct supervisers.—Securities traders candidates shall pass a qualification examination acceptable to the Exchange.

(6) Commodities solicitors.—Individuals who are engaged in the solicitation or handling of business in, or the sale of, commodities futures contracts shall demonstrate their competency by satisfying a solicitor's examination requirement of a national commodities exchange, which examination is acceptable to the Exchange.

NASD, para. 2162-2166

¶ 2162   Disclosure on Confirmations

Sec. 12. A member at or before the completion of each transaction with a customer shall give or send to such customer written notification disclosing (1) whether such member is acting as a broker for such customer, as a dealer for his own account, as a broker for some other person, or as a broker for both such customer and some other person; and (2) in any case in which such member is acting as a broker for such customer or for both such customer and some other person, either the name of the person from whom the security was purchased or to whom it was sold for such customer and the date and time when such transaction took place or the fact that such information will be furnished upon the request of such customer, and the source and amount of any commission or other remuneration received or to be received by such member in connection with the transaction.

Explanation of the Board of Governors

"Third Market" Confirmations

Members who act as brokers for customers in transactions in listed securities in the "third market", and members who make markets in such securities, have sought clarification and uniformity regarding the disclosures to be made to customers in situations in which the third market firms had confirmed to the retailing member plus or minus a differential, e.g., "20 plus 1/8" or "20 minus 1/8". In some such cases the confirmation from the retailing member to the customer has indicated that the transaction was effected for the customer at a price of 20 and that the total commission paid by the customer was received by the retailing member, and it failed to disclose that the retailing member, in effect, absorbed the 1/8 differential charged by the third market firm.

In cases such as those described above, where the retailing member effects an agency transaction for his customer with a third market firm at a price which is in line with the then current price on the exchange plus or minus a differential, with the retailer absorbing the differential charged by the third market firm, the following legend should be used by the retailing member to insure adequate disclosure on the confirmation to the customer:

We executed this transaction for you with a dealer who confirmed to us at the above price, plus (in the event you purchased) or less (in the event you sold) a fraction of . . .* per share. This fraction was absorbed by us out of the amount shown as our commission. Full details of this transaction are available upon request.

* The fractional amount absorbed may be shown, for example, as 1/8 or written one-eighth.

Failure to send an appropriate confirmation which conforms to the provisions hereof may involve not only conduct inconsistent with high standards of commercial honor and just and equitable principles of trade, but also violations of rules of the Securities and Exchange Commission, particularly the confirmation rule.

¶ 2163   Disclosure of Control

Sec. 13. A member controlled by, controlling, or under common control with, the issuer of any security, shall, before entering into any contract with or for a customer for the purchase or sale of such security, disclose to such customer the existence of such control, and if such disclosure is not made in writing, it shall be supplemented by the giving or sending of written disclosure at or before the completion of the transaction.

¶ 2164   Disclosure of Participation or Interest in Primary or
Secondary Distribution

Sec. 14. A member who is acting as a broker for a customer or for both such customer and some other person, or a member who is acting as a dealer and who receives or has promise of receiving a fee from a customer for advising such customer with respect to securities, shall, at or before the completion of any transaction for or with such customer in any security in the primary or secondary distribution of which such member is participating or is otherwise financially interested, give such customer written notification of the existence of such participation or interest.

¶ 2166   Offerings "At the Market"

Sec. 16. A member who is participating or who is otherwise financially interested in the primary or secondary distribution of any security which is not admitted to trading on a national securities exchange, shall make no representation that such security is being offered to a customer "at the market" or at a price related to the market price unless such member knows or has reasonable grounds to believe that a market for such security exists other than that made, created, or controlled by such member, or by any person for whom he is acting or with whom he is associated in such distribution, or by any person controlled by, controlling or under common control with such member.

NASD, para. 2197

¶ 2197   Operating Rules For ITS/CAES and CAES

Sec. 37. The Board of Governors is authorized to adopt rules, regulations and procedures required for the operation of the Computer Assisted Execution System including rules, regulations and procedures required for implementation of the linkage of the Computer Assisted Execution System and the Intermarket Trading System and the Intermarket Trading System Plan pursuant to which that linkage was consummated. The rules, regulations and procedures adopted hereunder shall be entitled "CAES Operating Rules" or "ITS/CAES Operating Rules" as the case may be. The Board of Governors shall have the power to alter, amend, supplement or modify the provisions of these rules, regulations and procedures from time to time without recourse to the membership for approval as otherwise would be required by Article IV of the By-Laws.

NASD, para. 2501–2510

301 4-90   **2501**

NATIONAL ASSOCIATION OF SECURITIES DEALERS, INC.

ITS/CAES RULES

... Rules of Practice and Procedure for Intermarket Trading System/Computer Assisted Execution System Automated Interface ...

TABLE OF CONTENTS

RULES OF PRACTICE AND PROCEDURE FOR INTERMARKET TRADING SYSTEM/COMPUTER ASSISTED EXECUTION SYSTEM AUTOMATED INTERFACE

¶ 2501

(a) DEFINITIONS

(1) The term "Participant Market" shall mean the securities trading floor of each participating ITS Exchange and the markets of ITS/CAES Market Makers in ITS securities.

(2) The term "ITS/CAES Market Maker" shall mean a member of the Corporation that is registered as a market maker with the Corporation for the purposes of participation in ITS through CAES with respect to one or more specified ITS securities in which he is then actively registered.

(3) The term "ITS Participant Exchange" shall mean a participant in the ITS Plan that is a national securities exchange.

(4) The term "ITS Plan" shall mean the plan agreed upon by the ITS participants, as from time to time amended in accordance with the provisions therein, and approved by the Securities and Exchange Commission pursuant to Section 11A(a)(3)(B) of the Securities Exchange Act of 1934, as amended (the Act) and Rule 11Aa3-2 thereunder.

(5) The term "ITS System" shall mean the communications network and related equipment that links electronically the ITS Participant Exchanges and ITS/CAES Market Makers as described in the Plan.

(6) The term "ITS Security" shall mean any security which may be traded through the System by an ITS/CAES Market Maker.

(7) The term "Pre-Opening Application" shall mean the application of the System which permits a specialist or ITS/CAES Market Maker who wishes to open his market in an ITS Security to obtain pre-opening interests from other specialists and ITS/CAES Market Makers.

(8) A "third participating market center trade-through", as that term is used in this Rule, occurs whenever an ITS/CAES Market Maker initiates the purchase of an ITS Security by sending a commitment to trade-through the System and such commitment results in an execution at a price which is higher than the price at which the security is being offered (or initiates the sale of such a security by sending a commitment to trade through the System and such commitment results in an execution at a price which is lower than the price at which the security is being bid for) at the time of the purchase (or sale) in another ITS participating market center as reflected by the offer (bid) then being displayed by ITS/CAES Market Makers from such other market center. The member described in the foregoing sentence is referred to in this Rule as the "member who initiated a third participating market center trade-through."

(9) The term "Previous Day's Consolidated Closing Price" as used in these Rules shall mean the last price at which a transaction in a security was reported by the consolidated last sale reporting system on the last previous day on which transactions were reported by such system; provided, however that the "previous day's consolidated closing price" for all Network A or Network B eligible Securities shall be the last price at which a transaction in the stock was reported by the New York Stock Exchange, Inc. ("NYSE") or the American Stock Exchange, Inc. ("Amex"), if, because of unusual market conditions, the NYSE or the Amex price is designated as such pursuant to the ITS plan.

¶ 2502

(b) ITS/CAES REGISTRATION

In order to participate in ITS, a market maker must be registered with the Corporation as an ITS/CAES Market Maker in each security in which a market will be made in ITS. Such registration shall be conditioned upon the ITS/CAES Market Maker's continuing compliance with the following requirements:

(1) registration as a CQS Third Market Maker pursuant to Part III of Schedule D and compliance with the rules in Part III;

(2) execution of an ITS/CAES Market Maker application agreement with the Corporation at least two days prior to the requested date of registration;

(3) compliance with SEC Rule 15c3-1;

(4) compliance with the ITS Plan, SEC Rule 11Ac1-1 and all applicable rules of the Corporation;

(5) the maintenance of continuous two-sided quotations in the absence of the grant of an excused withdrawal or a functional excused withdrawal by the Corporation;

(6) maintenance of the physical security of the equipment used to interface with the ITS System located on the premises of the ITS/CAES Market Makers to prevent the unauthorized entry of communications into the ITS System; and

(7) acceptance and settlement of each ITS System trade that the ITS System identifies as effected by such ITS/CAES Market Maker, or if settlement is to be made through another clearing member, guarantee of the acceptance of settlement of such identified ITS System trade by the clearing member on the regularly scheduled settlement date.

¶ 2503

(c) SUSPENSION OR REVOCATION OF ITS/CAES REGISTRATION

Failure by an ITS/CAES Market Maker to comply with the ITS Plan or any of the rules identified herein shall subject such ITS/CAES Market Maker to censure, fine, suspension or revocation of its registration as an ITS/CAES Market Maker or any other fitting penalty.

¶ 2504

(d) ITS OPERATIONS

(1) All transactions effected through ITS shall be on a "regular way" basis. Each transaction effected through ITS shall be cleared and settled through a clearing agency registered with the Securities and Exchange Commission which maintains facilities through which ITS transactions may be compared and settled.

(2) Any "commitment to trade," which is transmitted by an ITS/CAES Market Maker to another ITS participating market center through ITS, shall be firm and irrevocable for the period of either one or two minutes (specified in accordance with G below) following transmission by the sender. All such commitments to trade shall, at a minimum:

(A) include the number or symbol which identifies the ITS/CAES Market Maker;

(B) direct the commitment to a particular participant market;

(C) specify the security which is the subject of the commitment;

(D) designate the commitment as either a commitment to buy or a commitment to sell;

(E) specify the amount of the security to be bought or sold, which amount shall be for one unit of trading or any multiple thereof;

(F) specify (i) a price equal to the offer or bid price then being furnished by the destination Participant Market, which price shall represent the price at or below which the security is to be bought or the price at or above which the security is to be sold, respectively, (ii) a price at the execution price in the case of a commitment to trade sent in compliance with the block trade rule, or (iii) that the commitment is a commitment to trade "at the market;"

(G) specify either one minute or two minutes as the time period during which the commitment shall be irrevocable, but if the time period is not specified in the commitment, a two minute period shall be assumed. It should be noted that the period of time represented by these designations may be changed in the future by action of the ITS Operating Committee, whose decision as to the applicable period shall be binding upon ITS/CAES Market Makers;

(H) designate the commitment "short" or "short exempt" whenever it is a commitment to sell which, if it should result in an execution in the receiving market, would result in a short sale to which the provisions of paragraph (a) of Rule 10a-1 under the Act would apply.

(3) If a commitment to trade is directed to an ITS/CAES Market Maker, and the execution of such commitment exhausts the size of the quotation being displayed by the ITS/CAES Market Maker, then such ITS/CAES Market Maker shall be placed in a functional excused withdrawal state pending the input of a new two-sided quotation with size into the NASD Consolidated Quotation Service. The new two-sided quotation required of the ITS/CAES Market Maker will be entered as promptly as possible into the NASD Consolidated Quotation Service.

(4) Transactions in ITS securities executed in CAES by ITS/CAES Market Makers or received through the ITS System and executed by an ITS/CAES Market Maker are reported to the CTA Plan Processor by the CAES System at the price specified in the commitment or if executed at a better price, the execution price.

¶ 2505

(e) PRE-OPENING APPLICATION—OPENING BY ITS/CAES MARKET MAKER

The pre-opening application enables an ITS/CAES Market Maker or ITS Participant Exchange in any participant market who wishes to open his market in an ITS Security to obtain through the ITS System or CAES, any pre-opening interest of an ITS Participant Exchange or other ITS/CAES Market Makers registered in that security and/or market makers in other participant markets.

(1) Notification Requirement

Whenever an ITS/CAES Market Maker, in an opening transaction in any ITS/CAES Security, anticipates that the opening transaction will be at a price that represents a change from the security's previous day's consolidated closing price of more than the "applicable price change" (as defined below), he shall notify the other Participant markets of the situation by sending a "pre-opening notification" through the System. Thereafter, the ITS/CAES Market Maker shall not open the security in his market until not less than three minutes* after his transmission of the pre-opening notification. The "applicable price changes" are:

Security	Consolidated Closing Price	Applicable Price Change (More Than)
Network A	Under $15	$\frac{1}{8}$ point
	$15 or over**	$\frac{1}{4}$ point
Network B	$5 or over	$\frac{1}{8}$ point
	Under $5	$\frac{1}{4}$ point

(2) Applicability Following Regulatory Halt

The procedures for and the provisions of the Pre-Opening Application shall also apply prior to any resumption of trading in any Eligible ITS/CAES Security following the initiation of a "Regulatory Halt" by any Participant if both trading has been halted in all exchange markets and, when the affected security is also eligible for trading through the interface between the System and the NASD's Computer Assisted Execution System ("CAES"), the NASD has suspended quotations in the affected security. In such a circumstance, the determination of whether an ITS/CAES Market Maker must send a pre-opening notification shall be made with reference to the price reported by the consolidated last sale reporting system that pertains to the last transaction in the affected security prior to the Regulatory Halt. The Pre-Opening Application shall not apply when trading is resumed (A) following the initiation of a Regulatory Halt if either trading has not been halted in all exchange markets or, when the affected security is also eligible for trading through the interface between the System and CAES, the NASD has not suspended quotations in the affected security or (B) following any other type of halt in trading for any other reason.

(3) Form of Notification

A pre-opening notification shall

(A) be designated as a pre-opening notification ("POA")

(B) identify the ITS/CAES Market Maker and the security involved, and

(C) indicate the "applicable price range" by being formatted as a standard-ized pre-opening administrative message as follows:

POA MMID/XYZ [RANGE]

The price range shall not exceed the "applicable price range" shown below:

Security	Consolidated Closing Price	Applicable Price Range
Network A	Under $50	$\frac{1}{2}$ point
	$50 or over***	1 point
Network B	Under $10	$\frac{1}{2}$ point
	$10 or over	1 point

The price range also shall not straddle the previous day's consolidated closing price, although it may include it as an endpoint (e.g., a $\frac{1}{8}$-$\frac{5}{8}$ price range would be permissible if the previous day's consolidated closing price were $\frac{1}{8}$ or $\frac{5}{8}$, but not if the closing price were $\frac{1}{4}$, $\frac{3}{8}$ or $\frac{1}{2}$).

(4) Decision on Opening Transaction

If an ITS/CAES Market Maker who has issued a pre-opening notification receives "pre-opening responses" through the system containing "obligations to trade" from market-makers in other Participant markets ("responding market-makers"), he shall combine those obligations with orders he already holds in the security and, on the basis of this aggregated information, decide upon the opening transaction in the security. If the ITS/CAES Market Maker has received more than one pre-opening response from a

Participant market, he shall include in such combination only those obligations to trade from such Participant market as are specified in the most recent response, whether or not the most recent response expressly cancels the preceding response(s). An original or revised response received after the ITS/CAES Market Maker has effected his opening transaction shall be to no effect.

(5) Allocation of Imbalances

Whenever pre-opening responses from one or more responding market-makers include obligations to take or supply as principal more than 50 percent of the opening imbalance, the ITS/CAES Market Maker may take or supply as principal 50 percent of the imbalance at the opening price, rounded up or down as may be necessary to avoid the allocation of odd lots. In any such case, where the pre-opening response is from more than one responding market-maker, the ITS/CAES Market Maker shall allocate the remaining imbalance (which may be greater than 50 percent if the ITS/CAES Market Maker elects to take or supply less than 50 percent of the imbalance) among them in proportion to the amount each obligated himself to take or supply as principal at the opening price in his pre-opening response, rounded up or down as may be necessary to avoid the allocation of odd lots. For the purpose of this paragraph, multiple responding market-makers in the same ITS Security in the same Participant market shall be deemed to be a single responding market-maker.

(6) Subsequent Notifications

If, after sending a pre-opening notification, the situation in an ITS/CAES Market Maker's market changes he may have to issue a subsequent pre-opening notification. The three situations requiring subsequent notifications are described below. Subsequent pre-opening notifications shall be standardized pre-opening administrative messages. After sending a subsequent notification, the ITS/CAES Market Maker shall wait either (1) one minute or (2) until the balance of the original three-minute waiting period expires* whichever is longer, before opening his market (i.e., if more than one minute of the initial waiting period has not yet expired at the time the subsequent notification is sent, the ITS/CAES Market Maker must wait for the rest of the period to pass before opening his market).

(A) Increase or Decrease in Applicable Price Range—Where, prior to the ITS/CAES Market Maker's opening of his market in the security, his anticipated opening price shifts so that it (1) is outside of the price range specified in his pre-opening notification but (2) still represents a change from the previous day's consolidated closing price of more than the applicable price change, he shall issue a replacement pre-opening notification (an "additional" notification) before opening his market in the security. An additional notification contains the same kind of information as is required in an original pre-opening notification.

(B) Shift to within Applicable Price Change Parameter—The ITS/CAES Market Maker shall, by issuing a "cancellation" notification, notify the Participant market(s) of the receiving market-maker(s) prior to opening the security if the price at which he anticipates opening his market shifts so that it (1) is outside of the price range specified in his pre-opening notification but (2) does not represent a change from the previous day's consolidated closing price of more than the applicable price change.

(C) Participation as Principal Precluded ("Second Look")—If a responding market-maker who has shown in his pre-opening response interest as a principal at a price better than the anticipated opening price would be precluded from participation as principal in the opening transaction (e.g., his responding principal interest is to sell at a price $1/8$ or more below the opening price established by paired agency orders), the ITS/CAES Market Makers shall send a "second look" notification notifying such responding market-maker of the price and size at which he could participate as principal (i.e., in the parenthetical example above, the total amount of the security that he would have to sell at the $\frac{1}{8}$-better price to permit the opening transaction to occur at that price).

(7) Treatment of Obligations to Trade

In receiving a pre-opening response, an ITS/CAES Market Maker shall accord to any obligation to trade as agent included in the response the same treatment as he would to an order entrusted to him as agent at the same time such obligation was received.

(8) Responses Increasing the Imbalances

An ITS/CAES Market Maker shall not reject a pre-opening response that has the effect of further increasing the existing imbalance for that reason alone.

(9) Reports of Participation

Promptly following the opening in any security as to which an ITS/CAES Market Maker issued a pre-opening notification, the ITS/CAES Market Maker shall report to each Participant responsible for a market in which one or more responding market-makers are located (A) the amount of the security purchased and/or sold, if any, by the responding market-maker(s) in the opening transaction and the price thereof or (B) if the responding market-maker(s)'s response included principal interest at the opening price that did not participate in the opening transaction, the fact that such interest did not so participate.

(10) If either subparagraph (1) or subparagraph (2) requires the ITS/CAES Market Maker to send a pre-opening notification and the CTA Plan also requires that an "indication of interest" be furnished to the consolidated last sale reporting system, then the opening or re-opening indication of interest, if also transmitted through the System in the format of a standardized pre-opening administrative message, shall substitute for and satisfy the requirements of such paragraph. If any such situation, any subsequent indication of interest sent through the System in the format of a standardized pre-opening administrative message concurrently with the furnishing of the indication of interest to the consolidated last sale reporting system shall satisfy the requirements of subparagraphs (6)(A) and (B). For the purpose of subparagraphs (4), (5), (6)(C) and (7)-(9), "pre-opening notification" includes an indication of interest sent through the System in compliance with this subparagraph (10).

¶ 2506

(f) PRE-OPENING APPLICATION—OPENINGS ON OTHER PARTICIPANT MARKETS

(1) Pre-Opening Responses—Whenever an ITS/CAES Market Maker who has received a pre-opening notification from another ITS/CAES Market Maker or ITS Participant Exchange as provided in the ITS Plan in any ITS Security as to which he is registered as an ITS/CAES Market Maker wishes to participate in the opening of that security in the Participant market from which the pre-opening notification was issued, he may do so by sending obligations to trade through the System to such Participant market in a pre-opening response. A pre-opening response shall be designated as a pre-opening response ("POR"), identify the security, and show the ITS/CAES Market Makers' buy and/or sell, interest (if any), both as principal for his own account ("P") and as agent for orders left with him ("A"), at each price level within the price-range indicated in the pre-opening notification (e.g., $40\frac{3}{8}$), reflected on a netted share basis.

The pre-opening response shall be formatted as follows:

POR (MMID) BUY [SELL] A—P 40$\frac{3}{8}$

The response may also show market orders separately. For the purposes of this paragraph (f), "pre-opening notification" includes an "indication of interest" in the format of a standardized pre-opening administrative message received through the System in compliance with Exchange Participant rules concerning tape indications. Such rules provide, in relevant part, that an Exchange specialist sending a pre-opening notification that is required to furnish to the consolidated last sale reporting system an "indication of interest," either under the CTA Plan or the Exchange Rules may substitute for a pre-opening notification this indication of interest if also transmitted through the system in the format of a standardized pre-opening administrative message.

(2) Revised Responses—An ITS/CAES Market Maker may cancel or modify his pre-opening response by sending through the System a revised response that cancels the obligations to trade contained in his original response and, if a modification is desired, that substitutes new obligations to trade stating the ITS/CAES Market Maker's aggregate interest (i.e., his interest reflected in the original response plus any additional interest and/or minus any withdrawn interest) at each price level. Each succeeding response, even if it fails to expressly cancel its predecessor response, shall supersede the predecessor response in its entirety. Any revised response shall be to no effect if received in the Participant market from which the pre-opening notification was issued after the security has opened in such Participant market.

(3) No ITS/CAES Market Maker whether acting as principal or agent, shall send an obligation to trade, commitment to trade or order in any security through the System to any other participant market, prior to the opening of trading in such security on such other market (or prior to the resumption of trading in such security on such other market following a Regulatory Halt as referred to in Section X of the Consolidated Tape Plan) until a pre-opening notification as to such security has been issued from such other market or a quotation has been disseminated from such other market pursuant to Rule 11Ac1-1.

(4) Sole Means of Pre-Opening Routing—Once a pre-opening notification as to any security is received by the ITS/CAES Market Maker through the System, the ITS/CAES Market Makers in such security shall submit obligations to trade that security as principal for his own account to the market from which the pre-opening notification was issued only through the Pre-Opening Application and shall not send orders to trade that security for his own account to such market for participation at the opening in that market by any other means. However, this restriction shall not apply to any order sent to such market by the ITS/CAES Market Maker prior to the issuance of the pre-opening notification.

(5) Duration of Obligations to Trade—Responses to pre-opening notifications shall be voluntary, but each obligation to trade that an ITS/CAES Market Maker includes in any pre-opening response, or in any modification of a pre-opening response, shall remain binding on him, until the security has opened in the market from which the pre-opening notification was issued or until a cancellation or modification of such obligation has been received in such market, and until a subsequent cancellation or modification thereof has been received in such market.

(6) Request for Participation Report—The ITS Plan anticipates that an ITS/CAES Market Maker who has sent one or more obligations to trade in response to a pre-opening notification will request a report through the System as to his participation if he does not receive a report as required promptly following the opening. If, on or following trade date, he does request a report through the System as to his participation before 4:00 p.m. eastern time, and he does not receive a response by 9:30 a.m.

eastern time on the next trading day, he need not accept a later report. If he fails to so request a report, he must accept a report until 4:00 p.m. eastern time on the third trading day following the trade date (i.e., on T+3). The Association does not intend this paragraph to relieve him of the obligation, when he does not receive a report, to request a report as soon as he reasonably should expect to have received it.

¶ 2507

(g) OBLIGATION TO HONOR SYSTEM TRADES

If an ITS/CAES Market Maker or clearing member acting on his behalf is reported on the clearing tape (as adjusted) at the close of any trading day, or shown by the activity reports developed by CAES as constituting a side of a System trade, such ITS/CAES Market Maker or clearing member shall honor such trade on the scheduled settlement date.

¶ 2508

(h) TRADE-THROUGHS

(1) A member registered as an ITS/CAES Market Maker in an ITS/CAES security, shall avoid purchasing or selling such security, whether as principal or agent, at a price which is lower than the bid or higher than the offer displayed from an ITS Participant Exchange or ITS/CAES Market Maker ("trade-through"), unless the following conditions apply:

(A) the size of the bid or offer that is traded-through is for 100 shares;

(B) the ITS/CAES Market Maker is unable to avoid the trade-through because of the systems/equipment failure or malfunction;

(C) the transaction which constituted the trade-through is not a "regular way" contract;

(D) the bid or offer that is traded-through is being displayed from a Market Center whose members are relieved of their obligations under paragraph (c)(2) of Rule 11Ac1-1 with respect to such bid or offer;

(E) the bid or offer that is traded-through has caused a locked or crossed market in the ITS Security; or

(F) the commitment received by an ITS/CAES Market Maker which caused the trade-through was originated by an ITS Participant Exchange.

(G) (1) The transaction involves purchases and sales effected by ITS/CAES Market Makers participating in an opening (or reopening) transaction or (2) any "Block Transaction" as defined in the ITS/CAES Rules.

(H) In the case of a third participating market center trade-through, either:

(1) the ITS/CAES Market Maker who initiated the trade-through (a) had sent a commitment to trade promptly following the trade-through that satisfies the bid or offer traded-through and (b) preceded the commitment with an administrative message stating that the commitment was in satisfaction of a third participating market center trade-through; or

(2) a complaint with respect to the trade-through was not received by the Association through the System from the aggrieved party promptly following the trade-through, and, in any event, within ten (10) minutes from the time the aggrieved party sent a complaint through the System to the ITS participating market center that received the commitment to trade that caused the trade-

through, which first complaint must have been received within five (5) minutes from the time the report of the transaction that constituted the trade-through was disseminated over the high speed line of the consolidated last sale reporting system.

(2) If a trade-through occurs and a complaint is promptly received by the Corporation either through the ITS System from the appropriate ITS Participant Exchange whose member is the aggrieved party or from an ITS/CAES Market Maker, then:

(A) If ITS/CAES Market Makers are on both sides of a principal trade, the price of the transaction which constituted the trade-through shall be corrected, by agreement of the parties, to a price at which a trade-through would not have occurred and the price correction shall be reported through the consolidated last sale reporting system; otherwise (i) the initiating ITS/CAES Market Maker shall satisfy, or cause to be satisfied, the bid or offer traded-through in its entirety at the price of such bid or offer or at the price that caused the trade-through (as determined in accordance with (E) below, or, if the initiating ITS/CAES Market Maker elects not to do so, (ii) the transaction shall be voided.

(B) If an ITS/CAES Market Maker executed the transaction and the contra-side was not an ITS/CAES Market Maker (i) the ITS/CAES Market Maker registered in the security shall satisfy, or cause to be satisfied, the bid or offer traded-through in its entirety at the price of such bid or offer, or, if the ITS/CAES Market Maker elects not to do so, (ii) the price of the transaction which constituted the trade-through shall be corrected by the ITS/CAES Market Maker to a price at which a trade-through would not have occurred and the price correction shall be reported through the consolidated last sale reporting system.

(C) If ITS/CAES Market Makers are on both sides of a trade and one or both are acting as agent, the price of the transaction which constituted the trade-through shall be corrected, by agreement of the parties, to a price at which a trade-through would not have occurred and the price correction shall be reported through the consolidated last sale reporting system; otherwise, the ITS/CAES Market Maker that initiated the transaction shall satisfy, or cause to be satisfied, the bid or offer traded-through in its entirety at the price of such bid or offer.

(D) Whenever the provisions of paragraphs (B) and (C) apply, the customer's order or a portion thereof which was executed in the transaction which constituted the trade-through (whether such order or a portion thereof was executed by the member who initiated the trade-through or by the member on the contraside of the transaction, or both) shall receive the price which caused the trade-through, or the price at which the bid or offer traded-through was satisfied, if it was satisfied pursuant to clause (i) thereof, or the adjusted price, if there was an adjustment pursuant to clause (ii) thereof, whichever price is most beneficial to the order or a portion thereof. Money differences resulting from the application of this paragraph shall be the liability of the member who initiated the trade-through.

(E) the price at which the bid or offer traded-through shall be satisfied shall be the price of such bid or offer except if (i) the transaction that constituted the trade-through was of "block size" but did not constitute a "block trade" (as those terms are defined in the Block Trade Rule) and (ii) the ITS/CAES Market Maker who initiated the trade-through did not make every reasonable effort to satisfy, or cause to be satisfied, through the System the bid or offer traded-through at its price and in its entirety within two (2) minutes from the time the report of the transaction that constituted the trade-through was disseminated over the high speed line of the consolidated last sale reporting system. In the case of such exception, the price at which the bid or offer traded-through shall be satisfied shall be the price that caused the trade-through.

Such complaint shall be considered promptly received when no more than five minutes expire from the time the report of the transaction was disseminated over the high speed line of the consolidated last sale reporting system, unless the transaction is between an ITS/CAES Market Maker and another ITS/CAES Market Maker or ITS Participant Exchange. In the later case, the complaint must be received within ten minutes from the time the aggrieved party sent a complaint through the System to the ITS/CAES Market Maker or ITS Participant Exchange that received the commitment to trade that caused the trade-through, which first complaint must have been received within five minutes from the time the report of the transaction was disseminated over the high speed line of the consolidated last sale reporting system.

(3) (A) The Corporation shall notify the ITS/CAES Market Maker of any trade-through complaint received from an ITS Participant Exchange or ITS/CAES Market Maker. Upon receipt of such notification, the ITS/CAES Market Maker shall promptly respond to the complaining ITS Participant Exchange or ITS/CAES Market Maker. Such response shall set forth either, (i) the conditions specified in paragraph (h)(1) above, or (ii) the corrective action to be taken under paragraph (h)(2) above. If there is more than one ITS/CAES Market Maker that is registered in the ITS Security and participating in the transaction, then the ITS/CAES Market Maker that initiated the transaction will receive notification of the trade-through complaint.

(B) If it is ultimately determined that an ITS/CAES Market Maker has engaged in a trade-through but has not taken corrective action required by paragraph (h)(2) above, then the ITS/CAES Market Maker shall be liable for the lesser of (i) the actual loss proximately caused by the trade-through and suffered by the aggrieved party, or (ii) the loss proximately caused by the trade-through which would have been suffered by the aggrieved party had he purchased or sold the security subject to the trade-through in order to mitigate his loss and had such purchase or sale been effected at the "loss basis price." For purposes of this paragraph the "loss basis price" shall be the price of the next transaction, as reported by the high speed line of the consolidated last sale reporting system in the security in question, after one hour has elapsed from the time the complaint is received (or, if the complaint is so received within the last hour in which transactions are reported on the high speed line of the consolidated last sale reporting system on any day, then the price of the opening transaction in such security reported on such high speed line on the next day on which the security is traded).

(C) Any ITS/CAES Market Maker that becomes the subject of a trade-through by another ITS Participant Exchange or ITS/CAES Market Maker may take whatever steps are necessary to mitigate any potential loss resulting from the trade-through of his bid or offer. Such action shall be promptly communicated to the offending ITS Participant market.

(D) The provisions of this trade-through rule shall not apply in respect to any Participant Exchange which does not have in effect a similar rule imposing similar obligations and responsibilities.

(E) If a complaint of a purported trade-through is received by the Corporation and the complained-of transaction resulted from an ITS/CAES Market Maker's execution of a commitment to trade received from another ITS/CAES

Market Maker or ITS Participant Exchange, the ITS/CAES Market Maker should, if circumstances permit, make reasonable efforts to notify the complaining party, as promptly as practicable following receipt of the complaint, (A) that the transaction was not initiated by the ITS/CAES Market Maker and (B) of the identity of the ITS/CAES Market Maker or ITS Participant Exchange that originated the commitment. Neither compliance nor non-compliance with the preceding sentence shall be the basis for any liability of the ITS/CAES Market Maker for any loss associated with the complained-of transaction.

¶ 2509

(i) LOCKED OR CROSSED MARKETS

(1) A member registered as an ITS/CAES Market Maker in an ITS/CAES Security that makes a bid (offer) for such security at a price which equals the offering (bid) price at that time from an ITS Participant Exchange or ITS/CAES Market Maker has created what is referred to in this rule as a "locked market."

(2) A member registered as an ITS/CAES Market Maker in an ITS/CAES Security that makes a bid (offer) for such security at a price which exceeds (is less than) the offering (bid) price at that time from an ITS Participant Exchange or ITS/ CAES Market Maker has created what is referred to in this rule as a "crossed market."

(3) An ITS/CAES Market Maker who makes a bid or offer and in so doing creates a locked or crossed market with another ITS Participant or ITS/CAES Market Maker shall promptly send to such other ITS Participant Exchange or ITS/CAES Market Maker a commitment to trade seeking either the bid or offer which was locked or crossed, unless excused by operation of paragraph (4) below. Such commitment shall be for either the number of shares he has bid for (offered) or the number of shares offered (bid for) on the ITS Participant Exchange or by the ITS/CAES Market Maker, whichever is less.

(4) The provisions of paragraph (3) above shall not apply when:

(A) the bid or offer in the ITS Participating market center is for 100 shares;

(B) the issuance of the commitment to trade referred to above would be prohibited by SEC Rule 10a-1;

(C) the ITS/CAES Market Maker who causes a locked or crossed market is unable to comply with the provisions of paragraph (3) above because of a systems/ equipment failure or malfunction;

(D) the bid or offer that causes the locked or crossed market is not for a "regular way" contract;

(E) the locked or crossed market occurs at a time when, with respect to the ITS Security which is the subject of the locked or crossed market, members of the ITS participating market center to which the commitment to trade would be sent pursuant to paragraph (3) above are relieved of their obligations under paragraph (c)(2) of Rule 11Ac1-1.

(F) the transaction (1) involves purchases and sales effected by ITS/CAES Market Maker's participating in an opening or (reopening) transaction or (2) any "Block Transaction" as defined in the ITS/CAES Rules.

¶ 2510

(j) BLOCK TRANSACTIONS

(1) An ITS/CAES Market Maker who executes a "block transaction" in an ITS/CAES security in which he is registered as an ITS/CAES Market Maker at an execution price outside the best quotation for the security displayed by any ITS participant market or other ITS/CAES Market Maker, shall, upon executing the block trade, send to each other participant market and each ITS/CAES Market Maker displaying a bid or offer (as the case may be) superior to the execution price, a commitment to trade, at the execution price, to satisfy the number of shares displayed in that participant market's bid or offer.

(2) For purposes of this section, a block transaction shall be a trade that:

(A) involves 10,000 or more shares of a common stock traded through ITS (an "ITS Security") or a quantity of any such security having a market value of $200,000 or more ("block size").

(B) is effected at a price outside the bid or offer displayed from another ITS participating market center: and

(C) involves either.

(i) a cross of block size (where the member represents all of one side of the transaction and all or a portion of the other side), or

(ii) any other transaction of block size (i.e., in which the ITS/CAES Market Maker represents an order of block size on one side of the transaction only) that is not the result of an execution at the current bid or offer of the ITS/CAES Market Maker.

Contemporaneous transactions at the same price filling an order or orders then or theretofore represented by the ITS/CAES Market Maker (including transactions resulting from commitments to trade sent by the ITS/CAES Market Maker pursuant to paragraph (1) above) shall be deemed to constitute a single transaction for the purpose of this definition.

(3) A "current bid or offer" of the ITS/CAES Market Maker, as that term is used in paragraph (2)(C)(ii) above, means the price of the current quotation displayed by the ITS/CAES Market Maker established independently of the order to buy or sell.

(4) A "bid or offer" displayed from another ITS participating market center (or any derivative phrase), as that term is used in this Rule, means the current quotations from another ITS participating market center displayed to the ITS/CAES Market Maker as required by the ITS Plan, and does not include "away-from-the-market" limit orders or other interests that may be represented in such other ITS participating market center.

(5) Inapplicability—Paragraph (1) above shall not apply under the following conditions:

(A) the size of the better-priced bid or offer displayed by another ITS participating market center was for 100 shares;

(B) the ITS/CAES Market Maker representing the block-size order(s) made every reasonable effort to satisfy through ITS a better-priced bid or offer displayed by another ITS participating market center but was unable to because of a systems/equipment failure or malfunction;

(C) the block trade was not a "regular way" contract;

(D) the bid or offer that is traded-through is being displayed from a Market Center whose members are relieved of their obligations under paragraph (c)(2) of Rule 11Ac1-1 with respect to such bid or offer;

(E) the bid or offer that is traded-through has caused a locked or crossed market in the ITS Security; or

(F) the better-priced bid or offer was being displayed from an ITS participating market center whose members were relieved of their obligations with respect to such bid or offer under paragraph (c)(2) of Rule 11Ac1-1 pursuant to the "unusual market" except to paragraph (b)(3) of Rule 11Ac1-1;

(G) the better-priced bid or offer had caused a "locked or crossed market", in the ITS Security that was the subject of the block trade.

(k) Authority to Cancel or Adjust Transactions

(1) In circumstances in which the Association deems it necessary to maintain a fair and orderly market and to protect investors and the public interest, the Association may, pursuant to the procedures set forth in Section 70 of the Uniform Practice Code and Article IX of the NASD Code of Procedure, declare any transaction arising out of the use or operation of the ITS/CAES system, null and void on the grounds that one or more of the terms of the transaction are clearly erroneous; and the Association may reallocate stock between ITS/CAES Market Makers to correct an erroneous transaction.

(2) For purposes of this section, the terms of the transaction are clearly erroneous when there is an obvious error in any term, such as price, number of shares or other unit of trading, identification of the security, or if a specific commitment to trade has been executed with the wrong ITS/CAES market maker.

NASD, para. 2155

¶ 2155   Publication of Transactions and Quotations

Sec. 5. No member shall publish or circulate, or cause to be published or circulated, any notice, circular, advertisement, newspaper article, investment service, or communication of any kind which purports to report any transaction as a purchase or sale of any security unless such member believes that such transaction was a bona fide purchase or sale of such security; or which purports to quote the bid price or asked price for any security, unless such member believes that such quotation represents a bona fide bid for, or offer of, such security. If nominal quotations are used or given, they shall be clearly stated or indicated to be only nominal quotations.

Interpretation of the Board of Governors

Manipulative and Deceptive Quotations

Article III, Section 1 of the Rules of Fair Practice provides that:

"A member, in the conduct of his business, shall observe high standards of commercial honor and just and equitable principles of trade."

Article III, Section 5 of the Rules of Fair Practice provides that:

"No member shall publish or circulate, or cause to be published or circulated, any notice, circular, advertisement, newspaper article, investment service, or communication of any kind which purports to report any transaction as a purchase or sale of any security unless such member believes that such transaction was a bona fide purchase or sale of such security; or which purports to quote the bid price or asked price for any security, unless such member believes that such quotation represents a bona fide bid for, or offer of, such security. If nominal quotations are used or given, they shall be clearly stated or indicated to be only nominal quotations."

Article III, Section 18 of the Rules of Fair Practice provides that:

"No member shall effect any transaction in, or induce the purchase or sale of, any security by means of any manipulative, deceptive or other fraudulent device or contrivance."

It would be inconsistent with the above provisions for a member to publish or circulate or cause to be published or circulated, by any means whatsoever, any report of any securities transaction or of any purchase or sale of any security unless such member knows or has reason to believe that such transaction was a bona fide transaction, purchase or sale.

Similarly, it would be inconsistent with the above provisions for a member, for itself or for any other person, to publish or circulate or to cause to be published or circulated, by any means whatsoever, any quotation for any security without having reasonable cause to believe that such quotation is a bona fide quotation, is not fictitious and is not published or circulated or caused to be published or circulated for any fraudulent, deceptive or manipulative purpose.

For the purposes of this interpretation, the term "quotation" shall include any bid or offer or any formula, such as "bid wanted" or "offer wanted", designed to induce any person to make or submit any bid or offer.

NASD, para. 1919–1922

¶ 1917   Schedule G

This Schedule as been adopted pursuant to Article VII, Section I (a)(6) of the Corporation's By-Laws and shall apply to all over-the-counter transactions in listed securities that are required to be reported to the Consolidated Tape ("eligible securities"), as provided in the Plan filed by the Association pursuant to Rule 11Aa3-1 under the Securities Exchange Act of 1934 ("Plan").

¶ 1918

Section 1—Definitions

(a) Terms used in this Schedule shall have the meaning as defined in the By-Laws and Rules of Fair Practice, Rule 11Aa3-1 and the Plan, unless otherwise defined in this Schedule.

(b) "Consolidated Tape" means the consolidated transaction reporting system for the dissemination of last sale reports in eligible securities required to be reported pursuant to the Plan.

(c) "Designated Reporting Member" means a member of the Association that is registered as a Third Market Maker in an eligible security pursuant to Part III of Schedule D of the Association's By-Laws.

(d) "Eligible securities" means all common stocks, preferred stocks, long-term warrants, and rights entitling the holder to acquire an eligible security, listed or admitted to unlisted trading privileges on the American Stock Exchange or the New York Stock Exchange, and securities listed on regional stock exchanges, which substantially meet the original listing requirements of the New York Stock Exchange or the American Stock Exchange. A list of eligible securities listed on regional stock exchanges is attached to this Schedule.

(e) "Non-Designated Reporting Member" means all members of the Association which are not Designated Reporting Members.

¶ 1919

Section 2—Transaction Reporting

(a) When and How Transaction Reported

(1) Designated Reporting Members shall transmit through the NASDAQ Transaction Reporting System, within 90 seconds after execution, last sale reports of transactions in eligible securities during the trading hours of the Consolidated Tape otherwise than on a national securities exchange. Designated Reporting Members shall transmit through the NASDAQ Transaction Reporting System, within 90 seconds after execution, last sale reports of transactions in eligible securities executed in the United States otherwise than on a national securities exchange between 4:00 p.m. and 4:30 p.m. Eastern Time. Transactions not reported within 90 seconds after execution shall be designated as late.

(2) Non-Designated Reporting Members shall transmit through the Transactions Reporting System, or if such System is unavailable, via Telex, TWX or telephone, to the NASDAQ Department in New York City, within 90 seconds after execution, last sale reports of transactions in eligible securities executed during the trading hours of the Consolidated Tape otherwise than on a national securities exchange unless all of the following criteria are met:

(A) The aggregate number of shares of eligible securities which the member executed and is required to report does not exceed 1,000 shares in any one trading day; and

(B) The total dollar amount of shares of eligible securities which the member executed and is required to report does not exceed $25,000 in any one trading day; and

(C) The member's transactions in eligible securities have not exceeded the limits of (A) or (B) above on five or more of the previous ten trading days.

Non-Designated Reporting Members shall transmit through the NASDAQ Reporting System, or if such System is unavailable, via Telex, TWX or telephone, to the NASDAQ Department in New York City, within 90 seconds after execution, last sale reports of transactions in eligible securities executed in the United States otherwise than on a national securities exchange between the hours of 4:00 p.m. and 4:30 p.m. Eastern Time unless all of the criteria specified in paragraphs (A), (B) and (C) above are met.

Transactions not reported within 90 seconds after execution shall be designated as late. If the member has reason to believe its transactions in a given day will exceed the above limits, it shall report all transactions in eligible securities within 90 seconds after execution; in addition, if the member exceeds the above limits at any time during the trading day, it shall immediately report and designate as late any unreported transactions in eligible securities executed earlier that day.

(3) Non-Designated Reporting Members shall report weekly to the NASDAQ Department in New York City, on Form T, last sale reports of transactions in eligible securities which are not required by paragraph (2) to be reported within 90 seconds after execution.

(4) All Members shall report weekly to the NASDAQ Department in New York City, on Form T, last sale reports of transactions in eligible securities executed outside the hours of 9:30 a.m. and 4:30 p.m. Eastern Time.

(5) All trade tickets for transactions in eligible securities shall be time-stamped at the time of execution.

(b) Which Party Reports Transaction

(1) Transactions executed on an exchange are reported by the exchange and shall not be reported by members.

(2) In transactions between two Designated Reporting Members, only the member representing the sell side shall report.

(3) In transactions between a Designated Reporting Member and a Non-Designated Reporting Member, only the Designated Reporting Member shall report.

(4) In transactions between the Non-Designated Reporting Members, only the member representing the sell side shall report.

(c) Information To Be Reported

Each last sale report shall contain the following information:

(1) Stock symbol of the eligible security;

(2) Number of shares (odd lots shall not be reported);

(3) Price of the transaction as required by paragraph (d) below;

(4) A symbol indicating whether the transaction is a buy, sell, or cross.

(d) Procedures for Reporting Price and Volume

Members which are required to report pursuant to paragraph (b) above shall transmit last sale reports for all purchases and sales in eligible securities in the following manner:

(1) For agency transactions, report the number of shares and the price excluding the commission charged.

Example:

SELL as agent 100 shares at 40

less a commission of $12.50;

REPORT 100 shares at 40.

(2) For dual agency transactions, report the number of shares only once, and report the price excluding the commission charged.

Example:

SELL as agent 100 shares at 40

less a commission of $12.50;

BUY as agent 100 shares at 40 plus

a commission of $12.50;

REPORT 100 shares at 40.

(3) For principal transactions, except as provided below, report each purchase and sale transaction separately and report the number of shares and the price. For principal transactions which are executed at a price which includes a mark-up, mark-down or service charge, the price reported shall exclude the mark-up, mark-down or service charge. Such reported price shall be reasonably related to the prevailing market, taking into consideration all relevant circumstances including, but not limited to, market conditions with respect to the security, the number of shares invoved in the transaction, the published bids and offers with size at the time of the execution (including the reporting firm's own quotation), accessibility to market centers publishing bids and offers with size, the cost of execution and the expenses involved in clearing the transaction.

Example:

BUY as principal 100 shares from another member at 40 (no mark-down included).

REPORT 100 shares at 40.

Example:

BUY as principal 100 shares from a customer at $39\frac{3}{4}$, which includes a $\frac{1}{8}$ mark-down from prevailing market of $39\frac{7}{8}$;

REPORT 100 shares at $39\frac{7}{8}$.

Example:

SELL as principal 100 shares to a customer at $40\frac{1}{8}$, which includes a $\frac{1}{8}$ mark-up from the prevailing market of 40;

REPORT 100 shares at 40.

Exception:

A "riskless" principal transaction in which a member that is not a market maker in the security, after having received from a customer an order to buy, purchases the security as principal from another member or customer to satisfy the order to buy or, after having received from a customer an order to sell, sells the security as principal to another member or customer to satisfy the order to sell, shall be reported as one transaction in the same manner as an agency transaction, excluding the mark-up or mark-down. A riskless principal transaction in which a member purchases or sells the security on an exchange to satisfy a customer's order will be reported by the exchange and the member shall not report.

Example:

BUY as principal 100 shares from another member at 40 to fill an existing order;

SELL as principal 100 shares to a customer at 40 plus mark-up of $12.50;

REPORT 100 shares at 40.

Example:

BUY as principal 100 shares on an exchange at 40

to fill an existing order;

SELL as principal 100 shares to a customer at 40

plus a mark-up of $12.50.

DO NOT REPORT (will be reported by exchange)

(e) Transactions Not Required To Be Reported

The following types of transactions shall not be reported for inclusion on the Consolidated Tape:

(1) transactions executed on an exchange;

(2) odd-lot transactions;

(3) transactions which are part of a primary distribution by an issuer or of a registered secondary distribution (other than "shelf distributions") or of an unregistered secondary distribution effected off the floor of an exchange,

(4) transactions made in reliance on Section 4(2) of the Securities Act of 1933,

(5) transactions where the buyer and seller have agreed to trade at a price substantially unrelated to the current market for the security, e.g., to enable the seller to make a gift;

(6) the acquisition of securities by a member as principal in anticipation of making an immediate exchange distribution or exchange offering on an exchange;

(7) purchases of securities off the floor of an exchange pursuant to a tender offer; and

(8) purchases or sales of securities effected upon the exercise of an option pursuant to the terms thereof or the exercise of any other right to acquire securities at a pre-established consideration unrelated to the current market.

[Schedule G, Sec. 2 amended effective February 26, 1987 and December 17, 1986.]

¶ 1920

Section 3—Suspension of Trading

(a) Members shall promptly notify the Association whenever they have knowledge of any matter related to an eligible security or the issuer thereof which has not been adequately disclosed to the public or where they have knowledge of a regulatory problem relating to such security.

(b) Whenever any market for any eligible security halts or suspends trading in such security, members may continue to conduct trading in such security during the period of any such halt or suspension and shall continue to report all last sale prices reflecting transactions in such security.

¶ 1921

Section 4—Trading Practices

(a) No member shall execute or cause to be executed or participate in an account for which there are executed purchases of any eligible security at successively higher prices, or sales of any such security at successively lower prices, for the purpose of creating or inducing a false, misleading or artificial appearance of activity in such security or for the purpose of unduly or improperly influencing the market price for such security or for the purpose of establishing a price which does not reflect the true state of the market in such security.

(b) No member shall, for the purpose of creating or inducing a false or misleading appearance of activity in an eligible security or creating or inducing a false or misleading appearance with respect to the market in such security;

(1) execute any transaction in such security which involves no change in the beneficial ownership thereof, or

(2) enter any order or orders for the purchase of such security with the knowledge that an order or orders of substantially the same size, and at substantially the same price, for the sale of any such security, has been or will be entered by or for the same or different parties, or

(3) enter any order or orders for the sale of any such security with the knowledge that an order or orders of substantially the same size, and at substantially the same price, for the purchase of such security, has been or will be entered by or for the same or different parties.

(c) No member shall execute purchases or sales of any eligible security for any account in which such member is directly or indirectly interested, which purchases or sales are excessive in view of the member's financial resources or in view of the market for such security.

(d) No member shall participate or have any interest, directly or indirectly, in the profits of a manipulative operation or knowingly manage or finance a manipulative operation.

(1) Any pool, syndicate or joint account organized or used intentionally for the purpose of unfairly influencing the market price of an eligible security shall be deemed to be a manipulative operation.

(2) The solicitation of subscriptions to or the acceptance of discretionary orders from any such pool, syndicate or joint account shall be deemed to be managing a manipulative operation.

(3) The carrying on margin of a position in such securities or the advancing of credit through loans to any such pool, syndicate or joint account shall be deemed to be financing a manipulative operation.

(e) No member shall make any statement or circulate and disseminate any information concerning any eligible security which such member knows or has reasonable grounds for believing is false or misleading or would improperly influence the market price of such security.

(f) (1) No member shall (i) personally buy or initiate the purchase of an eligible security for its own account or for any account in which it or any person associated with it is directly or indirectly interested, while such member holds or has knowledge that any person associated with it holds an unexecuted market order to buy such security in the unit of trading for a customer, or (ii) sell or initiate the sale of any such security for any such account, while it personally holds or has knowledge that any person associated with it holds an unexecuted market order to sell such security in the unit of trading for a customer.

(2) No member shall (i) buy or initiate the purchase of any such security for any such account, at or below the price at which it personally holds or has knowledge that any person associated with it holds an unexecuted limited price order to buy such security in the unit of trading for a customer, or (ii) sell or initiate the sale of any such security for any such account at or above the price at which it personally holds or has knowledge that any person associated with it holds an unexecuted limited price order to sell such security in the unit of trading for a customer.

(3) The provisions of this section shall not apply (i) to any purchase or sale of any such security in an amount less than the unit of trading made by a member to offset odd-lot orders for customers, (ii) to any purchase or sale of any such security upon terms for delivery other than those spe cified in such unexecuted market or limited price order, or (iii) to any unexecuted order that is subject to a condition that has not been satisfied.

(g) No member or person associated with a member shall, directly or indirectly, hold any interest or participation in any joint account for buying or selling an eligible security, unless such joint account is promptly reported to the Association. The report should contain the following information for each account:

(1) Name of the account, with names of all participants and their respective interests in profits and losses;

(2) a statement regarding the purpose of the account;

(3) name of the member carrying and clearing the account; and

(4) a copy of any written agreement or instrument relating to the account.

(h) No member shall offer that a transaction or transactions to buy or sell an eligible security will influence the closing transaction on the Consolidated Tape.

(i) (1) No member shall accept a stop order in an eligible security.

(i) A buy stop order is an order to buy which becomes a market order when a transaction takes place at or above the stop price.

(ii) A sell stop order is an order to sell which becomes a market order when a transaction takes place at or below the stop price.

(2) Members may accept stop limit orders in eligible securities where the stop price and the limit price are the same. When a transaction occurs at the stop price, the order to buy or sell becomes a limit order at the stop price.

¶ 1922

Section 5—Eligible Securities

Transactions required to be reported on the Consolidated Tape (eligible securities) include all common stocks, preferred stocks, long-term warrants, and rights entitling the holder to acquire an eligible security, listed on the American Stock Exchange and/ or the New York Stock Exchange and the following securities listed on regional stock exchanges.

NASD, para. 1867

¶ 1867   REPORTING TRANSACTIONS IN NASDAQ NATIONAL MARKET SYSTEM DESIGNATED SECURITIES

Section 2—Transaction Reporting

(a) When and How Transaction Reported

(1) Registered Reporting Market Makers shall transmit through the Transaction Reporting System, within 90 seconds after execution, last sale reports of transactions in designated securities executed during the hours of the Transaction Reporting System. Transactions not reported within 90 seconds after execution shall be designated as late.

(2) Non-Registered Reporting Members shall transmit through the Transaction Reporting System, or if such System is unavailable, via Telex, TWX or telephone to the NASDAQ Operations Department in New York City, within 90

seconds after execution, last sale reports of transactions in designated securities executed during the trading hours of the Transaction Reporting System unless all of the following criteria are met:

(A) The aggregate number of shares of designated securities which the member executed and is required to report during the trading day does not exceed 1,000 shares; and

(B) The total dollar amount of shares of designated securities which the member executed and is required to report during the trading day does not exceed $25,000; and

(C) The member's transactions in designated securities have not exceeded the limits of (A) or (B) above on five or more of the previous ten trading days.

Transactions not reported within 90 seconds after execution shall be designated as late. If the member has reason to believe its transactions in a given day will exceed the above limits, it shall report all transactions in designated securities within 90 seconds after execution; in addition, if the member exceeds the above limits at any time during the trading day, it shall immediately report and designate as late any unreported transactions in designated securities executed earlier that day.

(3) Non-Registered Reporting Members shall report weekly to the NASDAQ Operations Department in New York City, on a form designated by the Board of Governors, last sale reports of transactions in designated securities which are not required by paragraph (2) to be reported within 90 seconds after execution.

(4) Last sale reports of transactions in designated securities executed between the hours of 4:00 p.m. and 5:00 p.m. Eastern Time shall be transmitted through the Transaction Reporting System no later than 5:00 p.m. Eastern Time.

(5) All members shall report weekly to the NASDAQ Operations Department in New York City, on a form designated by the Board of Governors, last sale reports of transactions in designated securities executed outside the hours of 9:30 a.m. and 5:00 p.m. Eastern Time.

(6) All trade tickets for transactions in eligible securities shall be time-stamped at the time of execution.

(b) Which Party Reports Transaction

(1) In transactions between two Registered Reporting Market Makers, only the member representing the sell side shall report.

(2) In transactions between a Registered Reporting Market Maker and a Non-Registered Reporting Member, only the Registered Reporting Market Maker shall report.

(3) In transactions between two Non-Registered Reporting Members, only the Member representing the sell side shall report.

(4) In transactions between a member and a customer, the member shall report.

(c) Information To Be Reported

Each last sale report shall contain the following information:

(1) NASDAQ symbol of the designated security;

(2) Number of shares (odd lots shall not be reported);

(3) Price of the transaction as required by paragraph (d) below.

(4) A symbol indicating whether the transaction is a buy, sell, or cross.

(d) Procedures for Reporting Price and Volume

Members which are required to report pursuant to paragraph (b) above shall transmit last sale reports for all purchases and sales in designated securities in the following manner:

(1) For agency transactions, report the number of shares and the price excluding the commission charged.

Example

SELL as agent 100 shares at 40

less a commission of $12.50;

REPORT 100 shares at 40.

(2) For dual agency transactions, report the number of shares only once, and report the price excluding the commission charged.

Example:

SELL as agent 100 shares at 40

less a commission of $12.50;

BUY as agent 100 shares at 40 plus

a commission of $12.50;

REPORT 100 shares at 40.

(3) For principal transactions, except as provided below, report each purchase and sale transaction separately and report the number of shares and the price. For principal transactions which are executed at a price which includes a mark-up, mark-down or service charge, the price reported shall exclude the mark-up, mark-down or service charge. Such reported price shall be reasonably related to the prevailing market, taking into consideration all relevant circumstances including, but not limited to, market conditions with respect to the security, the number of shares involved in the transaction, the published bids and offers with size at the time of the execution (including the reporting firm's own quotation), the cost of execution and the expenses involved in clearing the transaction.

Example:

BUY as principal 100 shares from another

member at 40 (no mark-down included).

REPORT 100 shares at 40.

Example:

BUY as principal 100 shares from a customer

at $39\frac{7}{8}$ which includes a $\frac{1}{8}$ mark-down

from prevailing market at 40;

REPORT 100 shares at 40.

Example:

SELL as principal 100 shares to a customer

at $40\frac{1}{8}$, which includes a $\frac{1}{8}$ mark-up

from the prevailing market of 40;

REPORT 100 shares at 40.

Example:

BUY as principal 10,000 shares from a
customer at $39\frac{3}{4}$, which includes a $\frac{1}{4}$
mark-down or service charge from the
prevailing market of 40;
REPORT 10,000 shares at 40.

Exception:

A "riskless" principal transaction in which a member that is not a market maker in the security after having received from a customer an order to buy, purchases the security as principal from another member or customer to satisfy the order to buy or, after having received from a customer an order to sell, sells the security as principal to another member or customer to satisfy the order to sell, shall be reported as one transaction in the same manner as an agency transaction, excluding the mark-up or mark-down.

Example:

SELL as principal 100 shares to another
member at 40 to fill an existing order;
BUY as principal 100 shares from a customer
at 40 minus a mark-down of $12.50;
REPORT 100 shares at 40.

(e) Transactions Not Required To Be Reported

The following types of transactions shall not be reported:

(1) transactions executed through the Computer Assisted Execution System ("CAES");

(2) odd-lot transactions;

(3) transactions which are part of a primary distribution by an issuer or of a registered secondary distribution (other than "shelf distributions") or of an unregistered secondary distribution;

(4) transactions made in reliance on Section 4(2) of the Securities Act of 1933;

(5) transactions where the buyer and seller have agreed to trade at a price substantially unrelated to the current market for the security, e.g., to enable the seller to make a gift;

(6) purchases or sales of securities effected upon the exercise of an option pursuant to the terms thereof or the exercise of any other right to acquire securities at a preestablished consideration unrelated to the current market.

(f) Aggregation of Transaction Reports

(1) Under the following conditions, individual executions of orders in a security at the same price may be aggregated, for transaction reporting purposes, into a single transaction report.

(A) Orders received prior to the opening of the reporting member's market in the security and simultaneously executed at the opening. Also, orders received during a trading or quotation halt in the security and executed simultaneously when trading or quotations resume. In no event shall a member delay its opening or resumption of quotations for the purpose of aggregating transactions.

Example: A firm receives, prior to its market opening, several market orders to sell which total 10,000 shares. All such orders are simultaneously executed at the opening at a reported price of 40. REPORT 10,000 shares at 40.

(B) Simultaneous executions by the member of customer transactions at the same price, e.g., a number of limit orders being executed at the same time when a limit price has been reached.

Example: A firm has several customer limit orders to sell which total 10,000 shares at a limit price of 40. That price is reached and all such orders are executed simultaneously. REPORT 10,000 shares at 40.

(C) Orders relayed to the trading department of the reporting member for simultaneous execution at the same price.

Example: A firm purchases a block of 50,000 shares from an institution at a reported price of 40. REPORT 50,000 at 40.

Subsequently, one of the firm's branch offices transmits to the firm's trading department for execution customer buy orders in the security totalling 12,500 shares at a reported price of 40. REPORT 12,500 at 40.

Subsequently, another branch office transmits to the firm's trading department for execution customer buy orders totalling 15,000 shares in the security at a reported price of 40. REPORT 15,000 at 40.

Example: Due to a major change in market conditions, a firm's trading department receives from a branch office for execution customer market orders to sell totalling 10,000 shares. All are executed at a reported price of 40. REPORT 10,000 at 40.

(D) Orders received or initiated by the reporting member which are impractical to report individually and are executed at the same price within 60 seconds of execution of the initial transaction; provided however, that no individual order of 10,000 shares or more may be aggregated in a transaction report and that the aggregated transaction report shall be made within 90 seconds of the initial execution reported therein. Furthermore, it is not permissible for a member to withhold reporting a trade in anticipation of aggregating the transaction with other transactions.

Examples: A reporting member receives and executes the following orders at the following times and desires to aggregate reports to the maximum extent permitted under this rule.

First Example

11:01:00 500 shares at 40

11:01:05 500 shares at 40

11:01:10 9,000 shares at 40

11:01:15 500 shares at 40

REPORT: 10,500 shares at 40 within ninety seconds of 11:01.

Second Example

11:01:00 100 shares at 40

11:01:10 11,000 shares at 40

11:01:30 300 shares at 40

REPORT: 400 shares within ninety seconds of 11:01 and 11,000 shares within ninety seconds of 11:01:10 (individual transactions of 10,000 shares or more must be reported separately).

Third Example

11:01:00 100 shares at 40

11:01:15 500 shares at 40

11:01:30 200 shares at 40

11:02:30 400 shares at 40

REPORT: 800 shares at 40 within ninety seconds of 11:01 and 400 shares at 40 within ninety seconds of 11:02:30 (the last trade is not within sixty seconds of the first and must, therefore, be reported separately).

(2) The reporting member shall identify aggregated transaction reports and order tickets of aggregated trades in a manner directed by the Corporation.

[Amended effective August 3, 1984; renumbered as Part X effective September 13, 1985; redesignated as Part XII effective July 20, 1987; amended effective October 1, 1987.]

NASD, para. 2156, 2158

¶ 2156   Offers at Stated Prices

Sec. 6. No member shall make an offer to buy from or sell to any person any security at a stated price unless such member is prepared to purchase or sell, as the case may be, at such price and under such conditions as are stated at the time of such offer to buy or sell.

Policy of the Board of Governors

Policy With Respect to Firmness of Quotations

Members and persons associated with members in the over-the-counter market make trading decisions and set prices for customers upon the basis of telephone and wire quotations as well as quotations in the National Quotation Bureau sheets. In some instances a dealer's quotations, purportedly firm, are, in fact, so qualified upon further inquiry as to constitute "backing away" by the quoting dealer. Further, dealers who place quotations in the sheets have been found to be unwilling to make firm bids or offers upon inquiry in such a way as to pose a question as to the validity of the quotations originally inserted. Such "backing away" from quotations disrupts the normal operation of the over-the-counter market.

Members, of course, change interdealer quotations constantly in the course of trading, but under normal circumstances where the member is making a "firm trading market" in any security, it is expected at least to buy or sell a normal unit of trading in the quoted stock at its then prevailing quotations unless clearly designated as not firm or firm for less than a normal unit of trading when supplied by the member. It should be realized, however, that at times contemporaneous transactions or substantial changes in inventory might well require dealers to quote a "subject market" temporarily.

In order to insure the integrity of quotations, every member has an obligation to correctly identify the nature of its quotations when they are supplied to others. In addition, each member furnishing quotations must insure that it is adequately staffed to respond to inquiries during the normal business hours of such member.

It shall be deemed conduct inconsistent with high standards of commercial honor and just and equitable principles of trade if a member fails to fulfill its obligations as outlined above.

¶ 2158   Securities Taken in Trade

Sec. 8. (a) A member engaged in a fixed price offering, who purchases or arranges the purchase of securities taken in trade, shall purchase the securities at a fair market price at the time of purchase or shall act as agent in the sale of such securities and charge a normal commission therefor.

(b) When used in this section—

(1) the term "taken in trade" means the purchase by a member as principal, or as agent for the account of another, of a security from a customer pursuant to an agreement or understanding that the customer purchase securities from the member which are part of a fixed price offering.

(2) the term "fair market price" means a price not higher than the price at which the securities would be purchased from the customer or from a similarly situated customer in the ordinary course of business by a dealer in such securities in transactions of similar size and having similar characteristics but not involving a security taken in trade.

(3) the term "normal commission" means an amount of commission which the member would normally charge to that customer or a similarly situated customer in the ordinary course of business in transactions of similar size and having similar characteristics but not involving a security taken in trade.

(c) For purposes of this Section a member shall be

(1) deemed, with respect to securities other than common stocks, to have taken such securities in trade at a fair market price when the price paid is not higher than the highest independent bid for the securities at the time of purchase, if such bid quotations for the securities are readily available.

(2) presumed, with respect to common stocks, to have taken such common stocks in trade at a fair market price when the price paid is not higher than the highest independent bid for the securities at the time of purchase, if such bid quotations for the securities are readily available.

(3) presumed to have taken a security in trade at a price higher than a fair market price when the price paid is higher than the lowest independent offer for the securities at the time of purchase, if such offer quotations for the securities are readily available.

(d) A member, in connection with every transaction subject to this Section, shall with respect to

(1) common stocks, which are traded on a national securities exchange or for which quotations are entered in an automated quotation system, obtain the necessary bid and offer quotations from the national securities exchange or from the automated quotation system; and

(2) other securities and common stocks not included in subparagraph (1) of this subsection (d) obtain directly or with the assistance of an independent agent bid and offer quotations from two or more independent dealers relating to the securities to be taken in trade or, if such quotations are not readily available, exercise its best efforts to

obtain such quotations with respect to securities having similar characteristics and of similar quality as those to be taken in trade.

(e) A member who purchases a security taken in trade shall keep or cause to be kept adequate records to demonstrate compliance with this Section and shall preserve the records for at least 24 months after the transaction. If an independent agent is used for the purpose of obtaining quotations, the member must request the agent to identify the dealers from whom the quotations were obtained and the time and date they were obtained or request the agent to keep and maintain for at least 24 months a record containing such information.

Interpretation of the Board of Governors

Safe Harbor and Presumption of Compliance

Subsection 8(c)(1) provides that, with respect to a security, other than a common stock, a member will be deemed to have paid the fair market price for a security taken in trade if the price paid is no higher than the highest independent bid for the securities at the time of purchase, if bid quotations are readily available. Subsection 8(c)(2) provides, with respect to common stock, that a member will be presumed to have paid no more than the fair market price for shares of common stock taken in trade if the price paid for the shares of common stock taken in trade is no higher than the highest independent bid for such shares at the time of purchase, if bid quotations are readily available. The presumption of compliance contained in Subsection (c)(2) may be rebutted by the Association upon a showing that the price paid, in fact, exceeded the fair market price as that term is defined in Subsection (b)(2). Inasmuch as a member is presumed to have complied with Section 8 when taking common stock in trade at a price no higher than the highest independent bid, the Association will have a heavier burden of demonstrating noncompliance in such circumstances than it has in the circumstances described below where there is neither a presumption of compliance nor one of noncompliance. Nonetheless, the factors described below in the sections "No Presumptions" and the "Presumption of Noncompliance," will be relevant in determining whether the Association has rebutted the presumption. Particular attention will be directed to the size of the transaction and the relative liquidity of the position.

Presumption of Noncompliance

Subsection 8(c)(3) establishes a presumption of noncompliance with Section 8 if securities for which offer quotations are readily available are taken in trade at prices higher than the lowest independent offer. While the presumption in Subsection 8(c)(3) is not conclusive, it may be rebutted by the member only in an exceptional or unusual case. To rebut the presumption of noncompliance, all factors relevant to the transaction must be taken into consideration, including, among other things, whether a customer of a member has given an indication of interest to purchase the securities taken in trade at a higher price; the member's pattern of trading in the securities or comparable securities at the time of the transaction; the member's position in, and the availability of, the securities taken in trade; the size of the transaction; and the amount by which the price paid exceeds the lowest independent offer.

The several factors described in the preceding paragraph will be relevant to determining whether the presumption of noncompliance has been rebutted. The existence of only one such factor, however, will not necessarily be sufficient to meet the heavy burden placed on a member, though in a given case it may be sufficient. In any event, all facts and circumstances must be considered. For example, a member may be able to satisfy the burden of demonstrating that fair market price was paid by showing that the price paid did not exceed the price, less an amount equal to a normal commission on an agency transaction, at which a customer had given the member an indication of interest to purchase the securities, or that the member held a short position in the security purchased, that it desired to cover that short position, that the availability of the security was scarce and that the amount of securities taken in trade could not have been acquired at a lower price.

No Presumptions

In instances when a member takes a security in trade at a price higher than the highest independent bid and not higher than the lowest independent offer, or when bid and offer quotations are not readily available, there shall be no safe harbor and there shall be neither a presumption of compliance nor one of noncompliance with Section 8. In such circumstances, whether the price paid is the fair market price will be determined by reference to the definition of fair market price in Subsection (b)(2).

Subsection (b)(2) states generally that fair market price is the price a dealer would pay for the amount of securities taken in trade if purchased from the customer in the ordinary course of business but not involving a security taken in trade. Accordingly, the price paid by a member or other dealers for the same security or a comparable security as that taken in trade but not in a transaction involving a security taken in trade will be relevant in determining compliance with Section 8. In comparing such transactions, all facts and circumstances will be considered, including such things as the size of the transactions being compared, the time of each transaction and the difference in price paid. In determining whether fair market price has been paid, other relevant factors, including those set forth above with respect to rebutting the presumption of noncompliance, will also be considered.

Quotations

Subsections 8(d) and (e) obligate members taking securities in trade to obtain and maintain records of bid and offer quotations. If the securities taken in trade are common stocks that are traded on a national securities exchange or for which quotations are entered in an automated quotation system, the quotations must be obtained from any such exchange or automated quotation system at the time of purchase.

Quotations for all other securities must be obtained from at least two independent dealers at the time of purchase. While the quotations from two dealers in such circumstances need not be for the specific size of the transaction, they must be for a size corresponding generally to the amount of the securities to be taken in trade. Quotations relating only to an odd lot, such as those typically available from a dealer in bonds on a national securities exchange, will not be acceptable for a transaction of a size normally traded by institutions.

If bid and offer quotations required by Subsection (d) are not readily available and a member is able to obtain such quotations for comparable securities, such quotations will be treated as though they are quotations for the securities taken in trade in determining whether the "safe harbor" in Subsection (c)(1) and the presumptions in Subsections (c)(2) and (c)(3) are applicable. In such circumstances, however, the member's determination of what constitutes comparable securities may be challenged.

Adequate Records

If the member purchases securities taken in trade at a price which is no higher than the lowest independent offer as determined according to this Section, it will have kept adequate records if it records the time and date quotations were received, the identity of the security to which the quotations pertain, the identity of the dealer from whom, or the exchange or quotation system from which, the quotations were obtained, and the quotations furnished. If a member uses the services of an independent agent to obtain the quotations and the agent does not disclose the identity of the dealers from whom quotations were obtained, the member will have kept adequate records if it otherwise complies with subsection (e) of Section 8 hereof and it records the time and date it received the quotations from the agent, the identity of the agent, and the quotations transmitted by the agent.

If a member takes a security in trade and pays more than the lowest independent offer, it will have kept adequate records if, in addition to the foregoing records, it keeps records of all relevant factors it considered important in concluding that the price paid for the securities was fair market price.

Fair Market Price at the Time of Purchase

Swap transactions that are arranged before the effectiveness of a fixed price offering are not generally viewed as being legally consummated until effectiveness of the fixed price offering. Nonetheless, the fair market price of securities taken in trade in such situations is normally determined at the time of the pricing of the fixed price offering, which occurs on the day before effectiveness usually in the afternoon, and the swap is arranged on the basis of that price. In such cases, for purposes of Section 8(a), the determination of the "fair market price at the time of purchase" of the securities to be taken in trade may be made as of the time of pricing of the fixed price offering. As to swaps agreed upon at a time after effectiveness of the offering, fair market price of the swapped securities must be determined as of the time the transaction is legally consummated.

NASD, para. 2196, 2157

¶ 2196　　　Transactions With Related Persons

Sec. 36

(a) Except as otherwise provided in Subsection (d) of this Section, no member engaged in a fixed price offering of securities shall sell the securities to, or place the securities with, any person or account which is a related person of the member unless such related person is itself subject to this Section or is a non-member foreign broker or dealer who has entered into the agreements required by Subsection 24(c) of this Article.

(b) For purposes of this Section 36, a "related person" of a member includes any person or account which directly or indirectly owns, is owned by or is under common ownership with the member.

(c) A person owns another person or account for purposes of this Section if the person directly or indirectly:

(1) has the right to participate to the extent of more than 25 percent in the profits of the other person; or

(2) owns beneficially more than 25 percent of the outstanding voting securities of the person.

(d) The prohibition contained in Subsection (a) does not apply to the sale of securities to, or the placement of securities in, a trading or investment account of a member or a related person of a member after termination of the fixed price offering if the member or the related person of the member has made a bona fide public offering of the securities. A member or a related person of a member is presumed not to have made a bona fide public offering for the purpose of this subsection if the securities being offered immediately trade in the secondary market at a price or prices which are at or above the public offering price.

Interpretation of the Board of Governors

Transactions With Related Persons

A member who is acting, or plans to act, as sponsor of a unit investment trust will not violate Section 36 if it accumulates securities with respect to which the member has acted as a syndicate member, selling group member or reallowance dealer in an account of the member or related person of the member if, at the time of accumulation, the member in good faith intends to deposit the securities into the unit investment trust as the public offering price and intends to make a bona fide public offering of the participation units of that trust. Members engaged in such activity, however, will continue to be subject to the Board of Governors Interpretation of Article III, Section 1 of the Rules of Fair Practice concerning Free-Riding and Withholding.

While Subsection (d) of Section 36 provides that a person is presumed not to have made a bona fide public offering if, immediately following the termination of the fixed price offering, the securities trade at or above the public offering price, there is no presumption that a person has made a bona fide public offering if, at such time, the securities trade below the public offering price. Whether a person has made a bona fide public offering will be determined on the basis of all relevant facts and circumstances.

¶ 2157   Disclosure of Price in Selling Agreements

Concessions

Sec. 7. Selling syndicate agreements or selling group agreements shall set forth the price at which the securities are to be sold to the public or the formula by which such price can be ascertained, and shall state clearly to whom and under what circumstances concessions, if any, may be allowed.

NASD, para. 2167

¶ 2167   Solicitation of Purchases on an Exchange to Facilitate a Distribution of Securities

Sec. 17. (a) No member, participating or otherwise financially interested in the primary or secondary distribution of any security of any issuer, shall,

(1) pay or offer or agree to pay, directly or indirectly, to any person any compensation for soliciting another to purchase any security of the same issuer on a national securities exchange, or for purchasing any security of the same issuer on any such exchange for any account other than the account of the member who pays or is to pay such compensation; or

(2) sell, offer to sell or induce an offer to buy such security, or deliver such security after sale, if, in connection with such distribution, such member has paid, or has offered or agreed to pay, directly or indirectly, to any person, any compensation for soliciting another to purchase any security of the same issuer on any national securities exchange, or for purchasing any security of the same issuer on any such exchange for any account other than the account of the member who has paid or is to pay such compensation.

(b) No member, participating or otherwise financially interested in the primary or secondary distribution of any security of any issuer, shall cause a purchase or sale of any security of the same issuer on a national securities exchange by paying or offering or agreeing to pay, directly or indirectly, to any person any compensation for soliciting another to purchase such security on any such exchange, or for purchasing such security on any such exchange for any account other than the account of the member who pays or is to pay such compensation.

(c) The provisions of this rule shall not apply in respect to any salary paid by a member to any person regularly employed by him whose ordinary duties include the solicitation or execution of brokerage orders on a national securities exchange, if such salary represents only ordinary compensation for the discharge by such person of such duties in the regular course of his employment, and is not paid, in whole or in part, directly or indirectly, for the inducement by such person of the purchase or sale on a national securities exchange of any security of the issuer of the security in the primary or secondary distribution of which such member is participating or otherwise financially interested.

NASD, para. 1782 1783

¶ 1782   Schedule C

This schedule has been prepared pursuant to the provisions of Section 2 of Article II of the Corporation's By-Laws and contains the requirements of registration with the Corporation of persons associated with a member, including the requirements for qualification examinations to be given.

¶ 1783   APPLICATIONS FOR MEMBERSHIP

(1) *Pre-Membership Interviews*

(a) An applicant for membership in the Corporation shall furnish to the District Office for the District in which it has or intends to have its principal place of business:

(1) a copy of its current submission to the Securities and Exchange Commission pursuant to Rule 15b1-2(c) under the Securities Exchange Act of 1934;

(2) its most recent trial balance, balance sheet, supporting schedules and computation of net capital;

(3) a copy of its written supervisory procedures;

(4) a list of all officers, directors, general partners, employees and other persons who will be associated with it at the time of admission to membership;

(5) a description of business activities in which it intends to engage; and

(6) such other relevant information and documents as may be requested by the District Office.

(b) Before an applicant shall be admitted to membership in the Corporation, and within a reasonable period of time after receipt of the foregoing information, the District Office shall schedule a pre-membership interview at which responsible personnel of the applicant, as determined by the District Office, shall personally appear at the District Office. At such interview, the applicant shall demonstrate, in accordance with the criteria listed in Section (1)(c) hereof, the appropriateness of its admission to membership in the Corporation to conduct the type of business intended in the manner specified in its submission.

(c) The pre-membership interview shall address the applicant's business plans to determine their adequacy and consistency with the federal securities laws and the rules of the Corporation; good business practices in the investment banking or securities business; a member's fiduciary obligation to its customers; and the public interest and the protection of investors. The pre-membership interview shall review, among other things,

(1) the nature, adequacy, source and permanence of applicant's capital and its arrangements for additional capital should a business need arise;

(2) the applicant's proposed recordkeeping system;

(3) the applicant's proposed internal procedures, including compliance procedures;

(4) the applicant's familiarity with applicable NASD rules and federal securities laws;

(5) the applicant's capability to properly conduct the type of business intended in view of the:

A. number, experience and qualifications of the persons to be associated with it at the time of its admission to membership;

B. its planned facilities;

C. arrangements, if any, with banks, clearing corporations and others, to assist it in the conduct of its securities business;

D. supervisory personnel, methods and procedures; and

(6) other factors relevant to the scope and operation of its business.

(d) Within thirty days after the conclusion of such pre-membership interview, or if further information and/or documents are requested, within thirty days of the receipt of such information or documents, the District Office shall notify the applicant in writing whether its application has been granted, denied, or granted subject to restrictions on its business activities, and provide the rationale for such determination.

(e) In all cases where restrictions are placed on its business activities, the applicant shall, prior to approval of membership, execute a written agreement with the Corporation agreeing to abide by the restrictions specified in the determination and agreeing not to modify its business activities in any way inconsistent with such agreement without first notifying the Corporation and receiving its written approval.

(2) Procedures for Review by the District Committee and the Board of Governors.

(a) The District Office's determination shall be reviewed by the relevant District Committee upon request made by the applicant within 15 days of receipt of the notification. Until completion of the District Committee's review, an applicant denied membership shall not be admitted to membership, and an applicant admitted to membership subject to restrictions on its business activities may engage in business consistent with such restrictions only after it has executed the agreement required by paragraph (1)(e) hereof.

(b) In connection with review by the District Committee, the applicant shall have the right to appear before a subcommittee of the District Committee, or the subcommittee may require such appearance. The applicant may present evidence and be represented by counsel. The subcommittee may request additional information to assist it in reaching a determination. A record shall be kept of the proceedings.

(c) The District Committee, after consideration of the record before it and the criteria contained in Section (1)(c), above, shall within a reasonable time after close of the record, notify the applicant in writing that its application has been granted, denied or granted subject to restrictions on its business activities and provide the rationale for such determination. The District Committee's determination shall be made independent of the determination of the District Office and shall not be limited thereby.

(d) The District Committee's determination shall be reviewed by the Board of Governors upon request made by the applicant within 15 days of receipt of the notification. The Board of Governors may call for review any District Committee determination within forty-five days of the date of the notification. During the pendency of such review, an applicant denied membership shall not be admitted to membership and an applicant admitted to membership subject to restrictions on its business activities may engage in business consistent with such restrictions only after it has executed the agreement required by paragraph (1)(e), above.

(e) In connection with review by the Board of Governors, the applicant shall have the right to appear before a subcommittee of the Board of Governors, or the subcommittee may require such appearance. The applicant may supplement the record developed before the District Committee and be represented by counsel. The subcommittee may request additional information to assist the Board of Governors in reaching a determination. A record shall be kept of the proceedings.

(f) The Board of Governors, after consideration of the record before it, and the criteria stated in Section (1)(c), above, shall within a reasonable period of time after close of the record before it, notify the applicant in writing that its application has been granted, denied or granted subject to restrictions on its business activities, and provide the rationale for such determination. The Board of Governors' determination shall be made independent of the determinations of the District Office and District Committee and shall not be limited thereby.

NASD, para. 1785

III

¶ 1785   REGISTRATION OF REPRESENTATIVES

(1) Registration Requirements

(a) *All Representatives Must be Registered*—All persons engaged or to be engaged in the investment banking or securities business of a member who are to function as representatives shall be registered as such with the Corporation in the category of registration appropriate to the function to be performed as specified in Part III, Section (2) hereof. Before their registrations can become effective, they shall pass a Qualification Examination for Representatives appropriate to the category of registration as specified by the Board of Governors. A member shall not maintain a representative registration with the Corporation for any person (i) who is no longer active in the member's investment banking or securities business, (ii) who is no longer functioning as a representative, or (iii) where the sole purpose is to avoid the examination requirement prescribed in Section (2)(c) hereof. A member shall not make application for the registration of any person as representative where there in no intent to employ such person in the member's investment banking or securities business. A member may, however, maintain or make application for the registration as a representative of a person who performs legal, compliance, internal audit, or similar responsibilities for the member, or a person who performs administrative support functions for registered personnel, or a person engaged in the investment banking or securities business of a foreign securities affiliate or subsidiary of the member.

(b) *Definition of Representative*—Persons associated with a member, including assistant officers other than principals, who are engaged in the investment banking or securities business for the member including the functions of supervision, solicitation or conduct of business in securities or who are engaged in the training of persons associated with a member for any of these functions are designated as representatives.

(c) *Requirement for Examination on Lapse of Registration*—Any person whose most recent registration as a representative or principal has been terminated for a period of two (2) or more years immediately preceding the date of receipt by the Corporation of a new application shall be required to pass a Qualification Examination for Representatives appropriate to the category of registration as specified in Part III, Section 2 hereof.

(2) *Categories of Representative Registration*

(a) *General Securities Representative*—

(i) Each person associated with a member who is included within the definition of a Representative in Part III, Section (1) hereof, shall be required to register with the Corporation as a General Securities Representative and shall pass an appropriate Qualification Examination before such registration may become effective unless his activities are so limited as to qualify him for one or more of the limited categories of representative registration specified hereafter. A person whose activities in investment banking or securities business are so limited is not, however, precluded from attempting to become qualified for registration as a General Securities Representative, and if qualified, may become so registered.

(ii) Except as provided in Part III, Section (1)(c) hereof:

(a.) Any person who was registered with the Corporation as a Representative prior to September 1, 1974, shall be qualified to be registered with the Corporation as a General Securities Representative.

(b.) A person who applied for registration as a Representative prior to September 1, 1974, and who became registered as a Representative prior to April 1, 1975 by virtue of having passed the Qualification Examination for Representatives (Test Series 1) shall be qualified to be registered as a General Securities Representative.

(c.) A person who applied for registration as a Representative on or after September 1, 1974, or who was registered as a Representative on or after April 1, 1975 by virtue of having passed the Qualification Examination for Registered Representatives (Test Series 1) shall be qualified to be registered only as a Limited Representative—

Investment Company and Variable Contracts Products and as a Limited Representative—Direct Participation Programs as defined in Part III, Sections 2(b) and 2(c) hereof.

(d.) A person who was registered as a Representative after September 1, 1974 by virtue of having passed the General Securities Representative Examination (Test Series 7) shall be qualified to be registered as a General Securities Representative.

(e) A person who was registered as a Registered Representative For Sale of Variable Contracts Only shall be qualified to be registered as a Limited Representative—Investment Company and Variable Contracts Products.

(iii) A person registered as a General Securities Representative shall not be qualified to function as a Registered Options Representative unless he is also qualified and registered as such pursuant to the provisions of Part III, Section 2(d) hereof.

(b) *Limited Representative—Investment Company and Variable Contracts Products—*

(i) Each person associated with a member who is included within the definition of a representative in Part III, Section (1) hereof may register with the Corporation as a Limited Representative—Investment Company and Variable Contract Products if:

a. his activities in the investment banking or securities business are limited to those activities enumerated in Part II, Section 2(c)(i)a. hereof, and,

b. he passes an appropriate Qualification Examination for Limited Representative—Investment Company and Variable Contracts Products.

(ii) A person qualified solely as a Limited Representative—Investment Company and Variable Contracts Products shall not be qualified to function as a representative in any area not prescribed in Part III, Section 2(c)(i)a. hereof.

(c) *Limited Representative—Direct Participation Programs*

(i) Each person associated with a member who is included within the definition of a representative in Part III, Section (1) hereof may register with the Corporation as a Limited Representative—Direct Participation Programs if:

a. his activities in the investment banking or securities business are limited to the solicitation, purchase and/or sale of direct participation programs as defined in Part II, Section (2)(d) hereof, and,

b. he passes an appropriate Qualification Examination for Limited Representative—Direct Participation Programs.

(ii) A person qualified solely as a Limited Representative—Direct Participation Programs shall not be qualified to function in any area not prescribed by Part III, Section 2(c)(i) hereof.

(d) *Registered Options Representative—*Each person associated with a member whose activities in the investment banking or securities business include the solicitation and/or sale of option contracts shall be required to be certified as a Registered Options Representative and to pass an appropriate certification examination for such or an equivalent examination acceptable to the Corporation. Registered Options Representatives qualified in either put or call options shall not engage in both put and call option transactions until such time as they are qualified in both such options. Members shall be required to report to the Corporation the names of any associated persons certified as Registered Options Representatives pursuant to an examination approved by the Corporation. Registered Options Representatives must also be qualified with the Corporation as either General Securities Representatives or as Limited

Representative—Corporate Securities; provided, however, Registered Options Representatives of members that are members of a national securities exchange which has standards of approval acceptable to the Corporation may be deemed to be approved by and certified with the Corporation, so long as such representatives are approved by and registered with such exchange.

(e) *Limited Representative—Corporate Securities*

(ii) Each person associated with a member who is included within the definition of a representative in Part III, Section (1) hereof may register with the Corporation as a Limited Representative—Corporate Securities if:

(a.) Such person's activities in the investment banking or securities business involve the solicitation, purchase, and/or sale of a "security," as that term is defined in Section 3(a)(10) of the Securities Exchange Act of 1934 (the "Act"), and do not include such activities with respect to the following securities unless such person is separately qualified and registered in the category or categories of registration related to these securities:

(1.) Municipal securities as defined in Section 3(a)(29) of the Act;

(2.) Option securities as defined in Article III, Section 33(d) of the NASD Rules of Fair Practice;

(3.) Redeemable securities of companies registered pursuant to the Investment Company Act of 1940, except for money market funds;

(4.) Variable contracts of insurance companies registered pursuant to the Securities Act of 1933; and/or,

(5.) Direct Participation Programs as defined in Part II, Section 2(d)(ii) hereof.

(b.) Such person passes an appropriate qualification examination for Limited Representative-Corporate Securities.

(ii) A person qualified solely as a Limited Representative—Corporate Securities shall not be qualified to function in any area not prescribed by Part III, Section 2(e)(i) hereof.

[Part II amended effective August 1, 1980; amended effective 1981; redesignated Part III effective July 26, 1984; Part III amended effective May 20, 1988 and August 25, 1988; amended effective July 17, 1989.]

IV

REGISTRATION OF ASSISTANT REPRESENTATIVES—ORDER PROCESSING

¶ 1785A

(1) Registration Requirements.

(a) *All Assistant Representatives—Order Processing Must Be Registered*—All persons associated with a member who are to function as Assistant Representatives—Order Processing shall be registered with the Corporation. Before their registrations can become effective, they shall pass a Qualification Examination for Assistant Representatives—Order Processing as specified by the Board of Governors.

(b) *Definition of Assistant Representative—Order Processing*—Persons associated with a member who accept unsolicited customer orders for submission for execution by the member are designated as Assistant Representatives—Order Processing.

(c) *Requirement for Examination on Lapse of Registration*—Any persons whose most recent registration as an Assistant Representative—Order Processing has been terminated for a period of two (2) or more years immediately preceding the date of receipt by the Corporation of a new application shall be required to pass a Qualification Examination for Assistant Representative—Order Processing.

(2) Restrictions

(a) *Prohibited Activities*—An Assistant Representative—Order Processing may not solicit transactions or new accounts on behalf of the member, render investment advice, make recommendations to customers regarding the appropriateness of securities transactions, or effect transactions in securities markets on behalf of the member.

Act of 1934, 15c3-1

NET CAPITAL RULE

¶ 4101   **Introduction**

On September 1, 1975, Rule 15c3-1 under the Securities Exchange Act of 1934 was amended for the purpose of establishing a uniform and comprehensive net capital standard for the securities industry. The amended rule discontinues the prior exemption for members of certain national securities exchanges. Also, pursuant to Securities Exchange Act Release No. 11854, dated November 20, 1975, the rule's applicability has been extended to cover broker-dealers engaged in municipal securities activities.

In most cases, the amended rule does not alter the minimum net capital requirements previously established for most types of broker-dealer activity. However, the method of computing net capital and aggregate indebtedness has been altered with the result that the entry level for certain prospective members of the Association seeking to do a business in the securities industry has been raised. Also, the rule introduces a debt-equity ratio requirement for the purpose of restricing or limiting the amount of subordinated debt that may be used to finance a firm's business activities. The amended provisions for the computation of net capital include an alternative method which permits a net capital requirement dependent on the Reserve Formula calculated pursuant to Rule 15c3-3 under the Securities Exchange Act of 1934. This requirement is optional and replaces the traditional ratio test of aggregate indebtedness to net capital. With the adoption of the alternative method of computing net capital, companion adjustments were also made in the custodial provisions and Reserve Formula requirements under Rule 15c3-3.

The rule as amended contains a table of contents, referencing each provision, followed by the rule itself and four appendixes dealing with areas unique to certain broker-dealers.

Following is the text of the Net Capital Rule:

¶ 4111   Net Capital Requirements for Brokers or Dealers
Rule 15c3-1
TABLE OF CONTENTS

Minimum Net Capital Requirements

Filing   subparagraph (c)(6)

Subordination Agreements in Effect Prior to Adoption   subparagraph (c)(7)

Reg. § 240.15c3-1. (a) No broker or dealer shall permit his aggregate indebtedness to all other persons to exceed 1500 percent of his net capital. No broker or dealer which has elected the provisions of paragraph (f) of this section (in which case he is not subject to the aggregate indebtedness limitation in this paragraph) shall permit his net capital to be less than 2 percent of aggregate debit items as computed in accordance with § 240.15c3-3a of this chapter. No broker or dealer registered as a futures commission merchant shall permit his net capital to be less than 4% of the funds required to be segregated pursuant to the Commodity Exchange Act and the regulations thereunder (less the market value of commodity options purchased by option customers on or subject to the rules of a contract market, each such deduction not to exceed the amount of funds in the option customer's account).

Brokers or Dealers Engaging in a General Securities Business

(1) No broker or dealer, except one who operates under paragraph (f) of this section, shall permit his aggregate indebtedness to all other persons to exceed 800 percentum of his net capital for 12 months after commencing business as a broker or dealer and, except as otherwise provided for in paragraph (a) or paragraph (f) of this section, the broker or dealer shall at all times have and maintain net capital of not less than $25,000 or, $25,000 plus the sum of each broker or dealer subsidiary's minimum net capital requirement which is consolidated pursuant to Appendix (C), 17 CFR 240.15c3-1c.

Brokers Who Do Not Generally Carry Customers' Accounts

(2) Notwithstanding the provisions of subparagraph (a)(1) hereof, a broker or dealer shall have and maintain net capital of not less than $5,000 if he does not hold funds or securities for, or owe money or securities to, customers and does not carry accounts of, or for, customers, except as provided for in subdivision (v) below, and he conducts his business in accordance with one or more of the following conditions and does not engage in any other securities activities;

(i) He introduces and forwards as a broker all transactions and accounts of customers to another broker or dealer who carries such accounts on a fully disclosed basis and (the introducing broker or dealer) promptly forwards all of the funds and securities of customers received in connection with his activities as a broker;

(ii) He participates, as broker or dealer, in underwritings on a "best efforts" or "all or none" basis in accordance with the provisions of 17 CFR 240.15c2-4(b)(2) and he promptly forwards to an independent escrow agent customers' checks, drafts, notes or other evidences of indebtedness received in connection therewith which shall be made payable to such escrow agent;

(iii) He promptly forwards, as broker or dealer, subscriptions for securities to the issuer, underwriter, sponsor or other distributor of such securities and receives checks, drafts, notes or other evidences of indebtedness payable solely to the issuer, underwriter, sponsor or other distributor who delivers the securities purchased directly to the subscriber;

(iv) He effects an occasional transaction in securities for his own investment account with or through another registered broker or dealer;

(v) He acts as broker or dealer with respect to the purchase, sale and redemption of redeemable shares of registered investment companies or of interests or participations in insurance company separate accounts, whether or not registered as an investment company, and he promptly transmits all funds and delivers all securities received in connection with such activities;

(vi) He introduces and forwards all customers and all principal transactions with customers to another broker or dealer who carries such accounts on a fully disclosed basis and promptly forwards all funds and securities received in connection with his activities as a broker or dealer and does not otherwise hold funds or securities for or owe money or securities to, customers and does not otherwise carry proprietary (except as provided in subdivision (a)(2)(iv) above) or customer accounts and his activities as dealer are limited to holding firm orders of customers and in connection therewith: (A) in the case of a buy order, prior to executing such customers' order, purchases as principal the same number of shares or purchases shares to accumulate the number of shares necessary to complete the order which shall be cleared through another broker or dealer or (B) in the case of a sell order, prior to executing such customers' order, sells as principal the same number of shares or a portion thereof which shall be cleared through another broker or dealer; or

(vii) He effects, but does not clear, transactions in securities as a broker on a registered national securities exchange for the account of another member of such exchange.

Brokers or Dealers Engaged Solely in the Sale of Redeemable Shares of Registered Investment Companies and Certain Other Share Accounts

(3) Net capital of not less than $2,500 shall be maintained by a broker or dealer who engages in no other securities activities except those prescribed in this subparagraph and who meets all of the following conditions:

(i) His dealer transactions are limited to the purchase, sale and redemption of redeemable shares of registered investment companies or of interests or participations in an insurance company separate account, except that he may also effect an occasional transaction in other securities for his own investment account with or through another registered broker or dealer;

(ii) His transactions as broker are limited to: (A) the sale and redemption of redeemable shares of registered investment companies or of interests or participations in an insurance company separate account whether or not registered as an investment company; (B) the solicitation of share accounts for savings and loan associations insured by an instrumentality of the United States; and, (C) the sale of securities for the account of a customer to obtain funds for immediate reinvestment in redeemable securities of registered investment companies; and

(iii) He promptly transmits all funds and delivers all securities received in connection with his activities as a broker or dealer, and does not otherwise hold funds or securities for, or owe money or securities to, customers.

Certain Additional Capital Requirements for Market Makers

(4) Notwithstanding the provisions of subparagraphs (a)(1), (2) and (3), a broker or dealer engaged in activities as a market maker as defined in subparagraph (c)(8) of this section shall maintain net capital in an amount not less than $2,500 for each security in which he makes a market (unless a security in which he makes a market has a market value of $5 or less in which event the amount of net capital shall be not less than $500 for each such security) based on the average number of such markets made by such broker or dealer during the 30 days immediately preceding the computation date, except that under no circumstances shall he have net capital less than that required by subparagraph (a)(1), or be required to maintain net capital of more than $100,000 unless otherwise required by the provisions of paragraphs (a) or (f) of this section.

Certain Additional Capital Requirements for Brokers or Dealers Engaged in the Sale of Options

(5) Notwithstanding the provisions of subparagraphs (a)(1)-(4) a broker or dealer who endorses or writes options, including but not limited to puts, calls, straddles, strips, or straps otherwise than on a registered national securities exchange or a facility of a registered national securities association shall have net capital of not less than $50,000.

Market Makers, Specialists and Certain Other Dealers

(6)(i) A dealer who meets the conditions of paragraph (a)(6)(ii) of this section may elect to operate under this paragraph (a)(6) and thereby not apply, except to the extent required by this paragraph (a)(6), the provisions of paragraphs (c)(2)(vi), (f)(3) or Appendix A, 17 CFR 240.15c3-1a, of this section to market maker and specialist transactions and, in lieu thereof, apply thereto the provisions of paragraph (a)(6)(iii) of this section.

(ii) This paragraph (a)(6) shall be available to a dealer who does not effect transactions with other than brokers or dealers, who does not carry customer accounts, who does not effect transactions in unlisted options, and whose market maker or specialist transactions are effected through and carried in a market maker or specialist account cleared by another broker or dealer as provided in paragraph (a)(6)(iv) of this section.

(iii) A dealer who elects to operate pursuant to this paragraph (a)(6) shall at all times maintain a liquidating equity in respect of securities positions in his market maker or specialist account at least equal to:

(A) An amount equal to 25 percent (5 percent in the case of exempted securities) of the market value of the long positions and 30 percent of the market value of the short positions; *provided, however,* in the case of long or short positions in options and long or short positions in securities other than options which relate to a bona-fide hedged position as defined in paragraph (c)(2)(x)(C) of this section, such amount shall equal the deductions in respect of such positions specified by paragraph (c)(2)(x)(A)(*1*)-(9) of this section.

(B) Such lesser requirement as may be approved by the Commission under specified terms and conditions upon written application of the dealer and the carrying broker or dealer.

(C) For purposes of this paragraph (a)(6)(iii), equity in such specialist or market maker account shall be computed by (1) marking all securities positions long or short in the account to their respective current market values, (2) adding (deducting in the case of a debit balance) the credit balance carried in such specialist or market maker account, and (3) adding (deducting in the case of short positions) the market value of positions long in such account.

(iv) The dealer shall obtain from the broker or dealer carrying the market maker or specialist account a written undertaking which shall be designated "Notice Pursuant to Section 240.15c3-1(a)(6) of Intention to Carry Specialist or Market Maker Account." Said undertaking shall contain the representations required by this paragraph (a)(6) and shall be filed with the Commission's Washington, D.C. Office, the regional office of the Commission for the region in which the broker or dealer has its principal place of business and the Designated Examining Authorities of both firms prior to effecting any transactions in said account. The broker or dealer carrying such account:

(A) Shall mark the account to the market not less than daily and shall issue appropriate calls for additional equity which shall be met by noon of the following business day;

(B) Shall notify by telegraph the Commission and the Designated Examining Authorities pursuant to 17 CFR 240.17a-11, if the market maker or specialist fails to deposit any required equity within the time prescribed in paragraph (a)(6)(iv)(A) above; said telegraphic notice shall be received by the Commission and the Designated Examining Authorities not later than the close of business on the day said call is not met;

(C) Shall not extend further credit in the account if the equity in the account falls below that prescribed in paragraph (a)(6)(iii) above, and

(D) Shall take steps to liquidate promptly existing positions in the account in the event of a failure to meet a call for equity.

(v) No such carrying broker or dealer shall permit the sum of (A) the deductions required by paragraph (c)(2)(x)(A) of this section in respect of all transactions in market maker accounts guaranteed, endorsed or carried by such broker or dealer pursuant to paragraph (c)(2)(x) of this section and (B) the equity required by paragraph (iii) of this paragraph (a)(6) in respect of all transactions in the accounts of specialists or market makers in options carried by such broker or dealer pursuant to this paragraph (a)(6) to exceed 1000 percent of such broker's or dealer's net capital as defined in paragraph (c)(2) of this section for any period exceeding five business days; *provided,* That solely for purposes of this paragraph (a)(6)(v), deductions or equity required in a specialist or market maker account in respect of positions in fully paid securities (other than options), which do not underlie options listed on the national securities exchange or facility of a national securities association of which the specialist or market maker is a member, need not be recognized. *Provided* further, That if at any time such sum exceeds 1000 percent of such broker's or dealer's net capital, then the broker or dealer shall immediately transmit telegraphic notice of such event to the principal office of the Commission in Washington, D.C., the regional office of the Commission for the region in which the broker or dealer maintains its principal place of business, and such broker's or dealer's Designated Examining Authority. *Provided* further, That if at any time such sum exceeds 1000 percent of such broker's or dealer's net capital, then such broker or dealer shall be subject to the prohibitions against withdrawal of equity capital set forth in paragraph (e) of this section, and to the prohibitions against reduction, prepayment and repayment of subordination agreements set forth in paragraph (b)(11) of section 240.15c3-1d, as if such broker or dealer's net capital were below the minimum standards specified by each of the aforementioned paragraphs.

Self-Clearing Options Specialists

(7) (i) A dealer who meets the conditions of paragraph (ii) of this paragraph (a)(7) may elect to operate under this paragraph (a)(7) and thereby not apply, except to the extent required by this paragraph (a)(7), the provisions of paragraphs (c)(2)(vi), (c)(2)(x), (c)(2)(xi), and (f)(3) of this section or Appendix A (17 CFR 240.15c3-1a) to this section and, in lieu thereof, apply the provisions of paragraph (a)(7)(iii) below.

(ii) This paragraph (a)(7) shall be available to a broker or dealer engaged solely in one or more of the following activities:

(A) His transactions as a dealer are limited to the business of effecting (as sole proprietor or through one or more natural persons associated with such dealer ("associated specialists")) and clearing specialist or market maker transactions in options listed on a national securities or a facility of a national securities association ("listed options"), or in the securities which underlie such options or which are exchangeable or convertible, without the payment of money, into such underlying securities ("underlying securities"); *provided,* That such dealer may also guarantee, endorse or carry listed options and underlying securities purchased or sold by a specialist or market maker who is not associated with such dealer (an "independent specialist") and who either is not subject to the provisions of this section 240.15c3-1 or operates under paragraph (a)(6) thereof.

(B) His transactions as a broker are limited to (1) effecting transactions in securities as agent for an independent specialist whose market maker account such broker carries pursuant to the provisions of this section, and (2) effecting transactions on the floor or a national securities exchange in options or securities other than options listed on such an exchange as agent for another broker or dealer.

(iii) A dealer electing to operate pursuant to this paragraph (a)(7) shall adjust its net worth by deducting, for positions in each class of option contracts in which the dealer, as sole proprietor or through associated specialists, is a market maker ("proprietary positions"), or each such independent specialist is a market maker (and for positions in other securities), an amount equal to:

(A) The deductions specified by paragraph (c)(2)(x)(A) of this section; *provided,* That for purposes of computing such deductions, proprietary positions, as well as positions in each such independent specialist's market maker account, shall be allocated in accordance with paragraph (c)(2)(x)(E) of this section; and *provided* further, That the deductions computed for each such independent specialist's positions pursuant to the foregoing shall be reduced by any liquidating equity, as defined in paragraph (c)(2)(x)(B)(2) of this section, that exists in such independent specialist's market maker account, and shall be increased to the extent of any liquidating deficit in such account; and *provided* further, That in no event shall the foregoing proviso be construed to increase the net capital of any dealer electing to operate under this paragraph (a)(7).

(B) Such lesser requirement as may be approved by the Commission under specified terms and conditions upon the written application of such dealer.

(iv) No dealer electing to operate under this paragraph (a)(7) shall permit the sum of the deductions required by paragraph (iii) of this paragraph (a)(7) in respect of all positions in the market maker accounts of independent specialists guaranteed, endorsed or carried by such dealer pursuant to this paragraph (a)(7), computed without regard to any liquidating equity or liquidating deficit in any such independent specialist's account, to exceed 1000 percent of such dealer's net capital as defined in paragraph (c)(2) of this section for any period exceeding five business days; *provided,* That solely for purposes of this paragraph (a)(7)(iv), deductions required in the market maker account of an independent specialist in respect of positions in fully paid securities (other than options), which do not underlie options listed on the national securities exchanges or facility of a national securities association of which the independent specialist is a member, need not be recognized; *provided* further, That if at any time such sum exceeds 1000 percent of such dealer's net capital, then the dealer shall immediately transmit telegraphic notice of such event to the principal office of the Commission in Washington, D.C., the regional office of the Commission for the region in which the dealer maintains its principal place of business, and such dealer's Designated Examining Authority; *provided* further, That if at any time such sum exceeds 1000 percent of such dealer's net capital, then the dealer shall be subject to the prohibitions against withdrawal of equity capital set forth in paragraph (e) of this section, and to the prohibitions against reduction, prepayment and repayment of subordination agreements set forth in paragraph (b)(11) of section 240.15c3-1d, as if such dealer's net capital were below the minimum standards specified by each of the aforementioned paragraphs.

(v) A dealer electing to operate under this paragraph (a)(7) shall comply in all respects with the requirements of paragraphs (c)(2)(x)(F) and (c)(2)(x)(G) of this section (or paragraph (a)(6)(iv) thereof) insofar as such dealer acts as the guarantor, endorser or carrying dealer for options written or purchased by an independent specialist not subject to the provisions of this section (or operating pursuant to paragraph (a)(6) thereof).

Municipal Securities Brokers' Brokers

(8) (i) A municipal securities brokers' broker, as defined in subsection (ii) of this paragraph (a)(8), may elect not to be subject to the limitations of paragraphs (c)(2)(ix) of this section provided that such brokers' broker complies with the requirements set out in subsections (iii), (iv) and (v) of this paragraph (a)(8).

(ii) The term municipal securities "brokers' broker" shall mean a municipal securities broker or dealer who acts exclusively as an undisclosed agent in the purchase or sale of municipal securities for a registered broker or dealer or registered municipal securities dealer, who has no "customers" as defined in this rule and who does not have or maintain any municipal securities in its proprietary or other accounts.

(iii) In order to qualify to operate under this paragraph (a)(8), a brokers' broker shall at all times have and maintain net capital of not less than $150,000.

(iv) For purposes of this paragraph (a)(8), a brokers' broker shall deduct from net worth 1% of the contract value of each municipal failed to deliver contract which is outstanding 21 business days or longer. Such deduction shall be increased by any excess of the contract price of the fail to deliver over the market value of the underlying security.

(v) For purposes of this paragraph (a)(8), a brokers' broker may exclude from its aggregate indebtedness computation indebtedness adequately collateralized by municipal securities outstanding for not more than one business day and offset by municipal securities failed to deliver of the same issue and quantity. In no event may a brokers' broker exclude any overnight bank loan attributable to the same municipal securities failed to deliver contract for more than one business day. A brokers' broker need not deduct from net worth the amount by which the market value of securities failed to receive outstanding longer than thirty (30) calendar days exceeds the contract value of those failed to receives as required by Rule 15c3-1(c)(2)(iv)(E).

Certain Additional Capital Requirements for Brokers or Dealers Engaging in Reverse Repurchase Agreements

(9) Notwithstanding the provisions of subparagraphs (a)(1)-(8), a broker or dealer shall maintain net capital in addition to the amounts required under paragraphs (a) or (f) of this section in an amount equal to 10 percent of:

(i) The excess of the market value of United States Treasury Bills, Bonds and Notes subject to reverse repurchase agreements with any one party over 105 percent of the contract prices (including accrued interest) for reverse repurchase agreements with that person; and

(ii) The excess of the market value of securities issued or guaranteed as to principal or interest by an agency of the United States or mortgage related securities as defined in Section 3(a)(41) of the Act subject to reverse repurchase agreements with any one party over 110 percent of the contract prices (including accrued interest) for reverse repurchase agreements with that person; and

(iii) the excess of the market value of other securities subject to reverse repurchase agreements with any one party over 120 percent of the contract prices (including accrued interest) for reverse repurchase agreements with that person.

Exemptions

(b) (1) The provisions of this section shall not apply to any specialist who does not transact a business in securities with other than members, brokers or dealers and who is in good standing and subject to the capital requirements of the American Stock Exchange (if he is not also a clearing member of the Options Clearing Corporation), the Boston Stock Exchange, the Midwest Stock Exchange, the New York Stock Exchange, the Pacific Stock Exchange, the PBW Stock Exchange (if he is not also a clearing member of the Options Clearing Corporation), or the Chicago Board Options Exchange (if he is not also a clearing member of the Options Clearing Corporation) provided that this exclusion as to a particular specialist of any exchange or as to the exchange itself, may be suspended or withdrawn by the Commission at any time, upon ten (10) days written notice to such exchange or specialist, if it appears to the Commission that such action is necessary or appropriate in the public interest or for the protection of investors.

(2) A member in good standing of a national securities exchange who acts as a floor broker (and whose activities do not require compliance with other provisions of this rule) may elect to comply, in lieu of the other provisions of this section, with the following financial responsibility standard: the value of the exchange membership of the member (based on the lesser of the most recent sale price or current bid price for an exchange membership) is not less than $15,000, or an amount equal to the excess of $15,000 over the value of the exchange membership is held by an independent agent in escrow; provided that the rules of such exchange require that the proceeds from the sale of the exchange membership of the member and the amount held in escrow pursuant to this paragraph shall be subject to the prior claims of the exchange and its clearing corporation and those arising from the closing out of contracts entered into on the floor of such exchange.

(3) The Commission may, upon written application, exempt from the provisions of this section, either unconditionally or on specified terms and conditions, any broker or dealer who satisfies the Commission that, because of the special nature of its business, its financial position, and the safeguards it has established for the protection of customers' funds and securities, it is not necessary in the public interest or for the protection of investors to subject the particular broker or dealer to the provisions of this section.

Definitions

(c) For the purpose of this section:

Aggregate Indebtedness

(1) The term "aggregate indebtedness" shall be deemed to mean the total money liabilities of a broker or dealer arising in connection with any transaction whatsoever, and includes, among other things, money borrowed, money payable against securities loaned and securities "failed to receive," the market value of securities borrowed to the extent to which no equivalent value is paid or credited (other than the market value of margin securities borrowed from customers in accordance with the provisions of 17 CFR 240.15c3-3 and margin securities borrowed from non-customers), customers' and non-customers' free credit balances, credit balances in customers' and non-customers' accounts having short positions in securities, equities in customers' and non-customers'

future commodities accounts and credit balances in customers' and non-customers' commodities accounts, but excluding:

Exclusions From Aggregate Indebtedness

(i) Indebtedness adequately collateralized by securities which are carried long by the broker or dealer and which have not been sold or by securities which collateralize a secured demand note pursuant to Appendix (D) to this section, 17 CFR 240.15c3-1d; indebtedness adequately collateralized by spot commodities which are carried long by the broker or dealer and which have not been sold; or, until October 1, 1976, indebtedness adequately collateralized by municipal securities outstanding for not more than one business day and offset by municipal securities failed to deliver of the same issue and quantity, where such indebtedness is incurred by a broker or dealer effecting transactions solely in municipal securities who is either registered with the Commission or temporarily exempt from such registration pursuant to 17 CFR 240.15a-1(T) or 17 CFR 240.15Ba2-3(T);

(ii) Amounts payable against securities loaned, which securities are carried long by the broker or dealer and which have not been sold or which securities collateralize a secured demand note pursuant to Appendix (D), 17 CFR 240.15c3-1d;

(iii) Amounts payable against securities failed to receive which securities are carried long by the broker or dealer and which have not been sold or which securities collateralize a secured demand note pursuant to Appendix (D), 17 CFR 240.15c3-1d or amounts payable against securities failed to receive for which the broker or dealer also has a receivable related to securities of the same issue and quantity thereof which are either fails to deliver or securities borrowed by the broker or dealer;

(iv) Credit balances in accounts representing amounts payable for securities or money market instruments not yet received from the issuer or its agent which securities are specified in subdivision (c)(2)(vi)(E) and which amounts are outstanding in such accounts not more than three (3) business days;

(v) Equities in customers' and non-customers' accounts segregated in accordance with the provisions of the Commodity Exchange Act and the rules and regulations thereunder;

(vi) Liability reserves established and maintained for refunds of charges required by Section 27(d) of the Investment Company Act of 1940, but only to the extent of amounts on deposit in a segregated trust account in accordance with 17 CFR 270.27d-1 under the Investment Company Act of 1940;

(vii) Amounts payable to the extent funds and qualified securities are required to be on deposit and are deposited in a "Special Reserve Bank Account for the Exclusive Benefit of Customers" pursuant to 17 CFR 240.15c3-3 under the Securities Exchange Act of 1934;

(viii) Fixed liabilities adequately secured by assets acquired for use in the ordinary course of the trade or business of a broker or dealer but no other fixed liabilities secured by assets of the broker or dealer shall be so excluded unless the sole recourse of the creditor for nonpayment of such liability is to such asset;

(ix) Liabilities on open contractual commitments;

(x) Indebtedness subordinated to the claims of creditors pursuant to a satisfactory subordination agreement, as defined in Appendix (D), 17 CFR 240.15c3-1d;

(xi) Liabilities which are effectively subordinated to the claims of creditors (but which are not subject to a satisfactory subordination agreement as defined in Appendix

(D) 17 CFR 240.15c3-1d), by non-customers of the broker or dealer prior to such subordination, except such subordinations by customers as may be approved by the Examining Authority for such broker or dealer;

(xii) Credit balances in accounts of general partners; and

(xiii) Deferred tax liabilities.

● ● ● *Selected NASD Notices to Members*

> 83-41 SEC Staff Issuance of No-Action Letter Providing Temporary Relief from Certain Provisions of Rules 15c3-1 and 15c3-3 Dealing with Municipal Securities
>
> (July 25, 1983)

Net Capital

(2) The term "net capital" shall be deemed to mean the net worth of a broker or dealer, adjusted by:

Adjustments to Net Worth Related to Unrealized Profit or Loss and Deferred Tax Provisions

(i)(A) Adding unrealized profits (or deducting unrealized losses) in the accounts of the broker or dealer;

(B)*(1)* In determining net worth, all long and all short positions in listed options shall be marked to their market value and all long and all short securities and commodities positions shall be marked to their market value.

(2) In determining net worth, the value attributed to any unlisted option shall be the difference between the option's exercise value and the market value of the underlying security. In the case of an unlisted call, if the market value of the underlying security is less than the exercise value of such call it shall be given no value and in the case of an unlisted put if the market value of the underlying security is more than the exercise value of the unlisted put it shall be given no value.

(C) Adding to net worth the lesser of any deferred income tax liability related to the items in *(1)*, *(2)*, and *(3)* below, or the sum of *(1)*, *(2)*, and *(3)* below;

(1) The aggregate amount resulting from applying to the amount of the deductions computed in accordance with subparagraph (c)(2)(vi) and Appendices (A) and (B), 17 CFR 240.15c3-1a and 240.15c3-1b or, where appropriate, paragraph (f) of this section, the appropriate Federal and State tax rate(s) applicable to any unrealized gain on the asset on which the deduction was computed;

(2) Any deferred tax liability related to income accrued which is directly related to an asset otherwise deducted pursuant to this section;

(3) Any deferred tax liability related to unrealized appreciation in value of any asset(s) which has been otherwise deducted from net worth in accordance with the provisions of this section; and,

(D) Adding, in the case of future income tax benefits arising as a result of unrealized losses, the amount of such benefits not to exceed the amount of income tax liabilities accrued on the books and records of the broker or dealer, but only to the extent such benefits could have been applied to reduce accrued tax liabilities on the date of the capital computation, had the related unrealized losses been realized on that date.

(E) Adding to net worth any actual tax liability related to income accrued which is directly related to an asset otherwise deducted pursuant to this section.

Subordinated Liabilities

(ii) Excluding liabilities of the broker or dealer which are subordinated to the claims of creditors pursuant to a satisfactory subordination agreement, as defined in Appendix (D), 17 CFR 240.15c3-1d.

Sole Proprietors

(iii) Deducting, in the case of a broker or dealer who is a sole proprietor, the excess of liabilities which have not been incurred in the course of business as a broker or dealer over assets not used in the business.

Assets Not Readily Convertible Into Cash

(iv) Deducting fixed assets and assets which cannot be readily converted into cash (less any indebtedness excluded in accordance with subdivision (c)(1)(viii) of this section) including, among other things:

Fixed Assets and Prepaid Items

(A) Real estate; furniture and fixtures; exchange memberships; prepaid rent, insurance and other expenses; goodwill, organization expenses;

Certain Unsecured and Partly Secured Receivables

(B) All unsecured advances and loans; deficits in customers' and non-customers' unsecured and partly secured notes; deficits in special omnibus accounts maintained in compliance with the requirements of 12 CFR 220.4(b) of Regulation T under the Securities Exchange Act of 1934, or similar accounts carried on behalf of another broker or dealer, after application of calls for margin, marks to the market or other required deposits which are outstanding 5 business days or less; deficits in customers' and non-customers' unsecured and partly secured accounts after application of calls for margin, marks to the market or other required deposits which are outstanding 5 business days or less, except deficits in cash accounts as defined in 12 CFR 220.4(c) of Regulation T under the Securities Exchange Act of 1934 for which not more than one extension respecting a specified securities transaction has been requested and granted, and deducting for securities carried in any of such accounts the percentages specified in paragraphs (c)(2)(vi) or (f) of this section or Appendix A (17 CFR 240.15c3-1a); the market value of stock loaned in excess of the value of any collateral received therefor; receivables arising out of free shipments of securities (other than mutual fund redemptions) in excess of $5,000 per shipment and all free shipiments (other than mutual fund redemptions) outstanding more than 7 business days, and mutual fund redemptions outstanding more than 16 business days; any collateral deficiencies in secured demand notes as defined in Appendix D (17 CFR 240.15c3-1d);

(C) Interest receivable, floor brokerage receivable, commissions receivable from other brokers or dealers (other than syndicate profits which shall be treated as required in subparagraph (c)(2)(iv)(E) of this section), mutual fund concessions receivable and management fees receivable from registered investment companies, all of which receivables are outstanding longer than thirty (30) days from the date they arise; dividends receivable outstanding longer than thirty (30) days from the payable date; good faith deposits arising in connection with a non-municipal securities underwriting, outstanding longer than eleven (11) business days from the settlement of the underwriting with the issuer; receivables due from participation in municipal securities underwriting syndicates and municipal securities joint underwriting accounts which are outstanding longer than sixty (60) days from settlement of the underwriting with the issuer and good faith deposits arising in connection with an underwriting of municipal securities, outstanding longer than sixty (60) days from settlement of the underwriting with the issuer; and receivables due from participation in municipal securities secondary trading joint accounts, which are outstanding longer than sixty (60) days from the date all securities have been delivered by the account manager to the account members.

Insurance Claims

(D) Insurance claims which, after seven (7) business days from the date the loss giving rise to the claim is discovered, are not covered by an opinion of outside counsel that the claim is valid and is covered by insurance policies presently in effect; insurance claims which after twenty (20) business days from the date the loss giving rise to the claim is discovered and which are accompanied by an opinion of outside counsel described above, have not been acknowledged in writing by the insurance carrier as due and payable; and insurance claims acknowledged in writing by the carrier as due and payable outstanding longer than twenty (20) business days from the date they are so acknowledged by the carrier; and,

Other Deductions

(E) All other unsecured receivables; all assets doubtful of collection less any reserves established therefore; the amount by which the market value of securities failed to receive outstanding longer than thirty (30) calendar days exceeds the contract value of such fails to receive outstanding longer than thirty (30) calendar days, and the funds on deposit in a "segregated trust account" in accordance with 17 CFR 270.27d-1 under the Investment Company Act of 1940, but only to the extent that the amounts on deposit in such segregated trust account exceeds the amount of liability reserves established and maintained for refunds of charges required by Sections 27(d) and 27(f) of the Investment Company Act of 1940; provided, that any amount deposited in the "Special Reserve Bank Account for the Exclusive Benefits of Customers" established pursuant to 17 CFR 240.15c3-3 and clearing deposits shall not be so deducted.

(F)(*1*) For purposes of this paragraph:

(*i*) The term "reverse repurchase agreement deficit" shall mean the difference between the contract price for resale of the securities under a reverse repurchase agreement and the market value of those securities (if less than the contract price).

(*ii*) The term "repurchase agreement deficit" shall mean the difference between the market value of securities subject to the repurchase agreement and the contract price for repurchase of the securities (if less than the market value of the securities).

(*iii*) As used in paragraph (F)(*1*), the term "contract price" shall include accrued interest.

(*iv*) Reverse repurchase agreement deficits and the repurchase agreement deficits where the counterparty is the Federal Reserve Bank of New York shall be disregarded.

(*2*)(*i*) In the case of a reverse repurchase agreement, the deduction shall be equal to the reverse repurchase agreement deficit.

(*ii*) In determining the required deductions under subsection (F)(*2*)(*i*), the broker or dealer may reduce the reverse repurchase agreement deficit by:

(*A*) any margin or other deposits held by the broker or dealer on account of the reverse repurchase agreement;

(*B*) any excess market value of the securities over the contract price for resale of those securities under any other reverse repurchase agreement with the same party;

(*C*) the difference between the contract price for resale and the market value of securities subject to repurchase agreements with the same party (if the market value of those securities is less than the contract price); and

(*D*) calls for margin, marks to the market, or other required deposits which are outstanding one business day or less.

(*3*)(*i*) In the case of repurchase agreements, the deduction shall be:

(*A*) The excess of the repurchase agreement deficit over 5 percent of the contract price for resale of United States Treasury Bills, Notes and Bonds, 10 percent of the contract price for the resale of securities issued or guaranteed as to principal or interest by an agency of the United States or mortgage related securities as defined in Section 3(a)(41) of the Act and 20 percent of the contract price for the resale of other securities and;

(*B*) The excess of the aggregate repurchase agreement deficits with any one party over 25 percent of the broker or dealer's net capital before the application of subparagraphs (c)(2)(vi) or (f)(3) of this section (less any deduction taken under subparagraph (F)(3)(i)(A) or, if greater;

(*C*) The excess of the aggregate repurchase agreement deficits over 300 percent of the broker or dealer's net capital before the application of subparagraphs (c)(2)(vi) or (f)(3) of this section.

(*ii*) In determining the required deduction under subsection (F)(3)(i), the broker or dealer may reduce a repurchase agreement deficit by:

(*A*) Any margin or other deposits held by the broker or dealer on account of a reverse repurchase agreement with the same party to the extent not otherwise used to reduce a reverse repurchase deficit;

(*B*) The difference between the contract price and the market value of securities subject to other repurchase agreements with the same party (if the market value of those securities is less than the contract price) not otherwise used to reduce a reverse repurchase agreement deficit; and

(*C*) Calls for margin, marks to the market, or other required deposits which are outstanding one business day or less to the extent not otherwise used to reduce a reverse repurchase agreement deficit.

Securities Borrowed

(G) 1% of the market value of securities borrowed collateralized by an irrevocable letter of credit.

(*H*) Any receivable from an affiliate of the broker or dealer (not otherwise deducted from net worth) and the market value of any collateral given to an affiliate (not otherwise deducted from net worth) to secure a liability over the amount of the liability of the broker or dealer unless the books and records of the affiliate are made available for examination when requested by the representatives of the Commission or the Examining Authority for the broker or dealer in order to demonstrate the validity of the receivable or payable. The provisions of this subsection shall not apply where the affiliate is a registered broker or dealer, registered government securities broker or dealer or bank as defined in Section 3(a)(6) of the Act or insurance company as defined in Section 3(a)(19) of the Act or investment company registered under the Investment Company Act of 1940 or federally insured savings and loan association or futures commission merchant registered pursuant to the Commodity Exchange Act.

Securities Differences

(v)(A) Deducting the market value of all short securities differences (which shall include securities positions reflected on the securities record which are not susceptible to either count or confirmation) unresolved after discovery in accordance with the following schedule:

Percentage of Market Value of Short Securities Differences	Number of Business Days After Discovery
25%	7
50%	14
75%	21
100%	28

(B) Deducting the market value of any long securities differences, where such securities have been sold by the broker or dealer before they are adequately resolved, less any reserves established therefor;

(C) The designated examining authority for a broker or dealer may extend the periods in (A) above for up to 10 business days if it finds that exceptional circumstances warrant an extension.

Securities Haircuts

(vi) Deducting the percentages specified in subdivisions (A)-(M) below (or the deductions prescribed for securities positions set forth in Appendix (A), 17 CFR 240.15c3-1a or, where appropriate, paragraph (f) of this section) of the market value of all securities, money market instruments or options in the proprietary or other accounts of the broker or dealer.

Government Securities

(A) *(1)* In the case of a security issued or guaranteed as to principal or interest by the United States or any agency thereof, the applicable percentages of the market value of the net long or short position in each of the categories specified below are:

Category 1

(i) Less than 3 months to maturity—0%;

(ii) 3 months but less than 6 months to maturity—$1/2$ of 1%;

(iii) 6 months but less than 9 months to maturity—$3/4$ of 1%;

(iv) 9 months but less than 12 months to maturity—1%.

Category 2

(i) 1 year but less than 2 years to maturity—$1^1/2$%;

(ii) 2 years but less than 3 years to maturity—2%.

Category 3

(i) 3 years but less than 5 years to maturity—3%;

(ii) 5 years but less than 10 years to maturity—4%;

Category 4

(i) 10 years but less than 15 years to maturity—$4^1/2$%;

(ii) 15 years but less than 20 years to maturity—5%;

(iii) 20 years but less than 25 years to maturity—$5^1/2$%;

(iv) 25 years or more to maturity—6%.

Brokers or dealers shall compute a deduction for each category above as follows: Compute the deductions for the net long or short positions in each subcategory above. The deduction for the category shall be the net of the aggregate deductions on the long positions and the aggregate deductions on short positions in each category plus 50% of the lesser of the aggregate deductions on the long or short positions.

(2) A broker or dealer may elect to deduct, in lieu of the computation required under paragraph (c)(2)(vi)(A)*(1)* of this section, the applicable percentages of the

market value of the net long or short positions in each of the subcategories specified in paragraph (c)(2)(vi)(A)*(1)* of this section.

(3) In computing deductions under paragraph (c)(2)(vi)(A)*(1)* of this section, a broker or dealer may elect to exclude the market value of a long or short security from one category and a security from another category, *Provided,* That:

(i) Such securities have maturity dates:

(A) Between 9 months and 15 months and within 3 months of one another.

(B) Between 2 years and 4 years and within 1 year of one another; or

(C) Between 8 years and 12 years and within 2 years of one another.

(ii) The net market value of the two excluded securities shall remain in the category of the security with the higher market value.

(4) In computing deductions under paragraph (c)(2)(vi)(A)*(1)* of this section, a broker or dealer may include in the categories specified in paragraph (c)(2)(vi)(A)*(1)* of this section, long or short positions in securities issued by the United States or any agency thereof that are deliverable against long or short positions in futures contracts relating to Government securities, traded on a recognized contract market approved by the Commodity Futures Trading Commission, which are held in the proprietary or other accounts of the broker or dealer. The value of the long or short positions included in the categories shall be determined by the contract value of the futures contract held in the account. The provisions of Appendix B to Rule 15c3-1 (17 CFR 240.15c3-1b) will in any event apply to the positions in futures contracts.

(5) In the case of a Government securities dealer which reports to the Federal Reserve System, which transacts business directly with the Federal Reserve System, and which maintains at all times a minimum net capital of at least $50,000,000, before application of the deductions provided for in paragraph (c)(2)(vi) or (f)(3) of this section, the deduction for a security issued or guaranteed as to principal or interest by the United States or any agency thereof shall be 75% of the deduction otherwise computed under subparagraph (c)(2)(vi)(A).

Municipals

(B) *(1)* In the case of any municipal security which has a scheduled maturity at date of issue of 731 days or less and which is issued at par value and pays interest at maturity, or which is issued at a discount, and which is not traded flat or in default as to principal or interest, the applicable percentages of the market value on the greater of the long or short position in each of the categories specified below are:

(i) Less than 30 days to maturity—0%.

(ii) 30 days but less than 91 days to maturity—$^1/_8$ of 1%.

(iii) 91 days but less than 181 days to maturity—$^1/_4$ of 1%.

(iv) 181 days but less than 271 days to maturity—$^3/_8$ of 1%.

(v) 271 days but less than 366 days to maturity—$^1/_2$ of 1%.

(vi) 366 days but less than 456 days to maturity—$^3/_4$ of 1%.

(vii) 456 days but less than 732 days to maturity—1%.

(2) In the case of any municipal security, other than those specified in paragraph (c)(2)(vi)(B)(1), which is not traded flat or in default as to principal or interest, the applicable percentages of the market value of the greater of the long or short position in each of the categories specified below are:

(i) Less than 1 year to maturity—1%.

(ii) 1 year but less than 2 years to maturity—2%

(iii) 2 years but less than $3^1/_2$ years to maturity—3%

(iv) $3^1/_2$ years but less than 5 years to maturity—4%

(v) 5 years but less than 7 years to maturity—5%

(vi) 7 years but less than 10 years to maturity—$5^1/_2$%

(vii) 10 years but less than 15 years to maturity—6%

(viii) 15 years but less than 20 years to maturity—$6^1/_2$%

(ix) 20 years or more to maturity—7%

Canadian Debt Obligations

(C) In the case of any security issued or unconditionally guaranteed as to principal and interest by the Government of Canada, the percentages of market value to be deducted shall be the same as in (A) above.

Certain Municipal Bond Trusts and Liquid Asset Funds

(D) *(1)* In the case of redeemable securities of an investment company registered under the Investment Company Act of 1940, which assets consist of cash or money market instruments and which is generally known as a "money market fund," the deduction shall be 2% of the market value of the greater of the long or short position.

(2) In the case of redeemable securities of an investment company registered under the Investment Company Act of 1940, which assets are in the form of cash or securities or money market instruments of any maturity which are described in paragraph (c)(2)(vi)(A) through (C) or (E) of this section, the deduction shall be 7% of the market value of the greater of the long or short positions.

(3) In the case of redeemable securities of an investment company registered under the Investment Company Act of 1940, which assets are in the form of cash or securities or money market instruments which are described in paragraphs (c)(2)(vi)(A) through (C) or (E) and (F) of this section, the deduction shall be 9% of the market value of the long or short position.

Commercial Paper, Bankers Acceptances and Certificates of Deposit

(E) In the case of any short term promissory note or evidence of indebtedness which has a fixed rate of interest or is sold at a discount, and which has a maturity date at date of issuance not exceeding nine months exclusive of days of grace, or any renewal thereof, the maturity of which is likewise limited and is rated in one of the three highest categories by at least two of the nationally recognized statistical rating organizations (provided, that effective January 1, 1977, and until September 1, 1977, this paragraph shall be deemed to require only one such rating), or in the case of any negotiable certificates of deposit or bankers acceptance or similar type of instrument issued or guaranteed by any bank as defined in Section 3(a)(6) of the Securities Exchange Act of 1934, the applicable percentage of the market value of the greater of the long or short position in each of the categories specified below are:

(1) less than 30 days to maturity—0 percent;

(2) 30 days but less than 91 days to maturity—$^1/_8$ of 1 percent;

(3) 91 days but less than 181 days to maturity—$^1/_4$ of 1 percent;

(4) 181 days but less than 271 days to maturity—$^3/_8$ of 1 percent;

(5) 271 days but less than 1 year to maturity—$^1/_2$ of 1 percent; and

(6) with respect to any negotiable certificate of deposit or bankers acceptance or similar type of instrument issued or guaranteed by any bank, as defined above, having 1 year or more to maturity, the deduction shall be on the greater of the long or short position and shall be the same percentage as that prescribed in subdivision (c)(2)(vi)(A) above.

Nonconvertible Debt Securities

(F)(*1*) In the case of nonconvertible debt securities having a fixed interest rate and fixed maturity date and which are not traded flat or in default as to principal or interest and which are rated in one of the four highest rating categories by at least two of the nationally recognized statistical rating organizations, the applicable percentages of the market value of the greater of the long or short position in each of the categories specified below are:

(*i*) Less than 1 year to maturity—2%

(*ii*) 1 year but less than 2 years to maturity—3%

(*iii*) 2 years but less than 3 years to maturity—5%

(*iv*) 3 years but less than 5 years to maturity—6%

(*v*) 5 years but less than 10 years to maturity—7%

(*vi*) 10 years but less than 15 years to maturity—7$1/2$%

(*vii*) 15 years but less than 20 years to maturity—8%

(*viii*) 20 years but less than 25 years to maturity—8$1/2$%

(*ix*) 25 years or more to maturity—9%;

(*2*) A broker or dealer may elect to exclude from the above categories long or short positions that are hedged with short or long positions in securities issued by the United States or any agency thereof or nonconvertible debt securities having a fixed interest rate and a fixed maturity date and which are not traded flat or in default as to principal or interest and which are rated in one of the four highest rating categories by at least two of the nationally recognized statistical rating organizations if such securities have maturity dates:

(*i*) Less than five years and within 6 months of each other;

(*ii*) Between 5 years and 10 years and within 9 months of each other;

(*iii*) Between 10 years and 15 years and within 2 years of each other; or

(*iv*) 15 years or more and within 10 years of each other.

The broker-dealer shall deduct the amounts specified in subparagraphs (3) and (4) below.

(*3*) With respect to those positions described in subparagraph (2) that include a long or short position in securities issued by the United States or any agency thereof, the broker or dealer shall exclude the hedging short or long United States or agency securities position from the applicable haircut category under paragraph (c)(2)(vi)(A). The broker or dealer shall deduct the percentage of the market value of the hedged long or short position in nonconvertible debt securities as specified in each of the categories below:

(*i*) Less than 5 years to maturity—1$1/2$%

(*ii*) 5 years but less than 10 years to maturity—2$1/2$%

(*iii*) 10 years but less than 15 years to maturity—2$3/4$%

(*iv*) 15 years or more to maturity—3%

(*4*) With respect to those positions described in paragraph (2) above that include offsetting long and short positions in nonconvertible debt securities, the broker or dealer shall deduct a percentage of the market value of the hedged long or short position in nonconvertible debt securities as specified in each of the categories below:

(*i*) Less than 5 years to maturity—1$3/4$%

(*ii*) 5 years but less than 10 years to maturity—3%

(*iii*) 10 years but less than 15 years to maturity—$3^1/_4\%$

(*iv*) 15 years or more to maturity—$3^1/_2\%$

(5) In computing deductions under paragraph (c)(2)(vi)(F)(*3*) of this section, a broker or dealer may include in the categories specified in paragraph (c)(2)(vi)(F)(*3*) of this section, long or short positions in securities issued by the United States or any agency thereof that are deliverable against long or short positions in futures contracts relating to Government securities, traded on a recognized contract market approved by the Commodity Futures Trading Commission, which are held in the proprietary or other accounts of the broker or dealer. The value of the long or short positions included in the categories shall be determined by the contract value of the futures contract held in the account.

The provisions of Appendix B to Rule 15c3-1 (17 CFR 240.15c3-1b) will in any event apply to the positions in futures contracts.

Convertible Debt Securities

(G) In the case of a debt security not in default which has a fixed rate of interest and a fixed maturity date and which is convertible into an equity security, the deductions shall be as follows: If the market value is 100 percent or more of the principal amount, the deduction shall be determined as specified in subdivision (I) below; if the market value is less than the principal amount, the deduction shall be determined as specified in subdivision (F) above if such securities are rated as required by subdivision (F) above.

Preferred Stock

(H) In the case of cumulative, nonconvertible preferred stock ranking prior to all other classes of stock of the same issuer, which is rated in one of the four highest categories by at least two of the nationally recognized statistical rating organizations and which are not in arrears as to dividends, the deduction shall be 10% of the market value of the greater of the long or short position.

Risk Arbitrage Positions

(I) In the case of each risk arbitrage transaction, the deduction shall be 30 percent (or such other percentage as required by this subdivision) on the long or equivalent short position, whichever has the greater market value. For the purposes of this subdivision (I), a "risk arbitrage transaction" shall mean the sale (either when issued, when distributed or short) of securities involved in a pending merger, consolidation, transfer of assets, exchange offer, recapitalization or other similar transaction which has been publicly announced and has not been terminated, in connection with a previous or approximately simultaneous offsetting purchase of other securities which upon consummation of the transaction will result in the equivalent of the securities sold.

All Other Securities

(J) In the case of all securities or evidence of indebtedness, except those described in Appendix (A), 17 CFR 240.15c3-1a and where appropriate, paragraph (f) of this section, which are not included in any of the percentage categories enumerated in subdivisions (A)-(I) above or (K)(*ii*) below, the deduction shall be 30 percent of the market value of the greater of the long or short positions and to the extent the market value of the lesser of the long or short position exceeds 25 percent of the market value of the greater of the long or short positions, there shall be a percentage deduction on such excess equal to 15 percent of the market value of such excess. Provided, that no deduction need be made in the case of *(1)* a security which is convertible into or exchangeable for other securities within a period of 90 days, subject to no conditions other than the payment of money, and the other securities into which such security is convertible or for which it is exchangeable, are short in the accounts of such broker or dealer or *(2)* a security which has been called for redemption and which is redeemable within 90 days.

Securities With A Limited Market

(K) In the case of securities (other than exempted securities, nonconvertible debt securities, and cumulative nonconvertible preferred stock) which are not: *(1)* traded on a national securities exchange; *(2)* designated as "OTC Margin Stock" pursuant to Regulation T under the Securities Exchange Act of 1934; *(3)* quoted on "NASDAQ"; or *(4)* redeemable shares of investment companies registered under the Investment Company Act of 1940, the deduction shall be as follows:

(i) in the case where there are regular quotations in an inter-dealer quotations system for the securities by three or more independent market-makers (exclusive of the computing broker or dealer) and where each such quotation represents a bona fide offer to brokers or dealers to both buy and sell in reasonable quantities at stated prices, or where a ready market as defined in subdivision (c)(11)(ii) is deemed to exist, the deduction shall be determined in accordance with subdivision (J) above;

(ii) in the case where there are regular quotations in an inter-dealer quotations system for the securities by only one or two independent market-makers (exclusive of the computing broker or dealer) and where each such quotation represents a bona fide offer to brokers or dealers both to buy and sell in reasonable quantities, at stated prices, the deduction on both the long and short position shall be 40 percent.

(L) Where a broker or dealer demonstrates that there is sufficient liquidity for any securities long or short in the proprietary or other accounts of the broker or dealer which are subject to a deduction required by subdivision (K) above, such deduction, upon a proper showing to the Examining Authority for the broker or dealer, may be appropriately decreased, but in no case shall such deduction be less than that prescribed in subdivision (J) above.

Undue Concentration

(M) In the case of money market instruments or securities of a single class or series of an issuer, including any option written, endorsed or held to purchase or sell securities of such a single class or series of an issuer (other than "exempted securities" and redeemable securities of an investment company registered pursuant to the Investment Company Act of 1940), which are long or short in the proprietary or other accounts of a broker or dealer, including securities which are collateral to secured demand notes defined in Appendix (D), 17 CFR 240.15c3-1d, for more than 11 business days and which have a market value of more than 10 percent of the "net capital" of a broker or dealer before the application of subparagraph (c)(2)(vi) or Appendix (A), 17 CFR 240.15c3-1a, there shall be an additional deduction from net worth and/or the Collateral Value for securities collateralizing a secured demand note defined in Appendix (D), 17 CFR 240.15c3-1d, equal to 50 percent of the percentage deduction otherwise provided by this subparagraph (c)(2)(vi) or Appendix (A), 17 CFR 240.15c3-1a, on that portion of the securities position in excess of 10% of the "net capital" of the broker or dealer before the application of subparagraph (c)(2)(vi) and Appendix (A), 17 CFR 240.15c3-1a. This provision shall apply notwithstanding any long or short position exemption provided for in subdivisions (I) or (J) of this subparagraph (except for long or short position exemptions arising out of the first proviso to subdivision (c)(2)(vi)(J) and the deduction on any such exempted position shall be 15% of that portion of the securities position in excess of 10% of net capital before the application of subparagraph (c)(2)(vi) and Appendix (A), 17 CFR 240.15c3-1a. Provided, that such additional deduction shall be applied in the case of equity securities only on the market value in excess of $10,000 or the market value of 500 shares, whichever is greater, or $25,000 in the case of a debt security. Provided, further, that any specialist which is subject to a deduction required by this subdivision (M), respecting his specialty stock, who can demonstrate to the satisfaction of the Examining Authority for such broker or dealer that there is sufficient liquidity for such specialists' specialty stock and that such deduction need not be applied in the public interest for the protection of investors may upon a proper showing to such Examining Authority have such undue concentration deduction appropriately decreased, but in no case shall the deduction prescribed in subdivision (J) above be reduced. Each such Examining Authority shall make and preserve for a period of not less than 3 years a record of each application granted pursuant to this subdivision, which shall contain a summary of the justification for the granting of the application.

Provided further, this provision will be applied to an issue of municipal securities having the same security provisions, date of issue, interest rate, day, month and year of maturity only if such securities have a market value in excess of $500,000 in bonds ($5,000,000 in notes) or 10% of tentative net capital, whichever is greater, and are held in position longer than twenty (20) business days from the date the securities are received by the syndicate manager from the issuer.

Non-Marketable Securities

→ *Rule 15c3-1(c)(2)(vii) is suspended as applied to municipal securities.*

(vii) Deducting 100 percent of the carrying value in the case of securities or evidence of indebtedness in the proprietary or other accounts of the broker or dealer, for which there is no ready market, as defined in subparagraph (c)(11) of this section, and securities, in the proprietary or other accounts of the broker or dealer, which cannot be publicly offered or sold because of statutory, regulatory or contractual arrangements or other restrictions.

Open Contractual Commitments

(viii) Deducting, in the case of a broker or dealer who has open contractual commitments (other than those option positions subject to Appendix (A), 17 CFR 240.15c3-1a), the respective deductions as specified in subdivision (c)(2)(vi) of this paragraph or Appendix (B), 17 CFR 240.15c3-1b, from the value (which shall be the market value whenever there is a market) of each net long and each net short position contemplated by any open contractual commitment in the proprietary or other accounts of the broker or dealer. In the case of a broker or dealer electing to operate pursuant to paragraph (f) of this section, the percentage deduction for contractual commitments in those securities which are treated in subdivision (f)(3)(ii) shall be 30%. Provided, that the deduction with respect to any single commitment shall be reduced by the unrealized profit, in an amount not greater than the deduction provided for by this section (or increased by the unrealized loss), in such commitment, and that in no event shall an unrealized profit on any closed transactions operate to increase net capital.

(ix) Deducting from the contract value of each failed to deliver contract which is outstanding 5 business days or longer (21 business days or longer in the case of municipal securities) the percentages of the market value of the underlying security which would be required by application of the deduction required by paragraph (c)(2)(vi) or, where appropriate, paragraph (f) of this section. Such deduction, however, shall be increased by any excess of the contract price of the failed to deliver contract over the market value of the underlying security or reduced by any excess of the market value of the underlying security over the contract value of the fail but not to exceed the amount of such deduction; *Provided,* however, That until January 1, 1983, the deduction provided for herein shall be applied only to those fail to deliver contracts which are outstanding 7 business days or longer (21 business days or longer in the case of municipal securities). The designated examining authority for the broker or dealer may, upon application by the broker or dealer, extend for a period of up to 5 business days, any period herein specified where it is satisfied that the extension is warranted. The designated examining authority upon expiration of the extension may extend for one additional period of up to 5 business days, any period herein specified when it is satisfied that the extension is warranted.

Brokers or Dealers Carrying Accounts of Option Specialists

(x)(A) With respect to any transaction in options listed on a registered national securities exchange or a facility of a registered national securities association for which a broker or dealer acts as a guarantor, endorser or carrying broker or dealer for options purchased or written by a specialist not otherwise subject to the provisions of this section, such broker or dealer shall adjust its net worth by deducting, for each class of option contracts in which each such specialist is a market maker, an amount equal to 50 percent of the market value of each option contract in a long position and 75 percent of the market value of each contract in a short position; provided, however, that:

(1) For the purpose of the above deductions, each option contract in a short position shall be deemed to have a market value of not less than $100.

(2) In the case of a bona fide hedged position as defined in this paragraph (c)(2)(x) involving a long position in a security, other than an option, and a short position in a call option, the deduction shall be 30 percent (or such other percentage required by paragraphs (A)-(K) of paragraph (c)(2)(vi) of this section or 15 percent if such broker or dealer operates pursuant to paragraph (f) of this section) of the market value of the long position reduced by any excess of the market value of the long position over the exercise value of the short option position; provided, that no such reduction shall operate to increase net capital.

(3) In the case of a bona fide hedged position as defined in this paragraph (c)(2)(x) involving a short position in a security, other than an option, and a long position in a call option, the deduction shall be the lesser of 30 percent of the market value of the short position or the amount by which the exercise value of the long option position exceeds the market value of the short position; however, if the exercise value of the long option position does not exceed the market value of the short position, no deduction shall be applied.

(4) In the case of a bona fide hedged position as defined in this paragraph (c)(2)(x) involving a short position in a security, other than an option, and a short position in a put option, the deduction shall be 30 percent (or such other percentage required by paragraphs (A)-(K) of paragraph (c)(2)(vi) of this section) of the market value of the short security position reduced by any excess of the exercise value of the short option position over the market value of the short security position; provided, that no such reduction shall operate to increase net capital.

(5) In the case of a bona fide hedged position as defined in this paragraph (c)(2)(x) involving a long position in a security, other than an option, and a long position in a put option, the deduction shall be the lesser of 30 percent (15 percent if such broker or dealer operates pursuant to paragraph (f) of this section) of the market value of such long security position or the amount by which the market value of such long security position exceeds the exercise value of the long option position; however, if the market value of the long security position does not exceed the exercise value of the long option position, no deduction shall be applied.

(6) In the case of a bona fide spread position as defined in this paragraph (c)(2)(x) in which the market value of the long position exceeds the market value of the short position, the deduction shall be 50 percent of the greater of the difference between the

market values of such long and short positions or $50 for each option contract included in the long position as part of such spread position; provided, that such endorser, guarantor or carrying broker or dealer need not deduct more in respect of any such spread position in a particular underlying security and in respect of option contracts for the same underlying security which are carried in a pure short position in such specialist's market maker account than the greater of the deduction required by this paragraph (6) in respect of the spread position or the deduction required by paragraphs (A) and (A)(1) of this paragraph (c)(2)(x) in respect of the pure short position.

(7) In the case of a bona fide spread position as defined in this paragraph (c)(2)(x) in which the market value of the short position equals or exceeds the market value of the long position, the deduction shall be 75 percent of the greater of the difference between the market values of such short and long positions or $50 for each option contract included in the long position as part of such spread position; *provided,* That if the option contracts in the short position expire no later than the option contracts in the long position, such deduction need not exceed the greater of 75 percent of $50 per long contract, or the amount by which the difference between the market values of the short and long positions is less than the amount by which the exercise value of the long position exceeds the exercise value of the short position; and *provided* further, That such endorser, guarantor or carrying broker or dealer need not deduct more in respect of any such spread position in a particular underlying security and in respect of option contracts for the same underlying security which are carried in a pure long position in such specialist's market maker account than the greater of the deduction required by this paragraph (7) in respect of the spread position or the deduction required by paragraph (A) of this paragraph (c)(2)(x) in respect of the pure long position.

(8) In the case of a bona fide straddle position as defined in this paragraph (c)(2)(x), the deduction shall be the greater of the deductions which this paragraph (c)(2)(x) would require in respect of the call option position and the put option if both positions were pure long (or short) positions.

(9) In the case of positions in securities which are not part of a bona-fide hedged, spread or straddle position as defined in this paragraph (c)(2)(x) and, in the case of options, which are not listed on the national securities exchange of which such specialist is a member, the deduction shall be that set forth in paragraph (c)(2)(vi) of this section, or, if such securities are options, the deduction shall be that set forth in Appendix A (17 CFR 240.15c3-1a) to this section.

(B) The deduction computed for each specialist's positions pursuant to paragraph (A) of this paragraph (c)(2)(x) shall be reduced by any liquidating equity, as defined in this paragraph (c)(2)(x), that exists in such specialist's market maker account with the broker or dealer, and shall be increased to the extent of any liquidating deficit in such account. Provided, that in no event shall this provision result in increasing the net capital of any such guarantor, endorser, or carrying broker or dealer.

(1) No such guarantor, endorser or carrying broker or dealer shall permit the sum of (*i*) the deductions required by paragraph (A) of this paragraph (c)(2)(x) in respect of all transactions in specialists' market maker accounts guaranteed, endorsed or carried by such broker or dealer and (*ii*) the equity required by paragraph (a) (6) (iii) of this section in respect of all transactions in the accounts of specialists or market makers in options carried by such broker or dealer pursuant to paragraph (a)(6) of this section to exceed 1000 percent of such broker's or dealer's net capital as defined in paragraph (c)(2) of this section for any period exceeding five business days; *provided,* That solely for purposes of this paragraph (c)(2)(x)(B)(*1*), the deductions or equity required in a specialist's or market maker's account in respect of positions in fully paid securities (other than options), which do not underlie options listed on the national securities exchange or facility of a national securities association of which such specialist or

market maker is a member, need not be recognized; *provided* further, That if at any time such sum exceeds 1000 percent of such broker's or dealer's net capital, then the broker or dealer shall immediately transmit telegraphic notice of such event to the principal office of the Commission in Washington, D.C., the regional office of the Commission for the region in which the broker or dealer maintains its principal place of business, and such broker's or dealer's Designated Examining Authority; *provided* further, That if at any time such sum exceeds 1000 percent of such broker's or dealer's net capital, then such broker or dealer shall be subject to the prohibitions against withdrawal of equity capital set forth in paragraph (e) of this section, and to the prohibitions against reduction, prepayment and repayment of subordination agreements set forth in paragraph (b)(11) of this section 240.15c3-1d, as if such broker or dealer's net capital were below the minimum standards specified by each of the aforementioned paragraphs.

(2) For purposes of this paragraph (c)(2)(x), equity in each such specialist's market maker account shall be computed by (i) marking all securities positions long or short in the account to their respective current market values, (ii) adding (deducting in the case of a debit balance) the credit balance carried in such specialist's market maker account, and (iii) adding (deducting in the case of short positions) the market value of positions long in such account.

(C) For purposes of this paragraph (c)(2)(x), a bona fide hedged position shall mean either (1) a long position in a security other than an option (an "underlying security"), or in a security which is currently exchangeable for or convertible into the underlying security if the conversion or exchange does not require the payment of money, which is offset by a short call option position or a long put option position for the same number of units of the same underlying security, or (2) a short position in an underlying security which is offset by a long call position or a short put position for the same number of units of the same underlying security.

(D)*(1)* For purposes of this paragraph (c)(2)(x), a bona fide spread position shall mean long and short positions in the same type (that is, put or call) of option contracts for the same number of units of the same underlying security.

(2) For purposes of this paragraph (c)(2)(x), a bona fide straddle position shall mean long put and long call (or short put and short call) positions for the same number of units of the same underlying security.

(E) For purposes of applying the deductions required by paragraph (A) of this paragraph (c)(2)(x) in respect of positions in each such specialist's market maker account, long and short positions in each such account shall be allocated in the following sequence:

(1) Bona-fide hedged positions as defined in paragraph (C) of this paragraph (c)(2)(x) shall be constituted by first matching long or short positions in securities, other than options, against offsetting long or short call options positions taken in order of increasing exercise value and any remaining long or short positions in securities, other than options, against offsetting long or short put options positions taken in order of decreasing exercise values; *provided that,* in the case of long (or short) options of equal exercise value, the option possessing the greatest time to expiration shall be matched first.

(2) Thereafter, bona fide spread positions as defined in paragraph (D) of this paragraph (c)(2)(x) shall be constituted by matching long options taken in order of increasing exercise values (decreasing exercise values in the case of puts) against offsetting short options taken in order of increasing exercise values (decreasing exercise values in the case of puts); provided, that in the case of long (or short) options of equal

exercise value, the option possessing the greatest time to expiration shall be matched first.

(3) Thereafter, bona fide straddle positions as defined in paragraph (D) of this paragraph (c)(2)(x) shall be constituted by matching long (or short) call options taken in order of increasing exercise values against offsetting long (or short) put options taken in order of decreasing exercise values; *provided,* That in the case of long (or short) call or (put) options of equal exercise value, the option possessing the greatest time to expiration shall be matched first.

(4) Thereafter, long or short positions not allocated pursuant to paragraphs (1), (2) or (3) above shall be treated in the manner prescribed by paragraphs (A), (A)(1) or (A)(9) of this paragraph (c)(2)(x).

(F) If at any time the deductions required in respect of any such specialist's market maker account pursuant to paragraph (A) of this paragraph (c)(2)(x) exceed the equity in the account computed pursuant to paragraph (B)(2) of this paragraph (c)(2)(x), then the broker or dealer guaranteeing, endorsing, or carrying options transactions in such account:

(1) Shall not extend further credit in the account, and

(2) Shall issue a call for additional equity which shall be met by noon of the following business day, and

(3) Shall notify by telegraph the principal office of the Commission in Washington, D.C., the regional office of the Commission for the region in which the broker or dealer maintains its principal place of business, and the Designated Examining Authorities of the specialist and the broker or dealer if the specialist fails to deposit any required equity within the time prescribed in (2) above; said telegraphic notice shall be received by the Commission's Washington, D.C. office, the Commission's regional office, and the Designated Examining Authorities not later than the close of business on the day said calls is not met.

(G) If at any time a liquidating deficit exists in any such specialist's market maker account, then the broker or dealer guaranteeing, endorsing or carrying options transactions in such account shall take steps to liquidate promptly existing positions in the account.

(H) Upon written application to the Commission by the specialist and the broker or dealer guaranteeing, endorsing, or carrying options transactions in such specialist's market maker account, the Commission may approve upon specified terms and conditions lesser adjustments to net worth than those specified by paragraph (A) of this paragraph (c)(2)(x).

Brokers or Dealers Carrying Specialists or Market Makers Accounts

(xi) With respect to a broker or dealer who carries a market maker or specialist account, or with respect to any transaction in options listed on a registered national securities exchange for which a broker or dealer acts as a guarantor or endorser of options written by a specialist in a specialist account, the broker or dealer shall deduct, for each account carried or for each class or series of options guaranteed or endorsed, any deficiency in collateral required by subparagraph (a)(6) of this Rule.

Deduction From Net Worth for Certain Undermargined Accounts

(xii) Deducting the amount of cash required in each customer's or non-customer's account to meet the maintenance margin requirements of the Examining Authority for the broker or dealer, after application of calls for margin, marks to the market or other required deposits which are outstanding 5 business days or less.

Deduction From Net Worth for Indebtedness Collateralized by Exempted Securities

(xiii) Deducting, at the option of the broker or dealer, in lieu of including such amounts in aggregate indebtedness, 4 percent of the amount of any indebtedness secured by exempted securities or municipal securities, if such indebtedness would otherwise be includable in aggregate indebtedness.

Exempted Securities

(3) The term "exempted securities" shall mean those securities deemed exempted securities by Section 3(a)(12) of the Securities Exchange Act of 1934 and rules thereunder.

Contractual Commitments

(4) The term "contractual commitments" shall include underwriting, when issued, when distributed and delayed delivery contracts, the writing or endorsement of puts and calls and combinations thereof, commitments in foreign currencies, and spot (cash) commodities contracts, but shall not include uncleared regular way purchases and sales of securities and contracts in commodities futures. A series of contracts of purchase or sale of the same security conditioned, if at all, only upon issuance may be treated as an individual commitment.

Adequately Secured

(5) Indebtedness shall be deemed to be adequately secured within the meaning of this section when the excess of the market value of the collateral over the amount of the indebtedness is sufficient to make the loan acceptable as a fully secured loan to banks regularly making secured loans to brokers or dealers.

Customer

(6) The term "customer" shall mean any person from whom, or on whose behalf, a broker or dealer has received, acquired or holds funds or securities for the account of such person, but shall not include a broker or dealer or a registered municipal securities dealer, or a general, special or limited partner or director or officer of the broker or dealer, or any person to the extent that such person has a claim for property or funds which by contract, agreement or understanding, or by operation of law, is part of the capital of the broker or dealer or is subordinated to the claims of creditors of the broker or dealer. *Provided, however,* That the term "customer" shall also include a broker or dealer, but only insofar as such broker or dealer maintains a special omnibus account carried with another broker or dealer in compliance with 12 CFR 220.4(b) of Regulation T under the Securities Exchange Act of 1934.

Non-Customer

(7) The term "non-customer" means a broker or dealer registered municipal securities dealer, general partner, limited partner, officer, director and persons to the extent their claims are subordinated to the claims of creditors of the broker or dealer.

Market Maker

(8) The term "market maker" shall mean a dealer who, with respect to a particular security, (i) regularly publishes bona fide, competitive bid and offer quotations in a recognized inter-dealer quotation system; or (ii) furnishes bona fide competitive bid and offer quotations on request; and, (iii) is ready, willing and able to effect transactions in reasonable quantities at his quoted prices with other brokers or dealers.

Promptly Transmit and Deliver

(9) A broker or dealer is deemed to "promptly transmit" all funds and to "promptly deliver" all securities within the meaning of subparagraphs (a)(2)(v) and (a)(3) of this section where such transmission or delivery is made no later than noon of

the next business day after the receipt of such funds or securities. Provided, however, that such prompt transmission or delivery shall not be required to be effected prior to the settlement date for such transactions.

Forward and Promptly Forward

(10) A broker or dealer is deemed to "forward" or "promptly forward" funds or securities within the meaning of subdivisions (i) through (vi) of subparagraph (a)(2) only when such forwarding occurs no later than noon of the next business day following receipt of such funds or securities.

Ready Market

(11) (i) The term "ready market" shall include a recognized established securities market in which there exists independent bona fide offers to buy and sell so that a price reasonably related to the last sales price or current bona fide competitive bid and offer quotations can be determined for a particular security almost instantaneously and where payment will be received in settlement of a sale at such price within a relatively short time conforming to trade custom.

(ii) A "ready market" shall also be deemed to exist where securities have been accepted as collateral for a loan by a bank as defined in Section 3(a)(6) of the Securities Exchange Act of 1934 and where the broker or dealer demonstrates to its Examining Authority, that such securities adequately secure such loans as that term is defined in subparagraph (c)(5) of this section.

Examining Authority

(12) The term "Examining Authority" of a broker or dealer shall mean for the purposes of 17 CFR 240.15c3-1 and 240.15c3-1a-d the national securities exchange or national securities association of which the broker or dealer is a member of, if the broker or dealer is a member of more than one such self-regulatory organization, the organization designated by the Commission as the Examining Authority for such broker or dealer, or if the broker or dealer is not a member of any such self-regulatory organization, the Regional Office of the Commission where such broker or dealer has its principal place of business.

Municipal Securities

(14) The term "municipal securities" shall mean those securities included within the definition of "municipal securities" in Section 3(a)(29) of the Securities Exchange Act of 1934.

Debt-Equity Requirements

(a) No broker or dealer shall permit the total of outstanding principal amounts of its satisfactory subordination agreements (other than such agreements which qualify under this paragraph (d) as equity capital) to exceed 70 percent of its debt-equity total, as hereinafter defined, for a period in excess of 90 days or for such longer period which the Commission may, upon application of the broker or dealer, grant in the public interest or for the protection of investors. In the case of a corporation, the debt-equity total shall be the sum of its outstanding principal amounts of satisfactory subordination agreements, par or stated value of capital stock, paid in capital in excess of par, retained earnings, unrealized profit and loss or other capital accounts. In the case of a partnership, the debt-equity total shall be the sum of its outstanding principal amounts of satisfactory subordination agreements, capital accounts of partners (exclusive of such partners' securities accounts) subject to the provisions of paragraph (e) of this section, and unrealized profit and loss. In the case of a sole proprietorship, the debt-equity total shall include the sum of its outstanding principal amounts of satisfactory subordination agreements, capital accounts of the sole proprietorship and unrealized profit and loss. *Provided,* however, that a satisfactory subordination agreement entered into by a partner or stockholder which has an initial term of at least three years and has a remaining term of not less than 12 months shall be considered equity for the purposes of this paragraph (d) if: (1) it does not have any of the provisions for accelerated maturity provided for by subparagraphs (b)(9)(i), (b)(10)(i) or (b)(10)(ii) of Appendix (D), 17 CFR 240.15c3-1d, and is maintained as capital subject to the provisions restricting the withdrawal thereof required by paragraph (e) of this section or (2) the partnership agreement provides that capital contributed pursuant to a satisfactory subordination agreement as defined in Appendix (D), 17 CFR 240.15c3-1d, shall in all respects be partnership capital subject to the provisions restricting the withdrawal thereof required by paragraph (e) of this section.

Limitation on withdrawal of equity capital

(e) No equity capital of the broker or dealer or a subsidiary or affiliate consolidated pursuant to Appendix C (17 CFR 240.15c3-1c) may be withdrawn by action of a stockholder or partner, or by redemption or repurchase of shares of stock by any of the consolidated entities or through the payment of dividends or any similar distribution, nor may any unsecured advance or loan be made to a stockholder, partner, sole proprietor or employee if, after giving effect thereto and to any other such withdrawals, advances or loans and any Payments of Payment Obligations (as defined in Appendix D (17 CFR 240.15c3-1d)) under satisfactory subordination agreements which are scheduled to occur within six months following such withdrawal, advance or loan, either aggregate indebtedness of any of the consolidated entities exceeds 1000 percent of its net capital or its net capital would fail to equal 120 percent of the minimum dollar amount required thereby or would be less than 5 percent of aggregate debit items computed in accordance with 17 CFR 240.15c3-3a, or, if registered as a futures commission merchant, 7% of the funds required to be segregated pursuant to the Commodity Exchange Act and the regulations thereunder (less the market value of commodity options purchased by option customers on or subject to the rules of a contract market, each such deduction not to exceed the amount of funds in the option customer's account), if greater, or in the case of any broker or dealer included within such consolidation if the total outstanding principal amounts of satisfactory subordination agreements of the broker or dealer (other than such agreements which qualify as equity under paragraph (d) of this section) would exceed 70% of the debt-equity total as defined in paragraph (d). The term equity capital includes capital contributions by partners par or stated value of capital stock, paid-in capital in excess of par, retained earnings or other capital accounts. The term equity capital does not include securities in the securities accounts of partners' and balances in limited partners' capital accounts in excess of their stated capital contributions. This provision shall not preclude a broker or dealer from making required tax payments or preclude the payment to partners of reasonable compensation.

Alternative Net Capital Requirement

(f)(1) A broker or dealer who is not exempt from the provisions of 17 CFR 240.15c3-3 under the Securities Exchange Act of 1934 pursuant to paragraph (k)(1) or (k)(2)(i) may elect not to be subject to the limitations of paragraph (a) of this section respecting aggregate indebtedness as defined in paragraph (c)(1) of this section and certain deductions provided for in paragraph (c)(2) of this section. Such broker or dealer shall at all times maintain net capital equal to the greater of $100,000 ($25,000 in the case of a broker or dealer effecting transactions solely in municipal securities) or 2 percent of aggregate debit items computed in accordance with the Formula for Determination of Reserve Requirements for Brokers and Dealers (Exhibit A to Rule 15c3-3, 17 CFR 240.15c3-3a), or, if registered as a futures commission merchant, 4 percent of the funds required to be segregated pursuant to the Commodity Exchange Act, and the regulations thereunder (less the market value of commodity options purchased by option customers on or subject to the rules of a contract market, each such deduction not to exceed the amount of funds in the option customer's account), if greater. Such broker or dealer shall notify the Examining Authority for such broker or dealer and the Regional Office of the Commission in which the broker or dealer has its principal place of business, in writing, of its election to operate under this paragraph. Once a broker or dealer has determined to operate under this paragraph he shall continue to do so unless a change is approved upon application to the Commission.

(2) A broker or dealer who has consolidated one or more subsidiaries pursuant to Appendix C (17 CFR 240.15c3-1c), shall maintain net capital equal to its net capital requirement and the total of each consolidated broker or dealer subsidiary's minimum net capital requirements.

(3) A broker or dealer electing to operate pursuant to this paragraph (f) shall be subject to the deductions set forth in subparagraph (c)(2) of this section, except that he shall not be subject to the deductions required by subparagraphs (c)(2)(vi)(G), (c)(2)(vi)(J), (c)(2)(vi)(K)(i), and (c)(2)(vi)(M) and shall in lieu thereof deduct the following amounts under subparagraph (c)(2) in its computation of net capital:

Convertible Debt Securities

(i) In the case of a debt security not in default which has a fixed rate of interest and a fixed maturity date and which is convertible into an equity security, the deduction shall be as follows: If the market value is 100 percent or more of its principal amount, the deduction shall be determined as specified in (ii) below; if the market value is less than its principal amount the deduction shall be determined as in subdivision (c)(2)(vi)(F) of this section if such securities are rated as required by subdivision (c)(2)(vi)(F);

Other Securities

(ii) In the case of all securities or evidence of indebtedness, except as provided in Appendix (A), 17 CFR 240.15c3-1a, which are not included in any of the percentage categories specifically enumerated in subdivisions (A)-(H) or (K)(*ii*) of subparagraph (c)(2)(vi) of this section, the deduction shall be 15 percent of the market value of the long positions. To the extent the market value of short positions exceeds 25 percent of the market value of long positions, there shall be a percentage deduction equal to 30 percent of the market value of such excess. *Provided,* that no deduction need be made in the case of (A) a security which is convertible into or exchangeable for other securities within a period of 90 days, subject to no conditions other than the payment of money, and the other securities into which such security is convertible or for which it is exchangeable are short in the account of such broker or dealer or (B) a security which has been called for redemption and which is redeemable within 90 days. *Provided* further, that at the option of the broker or dealer, securities described in subdivision (c)(2)(vi)(I) of this section may be included in the computation of the deductions under this subdivision (f)(3)(ii) if a lesser deduction would result.

Undue Concentrations

(iii) In the case of money market instruments, or securities of a single class or series of an issuer, including any option written, endorsed or held to purchase or sell securities of such a single class or series of an issuer, (other than "exempted securities" and redeemable securities of an investment company registered pursuant to the Investment Company Act of 1940) and securities underwritten (in which case the deduction provided for herein shall be applied after 11 business days) which are long or short in the proprietary or other accounts of a broker or dealer, including securities which are collateral to secured demand notes defined in Appendix (D), 17 CFR 240.15c3-1d, and which have a market value of more than 10 percent of the "net capital" of a broker or dealer before the application of subparagraphs (c)(2)(vi), (f)(3) or Appendix (A), 17 CFR 240.15c3-1a, there shall be an additional deduction from net worth and/or the Collateral Value of securities collateralizing a secured demand note defined in Appendix (D), 17 CFR 240.15c3-1d, equal to 50 percent of the percentage deduction otherwise provided by this section or Appendix (A), 17 CFR 240.15c3-1a (in the case of securities described in subparagraph (f)(3)(i) which receive a 30% deduction or securities described in subparagraph (f)(3)(ii) the deduction required by this subdivision (f)(3)(iii) shall be 15%) on that portion of the securities position in excess of 10 percent of the "net capital" of the broker or dealer before the application of subparagraphs (c)(2)(vi), (f)(3)(i) and (ii) and Appendix (A), 17 CFR 240.15c3-1a. This provision shall apply notwithstanding any long or short position exemption provided for in subparagraphs (c)(2)(vi)(I) or (f)(3)(ii) (except for a long or short position exemption arising out of the first proviso to subparagraph (f)(3)(ii)) and the deduction of any such exemption position shall be 15% of that portion of the position in excess of 10% of net capital before the application of subparagraph (c)(2)(vi), subparagraphs (f)(3)(i) and (ii) and Appendix (A), 17 CFR 240.15c3-1a. *Provided,* that such additional deductions shall be applied in the case of equity securities only on the market value in excess of $10,000 or the market value of 500 shares, whichever is greater, or $25,000 in the case of a debt security. *Provided further,* that any specialist who is subject to a deduction required by this subdivision (f)(3)(iii) respecting his specialty stock, who can demonstrate to the satisfaction of the Examining Authority for such broker or dealer that there is sufficient liquidity for such specialist's specialty stock and that such deduction need not be applied in the public interest for the protection of investors may on a proper showing to such Examining Authority have such undue concentration deduction appropriately decreased but in no case shall the deduction prescribed in subdivision (f)(3)(ii) above be reduced. Each such Examining Authority shall make and preserve for a period of not less than 3 years a record of each application granted pursuant to this subdivision, which shall contain a summary of the justification for the granting of the application.

Provided further, this provision will be applied to an issue of municipal securities having the same security provisions, date of issue, interest rate, day, month and year of maturity only if such securities have a market value in excess of $500,000 in bonds ($5,000,000 in notes) or 10% of tentative net capital, whichever is greater, and are held in position longer than twenty (20) business days from the date the securities are received by the syndicate manager from the issuer.

(4) In the case of any deductions for open contractual commitments provided for in subparagraph (c)(2)(viii) of this section, the deduction for securities which are described in subparagraph (f)(2)(ii) shall be 30 percent.

(5) In addition to the foregoing, brokers or dealers electing this alternative shall:

(i) make the computation required by 17 CFR 240.15c3-3(e) and set forth in Exhibit A, 17 CFR 240.15c3-3a, on a weekly basis and, in lieu of the 1 percent reduction of certain debits items required by Note B(2) in the computation of their Exhibit A requirement, reduce aggregate debit items in such computation by 3 percent;

(ii) include in Items 7 and 8 of Exhibit A, 17 CFR 240.15c3-3a, the market value of items specified therein over 7 business days old;

(iii) exclude credit balances in accounts representing amounts payable for securities not yet received from the issuer or its agent which securities are specified in subdivision (c)(2)(vi)(A) and (E) of this section and any related debit items from the Exhibit A requirement for three business days.

(iv) Deduct from net worth in computing net capital 1% of the contract value of all failed to deliver contracts or securities borrowed which were allocated to failed to receive contracts of the same issue and which thereby were excluded from Items 11 or 12 of Exhibit A, 17 CFR 240.15c3-3a.

Act of 1934, 17a-11

¶ 4197   Supplemental Current Financial and Operational Reports to Be Made by Certain Exchange Members, Brokers and Dealers

Reg. § 240.17a-11. (a) Every member, broker or dealer subject to § 240.15c3-1, whose net capital at any time is less than the minimum required by any capital rule to which such person is subject and every member, broker or dealer subject to § 240.15c3-1 whose total outstanding principal amounts of satisfactory subordination agreements exceeds the maximum allowable for a period in excess of 90 days in accordance with the provisions of § 240.15c3-1(d), shall:

(1) Give telegraphic notice as set forth in paragraph (f) of this section that such person's net capital is less than is required by any such capital rule, identifying the applicable net capital rule or rules or that such person's total outstanding principal amounts of satisfactory subordinary agreements exceeds the maximum allowable in accordance with the provisions of § 250.15c3-1(d). The notice shall be given on the same day that such person's capital becomes less than required by any of the aforesaid rules to which such person is subject or, with respect to the total outstanding principal amounts of satisfactory subordination agreements, on the first day upon which such amount has exceeded the maximum allowable for a period in excess of 90 days.

(2) Within 24 hours thereafter file Part II or Part IIA of Form X-17A-5 (§ 249.617 of this chapter) as determined in accordance with the standards set forth in § § 240.17a-5(a)(2)(ii) and (a)(2)(iii), and such supplementary information as may be required.

(b)(1) If a computation made by a broker or dealer pursuant to the requirements of § 240.15c3-1(c) shows, at any point during the month, that his aggregate indebtedness is in excess of 1,200 per centum of his net capital, or that his total net capital is less than 120 per centum of the minimum net capital required of him, such person shall file a report on Part II or Part IIA of Form X-17A-5 (§ 249.617 of this chapter) as determined in accordance with the standards set forth in sections 240.17a-5(a)(2)(ii) and (a)(2)(iii), within 15 calendar days after the end of each month thereafter until 3 successive months shall have elapsed during which his aggregate indebtedness does not exceed 1,200 per centum of his net capital, and his total net capital does not fall below 120 per centum of the minimum net capital required of him.

(2) If a computation made by a broker or dealer pursuant to § 240.15c3-1(f) shows, at any point during the month, that his net capital is less than 5 percent of aggregate debit items computed in accordance with § 240.15c3-3 Exhibit A: Formula for the Determination of Reserve Requirements, or that his total net capital is less than 120 per centum of the minimum net capital required of him, such broker or dealer shall file a report on Part II or Part IIA of Form X-17A-5 (§ 249.617 of this chapter) as determined in accordance with the standards set forth in § § 240.17a-5(a)(2)(ii) and (a)(2)(iii), within 15 days after the end of each month thereafter until three successive months shall have elapsed during which his net capital is not less than 5 percent of aggregate debit items computed in accordance with § 240.15c3-3 Exhibit A, and his total net capital does not fall below 120 percentum of the minimum net capital required of him.

(3) If a dealer operating pursuant to paragraph (a)(6) of Rule 15c3-1(a)(6) fails to deposit in the specialist or market maker account collateral required thereunder within

the time limit therein prescribed, the broker or dealer carrying such account shall give immediate telegraphic notice of such fact to the principal office of the Commission for the region in Washington, D.C., the regional office of the Commission for the region in which the broker or dealer has its principal place of business, and the Designated Examining Authorities of the dealer and the broker or dealer carrying such account.

(4) If a member, broker or dealer subject to the requirements of § 240.15c3-1(c)(2)(x)(F)(*3*), § 240.15c3-1(c)(2)(x)(B)(*1*) or § 240.15c3-1d(c)(2) fails to comply with the financial responsibility standards set forth in any of the above provisions, such member, broker or dealer shall immediately give notice of such event as specified in such provision.

(c) At any time when a broker or dealer subject to Rule 17a-3 fails to make and keep current the books and records specified therein, he shall immediately give telegraphic notice of such fact, specifying the books and records which have not been made or which are not current, and within 48 hours of the telegraphic notice file a report stating what steps have been and are being taken to correct the situation.

(d) Whenever any broker or dealer discovers, or is notified by an independent public accountant, pursuant to paragraph (h)(2) of Rule 17a-5 of the existence of any material inadequacy as defined in paragraph (g) of Rule 17a-5, said broker or dealer shall give telegraphic notice of such material inadequacy within 24 hours, and within 48 hours of the telegraphic notice file a report stating what steps have been and are being taken to correct the situation.

(e) Whenever any national securities exchange or national securities association learns that a member broker or dealer has failed to file a notice or file a report as required by paragraph (a), (b), (c) or (d) of this section, such organization shall immediately report such failure as provided in paragraph (f) of this section.

(f) Every notice and report required to be given or filed by this section shall be given to or filed with the principal office of the Commission in Washington, D.C., with the regional office of the Commission for the region in which the broker or dealer has its principal place of business, with the designated examining authority of which such broker or dealer is a member, and with the Commodity Futures Trading Commission if such broker or dealer is registered with such Commission.

[As last amended in Release No. 34-18417, January 13, 1982, 47 F.R. 3512.]

> All telegraphic notices and reports required to be filed with the Association pursuant to the provisions of Rule 17a-11 should be directed to the NASD, 1735 "K" Street, N.W. Washington, D.C. 20006, to the attention of the Surveillance Department.

NASD, para. 2198

¶ 2198   Regulation of Activities of Members Experiencing Financial and/or Operational Difficulties

Sec. 38. (a) Application—For the purposes of this rule, the term "member" shall be limited to any member of the Association who is not designated to another self-regulatory organization by the Securities and Exchange Commission for financial responsibility pursuant to Section 17 of the Securities Exchange Act of 1934 and Rule 17d-1 thereunder. Further, the term shall not be applicable to any member who is subject to paragraphs (a)(2) and (a)(3) of SEC Rule 15c3-1, or is otherwise exempt from the provisions of said rule.

(b) A member, when so directed by the Association, shall not expand its business during any period in which:

(1) Any of the following conditions continue to exist, or have existed, for more than 15 consecutive business days:

(A) A firm's net capital is less than 150 percent of its net capital minimum requirement or such greater percentage thereof as may from time to time be prescribed by the Association;

(B) If subject to the aggregate indebtedness requirement under SEC Rule 15c3-1, a firm's aggregate indebtedness is more than 1,000 per centum of its net capital;

(C) If, in lieu of subparagraph (b)(1)(B) above, the specified percentage of the aggregate debit items in the Formula for Determination of Reserve Requirements for Brokers and Dealers under SEC Rule 15c3-3 (the alternative net capital requirement) is applicable, a firm's net capital is less than 5 percent of the aggregate debit items thereunder; or,

(D) The deduction of capital withdrawals including maturities of subordinated debt scheduled during the next six months would result in any one of the conditions described in (A), (B) or (C) of this subparagraph (1).

(2) The Association restricts the member for any other financial or operational reason.

(c) A member, when so directed by the Association, shall forthwith reduce its business:

(1) To a point enabling its available capital to comply with the standards set forth in subparagraphs (b)(1)(A), (B) or (C) of this rule if any of the following conditions continue to exist, or have existed, for more than fifteen (15) consecutive business days:

(A) A firm's net capital is less than 125 percent of its net capital minimum requirement or such greater percentage thereof as may from time to time be proscribed by the Association;

(B) If subject to the aggregate indebtedness requirement under SEC Rule 15c3-1, a firm's aggregate indebtedness is more than 1,200 per centum of its net capital;

(C) If, in lieu of subparagraph (c)(1)(B) above, the specified percentage of the aggregate debit items in the Formula for Determination of Reserve Requirements for Brokers and Dealers, under SEC Rule 15c3-3 (the alternative net capital requirement) is applicable, a firm's net capital is less than 4 percent of the aggregate debit items thereunder; or,

(D) If the deduction of capital withdrawals including maturities of subordinated debt scheduled during the next six months would result in any one of the conditions described in subparagraph (c)(1)(A), (B) or (C) of this rule.

(2) As required by the Association when it restricts a member for any other financial or operational reason.

[Section 38 adopted February 17, 1984.]

Explanation of the Board of Governors

Restrictions on a Member's Activity

This explanation outlines and discusses some of the financial and operational deficiencies which could initiate action under the rule. Subparagraphs (b)(2) and (c)(2) of the rule recognize that there are various unstated financial and operational reasons for which the Association may impose restrictions on a member so as to prohibit its expansion or to require a reduction in overall level of business. These provisions are deemed necessary in order to provide for the variety of situations and practices which do arise and, which if allowed to persist, could result in increased exposure to customers and to broker-dealers.

In the opinion of the Board of Governors, it would be impractical and unwise to attempt to identify and list all of the situations and practices which might lead to the imposition of restrictions or the types of remedial actions the Corporation may direct be taken because they are numerous and cannot be totally identified or specified with any degree of precison. The Board believes, however, that it would be helpful to members' understanding to list some of the other bases upon which the Corporation may conclude that a member is in or approaching financial difficulty.

Explanation of the Board of Governors

Explanation

(a) For purposes of subparagraphs (b)(2) and (c)(2) of the rule, a member may be considered to be in or approaching financial-or operational difficulty in conducting its operations and therefore subject to restrictions if it is determined by the Corporation that any of the parameters specified therein are exceeded or one or more of the following conditions exist:

(1) The member has experienced a reduction in excess net capital of 25% in the preceding two months or 30% or more in the three-month period immediately preceding such computation.

(2) The member has experienced a substantial change in the manner in which it processes its business which, in the view of the Corporation, increases the potential risk of loss to customers and members.

(3) The member's books and records are not maintained in accordance with the provisions of SEC Rules 17a-3 and 17a-4.

(4) The member is not in compliance, or is unable to demonstrate compliance, with applicable net capital requirements.

(5) The member is not in compliance, or is unable to demonstrate compliance, with SEC Rule 15c3-3 (Customer Protection Reserves and Custody of Securities).

(6) The member is unable to clear and settle transactions promptly.

(7) The member's overall business operations are in such a condition, given the nature and kind of its business that, notwithstanding the absence of any of the conditions enumerated in subparagraphs (1) through (6), a determination of financial or operational difficulty should be made, or

(8) The member is registered as a Futures Commission Merchant and its net capital is less than 7% of the funds required to be segregated

Explanation of the Board of Governors

pursuant to the Commodity Exchange Act and the regulations thereunder.

(b) If the Corporation determines that any of the conditions specified in subparagraph (a) of this Explanation exist, it may require that the member take appropriate action by effecting one or more of the following actions until such time as the Corporation determines they are no longer required:

(1) Promptly pay all free credit balances to customers.

(2) Promptly effect delivery to customers of all fully-paid securities in the member's possession or control.

(3) Introduce all or a portion of its business to another member on a fully-disclosed basis.

(4) Reduce the size or modify the composition of its inventory.

(5) Postpone the opening of new branch offices or require the closing of one or more existing branch offices.

(6) Promptly cease making unsecured loans, advances or other similar receivables, and, as necessary, collect all such loans, advances or receivables where practicable.

(7) Accept no new customer accounts.

(8) Undertake an immediate audit by an independent public accountant at the member's expense.

(9) Restrict the payment of salaries or other sums to partners, officers, directors, shareholders, or associated persons of the member.

(10) Effect liquidating transactions only.

(11) Accept unsolicited customer orders only.

(12) File special financial and operating reports and/or

(13) Be subject to such other restrictions or take such other action as the Corporation deems apropriate under the circumstances in the public interest and for the protection of members.

NASD, para. 4197

(c) Individual reports filed by, or on behalf of, brokers, dealers or members of national securities exchanges pursuant to this section are to be considered non-public information, except in cases where the Commission determines that it is in the public interest to direct otherwise.

(d) In the event any broker or dealer finds that it cannot file the annual report required by paragraph (a) of this section within the time specified without undue hardship, it may file with the Commission's principal office in Washington, D.C., prior to the date upon which the report is due an application for an extension of time to a specified date which shall not be later than 60 days after the close of the calendar year for which the report is to be made. The application shall state the reasons for the requested extension and shall contain an agreement to file the report on or before the specified date.

[As last amended in Release No. 34-18300, December 3, 1981, 46 F.R. 60193.]

¶ 4197   Supplemental Current Financial and Operational Reports to Be Made by Certain Exchange Members, Brokers and Dealers

Reg. § 240.17a-11. (a) Every member, broker or dealer subject to § 240.15c3-1, whose net capital at any time is less than the minimum required by any capital rule to which such person is subject and every member, broker or dealer subject to § 240.15c3-1 whose total outstanding principal amounts of satisfactory subordination agreements exceeds the maximum allowable for a period in excess of 90 days in accordance with the provisions of § 240.15c3-1(d), shall:

(1) Give telegraphic notice as set forth in paragraph (f) of this section that such person's net capital is less than is required by any such capital rule, identifying the applicable net capital rule or rules or that such person's total outstanding principal amounts of satisfactory subordinary agreements exceeds the maximum allowable in accordance with the provisions of § 250.15c3-1(d). The notice shall be given on the same day that such person's capital becomes less than required by any of the aforesaid rules to which such person is subject or, with respect to the total outstanding principal amounts of satisfactory subordination agreements, on the first day upon which such amount has exceeded the maximum allowable for a period in excess of 90 days.

(2) Within 24 hours thereafter file Part II or Part IIA of Form X-17A-5 (§ 249.617 of this chapter) as determined in accordance with the standards set forth in § § 240.17a-5(a)(2)(ii) and (a)(2)(iii), and such supplementary information as may be required.

(b)(1) If a computation made by a broker or dealer pursuant to the requirements of § 240.15c3-1(c) shows, at any point during the month, that his aggregate indebtedness is in excess of 1,200 per centum of his net capital, or that his total net capital is less than 120 per centum of the minimum net capital required of him, such person shall file a report on Part II or Part IIA of Form X-17A-5 (§ 249.617 of this chapter) as determined in accordance with the standards set forth in sections 240.17a-5(a)(2)(ii) and (a)(2)(iii), within 15 calendar days after the end of each month thereafter until 3 successive months shall have elapsed during which his aggregate indebtedness does not exceed 1,200 per centum of his net capital, and his total net capital does not fall below 120 per centum of the minimum net capital required of him.

(2) If a computation made by a broker or dealer pursuant to § 240.15c3-1(f) shows, at any point during the month, that his net capital is less than 5 percent of aggregate debit items computed in accordance with § 240.15c3-3 Exhibit A: Formula for the Determination of Reserve Requirements, or that his total net capital is less than 120 per centum of the minimum net capital required of him, such broker or dealer shall file a report on Part II or Part IIA of Form X-17A-5 (§ 249.617 of this chapter) as determined in accordance with the standards set forth in § § 240.17a-5(a)(2)(ii) and (a)(2)(iii), within 15 days after the end of each month thereafter until three successive months shall have elapsed during which his net capital is not less than 5 percent of aggregate debit items computed in accordance with § 240.15c3-3 Exhibit A, and his total net capital does not fall below 120 percentum of the minimum net capital required of him.

(3) If a dealer operating pursuant to paragraph (a)(6) of Rule 15c3-1(a)(6) fails to deposit in the specialist or market maker account collateral required thereunder within the time limit therein prescribed, the broker or dealer carrying such account shall give immediate telegraphic notice of such fact to the principal office of the Commission for the region in Washington, D.C., the regional office of the Commission for the region in

which the broker or dealer has its principal place of business, and the Designated Examining Authorities of the dealer and the broker or dealer carrying such account.

(4) If a member, broker or dealer subject to the requirements of § 240.15c3-1(c)(2)(x)(F)(*3*), § 240.15c3-1(c)(2)(x)(B)(*1*) or § 240.15c3-1d(c)(2) fails to comply with the financial responsibility standards set forth in any of the above provisions, such member, broker or dealer shall immediately give notice of such event as specified in such provision.

(c) At any time when a broker or dealer subject to Rule 17a-3 fails to make and keep current the books and records specified therein, he shall immediately give telegraphic notice of such fact, specifying the books and records which have not been made or which are not current, and within 48 hours of the telegraphic notice file a report stating what steps have been and are being taken to correct the situation.

(d) Whenever any broker or dealer discovers, or is notified by an independent public accountant, pursuant to paragraph (h)(2) of Rule 17a-5 of the existence of any material inadequacy as defined in paragraph (g) of Rule 17a-5, said broker or dealer shall give telegraphic notice of such material inadequacy within 24 hours, and within 48 hours of the telegraphic notice file a report stating what steps have been and are being taken to correct the situation.

(e) Whenever any national securities exchange or national securities association learns that a member broker or dealer has failed to file a notice or file a report as required by paragraph (a), (b), (c) or (d) of this section, such organization shall immediately report such failure as provided in paragraph (f) of this section.

(f) Every notice and report required to be given or filed by this section shall be given to or filed with the principal office of the Commission in Washington, D.C., with the regional office of the Commission for the region in which the broker or dealer has its principal place of business, with the designated examining authority of which such broker or dealer is a member, and with the Commodity Futures Trading Commission if such broker or dealer is registered with such Commission.

[As last amended in Release No. 34-18417, January 13, 1982, 47 F.R. 3512.]

All telegraphic notices and reports required to be filed with the Association pursuant to the provisions of Rule 17a-11 should be directed to the NASD, 1735 "K" Street, N.W. Washington, D.C. 20006, to the attention of the Surveillance Department.

NASD, para. 2171(a)

¶ 2171   Books and Records

Sec. 21.

Requirements

(a) Each member shall keep and preserve books, accounts, records, memoranda, and correspondence in conformity with all applicable laws, rules, regulations and statements of policy promulgated thereunder and with the rules of this Association.

Marking of Customer Order Tickets

(b)(i) A person associated with a member shall indicate on the memorandum for the sale of any security whether the order is "long" or "short," except that this requirement shall not apply to transactions in corporate debt securities. An order may be marked "long" if (1) the customer's account is long the security involved or (2) the customer agrees to deliver the security as soon as possible without undue inconvenience or expense.

(ii) A person associated with a member shall indicate on the memorandum for each transaction in a non-NASDAQ security, as that term is defined in Schedule H to the NASD By-Laws, the name of each dealer contacted and the quotations received to determine the best inter-dealer market.

Act of 1934, 17a3-17a4

KEEPING AND PRESERVATION OF RECORDS

¶ 4031   Introduction

Securities and Exchange Commission Rule 17a-3, adopted under the Securities Exchange Act of 1934, specifies the records which certain brokers and dealers shall make and keep current. Rule 17a-4 specifies the period of time during which these records and other documents pertaining to the business of a broker-dealer shall be preserved.

The rules apply not only to all members of national securities exchanges, broker-dealers who transact a business in securities through the medium of such members, but also to all brokers and dealers registered with the SEC.

● ● ● *Cross Reference*

See Rules of Fair Practice, Article III, Section 21 . . . . ¶ 2171
See Memorandum Re: Rule 17a-3 . . . . ¶ 4061

¶ 4041   **Records to Be Made by Certain Exchange Members, Brokers and Dealers**

Reg. § 240.17a-3. (a) Every member of a national securities exchange who transacts a business in securities directly with others than members of a national securities exchange, and every broker or dealer who transacts a business in securities through the medium of any such member, and every broker or dealer registered pursuant to Section 15 of the Securities Exchange Act of 1934, as amended, shall make and keep current the following books and records relating to his business:

(1) Blotters (or other records of original entry) containing an itemized daily record of all purchases and sales of securities, all receipts and deliveries of securities (including certificate numbers), all receipts and disbursements of cash and all other debits and credits. Such records shall show the account for which each such transaction was effected, the name and amount of securities, the unit and aggregate purchase or sale price (if any), the trade date, and the name or other designation of the person from whom purchased or received or to whom sold or delivered.

(2) Ledgers (or other records) reflecting all assets and liabilities, income and expense and capital accounts.

(3) Ledger accounts (or other records) itemizing separately as to each cash and margin account of every customer and of such member, broker or dealer and partners thereof, all purchases, sales, receipts and deliveries of securities and commodities for such account and all other debits and credits to such account.

(4) Ledgers (or other records) reflecting the following:

(i) securities in transfer;

(ii) dividends and interest received;

(iii) securities borrowed and securities loaned;

(iv) monies borrowed and monies loaned (together with a record of the collateral therefor and any substitutions in such collateral);

(v) Securities failed to receive and failed to deliver;

(vi) All long and all short securities record differences arising from the examination, count, verification and comparison pursuant to Rule 17a-13 and Rule 17a-5 hereunder (by date of examination, count, verification and comparison showing for each security the number of long or short count differences);

(vii) Repurchase and reverse repurchase agreements;

(5) A securities record or ledger reflecting separately for each security as of the clearance dates all "long" or "short" positions (including securities in safekeeping and securities that are the subjects of repurchase or reverse repurchase agreements) carried by such member, broker or dealer for his account of for the account of his customers or partners or others and showing the location of all securities long and the offsetting position to all securities short, including long security count differences and short security count differences classified by the date of the physical count and verification in which they were discovered, and in all cases the name or designation of the account in which each position is carried.

(6) A memorandum of each brokerage order, and of any other instruction, given or received for the purchase or sale of securities, whether executed or unexecuted. Such memorandum shall show the terms and conditions of the order or instructions and of any modification or cancellation thereof, the account for which entered, the time of entry, the price at which executed and, to the extent feasible, the time of execution or cancellation. Orders entered pursuant to the exercise of discretionary power by such member, broker or dealer, or any employee thereof, shall be so designated. The term "instruction" shall be deemed to include instructions between partners and employees of a member, broker or dealer. The term "time of entry" shall be deemed to mean the time when such member, broker or dealer transmits the order or instruction for execution or, if it is not so transmitted, the time when it is received.

(7) A memorandum of each purchase and sale for the account of such member, broker, or dealer showing the price and, to the extent feasible, the time of execution; and, in addition, where such purchase or sale is with a customer other than a broker or dealer, a memorandum of each order received, showing the time of receipt, the terms and conditions of the order, and the account in which it was entered.

(8) Copies of confirmations of all purchases and sales of securities, including all repurchase and reverse repurchase agreements, and copies of notices of all other debits and credits for securities, cash and other items for the account of customers and partners of such member, broker or dealer.

(9) A record in respect of each cash and margin account with such member, broker or dealer indicating (i) the name and address of the beneficial owner of such account, and (ii) Except with respect to exempt employee benefit plan securities as defined in §240.14a-1(d), but only to the extent such securities are held by employee benefit plans established by the issuer of the securities, whether or not the beneficial owner of securities registered in the name of such members, brokers or dealers, or a registered clearing agency or its nominee objects to disclosure of his or her identity, address and securities positions to issuers, and (iii) in the case of a margin account, the signature of

such owner, *Provided,* That, in the case of a joint account or an account of a corporation, such records are required only in respect of the person or persons authorized to transact business for such account.

(10) A record of all puts, calls, spreads, straddles and other options in which such member, broker or dealer has any direct or indirect interest or which such member, broker or dealer has granted or guaranteed, containing, at least, an identification of the security and the number of units involved.

(11) A record of the proof of money balances of all ledger accounts in the form of trial balances, and a record of the computation of aggregate indebtedness and net capital, as of the trial balance date, pursuant to § 240.15c3-1; *Provided, however,* (i) That such computation need not be made by any member, broker or dealer unconditionally exempt from § 240.15c3-1 by subparagraph (b)(1) or (b)(3), thereof; and (ii) that any member of an exchange whose members are exempt from § 240.15c3-1 by subparagraph (b)(2) thereof shall make a record of the computation of aggregate indebtedness and net capital as of the trial balance date in accordance with the capital rules of at least one of the exchanges therein listed of which he is a member. Such trial balances and computations shall be prepared currently at least once a month.

(12)(i) A questionnaire or application for employment executed by each "associated person" (as hereinafter defined) of such member, broker or dealer, which questionnaire or application shall be approved in writing by an authorized representative of such member, broker or dealer and shall contain at least the following information with respect to such person:

(a) His name, address, social security number, and the starting date of his employment or other association with the member, broker or dealer;

(b) His date of birth;

(c) A complete, consecutive statement of all his business connections for at least the preceding ten years, including whether the employment was part-time or full-time.

(d) A record of any denial of membership or registration, and of any disciplinary action taken, or sanction imposed, upon him by any federal or state agency, or by any national securities exchange or national securities association, including any finding that he was a cause of any disciplinary action or had violated any law;

(e) A record of any denial, suspension, expulsion or revocation of membership or registration of any member, broker or dealer with which he was associated in any capacity when such action was taken;

(f) A record of any permanent or temporary injunction entered against him or any member, broker or dealer with which he was associated in any capacity at the time such injunction was entered;

(g) A record of any arrest or indictment for any felony, or any misdemeanor pertaining to securities, commodities, banking, insurance or real estate (including, but not limited to, acting as or being associated with a broker-dealer, investment company, investment adviser, futures sponsor, bank, or savings and loan association), fraud, false statements or omissions, wrongful taking of property or bribery, forgery, counterfeiting or extortion, and the disposition of the foregoing.

(h) A record of any other name or names by which he has been known or which he has used;

provided, however, that if such associated person has been registered as a registered representative of such member, broker or dealer with, or his employment has been approved by, the National Association of Securities Dealers, Inc., or the American Stock Exchange, the Boston Stock Exchange, the Midwest Stock Exchange, the New York Stock Exchange, the Pacific Coast Stock Exchange, or the Philadelphia-Baltimore Stock Exchange, then retention of a full, correct, and complete copy of any and all applications for such registration or approval shall be deemed to satisfy the requirements of this subparagraph.

(ii) For purposes of subparagraph (12) of paragraph (a) of this rule the term "associated person" shall mean a partner, officer, director, salesman, trader, manager, or any employee handling funds or securities or soliciting transactions or accounts for such member, broker or dealer.

(13) Records required to be maintained pursuant to Rule 17f-2, paragraph (d).

(14) Copies of all Forms X-17F-1A filed pursuant to § 240.17f-1, all agreements between reporting institutions regarding registration or other aspects of § 240.17f-1, and all confirmations or other information received from the Commission or its designee as a result of inquiry.

(15) Records required to be maintained pursuant to paragraph (e) of § 240.17f-2.

(b)(1) This rule shall not be deemed to require a member of a national securities exchange, a broker or dealer who transacts a business in securities through the medium of any such member, or a broker or dealer registered pursuant to Section 15 of the Act, to make or keep such records of transactions cleared for such member, broker or dealer as are customarily made and kept by a clearing broker or dealer pursuant to the requirements of Rules 17a-3 and 17a-4, *Provided that* the clearing broker or dealer has and maintains net capital of not less than $25,000 and is otherwise in compliance with Rule 15c3-1 or the capital rules of the exchange of which such clearing broker or dealer is a member if the members of such exchange are exempt from Rule 15c3-1 by subparagraph (b)(2) thereof.

(2) This rule shall not be deemed to require a member of a national securities exchange, a broker or dealer who transacts a business in securities through the medium of any such member, or a broker or dealer registered pursuant to Section 15 of the Act, to make or keep such records of transactions cleared for such member, broker or dealer by a bank as are customarily made and kept by a clearing broker or dealer pursuant to the requirements of Rules 17a-3 and 17a-4, *Provided that* such member, broker or dealer obtains from such bank an agreement in writing to the effect that the records made and kept by such bank are the property of the member, broker or dealer, and *Provided further* that such bank files with the Commission a written undertaking in form acceptable to the Commission and signed by a duly authorized person, that such books and records are available for examination by representatives of the Commission as specified in Section 17(a) of the Act, and that it will furnish to the Commission, upon demand, at its principal office in Washington, D.C. or at any Regional Office of the Commission designated in such demand, true, correct, complete and current copies of any or all of such records. Such undertaking shall include the following provisions:

The undersigned hereby undertakes to maintain and preserve on behalf of [BD] the books and records required to be maintained and preserved by [BD] pursuant to Rules 17a-3 and 17a-4 under the Securities Exchange Act of 1934 and to permit examination of such books and records at any time or from time to time during business hours by examiners or other representatives of the Securities and Exchange Commission, and to furnish to said Commission at its principal office in Washington, D.C., or at any Regional Office of said Commission specified in a demand made by or on behalf of said Commission for copies of books and records, true, correct, complete and current copies of any or all, or any part, of such books and records. This undertaking shall be binding upon the undersigned, and the successors and assigns of the undersigned.

Nothing herein contained shall be deemed to relieve such member, broker or dealer from the responsibility that such books and records be accurately maintained and preserved as specified in Rule 17a-3 and Rule 17a-4.

(c) This rule shall not be deemed to require a member of a national securities exchange, or a broker or dealer registered pursuant to Section 15 of the Securities Exchange Act of 1934, as amended, to make or keep such records as are required by Paragraph (a) reflecting the sale of United States Tax Savings Notes, United States Defense Savings Stamps, or United States Defense Savings Bonds, Series E, F and G.

(d) The records specified in paragraph (a) of this rule shall not be required with respect to any cash transaction of $100.00 or less involving only subscription rights or warrants which by their terms expire within 90 days after the issuance thereof.

(e) For purposes of transactions in municipal securities by municipal securities brokers and municipal securities dealers, compliance with Rule G-8 of the Municipal Securities Rulemaking Board will be deemed to be compliance with this section.

¶ 4051 Records to Be Preserved by Certain Exchange Members, Brokers and Dealers

Reg. § 240.17a-4. (a) Every member, broker and dealer subject to § 240.17a-3 shall preserve for a period of not less than six years, the first two years in an easily accessible place, all records required to be made pursuant to paragraphs 1, 2, 3 and 5 of § 240.17a-3.

(b) Every such broker and dealer shall preserve for a period of not less than three years, the first two years in an accessible place:

(1) All records required to be made pursuant to paragraphs 4, 6, 7, 8, 9 and 10 of § 240.17a-3.

(2) All check books, bank statements, cancelled checks and cash reconciliations.

(3) All bills receivable or payable (or copies thereof), paid or unpaid, relating to the business of such member, broker or dealer, as such.

(4) Originals of all communications received and copies of all communications sent by such member, broker or dealer (including inter-office memoranda and communications) relating to his business as such.

(5) All trial balances, computations of aggregate indebtedness and net capital (and working papers in connection therewith), financial statements, branch office reconciliations, and internal audit working papers, relating to the business of such member, broker or dealer, as such.

(6) All guarantees of accounts and all powers of attorney and other evidence of the granting of any discretionary authority given in respect of any account, and copies of resolutions empowering an agent to act on behalf of a corporation.

(7) All written agreements (or copies thereof) entered into by such member, broker or dealer relating to his business as such, including agreements with respect to any account.

(8) Records which contain the following information in support of amounts included in the report prepared as of the audit date on Form X-17A-5 (§ 249.617 of this

chapter) Part II or Part IIA and in the annual financial statements required by §240.17a-5(i)(XV).

(i) money balance position, long or short, including description, quantity, price and valuation of each security including contractual commitments in customers' accounts, in cash and fully secured accounts, partly secured accounts, unsecured accounts and in securities accounts payable to customers;

(ii) money balance and position, long or short, including description, quantity, price and valuation of each security, including contractual commitments in non-customers' accounts, in cash and fully secured accounts, partly secured and unsecured accounts and in securities accounts payable to non-customers;

(iii) position, long or short, including description, quantity, price and valuation of each security, including contractual commitments included in the Computation of Net Capital as commitments, securities owned, securities owned not readily marketable, and other investments owned not readily marketable;

(iv) amount of secured demand note, description of collateral securing such secured demand note including quantity, price and valuation of each security and cash balance securing such secured demand note;

(v) description of futures commodity contracts, contract value on trade date, market value, gain or loss, and liquidating equity or deficit in customers' and non-customers' accounts;

(vi) description of futures commodity contracts, contract value on trade date, market value, gain or loss and liquidating equity or deficit in trading and investment accounts;

(vii) description, money balance, quantity, price and valuation of each spot commodity position or commitments in customers' and non-customers' accounts;

(viii) description, money balance, quantity, price and valuation of each spot commodity position or commitments in trading and investment accounts;

(ix) number of shares, description of security, exercise price, cost and market value of put and call options including short out of the money options having no market or exercise value, showing listed and unlisted put and call options separately;

(x) quantity, price, and valuation of each security underlying the haircut for undue concentration made in the Computation for Net Capital;

(xi) description, quantity, price and valuation of each security and commodity position or contractual commitment, long or short, in each joint account in which the broker or dealer has an interest, including each participant's interest and margin deposit;

(xii) description, settlement date, contract amount, quantity, market price, and valuation for each aged failed to deliver requiring a charge in the Computation of Net Capital pursuant to Rule 15c3-1;

(xiii) detail relating to information for possession or control requirements under Rule 15c3-3 and reported on the schedule in Part II or IIA of Form X-17A-5;

(xiv) detail of all items, not otherwise substantiated which are charged or credited in the Computation of Net Capital pursuant to Rule 15c3-1, such as cash margin deficiencies, deductions related to securities values and undue concentration, aged securities differences and insurance claims receivable; and

(xv) other schedules which are specifically prescribed by the Commission as necessary to support information reported as required by Rule 17a-5.

(9) The records required to be made pursuant to § 240.15c3-3(d)(4).

(c) Every such member, broker and dealer shall preserve for a period of not less than six years after the closing of any customer's account any account cards or records which relate to the terms and conditions with respect to the opening and maintenance of such account.

(d) Every such member, broker and dealer shall preserve during the life of the enterprise and of any successor enterprise all partnership articles or, in the case of a corporation, all articles of incorporation or charter, minute books and stock certificate books.

(e) Every such member, broker and dealer shall maintain and preserve in an easily accessible place:

(1) all records required under paragraph (a)(12) of Rule 17a-3 until at least three years after the "associated person" has terminated his employment and any other connection with the member, broker, or dealer.

(2) all records required under paragraph (a)(13) of Rule 17a-3 until at least three years after the termination of employment or association of those persons required by Rule 17f-2 to be fingerprinted;

(3) All records required pursuant to paragraph (a)(15) of § 240.17a-3 for the life of the enterprise.

(4) all records required pursuant to paragraph (a)(14) of § 240.17a-3 for three years.

(f) The records required to be maintained and preserved pursuant to Rules 17a-3 and 17a-4 may be immediately produced or reproduced on microfilm and be maintained and preserved for the required time in that form. If such microfilm substitution for hard copy is made by a member, broker, or dealer, he shall (1) at all times have available for Commission examination of his records, pursuant to Section 17(a) of the Act, facilities for immediate, easily readable projection of the microfilm and for producing easily readable facsimile enlargements, (2) arrange the records and index and file the films in such a manner as to permit the immediate location of any particular record, (3) be ready at all times to provide, and immediately provide, any facsimile enlargement which the Commission by its examiners or other representatives may request, and (4) store separately from the original one other copy of the microfilm for the time required.

(g) If a person who has been subject to § 240.17a-3 ceases to transact a business in securities directly with others than members of a national securities exchange, or ceases to transact a business in securities through the medium of a member of a national securities exchange, or ceases to be registered pursuant to Section 15 of the Securities Exchange Act of 1934, as amended, such person shall, for the remainder of the periods of time specified in this rule, continue to preserve the records which he theretofore preserved pursuant to this rule.

(h) For purposes of transactions in municipal securities by municipal securities brokers and municipal securities dealers, compliance with Rule G-9 of the Municipal Securities Rulemaking Board will be deemed to be compliance with this section.

(i) If the records required to be maintained and preserved pursuant to the provisions of § § 240.17a-3 and 240.17a-4 are prepared or maintained by an outside service bureau, depository, bank which does not operate pursuant to § 240.17a-3(b)(2), or other recordkeeping service on behalf of the member, broker or dealer required to maintain and preserve such records, such outside entity shall file with the Commission a written undertaking in form acceptable to the Commission, signed by a duly authorized person, to the effect that such records are the property of the member, broker or dealer required to maintain and preserve such records and will be surrendered promptly on request of the member, broker or dealer and including the following provision:

> With respect to any books and records maintained or preserved on behalf of [BD], the undersigned hereby undertakes to permit examination of such books and records at any time or from time to time during business hours by representatives or designees of the Securities and Exchange Commission, and to promptly furnish to said Commission or its designee true, correct, complete and current hard copy of any or all or any part of such books and records.

Agreement with an outside entity shall not relieve such member, broker or dealer from the responsibility to prepare and maintain records as specified in this section or in Section 240.17a-3.

(j) Every member, broker or dealer subject to this Section shall furnish promptly to a representative of the Commission such legible, true and complete copies of those records of the member, broker or dealer, which are required to be preserved under this Section, as are requested by the representative of the Commission.

[As last amended in Release No. 34-19268, November 18, 1982, 47 F.R. 54057.]

Memorandum of the Board of Governors

¶ 4061   Rule 17a-3

The rule applies not only to all members of national securities exchanges, brokers or dealers who transact a business in securities through the medium of such members, but also to all brokers and dealers registered with the S. E. C.

Generally speaking, the rule represents a codification of bookkeeping practices now followed by many exchange firms and over-the-counter brokers and dealers in that it specifies the various items of information which must be reflected upon the firm's books. The rule does not, however, require that the various books or records specified therein must be kept on any prescribed form or type of book, ledger or card system. Nor does the rule regulate accounting practices.

¶ 4062   Blotters or similar records

Paragraph 1 of the rule requires that "blotters," or other records of original entry, contain an itemized daily record of all purchases and sales as well as receipts and deliveries of securities (including certificate numbers), all receipts and disbursements of cash, and all other debits and credits. Such blotters, or comparable records of original entry, should show the account for which each such transaction was effected, number of shares (or principal amount in the case of bonds), the name of the security, the unit and aggregate purchase or sales price (if any), the trade date, and the name or other designation of the person from whom purchased or received or to whom sold or delivered.

The "blotter," as it is often called, is a broker's or dealer's book of original entry and contains an historical account of *all* the daily transactions of the firm or its customers. The term "blotter" is often used synonymously with "diary," "journal," or "day book." Larger firms may keep a number of different blotters, each to record a separate type of transaction. For instance, a member firm of a securities exchange ordinarily maintains a clearing house blotter in which are recorded the purchases and sales of cleared securities in lots of 100 shares or more and an "ex-clearing blotter" or several other blotters in which are recorded transactions in odd lots, unlisted securities, bonds, cash, receipts and deliveries, and journal entries. Over-the-counter houses may also keep separate blotters for special kinds of business such as a "cash book" showing only payments and receipts of cash. Blotters are either "To Receive" blotters, in which are recorded purchases, receipt of securities and payments of cash, or "To Deliver" blotters, in which are recorded sales, deliveries of securities and receipts of cash.

The blotter is usually a loose-leaf affair showing on the bought (to receive) side, of whom bought, quantity, security, certificate numbers, price, amount, interest (if any), commission (if any), trade date, and the account for which bought.

The sold (to deliver) side shows to whom sold, quantity, security, certificate numbers, price, amount, tax, interest (if any), commission (if any), trade date, account for which sold. Blotters or similar records, besides being occasionally kept in bound ledgers, may also be kept on cards separated by days or may consist of carbon copies of customers' confirmations, arranged and bound by days, provided that all of the information specified by paragraph 1 of the rule is contained with respect to each entry.

¶ 4063   Firm's general ledgers

Paragraph 2 requires that ledgers or other records be maintained reflecting all of the firm's assets and liabilities, and its income and expense and capital accounts. This refers to what is usually known as the general ledger in which a record of all asset, liability and nominal accounts are kept and from which a trial balance can be abstracted in order to prepare financial statements showing the broker's or dealer's financial condition. Under present day double entry systems, this record requires but little explanation.

¶ 4064   Customers' accounts

Paragraph 3 requires ledger accounts (or other records) itemized separately as to *each* cash and margin account of every customer (regardless of the frequency of transactions with or for the customer), and as to each account (if any) of the firm and of its partners which should show all purchases and sales, and where securities or commodities are otherwise received in or delivered out of the account, all such receipts and deliveries. The records should also itemize all other debits and credits to each such account.

This item thus calls for what is commonly termed an account for each customer. Whether the bookkeeping system is maintained on machines, or the ledger is handwritten, the account pages, or account cards in the case of card systems, usually consist of columns for the date, number of shares bought or received into the account, number of shares sold or delivered out of the account, name of security, money debits and credits and usually a balance column and columns for calculating interest on balances. At the end of each month it is customary to bring down the debit or credit balance and the long and short position in each customer's account. Of course, it is not necessary under the rule even that a full page be devoted to each such account. It is only required that in some way the required information as to each account (whether it be kept in the form of a single record or several related secondary records) be kept separately as to that account.

¶ 4065   Secondary or subsidiary records

Paragraph 4 requires that ledgers or other records be maintained reflecting the following:

(A) Securities in transfer;

(B) Dividends and interest received;

(C) Securities borrowed and securities loaned;

(D) Monies borrowed and monies loaned, together with a record of the collateral therefor and any substitutions in such collateral;

(E) Securities failed to receive and failed to deliver.

All of the above are "secondary" or, as they are sometimes called, "subsidiary" records and are not records of original entry. These records are made up from the blotters or other records of original entry. Hence, the data appearing in such records is generally posted daily or at such intervals as the business requires. There follows a brief description of such subsidiary records.

¶ 4066   Securities in transfer

(A) The certificates of stock which a broker or dealer receives upon consummation of purchases may often be in a "street" name or in the names of individuals who may previously have owned the stock. When a broker or dealer receives instructions to have certificates registered in the name of the purchaser the certificates are sent to the transfer agent. The purpose of this paragraph of the rule is to require the keeping of a record showing all stocks "in transfer." This record usually shows the number borne by the transfer receipt received from the transfer agent, the number of shares, name of security, name in which it was registered, new name (i. e., the new name in which new certificates will be registered), date sent out to transfer, old certificate number, date received back from transfer, and new certificate number.

¶ 4067   Dividends and interest received

(B) For the purpose of this item of the rule it is necessary that a record be maintained by the firm with respect to dividends or interest paid by corporations on stock or bonds, respectively, carried by the broker for the account of customers but registered in some name other than that of the customer. The general practice, which would represent compliance with the rule, is to set up a sheet showing the name of the security, the ex-dividend date (or interest date), the rate per share and the payable date. Information is obtained from the "stock record" or, as it is sometimes called, the "securities position record," (the nature of which is explained hereafter) showing the names of both "long" and "short" customers. This information is then recorded on the dividend and interest register. All customers who are "long" are credited with their proportionate interest in monies received by the firm on account of the dividend or interest to which such customers are entitled. All customers who are "short" on the record dividend date, or the interest date in the case of bonds, are charged with the amount of the dividend or interest payable on their short position.

¶ 4068   Securities borrowed and securities loaned

(C) In borrowing securities to make deliveries against sales or in lending securities to other brokers or dealers, it is necessary, under paragraph 1 of the rule, to enter such transactions in the blotters, day book or other records of original entry. The requirements of paragraph 4(C) of the rule can be complied with by posting from the blotters or other records of original entry onto the securities borrowed and loaned records the date borrowed or date loaned, name of broker from whom borrowed or to whom loaned, number of shares, name of security, price, amount, and the date returned. In some cases securities borrowed and loaned records also provide an additional column showing the interest rate or premium on stock borrowed or loaned. The information may be kept on cards, in a loose-leaf or in a bound record, and the "date returned" may be stamped in with a regular date stamp.

¶ 4069   Monies borrowed, Monies loaned, etc.

(D) A record must be kept of all borrowings, regardless of whether customers' or the firm's securities are pledged as collateral. This record should show the name of the bank, the date, the interest rate, the amount of the loan, terms of the loan, and date when paid. Usually a separate page is made up for each loan. In connection with this information there must be kept a collateral record consisting of the number of shares, or principal amount in the case of bonds, name of the security, and certificate numbers in respect of all collateral pledged to secure the particular loan. Substitutions in collateral are usually shown on an additional column on the page or card kept for the particular loan. This information is obtained from the blotter, cash book, day book or other record of original entry and is transferred to the subsidiary record. Many houses find it convenient (and the rule so permits) to keep their loan records on a card index system which reflects the above information. Others keep only their record of collateral substitutions on cards, maintaining a loose-leaf or bound ledger for the other required details on such loans.

¶ 4070   Securities failed to receive or deliver

(E) These are also subsidiary records and are constructed from information contained on the blotters or other records of original entry. Upon learning that a broker or dealer on the other side of a transaction will fail to deliver on the date upon which delivery is due, either under clearing house rules or under the agreement between the buyer and the seller, this item requires that records must be made which should show the "fail date" (i.e., the date on which delivery was due but not made), number of shares (or principal amount of bonds), name of security, purchase price, broker or dealer from whom delivery is due, and date received. Conversely, when the firm fails to deliver it must set up records which should show the date on which delivery was due, number of shares (or principal amount of bonds), name of security, to whom sold, sales price and date on which delivery is made. An additional column may also provide for any remarks pertinent to the failure to receive or failure to deliver of that particular security. The total amount of open items in the "fail to receive" or "fail to deliver" records should agree with the "fail to receive" or "fail to deliver" account in the firm's general ledgers kept pursuant to paragraph 2 of the rule.

¶ 4071   Securities record or ledger

Paragraph 5 requires that a securities record or ledger (often called a "position book") be kept (or some comparable group of related secondary records), which will reflect separately for each security all long or short positions (including securities in safe-keeping) carried by the member broker or dealer either for his account or for the account of his customers or partners, and showing the location of all securities "long," and the offsetting position to all securities "short," and in all cases the name or designation of the account in which each position is carried. The rule requires that the securities record be posted currently so as to show all positions as of "clearance dates." The term "clearance date" refers to the date agreed upon by the buyer and seller (or the date fixed by applicable clearing house rules, if any) as the date upon which delivery is due. The securities record may, of course, be posted on the "trade" or execution date or any other date prior to the clearance date.

Houses which handle a large volume of business may keep separate "securities records" or "position records" as they are often called, for stocks and for bonds. The stock or securities record is seldom a bound record but it is usually kept in a loose-leaf book, or in the form of a group of cards or of related groups of cards, containing the above information. The typical stock record is a columnar record with a page or portion thereof for each security. The page should show the name of the security, the customers' and other accounts which are "long" and "short" that security, the daily changes in their position, the location of each security, and the total of the long or short position for the account of customers and the firm and partners. The more frequently recurring items often are printed on the form for speed in recording and in order to eliminate the necessity of writing in each item. Many forms for stock or securities position records are printed with or otherwise contain an appropriate space for the name of the account and a column for each business day in the month. The month-end securities balances may be carried forward to new sheets at the beginning of each new month.

In those houses which use the manifold or accounting machine methods of bookkeeping, the posting to the stock record is made from information typed simultaneously with the blotter.

¶ 4072   Memoranda of brokerage orders

Paragraph 6 requires that *brokers* maintain a memorandum of each *brokerage* order and of any other instruction, given or received for the purchase or sale of securities, whether executed or unexecuted. Such memoranda must show the terms and conditions of the Order or instructions and of any modification or cancellation thereof, the account for which entered, the time of entry, the price at which executed, and, to the extent feasible, the time of execution or cancellation. Orders entered pursuant to the exercise of discretionary power by such member, broker or dealer, or any employee thereof, shall be so designated.

The rule provides that the term "instruction" shall be deemed to include instructions between partners and employees of a member, broker or dealer. The term "time of entry" is specified to mean the time when the member, broker or dealer transmits the order or instruction for execution, or if it is not so transmitted, the time when it is received.

It is the usual practice (and probably the more desirable) to record all of the required information upon the face of the order ticket or other slip which records the brokerage order or instruction. If such order tickets or slips be filed together, they would themselves constitute the required record in respect of orders or instructions for the purchase or sale of securities.

¶ 4073   Memoranda of purchases and sales

Paragraph 7 which applies to *dealer transactions* requires a memorandum for each *purchase* and *sale* of securities for the account of such member, broker or dealer showing the price, and *to the extent feasible*, the time of execution. Paragraph 7, we understand, also serves to make it clear that memoranda or other records need not be made of dealers' quotations, or bids or offers made in the course of trading.

¶ 4074   Confirmations and notices

Paragraph 8 requires that brokers and dealers must make copies of confirmations of all purchases and sales of securities and copies of notifications of all other debits and credits for cash securities, or other items for the account of customers including partners of the member, broker or dealer. Note that paragraph 4 of Rule 17a-4 requires that the broker or dealer preserve copies of such confirmations or notices which he sends to his customers. In the event a firm uses the manifold system of bookkeeping, one of the several carbon copies so made would meet the above requirements provided it contained all the material information as contained on the simultaneously typed customer's copy of the confirmation.

¶ 4075   Records re cash and margin accounts

Paragraph 9 requires that a record in respect of each cash and margin account with such member, broker or dealer contain the name and address of the beneficial owner of such account, and, in the case of a margin account, the signature of such owner; provided that, in the case of a joint account or an account of a corporation, such records are required only in respect of the person or persons authorized to transact business for such account. This provision refers to what is commonly known as the customers' account card; many houses use an ordinary 3 × 5 card with the required data printed thereon and filled out at the time of opening the account with a customer.

Some questions have been raised in connection with "omnibus accounts" or similar accounts in which a bank, trustee or another broker or dealer effects transactions which the bank, trustee or broker or dealer may later allocate to the particular beneficiary or customer for whom it is acting. Where such an account is carried with the member, broker or dealer by a second party, such as a bank, trust company or another broker, the second party only, generally speaking, should be regarded as the "beneficial owner" of that account for purposes of this paragraph of the rule. In other words, the customers of the second party, at least under normal circumstances, are not regarded as the customers of the member, broker or dealer with whom the second party carries such an omnibus or general account. The phrase in paragraph 9 of Rule 17a-3 "a record in respect of each cash or margin account with such member, broker or dealer" has reference to accounts only of customers of that member, broker or dealer. Consequently, this item does not require broker or dealer "A" to make records with respect to the customers of broker or dealer "B" whose transactions may be effected by "A" in one or more accounts which "B" carries with "A." However, "B" must of course keep the specified information with respect to the accounts of his customers.

Where, on the other hand, a trustee, nominee or other fiduciary opens and maintains an account with a member, broker or dealer as a representative of one or more particular beneficiaries and where all transactions effected in that trust account are solely for the particular predetermined beneficiaries for whom the account is maintained, such beneficiaries (who thus have ownership of *the account itself* as distinguished from an interest in particular *securities or credits* which may happen to be recorded therein) should be regarded as beneficial owners of the account. Consequently, in this latter situation where the agent's or trustee's transactions on behalf of a trust or particular individuals are of such volume and importance as to warrant the opening of a separate account for the particular trust or individuals, it is our understanding that paragraph 9 of Rule 17a-3 does apply, and that the name and address either of the particular trust or of the beneficiaries should be obtained.

¶ 4076   Puts, calls, straddles and other options

Paragraph 10 requires the record of all puts, calls, spreads, straddles and other options in which such member, broker or dealer has any direct or indirect interest, or which such member, broker or dealer has granted or guaranteed containing at least an identification of the security and the number of units involved. Such a memorandum may be kept in any suitable record which shows the date, details regarding the option, name of security, number of shares, expiration date. Letters pertaining to such options, including those received from and addressed to customers, should be kept together with the memorandum.

¶ 4077   Monthly trial balances and net capital
computations

Paragraph 11 requires the preparation of a record of the proof of money balances in all ledger accounts in the form of trial balances currently at least once a month, and the preparation of a record of the computation of aggregate indebtedness and net capital as of the trial balance date currently at least once a month. Such trial balances and computations will serve as a check upon the current status and accuracy of the ledger accounts which members are required to maintain and keep current and will also help to keep members currently informed of their capital positions.

¶ 4078   Employment applications

Paragraph 12 requires a questionnaire or employment application for each "associated person" which must list various items of information with respect to such person, and must be approved in writing by an authorized representative of the member. Retention of a complete copy of a registration application filed by the member on behalf of such person with the Association or certain securities exchanges will satisfy this requirement.

¶ 4079   Inquiries concerning rules

Any inquiries with respect to the provisions of Rules 17a-3 and 4 and whether or not the bookkeeping system now in use by your firm meets the requirements of the rule should be addressed either to the National Association of Securities Dealers, Inc., 1735 K Street, N. W., Washington, D. C. 20006, or to the Division of Market Regulation, Securities and Exchange Commission, 500 No. Capitol St., Washington, D. C. 20549.

NASD, para. 2180

¶ 2180   Margin Accounts

Sec. 30.

Prohibition

(a) A member shall not effect a securities transaction in a margin account in a manner contrary to the requirements adopted by the Board of Governors pursuant to authority granted by this rule nor shall a member in connection with such a transaction otherwise act in a manner inconsistent with requirements adopted hereunder.

Requirements

(b) The Board of Governors is authorized (1) to establish the minimum amounts of initial and maintenance margin required to be obtained by members from customers for or with whom such members effect transactions on a margin or cash basis, and (2) to establish other specific requirements or prohibitions, including record-keeping, reporting or other requirements necessary for the proper implementation of the initial and margin maintenance provisions.

Amount required

(c) The amounts of margin required, and other requirements authorized hereby, shall be set forth in Appendix A attached to and made part of this rule. The Board of Governors may from time to time alter, amend, supplement or modify the said Appendix A.

Special margin requirements

(d) Whenever the Board of Governors determines that unusual or extraordinary conditions warrant, it may prescribe special margin requirements for specific securities. The membership shall be promptly informed by notice to it of any such special margin requirements.

[Sec. 30 added effective July 1, 1972.]

Annotation of selected SEC decision

.10 Margin Rules, Inadequate Supervision, Special Omnibus Account.—A member firm violated Article III, Section 30 and Regulation T, Section 4(b) when it improperly purchased call options on credit for a special omnibus account which was supposed to be carried solely for accounts of the firm's customers but which was, in fact, beneficially owned by the firm's officers.

It violated Article III, Section 27 in failing to provide adequate supervision over its treasurer when it improperly allowed him to use CBOE margin rules even though the firm was no longer a CBOE member.

Prince, Langheinrich & Greer, Inc., SEC Release No. 34-16898 (1980).

NASD, para. 2180A

¶ 2180A   APPENDIX A

Sec. 1.

Exception

Members of the American Stock Exchange, Chicago Board Options Exchange, Midwest Stock Exchange, New York Stock Exchange, Pacific Stock Exchange, and the PBW Stock Exchange are exempt from the provisions hereof.

[As amended effective July 1, 1974.]

Sec. 2.

Initial Margin

For the purpose of effecting and carrying new securities transactions the following provisions shall apply:

(a) Any member who effects a securities transaction, including transactions in "when issued" securities, for a customer in a margin account must obtain from the customer no later than settlement date, initial margin in an amount consistent with the provisions of Regulation T of the Board of Governors of the Federal Reserve System and Section 4 hereof. Every margin account shall have a minimum equity deposit in the account of $2,000, except that cash need not be deposited in excess of the cost of any security purchased.

(b) Withdrawals of cash or securities in accordance with Regulation T may be made from any account provided that such withdrawal does not reduce the equity in the account below $2,000 or the amount required by Section 4 hereof, whichever is greater. Provided, however, Special Subscriptions Accounts and Special Equity Funding Accounts maintained in accordance with Sections 4(h) and 4(k), respectively, of Regulation T shall be exempt from the $2,000 minimum equity requirement.

Sec. 3.

Valuation of Securities

For purposes of this Appendix, securities shall be valued at current market prices determined by a reasonable and consistent method. Securities listed on a national securities exchange shall be valued at current market prices as reported by the exchange. OTC marginable securities listed on NASDAQ shall be valued at the current representative market reflected on that system.

Substantial additional margin may be required by the Association when the margin account being carried has any security in such concentrated quantities that its liquidation cannot be accomplished promptly in relation to the volume of trading in the security or if the security is subject to unusually rapid or violent changes in value.

Sec. 4.

Minimum Margin

(a) The minimum margin to be maintained in the margin account of a customer shall be as follows:

(1) 25% of the market value of all securities "long" in the account, except securities exempted under Section 2 (g) of Regulation T; and,

(2) $2.50 per share or 100% of the market value, whichever is greater, of each stock "short" in the account with a market value of less than $5.00 per share; and,

(3) $5.00 per share or 30% of the market value, whichever is greater, of each stock "short" in the account with a market value of $5.00 per share or above; and,

(4) Minimum maintenance requirements for any put or call issue, guaranteed or carried "short" in a customer's account shall be:

(i) Listed Stock Options. In the case of puts and calls listed or traded on a registered national securities exchange, displayed in the NASDAQ System, or issued by a registered clearing corporation, 100% of the current market value of the option contract plus 20% of the current value of the equivalent number of shares of the underlying security. In each case, the amount shall be decreased by any excess of the aggregate exercise price of the option over the current market value of the equivalent number of shares of the underlying security in the case of a call, or any excess of the current market value of the equivalent number of shares of the underlying securities over the aggregate exercise price of the option in the case of a put; provided, however, that the minimum margin required on each such option contract shall not be less than 100% of the current market value of the option contract plus 10% of the value of the equivalent number of shares of the underlying security.

(ii) Unlisted Stock Options. In the case of puts and calls which are not listed or traded on a registered national securities exchange, displayed in the NASDAQ System, or issued by a registered clearing corporation, 100% of the current market value of the option contract plus 45% of the current value of the equivalent number of shares of the underlying security. In each case, the amount shall be decreased by any excess of the aggregate exercise price of the option over the current market value of the equivalent number of shares of the underlying security in the case of a call, or any excess of the current market value of the equivalent number of shares of the underlying securities over the aggregate exercise price of the option in the case of a put; provided, however, that the minimum margin required on each such option contract shall not be less than 100% of the current market value of the option contract plus 10% of the value of the equivalent number of shares of the underlying security.

(iii) Market Index Options. In the case of puts and calls listed or traded on a registered national securities exchange or displayed in the NASDAQ System and representing options on a market index carried in a short position in an account, 100% of the current market value of the option contract plus 15% of the product of the current index group value and the index multiplier applicable to the option contract. In each case, the amount shall be decreased by any excess of the aggregate exercise price of the option over the product of the current index group value and the applicable index multiplier in the case of a call, or any excess of the product of the current index group value and the applicable index multiplier over the aggregate exercise price of the option in the case of a put; provided, however, that the minimum margin required on each such option contract shall not be less than 100% of the current market value of the option contract plus 10% of the product of the current index group value and the applicable index multiplier;

(iv) Industry Index Options. In the case of puts and calls listed or traded on a registered national securities exchange or displayed in the NASDAQ System and representing options on an industry index carried in a short position in an account, 100% of the current market value of the option contract plus 20% of the product of the current index group value and the index multiplier applicable to the option contract. In each case, the amount shall be decreased by any excess of the aggregate exercise price of the option over the product of the current index group value and the applicable index multiplier in the case of a call, or any excess of the product of the current index group value and the applicable index multiplier over the aggregate exercise price of the option in the case of a put; provided, however, that the minimum margin required on each such option contract shall not be less than 100% of the current market value of the option contract plus 10% of the product of the current index group value and the applicable index multiplier;

The requirements set forth in paragraphs (iii) and (iv) hereof are subject to the following exceptions, which in each case may be applied at the discretion of the member organization with which the account is maintained.

(1) In the case of long call index options (or long put index options) which are offset by positions in short call index options (or short put index options) for the same underlying index with the same index multiplier, provided that the expiration date of the long calls (or long puts) is the same as or subsequent to the expiration date of the offsetting short calls (or short puts), the treatment shall be as follows:

(A) When the exercise price of the long call index option (or short put index option) is less than or equal to the exercise price of the offsetting short call index option (or long put index option), no margin is required.

(B) When the exercise price of the long call index option (or short put index option) is greater than the exercise price of the offsetting short call index option (or long put index option) margin is required equal to the difference in aggregate exercise prices.

(2) In the case of accounts carrying positions in short put index options which are offset by positions in short call index options for the same underlying index with the same index multiplier, the margin required shall be the margin required for the short put option contract or the margin required for the short call option contract (pursuant to subparagraphs (iii) and (iv) of this Rule), whichever is greater, as determined by (iii) and (iv) above, plus 100% of the current market value of the other option contract.

(v) Foreign Currency Options. In the case of puts and calls listed or traded on a registered national securities exchange or displayed in the NASDAQ System and representing options on foreign currencies carried in a short position in an account, 100% of the current market value of the option contract plus 4% of the value of the underlying foreign currency at the current spot market price. In each case, the amount shall be decreased by any excess of the aggregate exercise price of the option over the value of the underlying foreign currency at the current spot market price in the case of a call, or any excess of the value of the underlying foreign currency at the current spot market price over the aggregate exercise price of the option in the case of a put; provided, however, that the minimum margin required on each such option contract shall not be less than 100% of the current market value of the option contract plus 3/4% of the value of the underlying foreign currency.

(vi) Treasury Security Options. In the case of puts and calls listed or traded on a registered national securities exchange or displayed in the NASDAQ System and representing options on U.S. Treasury Securities carried in a short position in an account, 100% of the current market value of the option contract plus .35% of the underlying principal amount in the case of options on Treasury Bills with a maturity of 95 days or less; 3% of the underlying principal amount in the case of options on Treasury Notes and 3.5% of the underlying principal amount in the case of options on Treasury Bonds. In each case, the amount shall be decreased by any excess of the aggregate exercise price of the option over the current market value of the underlying principal amount in the case of a call, or any excess of the current market value of the underlying principal amount over the aggregate exercise price of the option in the case of a put; provided, however, that the minimum margin required on each such option contract shall not be less than 100% of the current market value of the option contract plus $1/20$% of the underlying principal amount in the case of Treasury Bills with a maturity of 95 days or less and $1/2$% of the underlying principal amount in the case of Treasury Notes and Bonds.

[Amended effective September 28, 1985; and October 5, 1988.]

(5) 5% of the principal amount or 30% of the market value, whichever is greater, of each debt security "short" in the account, except securities exempted under Section 2 (g) of Regulation T; and,

(6) 15% of the principal amount or 25% of the market value, whichever is lower, on each long and short position in securities exempted under Section 2(g) of Regulation T, except as covered in subsection (7); and,

(7) 5% of the principal amount of each long or short position in obligations issued or unconditionally guaranteed as to principal or interest by the United States Government or any agency thereof; and,

(8) Notwithstanding the provisions of paragraphs (1), (6) and (7) of this subsection (a), minimum maintenance requirements for securities exempted under Section 2(g) of Regulation T and for certain corporate debt securities shall be as follows concerning:

(i) obligations issued or unconditionally guaranteed as to principal or interest by the U.S. Government or any agency thereof with 10 years or less to maturity:
less than 1 year—$1/2$% of market value
1 to 2 years—1% of market value
2 to 3 years—$1 1/2$% of market value
3 to 4 years—2% of market value
4 to 5 years—$2 1/2$% of market value
5 to 10 years—3% of market value

(ii) other securities exempted under Section 2(g) of Regulation T and non-convertible corporate debt securities with 5 years or less to maturity which are in the first three ratings (e.g., AAA, AA, A) according to a nationally known statistical service, the Association may authorize lower requirements upon application.

Market Index Option Escrow Receipts[1]

(vi) no margin is required in respect of a call option contract on a market index carried in a short position where the customer has delivered promptly, after the options are written, to the member organization with which such position is maintained, a Market Index Option Escrow Receipt in a form satisfactory to the Association, issued by a bank or trust company pursuant to specific authorization

---

[1] This section has been approved by the SEC for a one-year pilot period commencing August 13, 1985. During the pilot period, the Board of Governors may, pursuant to its normal rulemaking procedures, at any time on its own initiative, or at the direction of the Securities and Exchange Commission or the Board of Governors of the Federal Reserve System, suspend, terminate or otherwise modify the provisions of this section.

from the customer which certifies that the issuer of the agreement holds for the account of the customer (1) cash, (2) cash equivalents, (3) one or more qualified equity securities, or (4) a combination thereof; that such deposit has an aggregate market value, at the time the option is written, of not less than 100% of the aggregate current index value; and that the issuer will promptly pay the member organization the exercise settlement amount in the event the account is assigned an exercise notice.

(1) Association approved broad-based index option escrow receipts are those that are provided by the Options Clearing Corporation ("OCC"). From time to time the Association may approve additional forms provided they do not differ substantively from the OCC form. An acceptable index option escrow receipt must stipulate the following:

(A) A certification that the bank/trust company is holding (1) cash, (2) cash equivalents, (3) one or more qualified equity securities, or (4) any combination thereof; and that such deposit has an aggregate market value, at the time the option is written, of not less than 100% of the aggregate current index value for each contract covered by the receipt.

(B) A commitment from the bank/trust company to pay the exercise settlement amount plus all applicable commissions out of the collateral or the proceeds thereof.

(C) Each deposited security is traded on a national securities exchange or is traded Over-the-Counter and is included on the Federal Reserve Board's List of Over-the-Counter Margin Stocks.

(D) The customer or its agent has duly authorized the bank to liquidate any securities included in the collateral to the extent necessary to perform the bank's obligations; and the bank maintains a written affirmation from the customer or its agent stating that all index call options written for the customer's account and covered by index option escrow receipts issued by the bank are written against a diversified stock portfolio.

(E) The bank shall not subject nor permit the customer to subject the collateral or any portion thereof to any lien or encumbrance.

(F) When one or more securities are substituted for securities held by the bank or trust company, the substitution shall not impair the value of the collateral held by the bank at the time the substitution is made.

(G) Should the collateral value drop below 55% of the aggregate current index value, the bank shall notify the customer or its agent and promptly obtain additional collateral. OCC and the broker-dealer shall be immediately notified by the bank should the collateral's value fall below 50% of the current underlying index value.

(2) Upon notification that the collateral value is deficient, an index option escrow receipt is no longer deemed to be an acceptable deposit in lieu of the margin required to be maintained by the broker-dealer. If the collateral is not promptly supplemented to a level in excess of 55% of the aggregate current index value, the broker-dealer must take steps to promptly liquidate the short index call(s) covered by the receipt.

(3) The term "aggregate current index value" means the current index value times the index multiplier, the term "aggregate exercise price" means the exercise price times the index multiplier; and the term "exercise settlement amount" means the difference between the aggregate exercise price and the aggregate current index value (as such terms are defined in Article XVII of the By-Laws of OCC).

(4) For purposes of Appendix A, Section 4(a)(4)(vi), a bank or trust company is qualified to issue a Market Index Option Escrow Receipt if it is a corporation organized under the laws of the United States or a State thereof and is regulated and examined by federal or state authorities having regulatory authority over banks or trust companies. The issuing bank or trust company must be approved by OCC if Market Index Option Escrow Receipts are to be forwarded to OCC for the purpose of meeting margin requirements.

(5) A security is qualified if:

(A) Exchange securities: it is an equity security (with the exception of warrants, rights and options) traded on the New York Stock Exchange, or on another national securities exchange and it substantially meets the listing standards of the New York Stock Exchange or the American Stock Exchange; or

(B) OTC Securities: it is an equity security (with the exception of warrants, rights and options) listed on the current list of Over-the-Counter Margin Stocks published by the Board of Governors of the Federal Reserve System.

(6) The term "cash equivalent" is defined in Regulation T, Section 220.8(a)(3)(ii), to mean securities issued or guaranteed by the United States or its agencies, negotiable bank certificates of deposit, or bankers' acceptances issued by banking institutions in the United States and payable in the United States with one year or less to maturity.

(7) When one or more securities are substituted for securities held by the bank or trust company, the substitution should not impair the value of the collateral held by the bank at the time the substitution is made.

[Adopted effective November 20, 1985.]

(b) Notwithstanding the provisions of paragraph (a) hereof, the minimum margin to be maintained in a margin account shall be 10% of the market value of the "long" securities in the following situations:

(1) When a security carried in a "long" position is exchangeable or convertible within a reasonable time and without restriction other than payment of money, into a security carried in a short position; or

(2) When there are offsetting "long" and "short" positions in the same security. In such cases "short" positions must be marked to the market in determining the required minimum margin.

(3) The Association may, for specific securities when it deems circumstances warrant, either at the time of establishing the special initial margin or thereafter, require special initial margin of up to 100% to be deposited in all margin accounts on new transactions within 5 business days of the trade date.

[As amended effective May 11, 1977; amended effective April 13, 1984.]

Sec. 5.

When Issued Securities

(a) For purposes of this Appendix, the minimum amount of margin on any transaction or net position in each "when issued" security shall be the same as if such security were issued.

(b) Each position in a "when issued" security must be computed separately, and any unrealized profit shall be applied only to the amount of margin required on the position in the particular security.

(c) When an account has both a "short" position in a "when issued" security and a long position in the securities with respect to which the "when issued" security may be issued, such "short" position must be marked to the market and the balance in the account adjusted for any unrealized loss.

Sec. 6.

Sec. 6.

Certain Purchases in Special Cash Accounts

Transactions in the following types in special cash accounts are subject to the margin requirements hereof except when the account is that of a broker/dealer, banker, trust company, investment company, investment trust, insurance company, charitable or non-profit educational institution, or similar fiduciary type account or of any person (as defined in Section 3(a)(9) of the Securities Exchange Act of 1934), having net tangible assets of sixteen million dollars ($16,000,000) or more:

(a) Purchases of issued securities exempted under Section 2(g) of Regulation T when payment is not made promptly after presentation of the securities to the customer, except that the $2,000 minimum equity requirement does not apply; provided however, the Association may waive or extend the above requirements upon application by the creditor made in good faith and in exceptional circumstances;

(b) Transactions in "when issued" securities when payment is not made promptly unless,

(i) such is the subject of a primary distribution in connection with a *bona fide* offering by the issuer to the general public for "cash," or

(ii) such is exempt by the Association as involving a primary distribution or a registered secondary offering.

The term "when issued" herein also means "when distributed."

[Amended effective May 22, 1987.]

Sec. 7.

Put and Call Options

(a) Each put or call shall be margined separately. Any difference between the market price of the underlying security and the exercise price of a put or call will be of value only in providing margin on that particular put or call. Substantial additional margin must be required on options issued, guaranteed or carried "short" with an unusually long period of time to expiration (generally, more than six months and ten days), or written on securities subject to unusually rapid or abrupt changes in value, or which do not have an active market, or when the securities subject to the option cannot be liquidated promptly.

(b) If both a put and a call for the same number of shares of the same security are issued, guaranteed or carried "short" for a customer, the margin shall be the greater of that required on either the put or the call, except that:

(i) The $250 minimum margin requirement shall apply to only one of the options, and

(ii) if there is unrealized loss on the other option, the amount of margin required shall include that unrealized loss.

(c) When a call that is listed or traded on a registered national securities exchange or displayed in the NASDAQ system is carried "long" for a cus tomer's account and the account is also "short" a call listed or traded on a registered national securities exchange or displayed in the NASDAQ system expiring on or before the date of expiration of the "long" listed call and written on the same number of shares of the same security, the margin required on the "short" call shall be the lower of

(i) the margin required pursuant to Section 4(a)(4)(ii) above, or

(ii) the amount by which the exercise price of the "long" call exceeds the exercise price of the short call.

(d) When a put that is listed or traded on a registered national securities exchange or displayed in the NASDAQ system is carried "long" for a customer's account and the account is also "short" a put listed or traded on a registered national securities exchange or displayed in the NASDAQ system expiring on or before the date of expiration of the "long" listed put and written on the same number of shares of the same security, the margin required on the "short" put shall be the lower of:

(i) the margin required pursuant to Section 4(a)(4)(ii) above, or

(ii) the amount by which the exercise price of the "short" put exceeds the exercise price of the "long" put.

(e) When a call is issued, guaranteed or carried "short" against an existing net "long" position in the security under option or in any security exchangeable or convertible into the security under option within a reasonable time without restriction other than the payment of money, no margin need be required on the call, provided:

(i) such net "long" position is adequately margined in accordance with this Rule, and

(ii) the right to exchange or convert the net "long" position does not expire on or before the date of expiration of the "short" call and

(iii) the conversion price of the exchangeable or convertible security does not exceed the exercise price of the call.

(f) When a call is issued, guaranteed or carried short against a net "long" position in an exchangeable or convertible security, as outlined above, margin shall be required on the call equal to any amount by which the conversion price of the "long" security exceeds the exercise price of the call.

(g) When a put is issued, guaranteed or carried "short" against an existing net "short" position in the security under option, no margin need be required on the put, provided such net "short" position is adequately margined in accordance with this Rule.

(h) When determining net "long" and net "short" positions, offsetting "long" and "short" positions in exchangeable or convertible securities or in the same security shall be deducted. When computing margin on such an existing net stock position carried against a put or call, the current market price used shall not be greater than the call price in the case of a call or less than the put price in the case of a put. If a payment of money is required to exchange or convert the net "long" security, such security shall have no value for the purposes of this Rule.

(i) When a member issues or guarantees an option to receive or deliver securities for a customer, such option shall be margined as if it were a put or call.

(j) An exchangeable or convertible security shall cease to have margin purposes as of its expiration date and cannot be used thereafter for purposes of this Rule.

[As amended effective May 11, 1977.]

Sec. 8.

Guaranteed Customer Accounts

Any account guaranteed by another account of a public customer in writing, may be consolidated with the other account and the required margin may be computed on the net position of both accounts if the guarantee permits the member, without restriction, to use the money and securities in the guaranteeing account to carry the guaranteed account or to pay any deficit therein; provided however, a guaranteeing account shall not be owned directly or indirectly by (a) a partner or a stockholder in the organization carrying the account, or (b) a member, partner or stockholder therein having a definite arrangement for participating in the commissions earned on the guaranteed account. The guarantee of a limited partner or of a stockholder if based upon his resources other than his capital contribution to, or other than his interest in a member organization, shall not be affected by the foregoing prohibition, and such a guarantee may be taken into consideration in computing margin in the guaranteed account.

Sec. 9.

Consolidation of Accounts

When two or more accounts are carried for the same person or entity, the required margin may be computed on the net position of such accounts, provided the customer has consented in writing that the money and securities in each of the accounts may be used to carry or pay any deficit in all such accounts.

Sec. 10.

Deferred Payment Prohibited

No member shall permit a customer to effect transactions requiring margin and then either defer the payment of margin beyond regular settlement date, or meet such demand for margin by the liquidation of the same or other commitments in the account, except that the provisions of this section shall not apply to any account maintained for another broker/dealer in which are carried only the commitments of public customers of the other broker/dealer, provided that the latter has agreed in writing that he will maintain a record in accordance with Section 11 hereof.

Sec. 11.

Recordkeeping Requirements

Any member carrying securities margin accounts for customers shall make a daily record of each case in which initial or additional margin must be deposited in a customer's account because of transactions in the account on that day. The record shall show, for each account, the amount of margin required and the time when, and the manner in which, such margin is obtained.

Sec. 12.

OTC Market Maker

The account of a member in which are effected only transactions in securities in which he is an "OTC Market Maker", as defined in Rule 17a-12 under the Securities Exchange Act of 1934, may be carried upon a margin basis which is mutually agreeable to the market maker and the carrying member.

Sec. 13.

Prompt Payment Required

The amount of margin, deposit, or "mark to market" required by any provision of this rule shall be obtained as promptly as possible.

Sec. 14.

Margin Account Defined

"Margin account" shall mean every account established pursuant to Regulation T in which a broker/dealer creditor extends or maintains credit, except as otherwise provided by the Association.

Sec. 15.

Accrued Interest

(a) Accrued interest may not be credited to an account except as provided in paragraph (b).

(b) A member may credit to a customer's account accrued interest in obligations issued or unconditionally guaranteed by the U.S. Government or any agency thereof provided that such securities are registered in the member's name or that of its nominee or, in the case of bearer bonds, are in the possession of the member and, provided further, that on a concurrent basis accrued interest on the outstanding debit balance in that account is entered as of the same date.

NASD, para. 2183

¶ 2183   Options

Sec. 33

(a) A member or a person associated with a member shall not effect any transaction in an option contract, including an option displayed on the NASDAQ System, except in accordance with the provisions of rules, regulations and procedures adopted by the Board of Governors pursuant to the authorization granted in subsection (b) hereof.

(b) The Board of Governors is authorized, for the purpose of preventing fraudulent and manipulative acts and practices, promoting just and equitable principles of trade, providing safeguards against unreasonable profits or unreasonable rates of commission or other charges, and for the protection of investors and the public interest, to adopt rules, regulations and procedures for transactions in options relating to:

(1) transactions in option contracts, including options displayed on the NASDAQ System, by members for their own account or the accounts of public customers;

(2) the comparison—clearance and settlement of transactions in options;

(3) the reporting of transactions in options;

(4) the qualifications and standards for registered market makers in options;

(5) the standards for authorization of underlying securities eligible to be subject to options displayed on the NASDAQ System;

(6) the endorsement and guarantee of performance options; and,

(7) such other areas of options activity and trading as may be required to achieve the above-stated purposes.

(c) The rules, regulations and procedures authorized by subsection (b) hereof shall be incorporated into Appendix E to be attached to and made a part of these Rules of Fair Practice. The Board of Governors shall have the power to adopt, alter, amend, supplement or modify the provisions of Appendix E from time to time without recourse to the membership for approval, as would otherwise be required by Article VII of the By-Laws, and Appendix E shall become effective as the Board of Governors may prescribe unless disapproved by the Securities and Exchange Commission.

(d) For purposes of this section, the term "option" shall mean any put, call, straddle or other option or privilege, which is a "security" as defined in Section 2(1) of the Securities Act of 1933, as amended, but shall not include any tender offer, registered warrant, right, convertible security or any other option in respect to which the writer is the issuer of the security which may be purchased or sold upon the exercise of the option.

NASD, para. 2184

¶ 2184   APPENDIX E

Sec. 1.

General

(a) Applicability—The Rules in this Appendix E shall be applicable (1) to the trading of options contracts issued by The Options Clearing Corporation and displayed on the NASDAQ System and to the terms and conditions of such contracts; (2) to the extent appropriate unless otherwise stated herein, to the conduct of accounts, the execution of transactions, and the handling of orders in exchange-listed options by members who are not members of an exchange on which the option executed is listed; (3) to the extent appropriate unless otherwise stated herein, to the conduct of accounts, the execution of transactions, and the handling of orders in conventional options; and (4) other matters related to options trading.

Unless otherwise indicated herein, Sections 3 through 12 of this Appendix E shall apply only to options displayed on the NASDAQ System and standardized and conventional options on common stock and Sections 13 through 24 of this Appendix E shall apply to transactions in all options as defined in paragraph (d) of Article III, Section 33 of the Rules of Fair Practice, including common stock.

(b) Except to the extent that specific sections in this Appendix govern, or unless the context otherwise requires, the provisions of the By-Laws and Rules of Fair Practice and all other interpretations and policies of the Board of Governors shall also be applicable to the trading of option contracts.

(c) Local Time—All times are stated in these Rules in terms of the local time in effect in New York City (Eastern Time) or as otherwise specified.

[Amended effective September 13, 1985.]

Sec. 2.

Definitions

The following terms shall, unless the context otherwise requires, have the stated meanings:

(a) The Options Clearing Corporation—The term "The Options Clearing Corporation" means The Options Clearing Corporation, the issuer of exchange-listed options and options displayed on the NASDAQ System.

(b) Rules of The Options Clearing Corporation—The term "rules of The Options Clearing Corporation" means the by-laws and the rules of The Options Clearing Corporation, and all written interpretations thereof as may be in effect from time to time.

(c) Clearing Member—The term "clearing member" means a member of the Corporation which has been admitted to membership in The Options Clearing Corporation pursuant to the provisions of the rules of The Options Clearing Corporation.

(d) Participating Organization—The term "participating organization" means a national securities exchange or association which has qualified for participation in The Options Clearing Corporation pursuant to the provisions of Article VII of the By-Laws of The Options Clearing Corporation.

(e) Options Contract—The term "options contract" means any option as defined in paragraph (d) of Article III, Section 33 of the Rules of Fair Practice. For purposes of Sections 3 through 12 of this Appendix E, an option to purchase or sell common stock shall be deemed to cover 100 shares of such stock at the time the contract granting such option is written. A NASDAQ index option shall be deemed to cover a dollar equivalent to the numerical value of the underlying index multiplied by the applicable index multiplier. If a stock option is granted covering some other number of shares, then for purposes of Sections 3 through 12 of the Appendix E, it shall be deemed to constitute as many option contracts as that other number of shares divided by 100 (e.g., an option to buy or sell five hundred shares of common stock shall be considered as five option contracts). A stock option contract which, when written, grants the right to purchase or sell 100 shares of common stock shall continue to be considered as one contract throughout its life, notwithstanding that, pursuant to its terms, the number of shares which it covers may be adjusted to reflect stock dividends, stock splits, reverse splits, or other similar actions by the issuer of such stock.

(f) Option Transaction—The term "option transaction" means a transaction effected by a member for the purchase or sale of an option contract, or for the closing out of a long or short position in such option.

(g) NASDAQ Option Transaction—The term "NASDAQ option transaction" means a transaction effected by a member of the Association for the purchase or sale of an option contract which is displayed on the NASDAQ System or for the closing out of a long or short position in such option contract.

(h) Type of Option—The term "type of option" means the classification of an option contract as either a put or a call.

(i) Call—The term "call" means an option contract under which the holder of the option has the right, in accordance with the terms of the option, to purchase the number of units of the underlying security or to receive a dollar equivalent of the underlying index covered by the option contract. In the case of a "call" issued by The

Options Clearing Corporation on common stock or on an option displayed on the NASDAQ System, it shall mean an option contract under which the holder of the option has the right, in accordance with the terms of the option, to purchase from The Options Clearing Corporation the number of units of the underlying security or receive a dollar equivalent of the underlying index covered by the option contract.

(j) Put—The term "put" means an option contract under which the holder of the option has the right, in accordance with the terms of the option, to sell the number of units of the underlying security or deliver a dollar equivalent of the underlying index covered by the option contract. In the case of a "put" issued by The Options Clearing Corporation on common stock or on an option displayed on the NASDAQ System, it shall mean an option contract under which the holder of the option has the right, in accordance with terms of the option, to sell to The Options Clearing Corporation the number of units of the underlying security covered by the option contract or to tender the dollar equivalent of the underlying index.

(k) Class of Options—The term "class of options" means all option contracts of the same type of option covering the same underlying security or index.

(l) Series of Options—The term "series of options" means all option contracts of the same class of options having the same exercise price and expiration date and which cover the same number of units of the underlying security or index.

(m) Underlying Security—The term "underlying security" in respect of an option contract means the security which The Options Clearing Corporation or another person shall be obligated to sell (in the case of a call) or purchase (in the case of a put) upon the valid exercise of such option contract.

(n) Exercise Price—The term "exercise price" in respect of an option contract means the stated price per unit at which the underlying security may be purchased (in the case of a call) or sold (in the case of a put) upon the exercise of such option contract.

(o) Aggregate Exercise Price—The term "aggregate exercise price" means the exercise price of an option contract multiplied by the number of units of the underlying security covered by such option contract.

(p) Expiration Month—The term "expiration month" in respect of an option contract means the month and year in which such option contract expires.

(q) Expiration Date—The term "expiration date" of an option contract issued by The Options Clearing Corporation means the day and time fixed by the rules of The Options Clearing Corporation for the expiration of all option contracts having the same expiration month as such option contract. The term "expiration date" of all other option contracts means the date specified thereon for such.

(r) Long Position—The term "long position" means the number of outstanding option contracts of a given series of options held by a person (purchaser).

(s) Short Position—The term "short position" means the number of outstanding option contracts of a given series of options with respect to which a person is obligated as a writer (seller).

(t) Opening Purchase Transaction—The term "opening purchase transaction" means an option transaction in which the purchaser's intention is to create or increase a long position in the series of options involved in such transaction.

(u) Opening Writing Transaction—The term "opening writing transaction" means an option transaction in which the seller's (writer's) intention is to create or increase a short position in the series of options involved in such transaction.

(v) Closing Sale Transaction—The term "closing sale transaction" means an option transaction in which the seller's intention is to reduce or eliminate a long position in the series of options involved in such transaction.

(w) Closing Purchase Transaction—The term "closing purchase transaction" means an option transaction in which the purchaser's intention is to reduce or eliminate a short position in the series of options involved in such transaction.

(x) Covered—The term "covered" in respect of a short position in a call option contract means that the writer's obligation is secured by a "specific deposit" or an "escrow deposit," meeting the conditions of Rules 610(e) or 610(h), respectively, of the Rules of The Options Clearing Corporation, or the writer holds in the same account as the short position, on a unit-for-unit basis, a long position either in the underlying security or in an option contract of the same class of options where the exercise price of the option contract in such long position is equal to or less than the exercise price of the option contract in such short position. The term "covered" in respect of a short position in a put option contract means that the writer holds in the same account as the short position, on a unit-for-unit basis, a long position in an option contract of the same class of options having an exercise price equal to or greater than the exercise price of the option contract in such short position.

(y) Uncovered—The term "uncovered" in respect of a short position in an option contract means the short position is not covered. For purposes of Section 16 (Opening of Accounts), Section 20 (Supervision of Accounts) and Section 11 (Delivery of Current Disclosure Document(s)), the term "writing uncovered short option positions" shall include combinations and any other transactions which involve uncovered writing.

(z) Outstanding—The term "outstanding" in respect of an option contract means an option contract which has neither been the subject of a closing sale transaction nor has been exercised nor reached its expiration date.

(aa) Member and Person Associated with a Member—The terms "member" and "person associated with a member" shall have the meanings as specified in Article I, Section 3 of the By-Laws of the Corporation.

(bb) Options Trading—The term "options trading" means trading (1) in any option issued by The Options Clearing Corporation, and (2) in any conventional option.

(cc) Premium—The term "premium" means the aggregate price of the option contracts agreed upon between the buyer and writer/seller or their agents.

(dd) Escrow Receipt—The term "escrow receipt" means a representation of an issuing bank to The Options Clearing Corporation that a particular customer's securities are on deposit with the bank and will be delivered upon exercise of the option for which the receipt is issued.

(ee) Current Prospectus—The term "current prospectus" shall mean edition of the prospectus of The Options Clearing Corporation as registered which at the time it is to be furnished to a given customer meets the requirements of Section 10(a)(3) of the Securities Act of 1933.

(ff) Spread Order—The term "spread order" means an order to buy a stated number of option contracts and to sell the same number of option contracts, or contracts representing the same number of units at option, of the same class of options.

(gg) Conventional Option—The term "conventional option" shall mean any option contract not issued, or subject to issuance, by The Options Clearing Corporation.

(hh) Beneficial Owner—The term "beneficial owner" means the person who has or shares the power to direct the voting or the disposition of securities, or who has or shares the right to receive or the power to direct the receipt of dividends or the proceeds from the sale of securities.

(ii) Aggregate Long and Aggregate Short—The terms "aggregate long" or "aggregate short" mean a person's total interest as the holder or writer of option contracts of a particular class of options.

(jj) Controls, Is Controlled by or Is Under Common Control With—The terms "controls," "is controlled by" and "is under common control with" shall have the meanings specified in SEC Rule 405 under the Securities Act of 1933.

(kk) Advertisement—The term "advertisement" means material published, or designed for use in, a newspaper, magazine or other periodical, radio, telephone or tape recording, motion picture, television, videotape display, signs or billboards, telephone directories (other than routine listings), or other public media.

(ll) Sales Literature—The term "sales literature" means any notice, circular, report (including research report), newsletter (including market letter), form letter or reprint or excerpt of the foregoing or of any published article, or any other promotional literature designed for use with the public which material does not meet the definition of "advertisement." A form letter shall include one of a series of identical letters, or individually typed or prepared letters which contain essentially identical statements or repeat the same basic theme and which are sent to 25 or more persons.

(mm) Unit—The term "unit" shall mean the smallest interest in a particular security which can be purchased or sold, such as one share of stock, one warrant, one bond, and so forth.

(nn) Disclosure Document(s)—The term "disclosure document" or "disclosure documents" shall mean those documents filed with the Securities and Exchange Commission, prepared by one or more options markets and meeting the requirements of Rule 9b-1 under the Securities Exchange Act of 1934. They shall contain general explanatory information relating to the mechanics of buying, writing and exercising options; the risks involved, the uses of and market for the options; transaction costs and applicable margin requirements; tax consequences of trading options; identification of the options issuer and the instrument underlying the options class; and the availability of the prospectus and the information in Part II of the registration statement.

(oo) Current Index Value—The term "current index value" means the level of a particular index (derived from the current market prices of the underlying securities in the index group) at the close of trading on any trading day, or any multiple or fraction thereof specified by the Corporation as such value is reported by the reporting authority.

(pp) Index Multiplier—The term "index multiplier" as used in reference to an index option contract means the dollar amount (as specified by the Corporation) by which the current index value is to be multiplied to obtain the aggregate index value. Such term replaces the term "unit of trading" used in reference to other kinds of options.

(qq) Index Dollar Equivalent—The term "index dollar equivalent" is the dollar amount which results when the index value is multiplied by the appropriate index multiplier.

(rr) Aggregate Current Index Value—The term "aggregate current index value" means the value required to be delivered to the holder of a call or by the holder of a put (against payment of the aggregate exercise price) upon the valid exercise of an index option. Such value is equal to the index dollar equivalent on the trading day on which an exercise notice is properly tendered to The Options Clearing Corporation; or, if the day on which such notice is so tendered is not a trading day, then on the most recent trading day.

(ss) Index Option Exercise Price—The term "exercise price" in respect of an index option means the specified index value which, when multiplied by the index multiplier, will yield the aggregate exercise price at which the aggregate current index value may be purchased (in the case of a call) or sold (in the case of a put) upon the exercise of such option.

(tt) Aggregate Exercise Price—The term "aggregate exercise price" in respect of an index option means the exercise price of such option times the index multiplier.

(uu) Index Option Premium—The term "index option premium" means the price of each such option (expressed in points), as agreed upon by the purchaser and seller in such transaction, times the index multiplier and the number of options subject to the transaction.

(vv) Underlying Index—The term "underlying index" means an index upon which a NASDAQ index option contract is based.

(ww) Index Group—The term "index group" means a group of securities whose inclusion and relative representation in the group is determined by the inclusion and relative representation of their current market values in a securities index specified by the Corporation.

(xx) NASDAQ Market Index Option—The term "NASDAQ market index option" means an option contract issued by The Options Clearing Corporation and displayed on the NASDAQ System based upon an underlying index which has been deemed by the Securities and Exchange Commission to be a market index.

(yy) Registered NASDAQ Index Options Market Maker—The term "registered NASDAQ index options market maker" means a member who meets the qualifications for such, as set forth in Section 3 of Appendix E to Section 33 in the Rules of Fair Practice, is willing and able to serve as such in connection with NASDAQ index option contracts and who is authorized by the Corporation to do so.

(zz) Control—The term "control" means the power or ability of an individual or entity to (a) make investment decisions for an account or accounts, or (b) influence directly or indirectly the investment decisions of any person or entity who makes investment decisions for an account. In addition, control will be presumed in the following circumstances:

(a) among all parties to a joint account who have authority to act on behalf of the account;

(b) among all general partners to a partnership account;

(c) when a person or entity (1) holds an ownership interest of 10 percent or more in an entity (ownership interest of less than 10 percent will not preclude aggregation), or (2) shares in 10 percent or more of profits and/or losses of an account;

(d) when accounts have common directors or management;

(e) where a person or entity has the authority to execute transactions in an account.

Control, presumed by one or more of the above powers, abilities or circumstances, can be rebutted by proving the factor does not exist or by showing other factors which negate the presumption of control. The rebuttal proof must be submitted by affidavit and/or such other evidence as may be appropriate in the circumstances.

The Corporation will also consider the following factors in determining if aggregation of accounts is required:

(1) similar patterns of trading activity among separate entities;

(2) the sharing of kindred business purposes and interests;

(3) whether there is common supervision of the entities which extends beyond assuring adherence to each entity's investment objectives and/or restrictions;

(4) the degree of contact and communication between directors and/or managers of separate accounts.

[Section 2 amended effective August 2, 1983; amended effective September 13, 1985; amended effective October, 1986; January 7, 1987 and June 28, 1989.]

Sec. 3.

Position Limits

(a) Stock Options—Except in highly unusual circumstances and with the prior written approval of the Corporation in each instance, no member shall effect for any account in which such member has an interest, or for the account of any partner, officer, director or employee thereof, or for the account of any customer, an opening transaction through the NASDAQ System, the over-the-counter market or on any exchange in a stock option contract of any class of stock options if the member has reason to believe that as a result of such transaction the member or partner, officer, director or employee thereof, or customer would, acting alone or in concert with others, directly or indirectly, hold or control or be obligated in respect of an aggregate position in excess of:

(1) 3,000 option contracts of the put class and the call class on the same side of the market covering the same underlying security, combining for purposes of this position limit long positions in put options with short positions in call options, and short positions in put options with long positions in call options; or

(2) 5,500 options contracts of the put class and the call class on the same side of the market covering the same underlying security, providing that the 5,500 contract position limit shall only be available for option contracts on securities which underly NASDAQ or exchange-traded options qualifying under applicable rules for a position limit ot 5,500 option contracts; or

(3) 8,000 option contracts of the put class and the call class on the same side of the market covering the same underlying security providing that the 8,000 contract position limit shall only be available for option contracts on securities which underly NASDAQ or exchange-traded options qualifying under applicable rules for a position limit of 8,000 option contracts; or

(4) such other number of stock options contracts as may be fixed from time to time by the Corporation as the position limit for one or more classes or series of options provided that reasonable notice shall be given of each new position limit fixed by the Corporation.

(5) The following positions, where each option contract is "hedged" by 100 shares of stock or, in the case of an adjusted option contract, the same number of shares represented by the adjusted contract, shall be exempted from established limits contained in (1) through (4) above: (i) long call and short stock; (ii) short call and long stock; (iii) long put and long stock; (iv) short put and short stock. In no event, however, may position limits for any class of stock options exceed twice the limits established by this Section 3.

The following examples illustrate the operation of position limits established by Section 3:

(a) Customer A, who is long 3,000 XYZ calls, may at the same time be short 3,000 XYZ calls, since long and short positions in the same class of options (i.e., in calls only, or in puts only) are on opposite sides of the market and are not aggregated for purposes of Section 3.

(b) Customer B, who is long 3,000 XYZ calls, may at the same time be long 3,000 XYZ puts. Section 3 does not require the aggregation of long call and long put (or short call and short put) positions, since they are on opposite sides of the market.

(c) Customer C, who is long 1,700 XYZ calls, may not at the same time be short more than 1,300 XYZ puts, since the 3,000 contract limit applies to the aggregation of long call and short put positions in options covering the same underlying security. Similarly, if Customer C is also short 1,600 XYZ calls, he may not at the same time be long more than 1,400 puts, since the 3,000 contract limit applies separately to the aggregation of short call and long put positions in options covering the same underlying security.

(b) Index Options—Except in highly unusual circumstances and with the prior written approval of the Corporation in each instance, no member shall effect for any account in which such member has an interest, or for the account of any partner, officer, director or employee thereof, or for the account of any customer, an opening transaction in an option contract of any class of index options displayed on the NASDAQ system or dealt in on an exchange if the member has reason to believe that as a result of such transaction the member or partner, officer, director or employee thereof, or customer, would, acting alone or in concert with others, directly or indirectly, hold or control or be obligated in respect of an aggregate position in excess of position limits established by the Corporation, in the case of NASDAQ Index Options, or the exchange on which the option trades.

In determining compliance with this Section 3, option contracts on a market index displayed in the NASDAQ System shall be subject to a contract limitation fixed by the Corporation, which shall not be larger than the equivalent of a $300 million position. For this purpose, a position shall be determined by the product of the closing index value times the index multiplier times the number of contracts on the same side of the market.

(c) Index option contracts shall not be aggregated with option contracts on any stocks whose prices are the basis for calculation of the index.

(d) The Corporation will notify the Securities and Exchange Commission at any time it approves a request to exceed the limits established pursuant to this Section.

[Section 3 amended effective November 30, 1983; amended effective April 1, 1985; amended effective September 13, 1985; amended effective October, 1986; amended effective February 9, 1990.]

Sec. 4.

Exercise Limits

Except in highly unusual circumstances and with the prior written approval of the Corporation, in each instance, no member or person associated with a member shall exercise, for any account in which such member or person associated with a member has an interest, or for the account of any partner, officer, director or employee thereof or for the account of any customer, any option contract if as a result thereof such member or partner, officer, director or employee thereof or customer, acting alone or in concert with others, directly or indirectly, has or will have exercised within any five (5) consecutive business days a number of option contracts of a particular class of options in excess of the limits for options positions in Section 3 of this Appendix E. The Corporation may institute other limitations concerning the exercise of option contracts from time to time by action of the Corporation. Reasonable notice shall be given of each new limitation fixed by the Corporation. [Section 4 amended effective November 30, 1983; amended effective April 1, 1985.]

Sec. 5.

Reporting of Options Positions

(a) Each member shall file with the Corporation a report with respect to each account in which the member has interest, each account of a partner, officer, director or employee or such member, and each customer account, which has established an aggregate position of 200 or more option contracts (whether long or short) of the put class and the call class on the same side of the market covering the same underlying security or index, combining for purposes of this Section long positions in put options with short positions in call options and short positions in put options with long positions in call options.

Such report shall identify the person or persons having an interest in such account and shall identify separately the total number of option contracts of each such class comprising the reportable position in such account. The report shall be in such form as may be prescribed by the Corporation and shall be filed no later than the close of business on the next business day following the day on which the transaction or transactions requiring the filing of such report occurred. Whenever a report shall be required to be filed with respect to an account pursuant to this subsection, the member filing such shall file with the Corporation such additional periodic reports with respect to such account as the Corporation may from time to time prescribe.

(b) In addition to the reports required by subsection (a) of this Section, each member shall report promptly to the Corporation any instance in which such member has a reason to believe that a person, acting alone or in concert with others, has exceeded or is attempting to exceed the position limits or the exercise limits set forth in Sections 3 and 4 hereof.

[Amended effective September 13, 1985.]

Sec. 6.

Liquidation of Positions and Restrictions on Access

(a) Whenever the Corporation determines that a person or group of persons acting in concert holds or controls, or is obligated in respect of, an aggregate position in option contracts covering any underlying security or index in excess of the position limitations established by Section 3 hereof, it may, when deemed necessary or appropriate in the public interest and for the protection of investors, direct:

(1) any member or all members carrying a position in option contracts covering such underlying security or index for such person or persons to liquidate such position or positions, or portions thereof, as expeditiously as possible and consistent with the maintenance of an orderly market, so as to bring such person or persons into compliance with the position limitations contained in Section 3;

(2) that such person or persons named therein not be permitted to execute an opening transaction, and that no member shall accept and/or execute for any person or persons named in such directive, any order for an opening transaction in any option contract, unless in each instance express approval therefor is given by the Corporation, the directive is rescinded, or the directive specifies another restriction appropriate under the circumstances.

(b) Prior to the issuance of any directive provided for in subsection (a) hereof, the Corporation shall notify, in the most expeditious manner possible, such person, or group of persons of such action, the specific grounds therefor and provide them an opportunity to be heard thereon. In the absence of unusual circumstances, in the case of a directive pursuant to the provisions of subsection (a)(1) hereof, the hearing shall be held within one business day of notice. In the case of a directive pursuant to the provisions of subsection (a)(2) hereof, the hearing shall be held as promptly as possible under the circumstances. In any such proceeding a record shall be kept. A determination by the Corporation after hearing or waiver of hearing, to implement such directive shall be in writing and shall be supported by a statement setting forth the specific grounds on which the determination is based. Any person aggrieved by action taken by the Corporation pursuant to this Section may make application for review to the Securities and Exchange Commission in accordance with Section 19 of the Securities Exchange Act of 1934, as amended.

[Amended effective September 13, 1985.]

Sec. 7.

Limit on Uncovered Short Positions

Whenever the Corporation shall determine in light of current conditions in the markets for options, or in the markets for underlying securities, that there are outstanding a number of uncovered short positions in option contracts of a given class in excess of the limits established by the Corporation for purposes of this Section or that a percentage of outstanding short positions in option contracts of a given class are uncovered, in excess of the limits established by the Corporation for purposes of this Section, the Corporation, upon its determination that such action is in the public interest and necessary for the protection of investors and the maintenance of a fair and orderly market in the option contracts or underlying securities, may prohibit any further opening writing transactions in option contracts of that class unless the resulting short position will be covered, and it may prohibit the uncovering of any existing covered short position in option contracts of one or more series of options of that class. The Corporation may exempt transactions in NASDAQ options by registered NASDAQ options market makers from restrictions imposed under this Section and it shall rescind such restrictions upon its determination that they are no longer appropriate.

[Amended effective September 13, 1985.]

Sec. 8.

Restrictions on Option Transactions and Exercises

The Corporation may impose from time to time such restrictions on option transactions or the exercise of option contracts in one or more series of options of any class which it determines are necessary in the interest of maintaining a fair and orderly market in option contracts, or in the underlying securities covered by such option contracts, or otherwise necessary in the public interest or for the protection of investors. During the period of any such restriction, no member shall effect any option transaction or exercise any option contract in contravention of such restriction. Notwithstanding the foregoing, during the ten (10) business days prior to the expiration date of a given series of options, no restriction established pursuant to this Section on the exercise of option contracts shall remain in effect with respect to that series of options.

[Section 8 renumbered effective October 22, 1980.]

Sec. 9.

Rights and Obligations of Holders and Writers

Subject to the provisions of Sections 4, 6, and 8 of this Appendix E, the rights and obligations of holders and writers of option contracts of any class of options issued by The Options Clearing Corporation shall be set forth in the rules of The Options Clearing Corporation.

[Section 9 renumbered effective October 22, 1980; amended effective September 13, 1985.]

Sec. 10.

Open Orders on "Ex-Date"

Open orders for one or more option contracts of any class of options issued by The Options Clearing Corporation held by members prior to the effective date of an adjustment by The Options Clearing Corporation to the terms of a class of options pursuant to Article VI, Section 11 of the By-Laws of The Options Clearing Corporation shall be adjusted on the "ex-date" by such amount as The Options Clearing Corporation shall specify, unless otherwise instructed by the customer.

[Section 10 renumbered effective October 22, 1980.]

Sec. 11.

Delivery of Current Disclosure Document(s)

Every member shall deliver the appropriate current disclosure document(s) to each customer at or prior to the time such customer's account is approved for trading in the category of options issued by The Options Clearing Corporation to which such disclosure document relates. In the case of customers approved for writing uncovered short options transactions, the disclosure document required by Section 16 shall be in a format prescribed by the Corporation. Thereafter, each new or revised current disclosure document(s) shall be distributed to every customer having an account approved for such trading or in the alternative, shall be distributed not later than the time a confirmation of a transaction is delivered to each customer who enters into a transaction in options issued by The Options Clearing Corporation. The Corporation will advise members when a new or revised current disclosure document meeting the requirements of Rule 9b-1 of the Securities Exchange Act of 1934 is available.

Where a broker or dealer enters his orders with another member in a single omnibus account, the member holding the account shall take reasonable steps to assure that such broker or dealer is furnished reasonable quantities of current disclosure documents, as requested by him in order to enable him to comply with the requirements of Rule 9b-1 of the Securities Exchange Act of 1934.

Where an introducing broker or dealer enters orders for his customers with, or clears transactions through, a member on a fully disclosed basis and that member carries the accounts of such customers, the responsibility for delivering the current disclosure document(s) as provided in this Section shall rest with the member carrying the accounts. However, such member may rely upon the good faith representation of the introducing broker or dealer that the current disclosure document(s) has been delivered in compliance with this Section.

[Section 11 renumbered effective October 22, 1980; amended effective August 2, 1983 and June 28, 1989.]

Sec. 12.

Confirmations

Every member shall promptly furnish to each customer a written confirmation of each transaction in option contracts for such customer's account. Each such confirmation shall show the type of option, the underlying security or index, the expiration month, the exercise price, the number of option contracts, the premium, the commission, the trade and settlement dates, whether the transaction was a purchase or a sale (writing) transaction, whether the transaction was an opening or a closing transaction, whether the transaction was effected on a principal or agency basis and for other than options issued by The Options Clearing Corporation the date of expiration. The confirmation shall by appropriate symbols distinguish between exchange listed and NASDAQ option transactions and other transactions in option contracts.

[Section 12 renumbered effective October 22, 1980; amended effective September 13, 1985.]

Sec. 13.

Transactions with Issuers

No member under any circumstances shall enter a transaction for the sale (writing) of a call option contract for the account of any corporation which is the issuer of the underlying security thereof.

[Section 13 renumbered effective October 22, 1980.]

Sec. 14.

Restricted Stock

For the purposes of covering a short position in a call option contract, delivery pursuant to the exercise of a put option contract, or satisfying an exercise notice assigned in respect of a call option contract, no member shall accept shares of an underlying stock, which may not be sold by the holder thereof except upon registration pursuant to the provisions of the Securities Act of 1933 or pursuant to SEC rules promulgated under the Securities Act of 1933, unless, at the time such securities are accepted and at any later time such securities are delivered, applicable provisions of the Securities Act of 1933 and the rules thereunder have been complied with by the holder of such securities.

[Section 14 renumbered effective October 22, 1980.]

Sec. 15.

Statements of Account

Statements of account showing security and money positions, entries, interest charges and any special charges that have been assessed against such account during the period covered by the statement shall be sent no less frequently than once every month to each customer in whose account there has been an entry during the preceding month with respect to an option contract and quarterly to all customers having an open option position or money balance. Interest charges and any special charges assessed during the period covered by the statement need not be specifically delineated if they are otherwise accounted for on the statement and have been itemized on transaction confirmations. With respect to options customers having a general (margin) account, such statements shall also provide the mark-to-market price and market value of each option position and other security position in the general (margin) account, the total market value of all positions in the account, the outstanding debit or credit balance in the account, and the general (margin) account equity. The statements shall bear a legend stating that further information with respect to commissions and other charges related to the execution of option transactions has been included in confirmations of such transactions previously furnished to the customer, and that such information will be made available to the customer promptly upon request. The statements shall also bear a legend requesting the customer promptly to advise the member of any material change in the customer's investment objectives or financial situation.

For purposes of this Section, general (margin) account equity shall be computed by subtracting the total of the "short" security values and any debit balance from the total of the "long" security values and any credit balance.

[Section 15 renumbered effective October 22, 1980.]

Sec. 16.

Opening of Accounts

(a) Approval Required—No member or person associated with a member shall accept an order from a customer to purchase or write an option contract relating to an options class that is the subject of an options disclosure document, or approve the customer's account for the trading of such option, unless the broker or dealer furnishes or has furnished to the customer the appropriate options disclosure document(s) and the customer's account has been approved for options trading in accordance with the provisions of subsections (b) through (d) hereof.

(b) Diligence in Opening Accounts

In approving a customer's account for options trading, a member or any person associated with a member shall exercise due diligence to ascertain the essential facts relative to the customer, his financial situation and investment objectives. Based upon such information, the branch office manager or other Registered Options Principal shall specifically approve or disapprove in writing the customer's account for options trading; provided, that if the branch office manager is not a Registered Options Principal, account approval or disapproval shall within ten (10) business days be submitted to and approved or disapproved by a Registered Options Principal. A record of the information obtained pursuant to this Section and of the approval or disapproval of each such account shall be maintained by the member as part of its permanent records in accordance with Section 18 of this Appendix E.

(c) Verification of Customer Background and Financial Information. The background and financial information upon which the account of every new options customer that is a natural person has been approved for options trading, unless the information is included in the customer's account agreement, shall be sent to the customer for verification within fifteen (15) days after the customer's account has been approved for options trading. A copy of the background and financial information on file with a member shall also be sent to the customer for verification within fifteen (15) days after the member becomes aware of any material change in the customer's financial situation.

(d) Account Agreement—Within fifteen (15) days after a customer's account has been approved for options trading, a member shall obtain from the customer a written agreement that the customer is aware of and agrees to be bound by the rules of the Corporation applicable to the trading of option contracts and, if he desires to engage in transactions in options issued by The Options Clearing Corporation, that the customer has received a copy of the current disclosure document(s) required to be furnished under this section and that he is aware of and agrees to be bound by the rules of The Options Clearing Corporation. In addition, the customer should indicate on such written agreement that he is aware of and agrees not to violate the position limits established pursuant to Section 3 and the exercise limits established pursuant to Section 4 of this Appendix E.

(e) Uncovered Short Option Contracts—Each member transacting business with the public in writing uncovered short option contracts shall develop, implement and maintain specific written procedures governing the conduct of such business which shall include, at least, the following:

1. Specific criteria and standards to be used in evaluating the suitability of a customer for writing uncovered short option transactions;

2. Specific procedures for approval of accounts engaged in writing uncovered short option contracts, including written approval of such accounts by a Registered Options Principal;

3. Designation of the Senior Registered Options Principal and/or Compliance Registered Options Principal as the person responsible for approved customer accounts that do not meet the specific criteria and standards for writing uncovered short option transactions and for maintaining written records of the reasons for every account so approved;

4. Establishment of specific minimum net equity requirements for initial approval and maintenance of customer accounts writing uncovered short option transactions; and

5. Requirements that customers approved for writing uncovered short options transactions be provided with a special written statement for uncovered option writers approved by the Association that describes the risks inherent in writing uncovered short option transactions, at or prior to the initial writing of an uncovered short option transaction.

[Section 16 renumbered effective October 22, 1980; amended effective August 2, 1983 and June 28, 1989.]

Interpretation of the Board of Governors

.01 In fulfilling their obligations pursuant to subsection (b) of this Section, with respect to options customers who are natural persons, members shall seek to obtain the following information at a minimum (information shall be obtained for all participants in a joint account):

1. Investment objectives (e.g., safety of principal, income, growth, trading profits, speculation);

2. Employment status (name of employer, self-employed or retired);

3. Estimated annual income from all sources;

4. Estimated net worth (exclusive of family residence);

5. Estimated liquid net worth (cash, securities, other);

6. Marital status; number of dependents;

7. Age; and,

8. Investment experience and knowledge (e.g., number of years, size, frequency and type of transactions) for options, stocks and bonds, commodities, others.

In addition, a customer's account records shall contain the following information, if applicable:

1. Source or sources of background and financial information (including estimates) concerning the customer;

2. Discretionary authorization agreement on file, name, relationship to customer and experience of person holding trading authority;

3. Date disclosure document(s) furnished to customer;

4. Nature and types of transactions for which account is approved (e.g., buying, covered writing, uncovered writing, spreading, discretionary transactions);

5. Name of registered representative;

6. Name of ROP approving account; date of approval; and,

7. Dates of verification of currency of account information.

Members should consider utilizing a standard account approval form so as to ensure the receipt of all the required information.

.02 Refusal of a customer to provide any of the information called for in Interpretation .01 shall be so noted on the customer's records at the time the account is opened. Information provided shall be considered together with the other information available in determining whether and to what extent to approve the account for options trading.

.03 The requirement of subsection (c) of this Section for the initial and subsequent verification of customer background and financial information is to be satisfied by sending to the customer the information required in Items 1 through 6 of Interpretation .01 above as contained in the member's records and providing the customer with an opportunity to correct or complete the information. In all cases, absent advice from the customer to the contrary, the information will be deemed to be verified.

Sec. 17.

Maintenance of Records

(a) In addition to the requirements of Section 21 of the Rules of Fair Practice, every member shall maintain and keep current a separate central log, index or other file for all options-related complaints, through which these complaints can easily be identified and retrieved. The central file shall be located at the principal place of business of the member or such other principal office as shall be designated by the member. At a minimum, the central file shall include: (i) identification of complainant; (ii) date complaint was received; (iii) identification of registered representative servicing the account; (iv) a general description of the matter complained of; and, (v) a record of what action, if any, has been taken by the member with respect to the complaint. For purposes of this Section, the term "options-related complaint" shall mean any written statement by a customer or person acting on behalf of a customer alleging a grievance arising out of or in connection with options. Each options-related complaint received by a branch office of a member shall be forwarded to the office in which the separate, central file is located not later than 30 days after receipt by the branch office that is the subject of the complaint. A copy of every options-related complaint shall also be maintained at the branch office that is the subject of the complaint.

(b) Background and financial information of customers who have been approved for options trading shall be maintained at both the branch office servicing the customer's account and the principal supervisory office having jurisdiction over that branch office. Copies of account statements of options customers shall also be maintained at both the branch office supervising the accounts and the principal supervisory office having jurisdiction over that branch for the most recent six-month period. Other records necessary to the proper supervision of accounts shall be maintained at a place easily accessible both to the branch office servicing the customer's account and to the principal supervisory office having jurisdiction over that branch office.

[Section 17 renumbered effective October 22, 1980.]

Sec. 18.

Discretionary Accounts

(a) Authorization and Approval—No member and no person associated with a member shall exercise any discretionary power with respect to trading in option contracts in a customer's account, or accept orders for option contracts for an account from a person other than the customer, except in compliance with the provisions of Section 15 of the Rules of Fair Practice and unless;

1. The written authorization of the customer required by Section 15 shall specifically authorize options trading in the account; and,

2. the account shall have been accepted in writing by a Registered Options Principal.

The Senior Registered Options Principal shall review the acceptance of each discretionary account to determine that the Registered Options Principal accepting the account had a reasonable basis for believing that the customer was able to understand and bear the risks of the strategies or transactions proposed, and shall maintain a record of the basis for such determination. Each discretionary order shall be approved and initialed on the day entered by the branch office manager or other Registered Options Principal, provided that if the branch office manager is not a Registered Options Principal, such approval shall be confirmed within a reasonable time by a Registered Options Principal. Each discretionary order shall be identified as discretionary on the order at the time of entry. Discretionary accounts shall receive frequent appropriate supervisory review by the Compliance Registered Options Principal. The provisions of this subsection shall not apply to discretion as to the price at which or the time when an order given by a customer for the purchase or sale of a definite number of option contracts in a specified security shall be executed.

(b) Record of Transactions—A record shall be made of every transaction in option contracts in respect to which a member or person associated with a member has exercised discretionary authority, clearly reflecting such fact and indicating the name of the customer, the designation and number of the option contracts, the premium and the date and time when such transaction was effected.

(c) Option Programs—Where the discretionary account utilizes options programs involving the systematic use of one or more options strategies, the customer shall be furnished with a written explanation of the nature and risks of such programs.

rules in respect of its options business. The CROP shall regularly furnish reports directly to the Compliance officer (if the CROP is not himself the Compliance officer) and to other senior management of the member. The requirement that the CROP have no sales functions shall not apply to a member that has received less that $1,000,000 in gross commissions on options business for either of the preceding two fiscal years or that currently has ten or fewer registered representatives.

(c) Branch Offices. No branch office of a member shall transact an options business unless the principal supervisor of such branch office accepting options transactions has been qualified as either a Registered Options Principal or a Limited Principal-General Securities Sales Supervisor; provided that this requirement shall not apply to branch offices in which no more than three registered representatives are located, so long as the options activities of such branch offices are appropriately supervised by either a Registered Options Principal or a Limited Principal-General Securities Sales Supervisor.

(d) Headquarters Review of Accounts. Each member shall maintain at the principal supervisory office having jurisdiction over the office servicing customer accounts, information to permit review of each customer's options account on a timely basis to determine (i) the compatibility of options transactions with investment objectives and with the types of transactions for which the account was approved; (ii) the size and frequency of options transactions; (iii) commission activity in the account; (iv) profit or loss in the account; (v) undue concentration in any options class or classes, and (vi) compliance with the provisions of Regulation T of the Federal Reserve Board.

[Section 20 renumbered effective October 22, 1980; amended effective December 7, 1981 and June 28, 1989.]

Sec. 21.

Violation of By-Laws and Rules of the Corporation or The Options Clearing Corporation

(a) In Corporation disciplinary proceedings, a finding of violation of any provision of the rules, regulations or by-laws of The Options Clearing Corporation by any member or person associated with a member engaged in transactions involving options issued, or subject to issuance, by The Options Clearing Corporation, may be deemed to be conduct inconsistent with just and equitable principles of trade and a violation of Article III, Section 1 of the Corporation's Rules of Fair Practice.

(b) In Corporation disciplinary proceedings, a finding of violation of any provision of the rules, regulations or by-laws of the Corporation by any member engaged in option transactions may be deemed to be conduct inconsistent with just and equitable principles of trade and a violation of Article III, Section 1 of the Corporation's Rules of Fair Practice.

[Section 21 renumbered effective October 22, 1980.]

Sec. 22.

Stock Transfer Tax

Any stock transfer or similar tax payable in accordance with applicable laws and regulations of a taxing jurisdiction upon the sale, transfer or delivery of securities pursuant to the exercise of an option contract shall be the responsibility of the seller (writer) to whom the exercise notice is assigned in the case of a call option contract or the exercising holder in the case of a put option contract except that (1) in the case of a call option contract where the incidents of the tax are attributable solely to the exercising holder, the member representing such holder or another member which acts on its behalf as a clearing member of The Options Clearing Corporation, the tax shall be the responsibility of the exercising holder, and (2) in the case of a put option contract where the incidents of the tax are attributable solely to the seller (writer) to whom the exercise notice is assigned, the member representing such seller (writer) or another member which acts on its behalf as a clearing member of The Options Clearing Corporation, the tax shall be the responsibility of such seller (writer). Each delivery of securities subject to such tax must be accompanied by a sales ticket stamped in accordance with the regulations of the State imposing such tax, or if required by applicable law, such tax shall be remitted by the clearing member having responsibility therefor to the clearing corporation through which it customarily pays stock transfer taxes, in accordance with the applicable rules of such clearing corporation.

[Section 22 renumbered effective October 22, 1980.]

Sec. 23.

Tendering Procedures for Exercise of Options

(a) Exercise of Options Contracts.

(1) Subject to the restrictions established pursuant to Section 4 hereof and such other restrictions which may be imposed by the Corporation, The Options Clearing Corporation or an options exchange pursuant to appropriate rules, an outstanding option contract issued by The Options Clearing Corporation may be exercised during the time period specified in the rules of The Options Clearing Corporation. An exercise notice may be tendered to The Options Clearing Corporation only by the clearing member in whose account the option contract is carried. Exercise instructions of their customers relating to exchange listed or NASDAQ option contracts shall not be accepted by members after 5:30 p.m. (Eastern Time) on the business day immediately prior to the expiration date of any option contract. Exercise instructions in respect of such option contracts carried in any proprietary account of a member shall similarly not be accepted by any other member with whom such member maintains an account after 5:30 p.m. (Eastern Time) on the business day immediately prior to the expiration date of any option contract.

(2) Notwithstanding the provisions of subsections (a)(1) hereof, members may receive and act on exercise instructions after the cut-off time for the acceptance of exercise instructions but prior to 5:00 p.m. (Eastern Time) on the expiration date of an option contract:

a. in the case of option contracts carried in an account maintained for another member in which only positions of customers of such other member are carried;

b. in order to remedy mistakes or errors made in good faith;

c. to take appropriate action as the result of a failure to reconcile unmatched option transactions; or

d. where extraordinary circumstances relating to a public customer's ability to communicate exercise instructions to the member (or the member's ability to receive exercise instructions) prior to such cut-off time warrant such action.

(3) This subsection (a) is intended as a means of providing for relatively uniform procedures in respect of exercise instructions and not to alter or affect in any way the expiration times for an option which are fixed in accordance with the rules of The Options Clearing Corporation or any other provisions of an option contract, and the exercise prior to expiration of an option contract in contravention of this subsection (a)

shall neither affect the validity of such exercise nor modify or otherwise affect any right or obligation of any holder or writer of any option contract of such series of options.

(b) Each member shall prepare a memorandum of every exercise instruction received from a customer showing the time such instruction was received. Such memoranda shall be subject to the requirements of SEC Rules 17a-3(a)(6) and 17A-4(b) under the Securities Exchange Act of 1934. In the event a member receives and acts on an exercise instruction pursuant to an exception set forth in clauses b., c. or d. of subsection (a) hereof, the member shall maintain a memorandum setting forth the circumstances giving rise to such exception. If the member is relying on clause b. or clause d. as the basis for an exception, it shall promptly file a copy of the memorandum with the Corporation.

(c) Allocation of Exercise Assignment Notices.

(1) Each member shall establish fixed procedures for the allocation to customers of exercise notices assigned in respect of a short position in option contracts in such member's customer accounts. Such allocation shall be on a "first in-first out" or automated random selection basis that has been approved by the Corporation or on a manual random selection basis that has been specified by the Corporation. Each member shall inform its customers in writing of the method it uses to allocate exercise notices to its customer's accounts, explaining its manner of operation and the consequences of that system.

(2) Each member shall report its proposed method of allocation to the Corporation and obtain the Corporation's prior approval thereof, and no member shall change its method of allocation unless the change has been reported to and been approved by the Corporation. The requirements of this subsection shall not be applicable to allocation procedures submitted to and approved by another self-regulatory organization having comparable standards pertaining to methods of allocation.

(3) Each member shall preserve for a three-year period sufficient workpapers and other documentary materials relating to the allocation of exercise assignment notices to establish the manner in which allocation of such exercise assignment notices is in fact being accomplished.

(d) Delivery and Payment

Delivery of the shares of an underlying security upon the exercise of an option contract and payment of the aggregate exercise price in respect thereto, shall be effected in accordance with the rules of The Options Clearing Corporation. As promptly as practicable after the exercise of an option contract by a customer, the member shall require the customer to make full cash payment of the aggregate exercise price in the case of a call option contract or to deposit the underlying stock in the case of a put option contract, or, in either case, to make the required margin deposit in respect thereto if such transaction is effected in a margin account, in accordance with the applicable regulations of the Federal Reserve Board and Section 30 of the Corporation's Rules of Fair Practice. As promptly as practicable after the assignment to a customer of an exercise notice, the member shall require the customer to deposit the underlying stock in the case of a call option contract if the shares of the underlying security are not carried in the customer's account, or to make full cash payment of the aggregate exercise price in the case of a put option contract, or, in either case, to make the required market deposit in respect thereof, if such transaction is effected in a margin account, in accordance with Section 30 of the Corporation's Rules of Fair Practice and the applicable regulations of the Federal Reserve Board.

(e) Exercise of NASDAQ Index Option Contracts

(1) With respect to NASDAQ index option contracts, clearing members are required to follow the procedures of The Options Clearing Corporation for tendering exercise notices, and member organizations also are required to comply with the following procedures:

a. A memorandum to exercise any NASDAQ index option contract issued or to be issued in a customer or market maker account at The Clearing Corporation must be received or prepared by the member organization no later than 4:10 p.m. (Eastern Time) and must be time-stamped at the time it is received or prepared. Member organizations must accept exercise instructions until 4:10 p.m. (Eastern Time) each business day.

b. A memorandum to exercise any NASDAQ option contract issued or to be issued in a firm account at The Options Clearing Corporation must be prepared by the member organization no later than 4:10 p.m. (Eastern Time) and must be time-stamped at the time it is prepared.

c. Any member or member organization that intends to submit an exercise notice for 25 or more contracts in the same series of NASDAQ index options on the same business day on behalf of an individual customer, registered NASDAQ options market maker or firm account must notify the Association of such exercises in a manner prescribed by the Association no later than 4:10 p.m. (Eastern Time) on that day. For purposes of this rule, exercises for all accounts controlled by the same individual must be aggregated.

(2) The provisions of paragraph 1(a) and 1(b) above are not applicable in respect to any series of NASDAQ index options on the last day of trading prior to the expiration date of such series.

[Section 23 deleted effective December 15, 1981; new Section 23 added effective September 13, 1985.]

● ● ● *Cross References*

Advertising and Sales Literature Standards . . . . ¶ 2195

"Tombstone Advertising" . . . . ¶ 5281

Sec. 24.

Options Transactions and Reports by Market Makers in Listed Securities

Every member who is an off-board market maker in a security listed on a national securities exchange shall report to the Association in accordance with such procedures as may be prescribed by the Board of Governors, transactions involving 50 or more option contracts on such listed securities which are either directly for the benefit of (a) the member or (b) any employee, partner, officer, or director of the member who, by virtue of his position with the member, is directly involved in the purchase or sale of the underlying security for the firm's proprietary account(s) or is directly responsible for supervision of such persons; or who by virture of his position in the firm, is authorized to, and regularly does, obtain information on the proprietary account(s) of the member in which the underlying security is traded. This rule shall apply to all options transactions including those executed on an exchange to which the member may belong.

[Section 24 amended effective July 5, 1983.]

NASD, para. 2191

¶ 2191   Direct Participation Programs

Sec. 34.

(a) A member or a person associated with a member shall not underwrite or participate in any way in the distribution to the public of units of a direct participation program, or sponsor a direct participation program, the provisions of which are inconsistent with rules, regulations and procedures prescribing standards of fairness and reasonableness in respect thereto adopted by the Board of Governors pursuant to the authorization granted in subsection (b) hereof.

(b) The Board of Governors is authorized, for the purpose of preventing fraudulent and manipulative acts and practices, promoting just and equitable principles of trade, providing safeguards against unreasonable profits or unreasonable rates of commissions or other charges, and for the protection of investors and the public interest, to adopt rules, regulations and procedures prescribing standards of fairness and reasonableness for direct participation programs relating to:

(1) the underwriting or other terms and conditions concerning, directly or indirectly, the distribution of units of such programs to the public, including, but not limited to, all elements of compensation in connection therewith, among other factors:

(2) the terms and conditions concerning the operations, structure and management of such programs in which a member or an affiliate of a member is a sponsor including, but not limited to:

a. the rights of participants in such programs;

b. conflicts or potential conflicts of interest of sponsors thereof, or others;

c. the financial condition of sponsors of such programs;

d. all elements of sponsor's compensation including but not limited to, working interests, net profit interests, promotional interests, program management fees, overriding royalty interests, sharing arrangements, interests in program revenues, and overriding interests of all other kinds, general and administrative expenses and organization and offering expenses;

e. the minimum unit value which may be offered and the minimum subscription amount per investor;

f. the retention and/or exchange of units of the program held by participants;

g. the assessments, mandatory, optional or otherwise, to be made on participants in a program in addition to the unit price;

h. the reinvestment of revenues derived from the operation of the program;

i. the duty of the program to render operational and financial reports to participants;

j. the liquidation of units in a program; and

k. any other terms, conditions or arrangements relating to the operation of the program which the Board of Governors determines are required for the protection of investors and the public interest;

(3) the standards of suitability for investment in such programs by investors;

(4) the content and filing with the Association of advertising and sales

literature to be used in connection with the distribution of direct participation programs; and

(5) the definitions of words commonly used in connection with such programs including words used in this section unless they are otherwise defined herein.

(c) The rules, regulations and procedures authorized by subsection (b) hereof shall be incorporated into Appendix F to be attached to and made a part of these Rules of Fair Practice. The Board of Governors shall have the power to adopt, alter, amend, supplement or modify the provisions of Appendix F from time to time without recourse to the membership for approval, as would otherwise be required by Article VII of the By-Laws, and Appendix F shall become effective as the Board of Governors may prescribe unless disapproved by the Securities and Exchange Commission.

(d) For the purposes of this section, the following terms shall have the stated meanings:

(1) Affiliate—when used with respect to a member or sponsor, shall mean any person which controls, is controlled by, or is under common control with, such member or sponsor, and includes:

a. any partner, officer or director (or person performing similar functions) of (a) such member or sponsor, or (b) a person which beneficially owns 50% or more of the equity interest in, or has the power to vote 50% or more of the voting interest in, such member or sponsor;

b. any person which beneficially owns or has the right to acquire 10% or more of the equity interest in or has the power to vote 10% or more of the voting interest in (a) such member or sponsor, or (b) a person which beneficially owns 50% or more of the equity interest in, or has the power to vote 50% or more of the voting interest in, such member or sponsor;

c. any person with respect to which such member or sponsor, the persons specified in subparagraph a. or b., and the immediate families of partners, officers or directors (or persons performing similar functions) specified in subparagraph a., or other person specified in subparagraph b., in the aggregate beneficially own or have the right to acquire 10% or more of the equity interest or have the power to vote 10% or more of the voting interest;

d. any person an officer of which is also a person specified in subparagraph a. or b. and any person a majority of the board of directors of which is comprised of persons specified in subparagraph a. or b.; or

e. any person controlled by a person or persons specified in subparagraphs a., b., c. or d.

(2) Direct participation program (program)—a program which provides for flow-through tax consequences regardless of the structure of the legal entity or vehicle for distribution including, but not limited to, oil and gas programs, real estate programs, agricultural programs, cattle programs, condominium securities, Subchapter S corporate offerings and all other programs of a similar nature, regardless of the industry represented by the program, or any combination thereof. A program may be composed of one or more legal entities or programs but when used herein and in any rules or regulations adopted pursuant hereto the term shall mean each of the separate entities or programs making up the overall program and/or the overall program itself. Excluded from this definition are real estate investment trusts, tax qualified pension and profit sharing plans pursuant to Sections 401 and 403(a) of the Internal Revenue Code and individual retirement plans under Section 408 of that Code, tax sheltered annuities pursuant to the provisions of Section 403(b) of the Internal Revenue Code, and any company,

including separate accounts, registered pursuant to the Investment Company Act of 1940.

(3) Equity interest—when used with respect to a corporation, means common stock and any security convertible into, exchangeable or exercisable for common stock, and, when used with respect to a partnership, means an interest in the capital or profits or losses of the partnership.

(4) Sponsor—a person who directly or indirectly provides management services for a direct participation program whether as general partner, pursuant to contract or otherwise.

APPENDIX II

EXAM

Compliance Test for All Participants

1. An RR is

    A. an employee of the broker-dealer.
    B. an agent of the broker-dealer.
    C. Both of the above
    D. Neither of the above

2. Which of the following is NOT true about penny stocks?

    A. They are the mainstay of boiler-room operations.
    B. They are suitable for most customers.
    C. Little public information is available about the companies.
    D. They are often sold by high-pressure operations.

3. Which of the following would NOT require an RR to register with the SEC as a broker-dealer?

    A. Possession of customers' stocks or bonds beyond transmittal time
    B. Cashing bond coupons for customers
    C. Entering buy and sell orders through your firm as an agent of your customer
    D. Buying or selling stock outside your broker-dealer's books and records

4. Which of the following is NOT an RR's duty to regulators?

    A. To be accurate in document filing
    B. To respond promptly and thoroughly to regulators' requests for information
    C. To be dually registered
    D. To pay fines and costs incurred because of rule violations

5. The RR has a duty to notify the employing broker-dealer when opening which of the following accounts?

   A. A personal account with another broker-dealer member of the same SRO
   B. An account with an NYSE member firm for an RR relative. The RR has written authority to enter orders in the account, but will not receive compensation.
   C. A personal account with a non-U.S. broker-dealer
   D. All of the above

6. Dual registration is registration with two

   A. regulators.
   B. or more states.
   C. broker-dealers.
   D. exchanges, in two different countries.

7. Investment suitability may be questioned if

   A. the client has not received appropriate information about the investment.
   B. the RR makes the investment decision without proper authorization.
   C. the customer's portfolio contains excessive risk.
   D. All of the above

8. The federal securities acts define a security

   A. narrowly.
   B. clearly.
   C. with an ambiguity that allows the courts to interpret the law.
   D. with enough clarity for lawyers and compliance officers to declare what is and what is not a security.

9. Which of the following apply (applies) to the calculation
   of markups and markdowns?

   I.   Markups and markdowns are calculated using the
         current market price; i.e., the high bid for sales by
         customers and the low offer for customer purchases.
   II.   Compensation on the proceeds of a sale is combined
         (when appropriate) with compensation on a buy-side
         transaction to calculate the markup percentage.
   III. No inventory profit or loss is included in the markup
         or markdown.

   A. I only
   B. I and III only
   C. II and III only
   D. I, II and III

10. Under the NASD markup rule

   A. a markup or commission of less than 1% is unfair.
   B. any markup of less than 5% is fair.
   C. the markup or markdown is calculated separately
       when one security is sold and the money is used to
       buy another security.
   D. a fair markup depends on many circumstances.

11. Which of the following is NOT a duty of the RR?

   A. Using the customer's money for the customer's
       purposes
   B. Recommending investments based on client suitability
   C. Gathering essential information in order to "know
       your customer"
   D. Entering discretionary orders with a verbal
       authorization

12 If the customer is the principal,

   A. the broker-dealer is the agent.
   B. the RR is the agent.
   C. Both of the above
   D. Neither of the above

13. The basic pieces of customer information are

    I.   objectives.
    II.   net worth.
    III. income.
    IV. risk tolerance.

    A. I and II only
    B. I and III only
    C. II, III and IV only
    D. I, II, III and IV

14. In order to confirm the receipt of options materials and accuracy of customer information, a broker-dealer may ask a client

    A. for positive verification.
    B. to phone the RR's branch manager.
    C. for negative verification.
    D. for either A or C.

15. Which of the following is NOT true?

    A. Most rules in the securities markets originate with the compliance officers of broker-dealer firms.
    B. RRs are responsible for their own behavior, but cannot be responsible for supervising themselves.
    C. The self-regulatory organizations (SROs) have been recognized by Congress and report to the Securities and Exchange Commission (SEC).
    D. Broker-dealers are required to supervise their own activities.

16. When a broker-dealer sends its clients documentation and requests a signature if the document information is incorrect, the firm is using

    A. positive verification.
    B. negative verification.
    C. a method of checking on the RR's compliance.
    D. an obsolete procedure.

17. Which of the following is NOT true?

    A. An RR may temporarily deposit a client's money in his/her own account until settlement date.

    B. The customer's money must be used for the customer's purpose.

    C. The RR may not share in the profit and losses of the customer's account.

    D. A RR's buy and sell recommendations are based on the client's objectives.

18. The RR is frequently in a position of conflict because

    A. the RR is an employee or principal of both the broker-dealer and the customer.

    B. the RR is an agent of both the customer and the broker-dealer.

    C. the RR is a principal in a dealer trade.

    D. the trade, principal or agency, determines the RR's position as principal or agent.

19. Which of the following is NOT relevant to a suitable recommendation?

    A. Past performance of the proposed investment

    B. The type of investment suggested

    C. The size of the investment

    D. The frequency of trading the investment

20. Trades in discretionary accounts

    A. must be marked "unsolicited."

    B. must be highly supervised.

    C. are allowed by all broker-dealers.

    D. are usually based on oral contracts.

21. An RR

    A. may occasionally cover a client's losses.

    B. may occasionally guarantee a client against loss.

    C. may share in the profits and losses of an account if he/she has a joint account with the client.

    D. may, under no circumstances, open an account with any client.

22. Under SEC regulations, the customer is required to sign the

    A. New Accounts form.
    B. Options Disclosure Document.
    C. Options Agreement.
    D. Prospectus for a new issue.

23. Insider information

    A. is part of the public domain.
    B. is subject to double damages on profits made.
    C. may be illegally used by accident as well as on purpose.
    D. can legally be used by foreign investors.

24. When placing a nondiscretionary order, the RR may assist in determining the

    A. time of the trade and the price of the trade.
    B. type of security and size of the trade.
    C. whether to buy or sell and the price of the trade.
    D. type of security and time of the trade.

25. The in-person compliance interview held annually with each of a firm's RRs need NOT include which of the following?

    A. A review of the RR's product mix and procedures
    B. A review of the firm's statement of financial condition and net capital
    C. An opportunity for the RR to ask questions and receive answers
    D. An update on new regulations, the firm's policies, and similar topics

26. A firm requires additional customer data for

    A. equities and limited partnerships.
    B. limited partnerships and options.
    C. bonds and equities.
    D. options and bonds.

27. Which of the following statements is true of public communications?

    I.   Advertising is any communication placed in a public medium.
    II. Sales literature is any public communication that is not advertising.
    III. All advertising must be approved by a registered principal prior to use.
    IV. Individual customer correspondence is neither advertising nor sales literature, but must be approved and a copy kept in a correspondence file for examination.

    A. I and II only
    B. I and IV only
    C. II and III only
    D. I, II, III and IV

28. Which of the following is NOT true of the "Chinese wall?"

    A. It refers to non-transmission of information from one part of the broker-dealer (underwriting and corporate finance) to another part (trading).
    B. It applies to nonpublic information.
    C. Broker-dealers must have supervisory procedures that look for evidence of such information transmissions.
    D. Federal law allows triple damages even if there is no action on the information.

29. Which of the following is NOT true of the Small Order Execution System (SOES)?

    A. Customers may enter orders through SOES terminals.
    B. Orders may not be divided into sizes which fit within the execution limits of the SOES.
    C. The SOES is intended to facilitate execution of agency orders for customers.
    D. SOES is not available for the execution of the firm's own trades

30. A corporate officer calls to enter an order for stock of his employer's issue. You should

    A. accept the order without question.
    B. suggest the customer contact the company's corporate counsel before entering the order.
    C. enter the order for the client and, if you purchase any for yourself, make sure the customer's order is filled first.
    D. refuse the order and tell your supervisor.

31. The NASDAQ system, like any other order transmission or execution system, is sometimes used for market manipulation. Which of the following is NOT an example of market manipulation?

    A. Marking the close of the market
    B. Using the final bid price or trade price for valuation of securities in margin accounts
    C. Entering market orders to buy the same security just before the market close each day
    D. Reporting NMS trades the day following the transaction

32. To participate in certain activities, RRs must notify their employers in writing and obtain the employer's prior permission. Which of the following is NOT permissible even after notification and permission?

    A. Private securities transactions
    B. Receipt of compensation from another firm
    C. Purchasing a new issue that trades at a premium in the aftermarket
    D. Selling a hot issue to a friend

33. The NASD markup policy applies to

    I. principal trades.
    II. agency trades.
    III. broker-dealer transaction compensation.
    IV. RR transaction compensation.

    A. I and III
    B. I and IV
    C. II and III
    D. I, II, III, and IV

34. Which of the following is true about or during an underwriting?

    I.   A broker-dealer may be unwilling to be an underwriter, because it does not want to spend the time, energy, or money performing due diligence duties.

    II.   The secondary market may be manipulated in fixed price offerings, at or below the market price, to stabilize the market.

    III.   There must be a bona fide offering of securities. Broker-dealers, RRs, and their immediate families may not buy an offering that trades at a premium in the secondary market.

    IV.   The RR may lose the selling compensation if the syndicate imposes a "penalty bid."

    A.   I and IV only
    B.   II and III only
    C.   III and IV only
    D.   I, II, III and IV

35. Your client buys stock in his father's public company. His tennis partner and her sister also purchase the same stock. The father neither buys nor sells any company shares. The stock goes up in value. A week later, the company announces a leveraged buy-out. The shares move substantially higher and all three people have large profits. An SEC investigation alleges the transfer of nonpublic information between father and son. Which of the following may be liable for triple damages?

    I.   Father
    II.   Son
    III.   Tennis partner
    IV.   Sister of tennis partner

    A.   I and II only
    B.   II only
    C.   II and III only
    D.   I, II, III and IV

Additional Questions For Supervisors

36. To be in compliance with regulations and securities laws, broker-dealer supervision must be

    A. perfect.
    B. reasonable.
    C. error free.
    D. total.

37. Which of the following is true of the guidelines in the NASD supervision rule?

    A. The supervisors should have the experience to know a violation when they see one.
    B. The supervisors should have access to the rules they are enforcing.
    C. The supervisors should not have to review the behavior of too many RRs in too many different places.
    D. All of the above

38. The broker-dealer's supervisory system

    A. is only required to cover public contacts; therefore, supervision covers only the sales force.
    B. must cover retail sales and trading.
    C. must cover retail sales, trading, and the underwriting or corporate finance departments.
    D. must cover all aspects of the firm's business, including retail, trading, underwriting, back office, and market services.

39. Which of the following is NOT true of the supervisory structure required by the NASD supervisory rule?

    A. A supervisor must be designated for each RR.
    B. One principal must be designated for each type of business in which the firm engages.
    C. Each nonbranch office must be supervised by an on-site principal.
    D. One or more compliance principals responsible for reviewing supervisory systems and reporting to management must be identified to the NASD.

40. The NASD must be notified promptly and in writing when which of the following occur?

   I.   Discipline of the broker-dealer or its RR
   II.   Termination of an RR
   III. Internal discipline of an RR or nonregistered person
   IV.   Termination for cause of a nonregistered person

   A. I and II only
   B. I and IV only
   C. II, III and IV only
   D. I, II, III and IV

41. Which of the following is NOT true of stock parking?

   A. Parking for the purposes of evading taxes is illegal.
   B. Parking is unethical under NASD and NYSE rules, but is not a problem under federal law.
   C. Parking for the purpose of concealing positions is illegal.
   D. Parking is the temporary sale of a stock to another firm with an agreement to repurchase the security at a set time and price.

42. Money received by a broker-dealer during a contingent offering

   I.   must be immediately deposited into an escrow account.
   II.   must be returned to the buyer if the escrow minimum is not met.
   III. may be deposited in the broker-dealer's customer account until the check has cleared, then to the escrow account within 24 hours.
   IV.   may be combined with credit extended under Reg T.

   A. I and II only
   B. I, II and IV only
   C. II and III only
   D. I, II, III and IV

43. A broker-dealer must exercise due diligence before distributing a new issue. Which of the following is true of due diligence?

   I.   The broker-dealer must take steps to verify relevant information.
   II. Other experts, such as accountants and engineers, must exercise due diligence in their areas of expertise.
   III. Assurance of disclosure of relevant information is the objective of due diligence.

   A. I only
   B. II only
   C. II and III only
   D. I, II and III

44. When a firm's net capital is less than required, the firm must

   A. accept no more public business.
   B. accept an immediate ruling that the firm is permanently closed.
   C. accept only sell orders that liquidate customer positions.
   D. accept only buy orders that liquidate customer positions.

45. A broker-dealer must have the following qualified options supervision before allowing options activities:

   I.   ROP (registered options principal)
   II. CROP (compliance registered options principal)
   III. SROP (senior registered options principal)

   A. I only
   B. I and III only
   C. II and III only
   D. I, II and III

46. Broker-dealers must notify regulators by telegraph

   I.   when the deposit to the customer's segregated account is not made.
   II. if the independent accountant informs the firm of "material inadequacies."
   III. if the broker-dealer's books and records are not current.
   IV. if net capital is less than required by any rule.
   V.   if the broker-dealer has too much leverage for more than 90 consecutive days.

   A. I and V only
   B. II and III only
   C. II, IV and V only
   D. I, II, III, IV and V

47. Where registered persons offer securities for sale, a location may be treated as a nonbranch

   I.   if it is identified solely by a telephone directory line listing.
   II. if it is identified solely by business cards or letterheads.
   III. if it is a permanent exhibit booth in a shopping mall.
   IV. if a substantial number of registered persons work at the location.

   A. I and II only
   B. II only
   C. III and IV only
   D. I, II, III and IV

48. Member firms must notify the NASD if they or their employees are the subject of any disciplinary action by a clearing organization, self-regulatory organization, etc. The notice must be prompt and

   A. in writing.
   B. by telegraph.
   C. by telephone followed by a written statement.
   D. by telegraph followed by a written statement.

49. Which of the following requires a firm to designate a location as an Office of Supervisory Jurisdiction (OSJ)?

 I.   Identification of the location to the public, such as a listing in a building directory
 II.   Identification of the location to the public solely by business cards identifying another location as a supervisory branch
 III. Supervision of a substantial number of registered persons at that location
 IV.   Wide geographic dispersal of registered persons who report to the location

 A. I and IV only
 B. II and III only
 C. III and IV only
 D. I, II, III and IV

50. If the net capital of a broker-dealer is within 120% of the required capital (less than $30,000 and more than the required minimum of $25,000), the broker-dealer must

 I.   give immediate telegraphic notice to the NASD or NYSE.
 II.   file FOCUS II or FOCUS IIA by the 15th of the following month.
 III. cease doing public business.

 A. I and II only
 B. I and III only
 C. II only
 D. I, II and III

Compliance Test Answer Key and Page Reference Numbers

RR and Supervisor Questions	Supervisory Only Questions
Answer #	*Answer #*

1.	C		36.	B
2.	B		37.	D
3.	C		38.	D
4.	C		39.	C
5.	D		40.	D
6.	C		41.	B
7.	D		42.	B
8.	C		43.	D
9.	D		44.	A
10.	D		45.	D
11.	D		46.	D
12.	C		47.	A
13.	D		48.	A
14.	D		49.	C
15.	A		50.	C
16.	B			
17.	A			
18.	B			
19.	A			
20.	B			
21.	C			
22.	C			
23.	C			
24.	A			
25.	B			
26.	B			
27.	D			
28.	D			
29.	A			
30.	B			
31.	B			
32.	C			
33.	D			
34.	D			
35.	D			

Index

K
Kennedy, John F., 40-43
Kennedy, Joseph P., 26
Kinnard, John G., 4-11, 13-14,
    66-68, 139

L
Levine, Dennis, 127, 180-81,
    182
Licensing procedures, 17
Limited partnerships, 106
Long-term government bond
    funds, recommending, 116

M
Making a market, 36
Maloney Act, 38
Manipulation, 25, 36
Marketplace, 13-19
    modern, 17-21
    traditional, 15-16
Market regulations, *See*
    Regulations
Marking the close of the
    market, 152
Metonymy, and Wall Street,
    175
Milken, Michael, 154, 156, 181,
    182
Mini/maxi underwritings, 163
Misappropriation of customer's
    money, 109-12
Mississippi Bubble, 19
Mississippi Company, 18-19
Modern marketplace, 17-21
    rules of the road for, 139
Municipal Securities
    Rulemaking Board
    (MSRB), 70, 145
Mutual funds, 115

N
National Association of
    Securities Dealers
    Automated Quotations
    (NASDAQ), 22, 23, 150-52
    growth of, 48
National Association of
    Securities Dealers (NASD),
    22, 26, 56, 59, 68, 78, 145,
    148-53, 170-71, 185
    Anti-Fraud Department, 126
    Best Efforts Distribution
        Reporting Program, 91
    disciplinary action,
        informing of, 145
    Free Riding and
        Withholding Program,
        91
    leverage over RRs, 73
    Market Surveillance
        Committee, 150-51
    New Issue Market
        Manipulation System,
        91
    and penny stock market,
        92-93
    and Series 7 exam, 70
    surveillance, increases in,
        91-92
    underwriting rules, 91
National Market System, 131
Negative verification, 105-6
Net capital requirements, 47,
    166-68
Newberg, Bruce Lee, 157, 181
New York Stock Exchange
    (NYSE), 38, 48-49, 53-54,
    59, 145
    and identification of sources
        of large trades, 53
    and Series 7 exam, 70
    Special Trust Fund, 45-47